Understanding International Sign

Ceil Lucas and Jordan Fenlon, Series Editors

VOLUME 1 Sociolinguistics in Deaf Communities
VOLUME 2 Multicultural Aspects of Sociolinguistics in Deaf Communities
VOLUME 3 Deaf Children in Public Schools
VOLUME 4 Pinky Extension and Eye Gaze: Language Use in Deaf Communities
VOLUME 5 Storytelling and Conversations: Discourse in Deaf Communities
VOLUME 6 Bilingualism and Identity in Deaf Communities
VOLUME 7 Sociolinguistic Variation in American Sign Language
VOLUME 8 Turn-Taking, Fingerspelling, and Contact in Signed Languages
VOLUME 9 Language and the Law in Deaf Communities
VOLUME 10 To the Lexicon and Beyond: Sociolinguistics in European Deaf Communities
VOLUME 11 The Rising of Lotus Flowers: Self-Education by Deaf Children in Thai Boarding Schools
VOLUME 12 Multilingualism and Sign Languages: From the Great Plains to Australia
VOLUME 13 Sign Languages in Contact
VOLUME 14 Hearing, Mother Father Deaf: Hearing People in Deaf Families
VOLUME 15 Extraordinary from the Ordinary: Personal Experience Narratives in American Sign Language
VOLUME 16 Language Policy and Planning for Sign Languages
VOLUME 17 Discourse in Signed Languages
VOLUME 18 Language Attitudes in the American Deaf Community
VOLUME 19 Form, Meaning, and Focus in American Sign Language
VOLUME 20 Teaching and Learning in Bilingual Classrooms: New Scholarship
VOLUME 21 International Sign: Linguistic, Usage, and Status Issues
VOLUME 22 Understanding International Sign: A Sociolinguistic Study

Understanding International Sign

A Sociolinguistic Study

Lori A. Whynot

GALLAUDET UNIVERSITY PRESS

Washington, DC

Sociolinguistics in Deaf Communities

Gallaudet University Press
Washington, DC 20002
http://gupress.gallaudet.edu

Printed in the United States of America

ISBN 978-1-56368-672-6
ISSN 1080-5494

∞ This paper meets the requirements of ANSI/NISO Z39.48-1992 (Permanence of Paper).

Dedicated to my mother, Peggy,
who departed far too soon but instilled in me
resilience and a childlike joie de vivre.

If you are brave enough to say "goodbye," life will reward you with a new "hello."

–Paulo Coehlo

Contents

Editors' Preface

For this 22nd volume of the *Sociolinguistics in Deaf Communities* series, I am very happy to announce that Dr. Jordan Fenlon will be taking over as the editor. After receiving his PhD from University College London in 2010, Jordan Fenlon worked as a postdoctoral researcher at the Deafness, Cognition and Language Research Centre on projects such as the British Sign Language Corpus and BSL Signbank. He has also taught at Gallaudet University and was recently a Mellon postdoctoral fellow at the University of Chicago. His research interests include the linguistics of sign languages from a sociolinguistic perspective and the use of sign language corpora. Currently, Jordan is an assistant professor of British Sign Language at Heriot-Watt University in the United Kingdom.

Welcome, Jordan! The series will be in very capable hands.

Ceil Lucas

Editorial Advisory Board

Acknowledgments

This volume is an edited version of my PhD dissertation completed at Macquarie University in Sydney between 2011 and 2015. The research project resulted from the alignment of several factors: chance meetings, opportunity, faith, friendship, support, love, and hard work. I thank my family for their love, and their faith in my decision to move far from home for the original PhD research undertaking that is the basis of this book.

My fortunate meeting of Trevor Johnston and Lindsay Ferrara at the Theoretical Issues in Sign Language Research (TISLR) conference in 2010 opened a door to doctoral study that I had wanted to pursue for some time. It is hard to quantify how much I learned in the process over those four short years. I am grateful for the supportive encouragement of Brenda Nicodemus who assured me that a PhD was certainly within my grasp and worth the effort even at a well-established point in my professional interpreting career.

I am indebted to Trevor Johnston whose support during my candidacy challenged me to be a better scholar, and who faithfully entrusted me with an opportunity for development as a new researcher.[1] To my associate supervisor, Jemina Napier, I owe much gratitude for reassuring advice when I needed it most, and for providing me an inspirational model for skilled time management of interpreting practice, research, teaching, and family. I thank Ceil Lucas for encouraging me to publish this work, and am appreciative of both her and Jordan Fenlon for their helpful editorial comments.

Most importantly, the project could not have happened without the gracious participation of several presenters and interpreters at the 2011 World Federation of the Deaf (WFD) Congress and the World Association of Sign Language Interpreters (WASLI) conference, who allowed me to capture their work in International Sign. I am also grateful to past president Markku Jokinen and current President Colin Allen of the World Federation of the Deaf for their assistance with participant recruitment for my source IS data collection. Equally important to this work was the

1. This research was funded by an International Macquarie University Research Excellence Scholarship iMQRES– No. 2010086.

willing, generous participation of 32 comprehension assessment participants; to you all I say, Obrigado! Arigato! Thanks! Děkuji! Cheers!

This research would have been impossible without the professional skill and work of several cultural liaisons and interpreters, many of whom welcomed me from afar, and helped recruit local participants and/or arranged for my housing or personally accommodated me during my round-the-world data collection. I sincerely appreciate your dedication to this project and your willingness to assist above and beyond the call of duty. I cannot thank you enough—Danny Gong, Takeshi Sunada, Alexandr Zvonek and family, Markéta Spilková, Nikola Novotna, Angela Russo, Edgar Correa Veras, Rubens Miranda, Neil Ray, James Blythe, Christopher Tester, and Rachel Judelson. I also wish to thank staff at Northeastern University—Anna Davis, Dennis Cokely; and staff at Masaryk University, Brno Czech Republic, Deaf Japan, Osaka; and Universidade Federal do Rio Grande do Sul, Porto Allegro, Brazil, for arranging research meeting space.

I thank Rachel Rosenstock for collegial discussions, support, and for being the first to test a difficult research question about IS.

An early conversation with my friend and colleague, Robert Lee, influenced my decision about my IS data (direct Deaf signers' IS lectures), and Rachel Sutton-Spence motivated me to learn about doing research, inspiring me as a linguist and also as a cycling buddy. Ted Supalla graciously offered time to discuss morphology and the IS "strategy" before I began this project. Also, along the way, I have benefitted from Adam Schembri's humor and style of explanation that helped me appreciate linguistic concepts.

To my fellow colleagues and friends, Lindsay Ferrara, Gabrielle Hodge, George Major, and Lily Wang, thank you for showing me the way, for moral support, and for helpful discussions; particularly, I thank George and Lindsay for reading and commenting on my early writing. Also, the hospitality and friendship of Della Goswell and encouragement from Gab and Lily were much appreciated, particularly in the last months and weeks of dissertation writing.

And finally, I am beholden to Neil Ray, the love of my life and best friend. Our chance meeting changed my life forever and has been a catalyst in my transformation—personally, emotionally, and professionally.

TABLE 1. *Annotation Conventions*

Annotation	Meaning
GLOSS(x)	English word used to gloss a sign; (x) indicates the origin of the sign (i.e., NOW[ASL] or HAVE[AUS]).
GLOSS(ASL)	An English word used to gloss a sign of ASL origin.
GLOSS(AUS)	An English word used to gloss a sign of Auslan origin.
GLOSS(WFD)	An English word used to gloss a sign listed in WFD resources or established IS usage.
GLOSS(GEST)	An English word used to gloss a sign listed in the 1975 *Gestuno* glossary.
GLOSS(UNKNOWN)	An English word used to gloss a sign that is either not known or suspected originates from another SL.
PT:PRO	A sign that points to a referent, with additional notation of first, second, or third person, (i.e., PT:PRO1 "me", or "I", PT:PRO3 "it" or "him" or "her," etc.). Adding a PL indicates plurality (i.e., PT:PRO3-pl to indicate "them"). Other points refer to previous referents or locations and these are glossed PT:DET (determiner) and PT:LOC (location).
PT:POSS	A sign that points to a possessor of a thing, and is additionally specified with (1), (2), (3) person singular (SG) or plural (PL) (i.e., PT:POSS2(PL) to indicate "(all of) yours").
DSL /S /M /H /G (HANDSHAPE):BRIEF-DESCRIPTION-OF-MEANING-OF-SIGN	A sign that depicts the Location/Size-shape/Movement or displacement/ Handling/Grounding of an entity. For example, DS = Depicting Sign, M = Movement or (DSM).
FS:TOKYO	A fingerspelled word.
NS:LONDON	A name sign for a proper noun (person, place, etc.).
G(FORM):MEANING	A type-like gesture that includes the handshape form and the meaning. For example, G(5-UP):WELL, or G(1-SHAKE):NO-NO.
G:DESCRIPTION-OF-MEANING	A gesture that conveys meaning within the utterance context (e.g., G:OH-WELL-SHRUG).
G(CA): MEANING	A type-like gesture that is enacted, with facial and body postures that show constructed action or dialogue. For example, G(CA):SURPRISED-PERSON.

(*Continued*)

TABLE 1. *(Continued)*

Annotation	Meaning
CA:ENTITY-ENACTED	A constructed action (CA) or dialogue (CD) annotated on the CA tier, where the signer's head and torso postures enact an entity (e.g., CA:NEGOTIATOR).
DS SEGMENT	An IS segment selected for comprehension test and that includes one or more depicting signs.

Note. Annotations of source IS presentation data were informed by the procedures used for annotating the Auslan Corpus, details for which are found in Johnston, 2014 Auslan Corpus Annotation Guidelines.

TABLE 2. *Transcription Conventions*

English transcription	Meaning
GLOSS	A word in small capitals denotes an English gloss for a sign form.
[MEANING]	A small capitalized word in brackets denotes the meaning of a sign or utterance.
PROGRESS-IS-FORWARD-MOVEMENT	A hyphenated phrase in small capitals denotes a metaphor.
ǀTOKEN SPACEǀ	Words surrounded by vertical bars denote an approximate location in signing space that is a placeholder "token" for a referent in signed discourse.
F-I-N-G-E-R-S-P-E-L-L-I-N-G	A word in small capital letters, separated by hyphens denotes a fingerspelled word.

TABLE 3. *Sign Language Abbreviations*

Abbreviation	Meaning
NSL(s)	Native signed language(s)
SL(s)	Signed language(s)
AlbSL	Albanian Sign Language
ASL	American Sign Language
Auslan	Australian Sign Language
BANZSL	British, Australian, and New Zealand Sign Language
BSL	British Sign Language
CSL	Chinese Sign Language
CZSL	Czech Sign Language
DGS	German Sign Language
DSGS	Swiss German Sign Language
FinSL	Finnish Sign Language
HKSL	Hong Kong Sign Language
HZJ	Croatian Sign Language
IPSL	Indo-Pakistani Sign Language
ISL	Israeli Sign Language
IrishSL	Irish Sign Language
JSL or NS	Japanese Sign Language
KAL	Kosovo Sign Language
KSL	Kenyan Sign Language
LIS	Italian Sign Language
LIBRAS	Brazilian Sign Language
LSE	Spanish Sign Language
LSF	French Sign Language
LSM	Mexican Sign Language
LSQ	Quebec Sign Language
NZSL	New Zealand Sign Language
NGT	Sign Language of the Netherlands
ÖGS	Austrian Sign Language
RSL	Russian Sign Language
TSL	Taiwanese Sign Language
TID	Turkish Sign Language
USL	Ugandan Sign Language

Chapter 1

Introduction

This volume is the result of a study that addressed several unknowns about a signed language contact phenomenon known as *International Sign.* International Sign (abbreviated IS) is a form of contact signing used in international settings where people who are deaf attempt to communicate with others who do not share the same conventional, native signed language (NSL).[1] The term has been broadly used to refer to a range of semiotic strategies of interlocutors in multilingual signed language situations, whether in pairs, or in small or large group communications.

The research herein focuses on one type of IS produced by deaf leaders when they give presentations at international conferences, which I consider to be a type of sign language contact in the form of *expository IS.* There has been very little empirical investigation of sign language contact varieties, and IS as a conference lingua franca is one example of language contact that has become widely recognized for its cross-linguistic communicative potential.

The larger piece of this research examines comprehension of expository IS lectures created by deaf people for other deaf people from different countries. By examining authentic examples of deaf people constructing messages with lecture IS, one can uncover features of more or less effective IS, and one can become better informed about IS as a sign language contact strategy. By investigating sociolinguistic features of IS contact, and identifying factors impacting its comprehension, one might ascertain optimal contexts for using IS as a means of linguistic accessibility. This research contributes to a limited literature about IS and aims to help

1. Following convention in the sign language literature, the capitalized word *Deaf* is used when referencing communities, languages, and the broad cultural-linguistic identity of members worldwide of the minority group of deaf SL users. The lowercase term *deaf* is used throughout in a general sense to refer to persons who do not hear, regardless of their identification with other deaf people, degree of audiological deafness, adherence to Deaf cultural norms, or fluency in their local SL.

stakeholders—deaf people, international deaf leaders, conference planners, IS trainers, and interpreters—improve our understanding of IS as a unique linguistic and cultural phenomenon.

The IS phenomenon has received increased attention in recent years (de Wit, 2010; Green, 2014; Hiddinga & Crasborn, 2011; Mesch, 2010; Mori, 2011; Whynot, 2013, 2015). Even as I was finishing this book, a timely new volume appeared, offering insights into the linguistic description, usage, and status of IS (Rosenstock & Napier, 2016).

IS is not a Deaf community sign language (one that is established with native users). It is not a conventional language, yet at international deaf events it functions as a contact language with some form-meaning conventions. The degree of effectiveness that an IS communication system achieves, however, remains elusive. Whether one refers to it as a "language of gestures" (British Deaf Association [BDA], 1975), an advanced or expanded contact pidgin (Supalla & Webb, 1995; Woll, 1990), a type of "foreigner talk" (Adam, 2012; Quinto-Pozos, 2007), or a lingua franca (Rosenstock, 2004), its customary use in global social and political contexts suggests that IS contact has semiotic value among some deaf people. Requests for IS interpreters have increased in recent years in Europe (Nardi, 2008), although interpreters have been asked to provide services into IS for communication access since 1977 (Scott-Gibson & Ojala, 1994). The European Union of the Deaf (EUD) provides a position paper on its website[2] regarding the use of IS as an auxiliary language for audiences of diverse SL backgrounds; it is used daily in many of their activities. The EUD emphasizes the priority of the rights of deaf people to have communication access in their "national or community" sign language (EUD website). They regard IS as an imperfect solution, arising out of a need for a common lingua franca among deaf persons in international contact.

It has grown customary for international conferences pertaining to deaf people to include interpreted and direct expository IS. Direct IS address is created by presenters; however, interpreted IS includes target messages between IS and the spoken and/or signed language of the conference. Conference planners typically limit interpreting services to the host country's sign language (English, for example), the host country's spoken/written language (if different than English), and increasingly,

2. URL (last accessed July 18, 2016): http://www.eud.eu/about-us/eud-position-paper/international-sign-guidelines/

International Sign. In some cases, IS is replacing conventional sign language as an official conference language.[3]

IS also appears frequently on informational websites either as a translation or as directly communicated content. (See Rosenstock & Napier, 2016, p. 2, for a detailed list.) In addition, it is recognized and used with increasing regularity in formal contexts for communication (direct and interpreted) in European Union institutions, the United Nations (UN), and other European government organizations (de Wit, 2016). This occurs in tandem with provision of NSL interpreting, as the Directorate General for Interpretation of the European Commission (SCIC—Service Commun Interprétation-Conférences) reports that 13 NSL interpreters and 10 IS interpreters are available to work for the European Commission (de Wit, 2016, p. 9). Notably, the profession of sign language interpreting is not controlled for quality, and it is not officially recognized in Europe (de Wit, 2016).

Due to the rising demand for this type of contact language interpretation, a special designation that identifies "qualified" IS interpreters was recently established by a World Association of Sign Language Interpreters (WASLI) and World Federation of the Deaf (WFD) task group "to regulate and monitor the standards of IS interpreting in international contexts" (Best, Napier, Carmichael, & Pouliot, 2016). The presence of IS alongside NSLs brings an interesting juxtaposition for provision of "language" access by sign language interpreters. There remains an ongoing need to assess empirically what constitutes effective interpretation from and into a mixed sign language contact variety and how this compares to provision of traditional NSL interpretation. Meanwhile, and perhaps as a point of departure, there is a need to understand the IS contact phenomenon as an example of meaning-making with sign language contact forms and features of language in the visual modality.

Meaning is a central theme in this research and recurs in the sparse IS literature, but meaning conveyance in IS has not been examined closely. Interpreters working in IS are challenged to achieve true semantic equivalence in their target interpretations, given the limitations of IS's "lexically limited and partially improvised" system (McKee & Napier, 2002, p. 50).

3. The 2016 International Gesture Studies Conference in Paris noted English and International Signs (interpreting services) as their two official conference languages. URL (last accessed January 12, 2016): http://isgs7.sciencesconf.org/?lang=en

At the same time, because some common features of NSLs are observed in IS, it is suggested that these aid in comprehension by varied signers in an audience. Interpreters are described as using a free approach to creating target IS (McKee & Napier, 2002), and by using their understanding of SLs, they produce "pared down" messages in a recognizable way to deaf audience members, who in turn rely on their life experiences and world knowledge to comprehend conveyed information (Scott-Gibson & Ojala, 1994). Common features of different SLs and adjustment techniques of IS interpreters (and perhaps deaf IS presenters) have yet to be connected to improved IS discourse comprehension. Without knowledge of linguistic (and other sociolinguistic) factors for improved IS comprehension, training and provision of IS for communication access run the risk of being less effective than desired.

Jordan and Battison (1976) were two of the earliest sign language researchers to question the long-held assumption that SLs are universal and that signers from all corners of the globe have little to no difficulty understanding each other. Forty years later there is a relative dearth of works on sign languages in contact and resulting phenomena to prove or disprove this assumption with respect to some form of "international sign." Nonetheless, IS has gained restrained acceptance to some degree as communicative access for international attendees with limited or no knowledge of conference languages. In other cases, IS is used as a lingua franca when deaf people gather without the use of conventional signed language interpreting services.

The topic of IS and the issues pertaining to it are prevalent in current discourse in international Deaf (and interpreting) communities. Rosenstock aptly notes that although IS usage previously was viewed as an ad hoc, "emergency" communication solution (Bergman, 1990 in Rosenstock, 2016), "the widespread and increasing use of IS today suggests it is no longer an emergency situation" (p. 99), but rather it indicates deaf peoples' highly valued desire for interconnectedness, and further, that there is a "need for this variety" of contact language (Lucas, in Rosenstock & Napier, 2016, p. 3).

It is my hope that linguistic examination of IS phenomena, usage contexts, and questions about comprehensibility will not be misconstrued as antithetical to manifestations of deaf collectivity (Ladd, 2003)—global Deaf identity—but rather, appreciated as timely in seeking to understand the unique sociolinguistic circumstances of signed language users in contact. Perhaps this study can contribute to a dialogue about where contact strategies like IS serve aims toward a desire for connectedness and where they are effective for language access.

PROBLEMS WITH DEFINING INTERNATIONAL SIGN

The nomenclature "International Sign" is a popular descriptor of contact signing, regardless of contexts and individuals or SLs involved in such contact. It is imperative to lay clear boundaries around SL contact phenomena in research endeavors so that public discourse moves toward a disciplined analysis of varied types of SL contact phenomena. Expository, presentation-style IS is one possible type. Therefore, what people are calling "IS" requires clearer definition and description as groundwork for empirical study.

Contact languages are complex communication systems. Even linguists seem to disagree on boundaries around contact phenomena befitting labels such as "pidgin, 'extended pidgin,' 'interlanguage,' 'imperfect second language (L2) learning,' 'jargon,' etc." (Winford, 2003, p. 268). Importantly, researchers of spoken language pidgins and contact varieties do not categorize all spoken language contact phenomena into a singular "International Speech." A special case worth mentioning is the spoken and written system "Esperanto," which is an example of an international, auxiliary contact language that has been in use by a small number of proponents since its creation by L. L. Zamenhof in 1887 (United Nations Educational, Scientific and Cultural Organization [UNESCO], 2003; Universal Esperanto Association [UEA], 2011). Esperanto is an artificial communication system, unlike the evolution of modern-day IS. However, some parallels can be seen in the early development of IS-type contact. Although in modern times IS is evolving naturally as a variety of SL contact, efforts between the late 1950s through 1975 tried to address the limited lexicon of what was an early international sign language pidgin.[4] Committees on standardization and planning created dictionaries for international signs, or what was promoted as *Gestuno:*

4. A pidgin is characterized as a simplified communication system resulting from contact between interlocutors who do not share the same language (Winford, 2003).

International sign language of the deaf (BDA, 1975; Supalla & Webb, 1995). As will be seen in this study, some of these promoted signs are still present in recent IS usage.

To date, a standard definition of IS has not been established in the literature. In 2007 the WFD General Assembly came to an agreement to use the term "International Sign" or IS, rather than "International Sign Language," identifying the need for further research to justify it as a language (Mesch, 2010). That same year, a WFD survey was conducted on the perspectives on and the definition of IS, which reported mixed assertions and opinions by laypersons, international deaf leaders, and several linguists. Conflicting claims and suggestions are noted, such as "It fulfills all criteria of human language," "[Its] temporary usage means the form of IS is too variable or unpredictable to be named 'a language' in the sense of a conventional system," "It has a sufficiently high level of conventionalization [....] lower than in national sign languages; but higher than in other kinds of cross-sign communication," and "It is a form of contact signing" (Mesch, 2010, p. 6). The report also notes a disagreement with characterizing IS as a pidgin or creole language,[5] given IS "expanded" grammar, simple lexicon, and lack of generational transmission. It is also suggested that there are two types of communication: conventionalized IS and informal communication between the users of national SLs (p. 13). This WFD publication clearly characterizes the lack of consensus about IS and demonstrates the need for more empirical investigations.

Supalla defines IS as "a contact language arising whenever two or more deaf people meet and communicate" (2008a, p. 1) and suggests that IS used in regular meetings of the WFD is a "standardized variety of pidgin language" (p. 2). The recent WFD survey report mentioned above makes a distinction between two types of IS communication (Mesch, 2010). The first is an informal *ad hoc* signing method between people who do not necessarily know each other's SLs. The second is a conventionalized form of IS by groups of signers. In this study I focused on the latter type, and even more specifically, on group communications that are in the form of presentations seen at global deaf conferences and meetings.

5. A creole language is typically characterized as a pidgin that has expanded over a generation and structurally developed via nativization (native speakers of the pidgin); however, the boundaries of creoles, their emergence, and difference from expanded pidgins are topics of debate in the contact language literature (Mufwene, 2007, 2008).

Discourse context cannot be neglected in a discussion about IS contact. Meanings are always produced and understood within subjective contexts and usage events (Janzen, 2014; Langacker, 1987; among many others). Because the nomenclature "International Sign" has been a popular descriptor of an assumed singular language-like variety—regardless of contexts and individuals or SLs involved in such contact—in my research, I drew clear boundaries around a specific discourse genre of IS, and then tested it for understanding.

As mentioned earlier, expository IS is a *contact language between more than two different SL users that occurs in the form of expository, formal discourses.* Expository IS is created by deaf presenters and interpreters who render a mixed SL system to a diverse SL-using audience in the form of unidirectional address, typically at global deaf conferences and meetings where large and small groups of mixed SL users convene. All references to IS forthwith refer to this contact variety of international contact signing.

Contact Language and IS

The reality for deaf people in varied communities around the world is economic and linguistic disparity. Deaf citizens experience disparity in their access to educational and economic opportunities, which is directly impacted by the success or lack of national recognition of their natively occurring languages and provision of services in those languages. Additionally, there are national discrepancies in government state wealth that also influence the extent of services available to deaf citizens, and this influences any outreach efforts to those citizens or others in neighboring communities.

Fewer than 5% of deaf people learn their sign language (i.e., American Sign Language) as a first language from deaf parents (Fischer, 1978; Schen & Delk, 1974 cited in Newport, 1999). Low numbers of native SL learning have been reported for many users of community or urban SLs in Australia and England (Schembri, Cormier, Fenlon, & Johnston, 2013), Europe, Latin America, and Africa (Brentari, 2010). A sociolinguistic reality of imperfect learning of one's native SL impacts second language (L2) learning as well. Imperfect learning of one's first language (L1) complicates phenomena where SLs are in contact.

Language contact phenomena involve a variety of structural and linguistic outcomes and are influenced by the status of the languages in contact, such as interlocutors' attitudes, characteristics, and bilingual skill, among other variables (Lucas & Valli, 1992). Contact between two SLs involves lexical borrowing, foreigner talk, code switching and interference, and the development of pidgins, creoles, and mixed systems (following Ferguson & DeBose, 1977; in Lucas & Valli, 1992). It is shown that signers quickly adapt their signing style depending on their interlocutor. Contact phenomena result from communicative accommodation where interlocutors exhibit degrees of convergence and divergence from each other (Giles, 1973). IS signing presenters and audience members are in a unique situation where numerous languages are in contact, and the communication is not targeted toward features of any *one* SL as an L2, but toward features that are assumed to be understood in all SLs.

Languages are imported through contact between groups of people, some of whom have money, social and political institutions, and large numbers of users (Mufwene, 2008). Contact is also a natural factor in the development of all languages. It is widely known that English is a global lingua franca (Crystal, 2003). English has an effect on deaf communities as well, through regular contact with speakers and the importation of English to international deaf communities (Kellett Bidoli & Ochse, 2008). In terms of SLs, most of the contact has arisen out of the sharing of educational methods and the work of religious missions from one country to another (Woll, Sutton-Spence, & Elton, 2001). French Sign Language (Langue des Signes Française, LSF) has had a profound influence on sign languages in North America and Europe, particularly American Sign Language (ASL), Russian Sign Language (RSL), and IrishSL (p. 30). ASL and British Sign Language (BSL) have impacted SLs in several African countries (Lule & Wallin, 2010).

The widespread influence of NSLs such as BSL and ASL is seen in contact situations that employ IS. Woll (1990) showed BSL prominence in the IS lexicon at one international venue. LSF and other European SLs influenced the original committee-created dictionary of *Gestuno* (the first attempt at capturing an international communication system of signs). Furthermore, ASL lexicon has been part of the instruction of IS training courses in Australia and Hong Kong.[6]

Both ASL and BSL have influenced the sign languages of countries in Africa and Asia through education and missionary work, as well as

6. IS intensives, Melbourne, Australia, 2011, and personal communication with Jenny Lam, UHK.

continued influence of "learned contact" with ASL via international programs and leadership graduates of Gallaudet University (Woll, Sutton-Spence, & Elton, 2001). Foreign forms are also sometimes more highly valued, and therefore, borrowing is one type of contact effect, such as the borrowing of Kenyan SL (KSL) into Ugandan SL (USL) after a period when educated deaf persons returned to Uganda from higher education institutions in Kenya (Lule & Wallin, 2010). Describing the transmission of SLs in Mediterranean Europe, Quer, Mazzoni, and Sapountzaki (2010) note that major urban centers in Rome, Athens, Madrid, and Barcelona helped maintain and develop each country's NSL, mainly due to the situation of deaf schools in these urban cities. They note:

> Nowadays, many signers have been exposed to foreign sign languages, mainly ASL, but also other European sign languages and International Sign (IS). In Spain Catalan signers have at least passive knowledge of LSE. This does not mean that there is a sign language bilingual situation in Catalonia, as LSC is the sign language used by Catalan signers almost exclusively. This is, for instance reflected in the curriculum for interpreter training in Catalonia, which devotes most of the sign language proficiency hours to LSC, with some additional LSE and IS learning. (Quer, Mazzoni, & Sapountzaki, 2010, pp. 98–99)

Many ASL video materials are available in web-based video repositories such as YouTube. Websites hosted in different countries stream Internet media for exchange of ideas and information, and creates easy access to foreign signed languages. A query of YouTube video archives in June 2016 using the search phrase "American Sign Language" prompted over a million results. A search for videos bearing the tag "British Sign Language" resulted in 77,500 results; "Língua Brasileira de Sinais" returned 20,000 items; Brazilian Sign Language 12,100 video items; "Japanese Sign Language" resulted in 74,800; "日本手話指文字" returned 6,940; while "Auslan" prompted 33,200.[7]

All of these factors impact the international contact between deaf people. Moreover, deaf people are subject to language contact trends

7. A query of the English phrase, "International Sign 'language'" prompted (121,000) results; however, only two-thirds of the hits show content related to IS phenomenon, with varied examples of what is called "International Sign (language)." It is likely that other queries in different languages (i.e., Spanish or Japanese) may return additional video examples of IS.

occurring within their surrounding spoken language communities. For example, political changes impact SLs in different ways. A lexical study of Taiwanese Sign Language (TSL) indicated evidence of influence from Japanese Sign Language (JSL) on modern TSL, which stemmed from periods of Japanese occupation between 1895 and 1945 and influence from Chinese Sign Language (CSL) beginning in 1949 from contact with deaf mainland China refugees (Sasaki, 2007).

Contact effects have also occurred with the spread of IS usage. Hoyer reported on the situation in Albania, when foreign signs in IS were brought into the country when its political and social economy began opening to the world in the late 1990s. External aid to a changing Communist country brought foreign forms into the long-suppressed Deaf community. As a result, IS signs now appear in Albanian Sign Language (AlbSL) (Hoyer, 2007).

The international Deaf community (via WFD) aims toward sign language rights, recognition, and access (Bergmann, 1990; Moody, 2007; Scott-Gibson & Ojala, 1994). Efforts continue toward the documentation, protection, and recognition of natively occurring SLs in many countries, and toward deaf persons' rights to civic access by way of their NSL. Meanwhile, the emerging IS contact system is used, ironically, in the international discourse on deaf persons' NSL access rights. Deaf people demonstrate a regular reliance on IS as a contact strategy in relatively high-stakes international meetings, as evidenced by IS interpreting provision over several decades of international conferences of the WFD and ongoing work of the EUD.[8] At the same time, the United Nations Convention on the Rights of Persons with Disabilities (UNCRPD), promotes Deaf people's rights to an NSL that is part of their country's cultural, social, historical, and religious heritage (WFD, 2014). The concurrent values of language diversity and language reduction/standardization through an auxiliary contact IS system present an interesting dichotomy of ideas, which may be further fleshed out in public discourse about IS in the coming years.

8. Personal communication with Mark Wheatley, executive director of the EUD, September 2011.

EMERGENCE OF IS CONTACT AND HISTORICAL CONTEXT FOR MODERN IS USAGE

Circumstances that are cultural, social, historical, political, and economic create separate, somewhat isolated populations of deaf people with distinct communities and native SLs. Yet, deaf people have a long history with contact signing strategies across SLs, which are first documented in Europe (Moody, 2002). Language contact often occurs between signed and spoken languages of deaf people's surrounding communities (Lucas & Valli, 1989, 1992). Contact between sign languages in Europe and other developing continents and countries was made by way of colonialism, and civic, religious, and educational missions (Brentari, 2010; Quinto-Pozos, 2007), but the languages used by deaf people in their local communities are mutually unintelligible to each other. This is true even when the national written and spoken language is shared, as is English for the United States and the United Kingdom, where ASL or BSL is the community language (Deuchar, 1984; Kyle & Woll, 1988).

Cross-linguistic contact is part of mankind's sociopolitical and economic histories (Mufwene, 2008), and deaf communities' SLs are not immune to these processes. Contact continues to occur more frequently over the past half century given modern advances benefitting deaf communities. One of the earliest documented SL contact systems was a variety of North American Native Indian sign language. It served as an intertribal lingua franca for indigenous speakers of varied native spoken languages in the 1800s–1900s, before English replaced this contact signing system (Davis, 2005, 2007). Additional evidence of deaf people in civic life 150 years ago points to the existence of some form of "universal" signing, a SL contact phenomenon between native users of different SLs (Moody, 2002). One such example comes from reports of banquets held in Paris, France, in the 19th century at the Institute Nationale des Jeunes Sourds (INJS) pertaining to the education of deaf persons. Reportedly at these banquets, "Sign is the only language permitted. Reports, minutes, correspondence, memoranda, everything is read in this language which deaf people from all parts of the world understand wonderfully well" (Ferdinand Berthier, 1850, trans. in Moody, 2002, p. 10).

Since Berthier's time, much more is known about the diverse, distinct SLs of the world. Assumptions about the phenomena of cross-linguistic contact signing noted above, particularly that they are easily understood, have yet to be fully investigated. It is unknown whether and to what extent attendees at these banquets understood one another. Most of the "international" contact in those years was between Europeans and North Americans and their colonies, which means there were regular communications and perhaps a more stable "trade" communication system through these connections. Evidently, enough content was conveyed in order for exchange of ideas regarding methods for the education of deaf people in those participating nations. These exchanges contributed to the foundational history of deaf people's education in Europe and the United States during the late 18th and early 19th centuries (Lane, 1985) and a sociopolitical organizing effort of deaf people in different countries (Moody, 2002, 2007).

Any contact variety of "international" signing observed in the mid-1800s has undoubtedly undergone much change during the past 160 years. Languages undergo gradual change over time and with natural evolution, and changes occur through competition, selection, and ecology (Mufwene, 2008). Regularly used trade contact varieties maintain the most robust elements of the languages in contact, and are less susceptible to the morpho-syntactic breakdown that accompanies contact (Mufwene, 2007). While Mufwene describes the nature of spoken language evolution in light of trade colonization and educational missions to non-Western countries, sporadic contact between different SL users for educational exchange created opportunities for SLs to interact and create structurally reduced language varieties. Without historical linguistic evidence, it is difficult to claim that the robust elements of early international signing contact resembles the expository IS used in conferences today. It is unlikely that these are the same "variety."

Most of the international sign language contact opportunities that continued into the 20th and 21st centuries only recently included host locations outside Europe or North American. The first Asian-based international deaf event took place in 1991 at the WFD Congress in Tokyo, Japan. Other non-Euro-American venues were chosen for events such as the 1989 Deaf Olympic Games in New Zealand, the 1999 WFD Congress, 2005 Deaflympics in Australia, the 2006 Theoretical Issues in Sign Language Research (TISLR) in Brazil, the 2009 Taiwan Deaflympics, and the 2011 WFD Congress in South Africa.[9] Therefore, the picture of

9. Data collected from World Federation of the Deaf website (https://wfdeaf.org) and Sign Language Linguistics Society (SLLS) events website (http://slls.eu/tislr-conferences/).

what people are referring to by "International Sign" is still very much what I assert to be a "moving target." Explanation of how it works and the level at which it works needs much more evidence-based description.

An important factor influencing the way IS emerges relates to the frequency and scope of language contact between users of different SLs. Regular, consistent cross-linguistic signing contact has taken place since the creation of the Comité International des Sports des Sourds (CISS) in 1924. CISS is the organization that hosts major international sporting competitions for deaf people from as many as 77 countries, notably the Summer and Winter Deaflympics. The Summer and Winter Deaflympics take place 2 years apart from each other, every 4 years, respectively, and are sanctioned by the International Olympic Committee (IOC) and World Deaf Championships for thousands of athletes, officials, volunteers, and spectators.

One of the primary contexts where IS is used is through the work of the WFD. The WFD was originally established in 1951 in Rome, Italy, at the first World Congress, under the auspices of the Italian Deaf Association and with the later support of the European Nation States. The WFD continues to serve its mission as an international nongovernmental organization representing approximately 70 million deaf people worldwide. The WFD has maintained ongoing consultative liaison work with UNESCO, the United Nations, and the World Health Organization (WHO) since 1958. Civic activity has spanned national borders for more than 50 years, stemming from the work of the WFD, which is currently based in Helsinki, Finland. WFD regional development initiatives have had major impact on sign languages in contact, in an effort toward quality of life improvements for the world's deaf communities.

Influences on IS and SL contact in general come from international development work by organizations and institutions serving deaf people. Several leaders active in the international deaf community of educators, researchers, national deaf associations, and the WFD were educated at Gallaudet University. Gallaudet University has positively impacted the educational and economic upward mobility of deaf Americans; it also contributes outreach work and promotes contact with other nations' deaf citizens. The university is globally recognized as the only liberal arts college founded to serve the higher education of deaf persons.[10] Prestige

10. Gallaudet University Office of Research Support and International Affairs (URL: http://www.gallaudet.edu/rsia/international-affairs.html)

is afforded the university by deaf people from countries that do not have the same amount of civic access and economic privilege. In one sense, it stands as a symbol to deaf people that a historically misunderstood, marginalized group of "disabled" people can achieve civic equality and impact their local and national community. In another view, the university's far-reaching influence is sometimes criticized, in social media and on website blogs. The university has international collaborations and influence through their Center for International Programs and Services Department, which creates additional opportunities for deaf people in varied countries to have contact with ASL users. Foreign SL influence on indigenous SLs from cross-cultural educational and civic exchanges has been previously noted in recent work on SL contact (Hoyer, 2007; Quinto-Pozos, 2007).

Additionally, in 1989 and 2002, two major international Deaf arts and culture conferences—Deaf Way I and Deaf Way II—took place in Washington, DC, in affiliation with Gallaudet University. There were more than 9,000 attendees from all over the world at Deaf Way II in 2002. It is interesting to note that even in the short 13-year gap between Deaf Way I and Deaf Way II, the number of different SLs present in the interpreting on stage in the opening plenary platforms had significantly reduced from as many as 12 SLs to 3 SLs. One rationale is the prohibitive cost to provide interpreting services in numerous different SLs. In recent years IS has been seen as a potential solution to providing access—albeit compromised—to diverse SL users (Scott-Gibson & Ojala, 1994).

There are other regularly occurring international conferences related to deaf communities and SLs. Many of these rely on IS as a lingua franca. Major events that have global impact on deaf people are Deaf History International (DHI), the International Congress on Education of the Deaf (ICED), TISLR, and the WASLI. A handful of additional international events are regularly listed on the WFD site. Many of the above-noted events are held in a host country every 2 to 4 years, and contribute to continuous annual international activity and forums for cross-linguistic contact.

Activities within major international deaf-related events offer opportunities for users of different world SLs to come into contact on a regular basis. A review of international deaf events over the past 80 years shows this trend of increased global contact opportunity among deaf leadership. In the 3-year period between 1924 and 1927 there were two international deaf events; between 1981 and 1983 there were three; between 2005 and 2007 there were seven; and between 2010 and 2013 there were 10 international deaf events where expository IS (and other forms of contact signing) served as an auxiliary conference "language." Therefore, opportunities for SL contact have quadrupled in the past 20 years with the potential to increase in the coming decades.

In addition to the venues and events outlined above, the modern-day advances of video technology and other infrastructural developments increase global contact between varied nations' citizens. This continues to influence the opportunities for contact between users of different SLs. Web-based video repositories such as YouTube and DeafRead, among several other online sites based in different countries, stream ongoing Internet sign language media. In 2009 an innovative website came online that offers a news journal and international deaf news programs and reporting, which the creators promote as "broadcasting in International Sign." The site, www.H3world.tv, has gained popularity in recent years and is promoted at major international Deaf conferences, where the media staff film and create on-location news stories for publication on the website. Deaf people with an Internet connection need not travel to meet and interact with other deaf people from a different SL background, thanks to web-based communication through Skype and other Internet protocol video conferencing.

Global interaction between users of varied SLs is on the rise in the past two decades with expanded contact with more than European and North American signers. This study considers some of the ways that sign languages create meaning, and in particular if these meaning-making mechanisms convey information in IS to different NSL signers.

SIGN LANGUAGES, DISTINCT YET SIMILAR

Sign language linguists increasingly understand more about the signed languages (SLs) used by deaf people in their local communities, that they are rich, distinctly different, and are mutually unintelligible from one another. It is known that many of them are distinct languages, but they share some similarities, due to the visual-spatial modality and shared articulators of hands, arms, face, and torso. An online resource *Ethnologue* reports more than 140 different SLs observed in numerous world communities;[11] while not all in this list have been verified to be NSLs,[12] many natively occurring and distinctly different signed languages are linguistically explored and described in the literature (among many, Smith, 1987; Smith & Tang, 1979, for Taiwan Sign Language [TSL]; Deuchar, 1984; Woll & Sutton-Spence, 1999, for British Sign language [BSL]; Fu & Mei, 1986, for Chinese Sign Language [CSL]; Stokoe, 2005 [1960, 2005]; Klima & Bellugi, 1979, for American Sign Language [ASL]; Johnston, 1989, Johnston & Schembri, 2007, for Australian Sign Language [Auslan]; Woodward, 1991, for SL varieties in Costa Rica; Corazza, 1993, for Italian Sign Language [LIS]; Zeshan, 2000, for Indo-Pakistani Sign Language [IPSL]; Boyes Braem, 2003–2005, for Swiss German Sign Language [DSGS]).

Research on SLs provides material and opportunities to explore language and cognition. In the SL literature, language universals are discussed within the modality as well as across modality. A justification is made for a sign language typology where visual-gestural language ought not be measured by traditional descriptions of spoken and written language (Slobin, 2005). Documented SLs are characterized as historically young compared to spoken languages, and the added differences in articulators and the perceptual system are also named as influential on the linguistic structures in SLs (Meier, 2002). In addition, some researchers suggest that the complex sociolinguistic situation of signing communities contributes to unique characteristics of SL grammars (Schembri et al., 2013). Others have assessed SL structure vis-à-vis the structure of spoken and written languages, contributing to the linguistic validity of

11. Ethnologue website URL: www.ethnologue.com/subgroups/sign-language

12. Fischer (1998) distinguished native sign languages from natural sign systems. A distinction is made here about native signed languages, which occur naturally and develop across generations. Natural sign systems are evolved systems deaf people use to communicate with hearing people. "Natural" is used in a semiotic sense and also signifies a highly iconic relationship between a spoken, written, or gestural sign (symbol) and its referent (Fischer, 2002). Both are also distinct from artificial codes for SLs created for deaf education. Natural is also used in the literature to refer to spontaneously occurring and spreading community SLs (Bavelier, Newport, & Supalla, 2003; Sandler & Lillo-Martin, 2001). Throughout this book I use the term *native signed language* to refer to conventional, established community SLs (i.e., JSL, BSL, etc.).

SLs (e.g., Aronoff, Meir, & Sandler, 2005; Klima & Bellugi, 1979; Sandler & Lillo-Martin, 2006).

Ease of understanding across SLs has yet to be proven, yet gestural roots, common grammatical and iconic features, are given as the reasons behind these claims. Significant to this study is recent evidence that both gesture and linguistic elements play complementary roles in the way SLs create meaning (de Beuzeville, Johnston, & Schembri, 2009: Ferrara, 2012; Liddell, 2003; Schembri, 2001), and a multimodal approach can enlighten us to the way linguistic and gestural elements contribute to all languages. Although the SLs of the world are relatively young and less studied than spoken languages, we do know that contact effects between signed and spoken language users impact the development and change in all SLs. Last, as mentioned earlier, SLs rely on a variety of semiotic devices that are linguistic and gestural to create meaning. This is important to the current study given that very little is known about the amount of gesture and linguistic material used to construct meaning in IS and comprehend it, particularly when compared to NSLs.

Signers appear to use resources from their own NSLs to communicate with foreign signers (Rosenstock, 2004; Woll, 1990). Linguistic and gestural elements from NSLs are observed in IS, as indicated in a small number of published studies (McKee & Napier, 2002; Rosenstock, 2004; Supalla & Webb, 1995). Because previous research suggests lexical signs, gestural elements, and depicting signs (Dudis, 2004, 2014)[13] to be important elements in meaning-making in IS, in the first part of this research (study one), I examined the frequency and distribution of these signs in expository IS. These elements were assumed to impact comprehension. The focus here was on fully lexical signs (whether borrowed or lexicalized by the users), partly lexical depicting signs, and nonlexical signs (gestures and enactments), following Johnston and Schembri (2010).

13. Schembri (2003), following Liddell (2003), makes a case that the "classifier" may be a problematic term for what Supalla (1986) and others have additionally referred to as "classifier structures" or "verbs of location and motion." Schembri calls them "polycomponential signs" (2001) or "depicting signs" (Johnston & Schembri, 2007). I adopt the term "depicting sign" here going forward, unless citing others who specifically use other terms.

The visibility and formal recognition of IS in varied cross-linguistic settings juxtaposes two incongruous views about signed languages. On one hand and contrary to myth, there is no singular, universal signed language. Laypeople often assume that visual-spatial languages can be simplified to a universal gestural communication system, which comes from the uninformed view of signed languages as nonlinguistic pantomimes. Naïve questions are often posed to deaf people and interpreters about whether "sign language" is a globally universal type. Typically taken with slight offense, we are quick to defend the fact that languages are diverse, whether signed, written, or spoken.

According to anecdotal evidence and practice, there are unique, shared qualities of SLs, whereby different signers appear to understand one another readily. Spoken language users do not seem to have the same ease of accommodation across language boundaries. Signed language users take pride in a rich, productive pantomimic and iconic motivation that underpins *seeing* a language, rather than *hearing* it. Further, transnational communication practiced by deaf people permits them to overcome linguistic borders and contributes to a "sense of connectedness between Deaf people of different origins" (Signs2Cross).[14] The International Sign phenomenon therefore has significant cultural power that must be appreciated, even if we do not fully understand how and to what extent it functions, yet.

The Impetus

The impetus to this study is three decades of living and working alongside deaf people, as a friend and as a multilingual interpreter. It has afforded me opportunities to interact with linguistically and culturally diverse deaf people in my multicultural home city of Boston; in my new home in Melbourne, Australia; at international conferences and international deaf sporting events; as well as when I visited, worked, or lived in foreign Deaf communities for periods of time. Experiences communicating with deaf people who use a different SL from my own occurred on many occasions. Through these, I had opportunities to act alone or with

14. Retrieved January 2016 from URL: http://www.acm5.com/signs2cross/international-sign/

deaf colleagues providing "visual gestural" interpreting (V-G), as it was called in the late 1980s and early 1990s in the Northeastern United States. It was suggested that this mixture of mime, ASL, and what is considered an iconic gestural approach was an effective way to communicate with deaf people who used a different sign language, who were immigrants, or who did not have fully formed ASL for a variety of social, educational, or cognitive reasons.

Trained deaf interpreters who hold national qualifications currently do much of this code-mixing work in many states in the United States and to some extent in Australia.[15] Personal conversations with colleagues indicate a set of shared intuitions and assumptions, which may or may not be correct, about gesture and universals of signed languages as key elements for communicating with other signers from different linguistic and cultural backgrounds. Numerous experiences have shown me that effective communication in these cases is not guaranteed, and when it appears to be effective, it is difficult to describe or explain.

While completing my master's degree in Intercultural Relations, I was intrigued by the interaction of cultural frame on communication, particularly in my daily work as an interpreter. The way interpreters represent diverse deaf people in multicultural communities of the United States and in international events has been a driving curiosity in my regular practice and is an underlying theme of this study. Moreover, as an ASL user living in Australia for over 5 years, I observe firsthand some of the challenges of communicating cross-linguistically and misunderstandings that arise from my own reliance on contact signing and interlanguage. When interpreting with deaf migrants in linguistic transition from an ASL-based sign language to Auslan, I observe successes and failures in their attempts to make meaning of sign language contact. This leaves me with many questions about the limits and affordances of sign language contact for interim and long-term solutions.

15. The U.S. Registry for Interpreters for the Deaf (RID) and the National Accreditation Authority of Translators and Interpreters in Australia (NAATI) have qualification processes recognizing this unique work of trained Deaf interpreters. Between 2012–2014 and 2016 I contributed to the NAATI Deaf interpreter recognition process and subsequent qualifications that identify a need for "non-conventional signed language" interpreting, which includes using IS-type contact as a form of language access.

Personal experience as a professional interpreter, including work with IS, also prompts my queries. As a conscientious practitioner and educator, I often reflect on the effectiveness of my own and others' interpretations, given the impact on deaf people's human rights and quality of life—socially, economically, and politically. There is an inherent responsibility to interpreting, and there is merit in regularly questioning whether our target interpretations are understood.

Interpreted IS is not, however, the main subject of this investigation, although it may be informed by the findings. In this research I choose to examine direct IS output from deaf, IS lecturers. I acknowledge that there are potential differences that would impact comprehension of IS created by interpreters (interpreted IS) from a source language compared to IS created by deaf signers (signed IS), as posited by Rosenstock (2004). Closer look at this warrants a valuable, yet slightly different study. Yet, interpreters adopt many of the signs and cross-linguistic communication strategies used by internationally active deaf individuals; therefore, it makes sense to assess how deaf people use IS to communicate with audiences of different SL users.

In a paper presented at the 2007 World Association of Sign Language Interpreter conference, Moody stated, "[...let us] never forget that IS was developed by Deaf people and belongs to Deaf people" (Moody, 2007, p. 8). This study is focused on the way deaf individuals communicate with IS, avoiding the additional processing layer that interpretation adds to the final target message created. Cokely (1992b) described the complex interpretive processes that are involved in decoding a source language message and rendering it into a target sign language interpretation. The interpreting process presents a complicating element to the already complex cognitive demands of communicating into a code-mixing system. Direct IS output from deaf, expository IS users is of interest, and findings here will likely inform the target IS construction decisions by interpreters.

IS Training and Research Gaps

As a result of increased opportunities for cross-linguistic SL contact during the past 25 years, there is interest in IS among members of Deaf communities and interpreters for learning how to use "it." IS has garnered growing attention by deaf people and interpreters across the world, and as a result, individuals and organizations offer ad hoc or formal short courses or training sessions in IS for the purpose of training interpreters and for personal use.[16] Woll (1990) was first to note that these offerings are made without sufficient research foundations.

To date, there is still no corpus-based dictionary or empirically described conventional IS linguistic system to inform curricula for IS training. Although certain skills such as multilingualism (Mesch, 2010), linguistic flexibility to improvise (McKee & Napier, 2002), and international travel experience (Moody, 2002) are important for IS interpreters to possess, the complex training needs for learners of IS (particularly those who wish to interpret with it) and proper preparation to do the work are a topic of current discourse (Oyserman, 2016; de Wit, 2016). Workshops and provision of IS interpreting and IS teaching materials continue to be offered, with an acknowledged need for additional research around specific "language" and practice competencies for effective IS communication.

Professional SL interpreting associations and policies about provision of interpreting have developed exponentially since initial foundations of the profession emerged in the middle of the 20th century in North America, Western Europe, and Australia (WASLI, http://wasli.org). Meanwhile, the use of International Sign (IS) as a cross-linguistic communication system is increasingly relied upon to meet a need for language access at conferences and in recent years has replaced provision of multiple NSL interpreting services.

Interpreters who work in international settings and interface with deaf leaders from distinct SL communities continue to incorporate contact strategies used by deaf people in these settings, with expository IS figuring more prominently every year. However, providing interpretation via an unstable contact language has not been without controversy.

The first attempts to provide IS interpreting at international conferences in 1977 and 1979 were met with much criticism, due to excessive pantomime renditions or otherwise robotic interpreter performances (Scott-Gibson & Ojala, 1994). In the following decade, IS interpretation still garnered controversy as a double-edged sword in the provision of cost-effective language access for participants who could not afford to bring their own interpreters. A debate centered on linguistic access for deaf people with no NSL interpreters. Concern arose about potentially

16. In recent years I have personally attended or have been asked to assist with provision of IS training.

undermining indigenous SLs by providing IS contact signing. These value conflicts and some debate about linguistic access continue.

In the past, some SL linguists have contended that there are limitations to communicating academic or scientific information with an IS contact system. *The Amsterdam Manifesto* originally raised concerns about accessibility to full conference content (Rathmann & Mathur, 2000). The document recommended reliance on full NSLs in academic forums, typically the host country SL and any other SL that is highly represented in conference attendees (e.g., BSL or ASL). The recommendations were aimed at academic and scientific communities, and not necessarily for sporting and cultural events such as Deaflympics and Deaf Way. Recent shifts in thinking about these recommendations are observed with the increased expectation that IS interpreters and conference presenters use IS. Notably, however, at the 2013 London TISLR conference, the decision was made to forgo the provision of IS interpreting and offer conference interpreting in only fully conventional languages: BSL, English, and ASL. This decision was controversial when a number of deaf attendees did not know BSL or ASL and could not access the conference content. Subsequent changes in expectations about conference language policies led to discussion among the Sign Language Linguistics Society (SLLS) and local organizers of TISLR 12 in Melbourne in 2016.[17] There appears to be no simple resolution; however, debates are important and indicate evolving shifts in thinking about linguistic access at international deaf conferences. Consideration for the most appropriate approaches to providing language access at international conferences continues to place IS as central to these discussions.

Thus, speculation and conjecture about IS contact varieties merit careful evaluation of the phenomena for linguistic access. Well-researched recommendations about contexts for usage are needed. This research is one such attempt to look closer at factors for IS comprehension and address implications for IS usage.

17. I personally served on the TISLR 12 local organizing committee primarily in the role of coordinator of interpreting services. The provision of IS interpreting was considered with much care and investigation into the sociolinguistic profile of attendees. As a result, a cost-benefit analysis led to the decision to not provide IS interpreting for the full academic program, and interpreting services were well received. I discuss the implications of this experience further in the concluding chapter of this book.

Problem Statement and Significance

Expository-genre IS functions as an auxiliary, second language for participants when their NSL is not one of the official conference languages. Yet, the quality of information conveyed by expository IS is not completely understood. Very little is known about factors for IS comprehension, and it has not been critically compared to NSLs. Given the UN Convention on the Rights of People with Disabilities (CRPD), which grants the right to language access in one's own native SL, it is important to examine differences between receiving information in the IS versus in one's NSL. Although some audience members may not understand it very well (Rosenstock, 2004), international events and conference policies continue to include expository IS (whether interpreted or direct) as an official conference "language." Consequently, the effectiveness of IS contact signing is often assumed, yet it remains untested. In addition, IS training programs are offered with limited research underpinnings, and there remains some degree of mystery around "qualifications" to provide IS interpreting. It is important to continue to evaluate the potential for gleaning information from formal IS presentations (and other IS contact forms).

The research presented in this volume looks at meaning-making NSL patterns in IS and whether they are understood by diverse IS audience members. It examines expository IS lectures by deaf presenters, makes comparisons to NSLs, and assesses sociolinguistic factors for IS comprehension, with an intent to seek a richer description of what varied audiences understand from IS lectures. New empirical information will inform international conference language policies, research-based training efforts, and IS interpreting and usage where it is recruited for communication access. The aim is to seek insights for potentially more effective IS and appropriate applications.

Research Questions

The primary aim of the study was to investigate the communicative effectiveness of IS by focusing on its comprehensibility across a variety of signers. It addressed the following research questions and their related subqueries:

1) How comprehensible is expository IS, and for whom?
    a) To what extent are global and detailed messages in IS understood?

b) How does comprehension of IS compare to comprehension of NSLs?
c) Do audience demographics play a role in IS lecture comprehension?

2) What is the distribution of linguistic elements in the IS lexicon, and does this affect comprehension?
a) Does increased comprehension of IS correlate with increased use of lexical signs sourced from a NSL (e.g., ASL)?
b) Do depiction and gesture influence intelligibility of expository IS?

3) How effective is IS for universal access to lectures?

Answering these questions can bring new insights to an issue that continues to confound many international stakeholders—deaf leaders and interpreters—who work to uphold the advancement of the rights of deaf people.

This research makes a unique contribution to what is known about IS comprehension and a description of signs and semiotic forms used by deaf IS lecture presenters. It identifies frequent sign forms through a corpus-based approach, reporting 200 high-frequency signs used in expository IS by deaf presenters who originate from 10 countries across five continents. It is also the first study undertaken that answers questions about the amount of lexicon, depicting signs, and gesture appearing in presentation IS and tests how these elements impact the effectiveness of IS discourses. It is the first study to assess comprehension of IS created by deaf presenters as opposed to target IS texts created by interpreters. This research extends Rosenstock's 2004 study of interpreted IS by describing IS used by deaf presenters and by using multiple approaches to assessing comprehension.[18] An overarching question remains regarding the communicative effectiveness of IS. This is the first study to examine the gap in communication between IS and what is communicated in a NSL.

18. Throughout this volume I will refer to the 2004 work as "the Rosenstock study."

Chapter 2

Prior Research on International Sign

A limited collection of existing literature on International Sign (IS) offers insights about deaf people using it to present information or for other negotiated contact. Only a handful of published papers and one thesis are devoted to the topic from different theoretical or analytical frameworks. Empirical research about IS is lacking, and varied settings of international sign contact are not clearly delineated. In this project, the genre of IS is defined by its usage setting—expository presentation discourse. This type of IS is often associated with the provision of sign language interpreting (as noted in the introduction), and a few studies of interpreted IS comprise the small collection of published works on the topic.

Prior studies describe interpreting into and from what people refer to as "IS," and others report on linguistic characteristics of deaf people's use of sign language contact strategies, using terms such as "international signs" (Battison & Jordan, 1976), "international gestures" (Moody, 1987), or "International Sign Pidgin" (McKee & Napier, 2002). Recently some insights come from work on "cross-signing" between deaf interlocutors (Bradford, Sagara, & Zeshan, 2013). Terminology for IS and cross sign language (SL) contact is quite varied, with the emergence of the name "International Sign" as an entity arising to describe SL contact in international exchanges sometime during the early 1990s. Recently there have been discussions of a "pan-European sign"[1] to distinguish a contact variety of IS that is influenced by European SLs, which may be different than an IS contact system used in the Asia-Pacific region (Mori, 2011).

Moody (2002) provides an historical account of IS with observations about linguistic material from a practitioner's point of view; he admits these are based on observations and not empirical data analysis.

1. In personal email discussion with Dr. Bencie Woll about terminology, she reports observations of this alternate name by people discussing IS in Europe in recent months; July 2014.

Other papers and publications by the same author outline communicating (and interpreting) with "international gestures" or "charades" (Moody, 1987, 1994). These works refer to the predominantly gestural resources that deaf people employ when they do not share a common SL as well as point to the variation in lexicon contributed to the mix depending on the participants. However, "international gesturing" as it had been called in the past referred to mostly face-to-face contact rather than an auxiliary system used for giving presentations as a form of unilateral contact communication.

Some of the earliest reports of the controversy around IS interpreting and linguistic access are made in Scott-Gibson and Ojala (1994) and again recently in Moody (2007), who questioned the system's ability to act as effectively as a native signed language (NSL). As a result, Moody advocated for the promotion of NSLs. In the late 1970s, interpreters were first recruited to work into IS, and reportedly, "Those watching indicated that it felt like watching a 'theatrical performance,' rather than a series of lectures" (Scott-Gibson & Ojala, 1994, p. 161). Observations of the quality of the signing suggested it was different from signing with an NSL. There has not been a quantitative, comparative study of IS to NSLs nor comparative comprehension research until this current one. The majority of IS investigation describes interpreted forms of it or strategies interpreters use when working with it. Deaf people in cross-linguistic contact are very much central to the phenomenon of IS, but there are only a handful of studies devoted to deaf people using IS as a contact strategy.

INTERNATIONAL CONTACT AND IS: CATEGORIZING LEXICAL PHENOMENA

I begin with an overview of prior studies about IS and situate it in terms of language contact—particularly SLs in contact. Early research into international (spontaneous) contact between SL users who do not share a common language is described in Battison and Jordan (1976) and Jordan and Battison (1976). They queried the notion of sign language universality and efforts by the World Federation of the Deaf (WFD) in the creation of the *Gestuno* sign glossary, claiming it constituted evidence that "deaf signers themselves believe in the universality of sign language or at least in its potential" (Battison & Jordan 1976, p. 53). The researchers interviewed informants, made observations, and video recorded unstructured conversations between North American and foreign signers to investigate these beliefs. They reported interview responses about one's ability to understand other SL users, such as

> An Italian and a Pole who have both travelled widely were in a casual conversation with five Americans. They made no attempt to imitate or use American signs; they stated flatly that they did not understand American signs; and they relied the entire time on an American who was skilled in using *international signs* [emphasis added] and signs from various European countries. (Battison & Jordan, 1976, p. 58)

This is one of the first references to "international signs" and it coincided around the time of the creation of the *Gestuno* sign glossary by the WFD. Supalla and Webb (1995) cite the first and second editions of this sign list (WFD, 1959, 1965) before the release of the expanded published *Gestuno* glossary by the British Deaf Association and the Unification of Signs Committee of the WFD (BDA, 1975). (The *Gestuno* glossary is no longer in print.) Supalla and Webb (1995) also refer to "International Sign" as a singular entity when reviewing historical contact between deaf users of different SLs as early as 1924. They defined IS as a "type of signing used when deaf signers communicate across mutually unintelligible language boundaries. Deaf individuals use IS primarily in international settings to become acquainted with each other and to communicate about affairs of concern to them" (p. 334).

The report by Jordan and Battison (1976) suggested that some signers who interact with different SL users may naïvely characterize foreign signs as "international signs." The authors reported: "In the course of introducing a Dane to some Americans, the Canadian introducer used a few Danish signs. One of the Americans remarked to him, '*Oh, you know International Sign Language!*'" (p. 60).

Although the authors were referring to North American deaf people's lack of travel and cross-linguistic experience compared to European deaf people, it is evidence of lacking methodology and research that identifies sign types and origins in IS-type contact. It also points to inconsistency in naming and describing the forms used in international SL contact in public discourse (past and present). This is also the case in published material. The book, *International Sign,* published in Korea (DeafPlus, 2012), lists many lexical forms that are ASL citation forms, which hints at a viewpoint that any "other" foreign signs (not from "my" SL) might qualify as "international signing." IS, as people refer to it, appears to be a catchall phrase to denote the signing phenomena of distinctly different SL users in contact with one another. The terminology is problematic for empirical description of a variety of complex contact phenomena that might occur between distinct SL users. These complexities are further outlined in the next few sections.

The quotes above imply that skill in communicating with different SL users requires knowledge of a collection of certain undescribed "international" signs and knowledge of different (European) SLs. Also, it has been shown that signers use resources from their own NSLs to communicate with foreign signers (Rosenstock, 2004; Woll, 1990). Linguistic and gestural elements from NSLs are observed in IS (McKee & Napier, 2002; Rosenstock, 2004; Supalla & Webb, 1995). For this reason, continued empirical study is needed on semiotic forms observed in varied IS type contact settings.

STUDIES ON INTERNATIONAL CONTACT SIGNING USE BY DEAF PEOPLE

Published works on deaf people in international contact come from Moody (1979; 2002), Woll (1990, 1995), Allsop, Woll, and Brauti (1995), and Supalla and Webb (1995). Moody refers to "some form of International Sign [...] in use for at least 150 years" (2002, p. 57). It is unlikely that all of these forms are best described by the singular term "IS," given variation in settings and languages in contact over those years. However, he reports that contact between deaf people from different SL origins has indeed been occurring for many decades.

In earlier work, Moody (1979; cited by Woll, 1990) suggested three kinds of communicative phenomena operate in the contact settings between deaf people. These are "mimed actions," "invented gestures"—nonce creations in the temporary context, and a collection of "international gestures" which are borrowed from other SLs or otherwise understood forms given context or explanation (p. 110). Using Moody's categories, Woll (1990) investigated the lexicon and grammar of contact phenomena occurring between eight international deaf researchers at a workshop in the UK, in order to answer questions about what happens when a number of deaf people with different SLs come into contact. She reported similarities between signs from five different SLs[2] represented by attendees at the workshop—British SL, American SL, Danish SL, Swedish SL, and Israeli SL. Comparisons were reported on 200 sign items that shared two out of three parameters, but actual signs used by all attendees in the contact setting were not compared. Woll analyzed the way BSL users communicated in the contact setting and classified the sign types they used. She applied Moody's (1979) suggested contact phenomena types and noted whether signs the BSL signers employed were from their own lexicon or whether they altered a native sign to a mimetic form or replaced them with an international gesture. She did forgo Moody's category of "invented gestures" but included these types within her category of "international gestures," mainly because it was difficult to separate forms that had been "previously accepted international signs" or invented in the meeting (p. 11).

Woll noted that the BSL signers continued to use many of their own BSL forms in international cross-linguistic communication—between 69% and 80% of signs—yet they altered their communication by using 6% to 11% mime, and 13% to 21% of what she labeled "international gestures" (p. 5). She did not report on the lexical signs used by the other SL users at the researcher's workshop, however she suggested the lexical choices to be much more varied than what Moody posed in his characterization of types. She pointed out frequent strategies in the data where the BSL signer employed duplication with different lexical sign variations of BSL and/or with different SLs, as well as with gestures. In fact, she noted that in the approximately 20% of instances where a BSL sign is replaced with an altered sign—mime or international gesture—half of them occurred paired with the BSL sign as well.

Woll also reported on some of the grammatical features appearing in the international contact between the workshop attendees who use any of the five different SLs represented. She provided examples of "quite complex" grammatical structures, including locating referents in space, directional verbs, modification of signs for aspect, and morphological changes to verb forms by reduplication, incorporating negation, use of

2. The figures reported are taken from the author's earlier study (Woll, 1984) comparing signs across several different SLs.

classifiers, and nonmanual marking of questions, negation, and rhetorical questions (Woll, 1990, p. 7). The only time the author referred to the phenomena as IS is in the conclusion of the paper in quotation marks. She predicts, "'International Sign' may become more formalized as a transnational language" (p. 13).

In the next few studies on IS, the label begins to be established. IS is referred to as sign language contact—whether between a deaf presenter to a large multilingual deaf audience (Supalla & Webb, 1995) or between individual signers who do not share a SL (Allsop et al., 1995). In 1994 and 1995 a handful of research papers on IS were written, which describe a limited lexicon (Allsop et al., 1995), negation in IS (Webb & Supalla, 1994; Woll, 1995), and grammatical material in IS produced by deaf people (Allsop et al., 1995; Supalla & Webb, 1995; Woll, 1995).

In addition to reporting borrowed and invented signs (noted above), Woll (1995) showed evidence of IS as an "expanded pidgin" given the use of manual negation in the final position of the sentence[3] being negated. The study compared BSL negation with IS negation in a story task between signers who share the same SL (BSL) and those who do not. The author predicted that IS would have more forms using multiple channels (e.g., a head shake simultaneously articulated with a manual negation), yet the findings claimed evidence to the contrary. Nonmanual headshakes occurred more often in BSL than in IS, and BSL preferred nonmanual negation to manual signs. Manual negation signs appeared to be preferred in IS for negating a sentence, typically occurring in the final position, but not always. Final position negation sign was also the most prevalent type in Supalla and Webb's data (1995), discussed below. Woll concluded that IS has the "lexical structure of a new pidgin, but some grammatical complexity and functional use of a more developed pidgin" (p. 8).

A second report from what authors called "the International Sign Project" (data from the same international event) described other elements of the project (Allsop et al., 1995). The researchers interviewed deaf signers from different SL origins using IS contact signing in a story retell task. They mention a comprehension assessment from the retell;

3. Signed languages are not written languages; therefore, it is difficult to apply the linear concept of "sentence" to simultaneous complex visual-gestural language phenomena. In this study, unless reporting in terms of a prior author, I use the term "signed utterances" to refer to sign sequences of varying length.

however, the retell was not explained and neither the analysis nor the results were reported. The published results focus on lexical examples, noting differences in duration of the retells. Many participants took longer to retell in IS than NSL retelling, mainly due to lexical expansion required for creating reference to objects in the story. The report mentions only two lexical items and concludes that signs in IS are shown to be highly varied, with a few conventions. Allsop et al. identified a conventional IS sign for "woman" but described expansive strategies used to convey concepts such as "skateboard" and "strawberry." The most interesting finding is what they call a "string of paraphrases" that IS signers employ to expand on ideas that seem to have no lexical sign. It is summarized that IS contact employs an "impoverished lexicon" but a rich and structured grammar, yet there is not an elaboration on how grammatical relationships operate.

In the only other study using the same genre of IS-type contact, Supalla and Webb (1995) analyzed expository IS presentations by two deaf leaders at an international workshop and claimed there are grammatical complexities in IS. Supalla and Webb analyzed IS sentences containing transitive verbs reporting that IS shows a degree of inflectional morphology that is similar to verbal inflections in full SLs. Inflections in IS, they asserted, are agreement devices to mark subject and object agreement "using not only movement between spatial loci, but also using eye gaze and reference shifting for marking complex grammatical relations"[4] (Supalla & Webb, 1995, p. 340). The authors characterized IS as a linguistic system exhibiting rule-governed grammatical structures, rather than a simple pidgin with features of a nonlinguistic system of expanded gestures or pantomime. They claimed that IS employs (subject-verb-object [SVO]) word order, with regular instances of pro-drop and to a lesser extent, object-fronting;[5] they observed verb inflections and clause negation structures, all of which are described in full SLs. Supalla and

4. In this current study referential role shifts are termed "enactment."

5. Pro-drop and object-fronting refer to utterance types described in some spoken and some SLs that are alternative to SVO orders. Pro-drop occurs where the pronoun is absent (implicitly realized or anaphoric from discourse context) and the utterance starts with the verb (e.g., GAVE IT). Object-fronting describes utterances that topicalize the object and then predicates it as a comment (e.g., BALL I THROW).

Webb made an agreement-based analysis[6] of IS utterances and identified several ways that IS by deaf presenters use similar linguistic features seen in NSLs.

It is evident from earlier work that several kinds of linguistic and semiotic material are relied upon to create meaning between different SL users, and some patterns emerge that resemble features typically robust in NSLs. The distribution of linguistic and nonlinguistic material is of interest in this study, as IS presenters attempt to convey meaning.

THE ROSENSTOCK STUDY

Rosenstock's doctoral study (2004) examines comprehension as well as IS linguistic structures. The work investigated IS created by conference interpreters. Rosenstock also administered a computerized, multiple-choice comprehension test from selected segments of her interpreted IS data to international and U.S. students at Gallaudet University. Her research is reported from a cognitive-linguistic frame. She primarily gives a description of structures observed in the data and an analysis of linguistic elements, using Liddell's (2003) work on ASL real space blending. (The same framework is assumed in this current study and discussed in the next chapter.) She suggested that IS functions as a lingua franca, and reported that similar grammatical devices found in natively occurring SLs are observed in IS target messages constructed by interpreters. These are depicting and indicating verbs, iconicity and metaphor in lexicon, as well as numerous spatial ways of grammatically structuring IS utterances, including buoys, tokens, and gesture-like surrogates. She described the numerical and fingerspelling system and an inventory of handshapes, and reported that some IS signs are shared across different SL families, as noted by native users of several SLs. The description is broad, with examples of several NSL-type features observed in IS; however, their distribution in IS discourse is not assessed, and details about IS sign tokens and types are not reported.

6. In this current study, the assumption is that verbs directed at referent locations are gestural points, following Liddell (1995). The linguistic analysis of IS by Rosenstock (2004) presents examples of IS grammatical features from a cognitive linguistic frame, also following Liddell (1995, 2003).

In a later work, Rosenstock (2008) presented examples from her 2004 study dataset where interpreters rely on iconic representations in their target IS. She posited that IS structure is iconically motivated in lexicon and grammar and that iconicity and economy (following Haiman, 1983) compete in IS on discourse-pragmatic, syntactic, and lexical levels. She concluded that iconic signs are "iconic only to those who share the relevant cultural knowledge" (Rosenstock, 2008, p. 144). Rosenstock's examples of reductions, omissions, and repetitions (among other meaning-making decisions) by interpreters support her argument regarding competing motivations in IS interpreters' constructions, and they reflect coping mechanisms noted by the above studies on interpreters' IS strategies. When interpreters construct unfamiliar concepts more transparently (iconic motivation) rather than reduce familiar concepts to a more opaque form, this is due to economic motivation.

Providing examples from the 2004 dataset, Rosenstock observed IS constructions by interpreters are simplified, semantically related to the intended referent, or are reductions or superordinate forms for specific source-language words. For example, the sign meaning [GROUP] is used to imply the source-language idea, "business" or "organization." She offered evidence of simplified complex phrase structures and reduced fixed phrases to indicate economic motivation behind interpreters' reduced constructions or omissions. IS interpreters also reduplicate signs to express plurality, or intensity of action, as well as present actions in chronological order. In addition, she noted expansions from English words into longer phrases in IS, which at times were iconic demonstrations (surrogate actions) to visibly show a concept that has no established sign in IS (2008, p. 145).

Haiman (1983) elaborated on comparative expressions of reflexive verbs, causative constructions, and clauses with indirect and direct objects that were reductions or regroupings of one another (within the same language). Notably, he demonstrated that different yet synonymous expressions, whose distinctions are motivated by coordination reduction, will not be completely synonymous (within the same language). Therefore, IS expressions, in their attempt to be equivalent (and synonymous) constructions of the intended message of a conventional source language, may have varied success communicating equivalent content.

The Rosenstock study (2004) is the only prior research on IS comprehension to date. It assessed comprehension of interpreted IS recorded at an international conference in the United States. The findings indicated that interpreted IS has varying degrees of intelligibility by deaf audience members, and showed performance differences between Euro-American participants, and those from non-Western or North American origins. The average performance on multiple-choice questions across all participants was 54%, with ASL signers scoring on average 74% for interpreted IS. The study used pre-recorded video clips from interpreters rendering conference lectures into IS at the international Deaf Way II conference in 2002 held in Washington, DC. All of the interpreters in the stimulus IS videos were users of either ASL or BSL. Rosenstock observed differences in comprehension of directly signed IS from that of interpreted IS and unknown foreign language (ASL). In Chapter 5 I discuss the comprehension testing and results from the Rosenstock study in more detail as it informs the design of the current project (outlined in the methodology sections in Chapter 6).

IS INTERPRETING: MEANING CREATION WITH CONTACT LANGUAGE IS CHALLENGING

There are two published works on IS that investigate interpreters' use of IS. These differed from Rosenstock's approach in that they examined interpreters' strategies for conveying meaning when working either from or into IS discourses (de Wit, 2010; McKee & Napier, 2002). De Wit described the coping strategies that interpreters employ to manage challenges while interpreting from IS monologues. These challenges come from the need to be familiar with not only one's own working language (a first SL), but also foreign SL vocabularies and signer styles and knowledge of cultural frames that interlocutors bring from different nationalities. In addition to fluency in source and target languages, interpreting involves applying one's cognitive resources and efforts for both comprehension and production (Gile, 2009). De Wit presents interpreter strategies from data recorded of an interpreter working into English from an IS monologue, given by a deaf presenter.

Some of the IS interpreting strategies reported by de Wit are omissions, paraphrasing, "reverse" paraphrasing, additions (as a type of explanatory expansion), repairs and reformulations, among others. Many of these strategies are practiced by NSL interpreters (Napier, 2002). Omissions in IS source to target English include missing lexical items or phrases that resulted from miscues or insufficient processing time. Target English required use of more or less words and phrases than found in the surface IS text level, in order to elaborate into English the specific meaning intended by the source IS message. Repairs and reformulations also were used to restructure the order of discourse elements, or to make a correction about a skewed, unintended target message that resulted from unrecognized or unconventional sign forms in the source IS (de Wit, 2010, p. 10). The challenges of interpreter comprehension of a deaf presenter's IS lecture are evident in de Wit's observations. The genre (lecture) does not allow interaction or intervention by the interpreter for clarifying source message; furthermore, IS comprehension is challenging given what is shown to be the need for relatively long processing time (compared to NSL to English) to construe and formulate target interpretations from source expository IS.

McKee and Napier (2002) outlined types of interpretation strategies and linguistic strategies employed by interpreters when working *into* IS target, which they suggest should be used with NSL interpretation for a more "free" and visually salient target. As with any contact language or mixing situation (see discussion below), interlocutors bring their own SL resources into the mix, and therefore, as noted by McKee and Napier, interpreters recruit a variety of NSL-type linguistic devices to convey meaning into IS target messages. This is especially challenging because "the cognitive environment of the target audience is mediated not by one language, but by many, and the message is not conveyed in any single one of these" (p. 32). The authors observed a variety of linguistic characteristics such as nonmanual grammatical markers for verb aspect and manner, as well as discourse cohesion devices, spatial metaphors, and an increased use of nonlexical resources. The reason given is that the conventional lexicon in IS is "impoverished," echoing what Allsop et al. report (1995).

McKee and Napier reported that IS-interpreted discourses are articulated more slowly and use larger signing space than in NSL discourse. Interpreted IS employs grammatical features observed in NSLs. This includes use of spatial reference, metaphors, and types of inflections that NSLs employ for aspect and manner of movements, nonmanual sentence markers, use of classifier handshapes (see depicting signs below), as well as mimetic enactments—which the authors refer to as "role-shifts" (p. 40). Varied terms are used in the SL literature to describe role shifting (Padden, 1986), constructed action (Metzger, 1995; Winston, 1991), constructed dialogue (Roy, 1989; following Tannen, 1986), and perspective shift (Janzen, 2004), among others. It is also reported that IS interpreters "incorporate a great deal of meaning into as few lexical signs as possible" (McKee & Napier, 2002, p. 41). This is given IS's varied lexicon that appears smaller than what is observed in developed NSLs (Allsop et al., 1995). Interpreters employ some de facto nonce sign creations for the duration of certain events, and they make creative use of gestures to convey meaning (McKee & Napier, 2002, p. 42).

McKee and Napier also described several examples where interpreters established referential loci by turning eye gaze or pointing to real objects in space or indexing in these ways to imagined objects established in real space. They identified the use of less specified signs (as opposed to established, lexical signs) for concepts. They report interpreters using "entity classifier handshapes" to describe actions and appearances of objects, the meanings of which they suggested participants are able to infer and understand from the discourse context. Additionally, "pantomime" and "role-shifting" (enactment in this study) are productive in interpreter-constructed IS discourse. Rosenstock (2004) (reviewed below) also reports similar types of meaning-making material in IS that is created by interpreters.

The two studies on IS interpreter strategies propose that most of the linguistic and translation decisions that IS interpreters use are similar to those produced by all professionally qualified interpreters in their aim toward appropriate target interpretations from source while working with NSLs. Many of these strategies are described in the translation and interpretation literature (Bartlomiejczyk, 2006; Cokely, 1992b; Gile, 2009; Metzger, 2005; Napier, 2002). Interpreting from IS into spoken English requires managing inevitable and sometimes deliberate omissions, additions, and substitutions, which requires more processing or "lag" time to comprehend, reduce errors, reformulate, and make repairs (de Wit, 2010). Interpreters also employ paraphrasing and use of fillers to create target English messages from an IS presentation. The approach to interpreting into IS is also characterized as "free"—that is, free from linguistic form, yet it aims to be equivalent in terms of message transfer (McKee & Napier, 2002; Napier, 2002). The authors admit they were not looking at equivalence or whether audiences understand interpreted IS, but posit that improvised linguistic strategies might assist comprehension. They suggested comprehension of interpreted IS needs empirical study, and this was addressed soon thereafter by Rosenstock (2004).

IS interpreters also make selective reductions of the source text, often omitting detailed information such as numbers and unfamiliar proper nouns, as well as omitting things that are determined to not be "vital" to the message, especially given time constraints and lexical limitations (McKee & Napier, 2002, p. 46). Interpreters rely on iconic signs that are "simpler in form and capture a root concept" (p. 48), and often they employ discourse analytical strategies that are reductions, such as processing and rendering *general* information rather than *specific* information. Interpreting between languages is a search for equivalent meaning rather than detailed word-for-word transfer (Seleskovich, 1978), and with limitations created by language to a contact pidgin, equivalent transfer is a challenge. Approaches that employ "detail-to-goal" processing are strategies available for transferring a less detailed message while conveying main objectives and goals[7] (Gish, 1987).

McKee and Napier observed that the literal tendencies to which NSL interpreters sometimes default are not typically seen in IS interpreting. This is because interpreters must actively hone in on message meaning and create a reduced version of main points that often must forgo details given the constraints of the medium. While working into target IS, interpreters make reductions that are visually meaningful to the audience with material that is "limited and partially improvised" (p. 50). They also make some expansions to adjust for cultural frames of reference. When working from IS into English, interpreters often compress these expanded IS sequences into succinct words or phrases (de Wit calls these examples of "reverse paraphrasing" [2010, p. 9]). A larger inventory of lexical items is more readily available in English than in SLs (Johnston & Schembri, 1999), a widely acknowledged observation. The lack of succinct, conventionally specified lexical signs in IS presents a challenge to conveying rich and equivalent messages.

It is evident from the two studies on IS interpreter strategies that working between a spoken language (English) and IS poses unique professional challenges that arise from the nature of working from and into a contact language rather than an established NSL. Interpreters who work from and into IS hold national qualification in at least one NSL; some have more than one national qualification. In addition to fluency in source and target languages, interpreters apply cognitive resources and

7. See Gish (1987) for more information about her model for general to specific "chunking" during processing source to target language interpretations.

efforts for both comprehension and production (Gile, 2009). The idea of "fluency" in a system that is not a conventional language is ill suited; therefore, "communicative skill" may be a more appropriate term. There is no established benchmark for communicative skill in IS, although given the recently established designation for "qualified" IS interpreters by World Association of Sign Language Interpreters (WASLI) and WFD, research endeavors are timelier. Given these descriptions about challenges, interpreters manage to create meaningful messages in IS, but questions surrounding the communicative effectiveness of expository IS remain unanswered.

IS LECTURE AS A CONTACT PHENOMENON

IS used in conference presentations is an example of language contact that is not easily characterized by typical definitions of contact phenomena, such as creoles and pidgins, which result from the voluntary and involuntary movement of groups of people and intermingling of daily living and trade. This is because the social and linguistic contexts of IS are markedly different than those of pidgin and creole phenomena. Situations that create language contact phenomena between groups and individuals are varied, including trade, war, intermarriage, and individual travel and exchange, and changing communities are affected by immigration and emigration patterns. Complex sociocultural, and economic shifts influence languages in contact (Heine & Kuteva, 2005; Mufwene, 2007, 2008; Thomason, 2001; Thomason & Kaufman, 1988). However, sign languages in contact have not been the subject of research investigation until recently (Quinto-Pozos, 2007; Zeshan, 2015). There is a lack of distinction in the limited literature between IS and other forms of sign language contact.

Provided as a summary overview, Table 4 on p. 39 presents contextual, social, and linguistic features of spoken language pidgins, creoles, and L2 learning, juxtaposed with what is known about IS. A comparison of contact language types suggests that the social context of IS presents as a complex contact language situation that is different from pidgins and creoles and from second language learning. Rosenstock characterized IS as a lingua franca stating, "Users of IS are generally not in longstanding contact with each other and the system is assumed to rely on nonce creations and contextual loans, rather than an increasingly stabilized lexicon"

(Rosenstock, 2004, p. 47). IS is not a stable, daily form of communication in any one geographic community. It involves more than two signed languages in temporary, limited contact situations and can vary depending on the communication context and the size and language profiles of the users in contact. It is therefore reasonable to characterize it as a unique example of language contact.

Supalla and Webb's (1995) characterization of IS as an "advanced" pidgin is based on what they observed to be inflections for person and number, and other examples of morphological complexity in IS presentations by two deaf conference lecturers. Supalla and Webb claim that evidence of complex, developed features in IS is not typically present

TABLE 4. *Comparative Features of Pidgins, Creoles, L2 Learning, and IS Contact*

Context of language contact	Pidgins	Creoles	L2 learning	International Sign
User profile	Monolingual L1 users cut off from their L1 community; interacting with superstrate powerful users of another language (L1). Lack of language choice	L1 acquisition of a pidgin (parents' use) since birth Lack of language choice	L1 user wanting to learn L2 or needing to learn due to migration or education	Varied L1 SL users with mixed degree of bi-/multi-lingualism Privileged interlocutors with financial and social means to travel Personal choice to connect with other L1 SL users
Frequency of contact	Daily	Daily	Varies: regular to intermittent	Varies (less often than daily up to once per 1–4 years)
Usage contexts	At home and in local community	At home and in local community	Varies depending on L1 circumstance (migrant or student)	Limited; in the workplace; small or large group exchange, and Internet broadcasts

(*Continued*)

TABLE 4. (*Continued*)

Context of language contact	Pidgins	Creoles	L2 learning	International Sign
Social features	Users have typical L1 acquisition from birth Prestige and power of one language	L1 use is derived from parental pidgin	Equal status of L1 and L2 language	Different L1 users have varied L1 acquisition history Multiple L1 in contact Varied L1 prestige status
Linguistic features	No native speakers Simplified lexicon Reduced phoneme inventory Lack of morphological inflection/modification Restructuring and reduction of syntax Borrowed lexicon, less marked and at times more marked features Fixed clause/word order	Native speakers Many similar features to pidgins plus: (1) expansion of syntax, i.e., relative clauses, (2) patterns of negation, tense and aspect, and (3) expanded lexicon (compounds and circumlocutions)	Interlanguage (L2 incompetency) L1 interference Code-mixing or switching (native L1 and developing L2 competencies): • Between clauses or sentences • Within clauses or sentences	No native speakers Lexicon from several SLs, minimal stable forms Evidence of negation and some sign modification types similar to NSLs Nonce creations Borrowed lexicon NSL grammatical features (use of space, buoys, etc.) No research on clause structure to date

in simple trade pidgins, which gives IS more communicative potential. Pidgin creation is characterized by simplifications into reduced vocabulary, absence of bound morphology, and a limited range of syntactic structures (Winford, 2003). Basic pidgins typically do not exhibit complex forms unless they develop further to be characterized as expanded pidgins or even vernaculars (Mufwene, 2007, p. 7).

Contact phenomena in spoken languages are shown to be complex, with volumes devoted to the topic in the past few decades

(Thomason, 2001; Winford, 2003). SLs are linguistically complex in their own way, owing to the visual gestural modality and given that all SLs are typically subject to contact influence by spoken languages, because deaf communities are situated within surrounding spoken, written language communities. Therefore, SLs in contact are involuntary first cousins to the effects of spoken-to-SL contact. Twenty years ago, Lucas noted this fact when she wrote,

> For example the Italian Sign Language (LIS) sign NEVER is a lexicalized fingerspelled sign, related to the spoken Italian word **mai**. The handshape is i, representative of the last letter of the written Italian word. American ASL users in contact with LIS users may learn and use this sign and use it in conversation with ASL-LIS bilinguals. It is the result of spoken-sign contact and gets used in sign-sign contact situations. (Lucas, 1994, p. 262)

Contact phenomena between SLs and spoken languages are different from contact pidgins created from spoken languages. In spoken language contact, grammar comes from the substrate and lexicon from a superstrate (e.g., French and an African indigenous language created Haitian Creole). In SL-spoken language contact such as with English-influenced signing[8] in the United States, the grammar often comes from the superstrate English, and the lexifier is ASL (Fischer, 1996 in Quinto-Pozos, 2007), but not always. Contact signing between English and ASL also can exhibit grammatical features of the substrate, ASL, such as the use of eye gaze or space to establish referents, or the simultaneous occurrence of English mouthings with ASL forms (Lucas, 1994).

It is expected that SL contact varieties will incorporate elaborate means for constructing meaning that are informed by both superstrate and substrate elements from the languages in the mix. With IS, it is unclear which languages in contact (signed or spoken) contribute to the lexicon and which contribute to grammatical forms, and whether any of the constructions are fully understood by mixed signing audiences. However, lexical signs that are common to several different signed languages appear in interpreter's presentation IS, and it also incorporates ways of making meaning that (such as use of topographic and referential space)

8. English-influenced ASL has been also known by terms such as Pidgin Signed English (PSE) (see Woodward, 1973) and a third system, contact signing (CS) (see Lucas & Valli, 1990).

resemble several other observed NSL features (Rosenstock, 2004). I take the stance that expository lecture IS is a form of sign language contact that is underdescribed.

DESCRIBING IS LEXICON AND GRAMMAR

The lexicon of this "generic" type of IS (Supalla & Webb, 1995: 338) has not been fully described but it is characterized as highly gestural and incorporates borrowed signs that tend to be iconically transparent and/or shared forms across different SLs. Rosenstock (2004) was the first to provide quantitative information about IS lexicon (used by interpreters) and noted that a number of IS signs appeared to be cognates, sharing similar parameters across several different signed languages. There were some limitations to her study and sign types were not elaborated, however, she found that most of the loan signs in interpreted IS were borrowed from Western SLs.

It is unclear whether expository IS exhibits a large number of signs instantiated from individual signers' NSLs, or if borrowed forms from BSL or ASL are the conventional forms regularly recruited in IS presentations. In the Woll study (1990), it is possible that the "other SL" users would have incorporated many of their own lexical forms rather than BSL.

> International Sign does not have a lexicon in the way that a Sign Language does. For a signer recounting a narrative in International Sign, choices must constantly be made about whether to use a sign from one's own Sign Language, or from another Sign Language, or whether to use mime, classifiers, or, in a few cases, a sign recognised as conventional in International Sign. (Allsop et al., 1995, p. 181)

A British-based media production, *Sign Forward,* notes several anecdotal opinions about IS lexicon and grammar in its DVD, *International Signs: An Introduction.* A Deaf user of IS replied when asked, "What is International Sign?":

> Whether from Australia, Spain, Russia, North or South America, deaf people use International Sign by using visual and spatial information, gesture, and some of one's own native signs to communicate. Different people are able to match and understand each other by taking parts of their own grammar, and their own language, as well as gesturing

or using mime. These different SL users adapt their signing style, use a one-handed fingerspelling system and find a balance using some signs—more or less—that may be similar or different from their own native SL. International Sign is an interesting, universal way for deaf people around the world to communicate [translations by the author].

These observations that IS employs a variety of meaning-making resources (that languages have at their disposal) are repeatedly noted in recently reviewed prior work on IS. Yet, there is very little known about what exactly is conventional enough to be "universally" understood (as is posited about IS)—be that in lexicon or grammatical forms. This same resource states that IS is not ASL, even when other sources concede that Western sign languages like ASL contribute productively to the lexical items observed in IS. The quotes above illustrate the vagaries of IS. In particular, there does not seem to be any clear documentation about which of "one's own native signs" one might use in IS and, moreover, whether specific forms contribute to comprehension.

Historical descriptions of IS lexicon mention an early attempt to unify signs used in international forums in Europe in the 1950s (Moody, 2002, p. 15). IS glossaries are discussed in the next section. In the published literature, the lexicon of IS is referred to in a few studies, often in general terms and typically absent of corpus-informed methods. To date, there remains a gap in the literature for quantitative and qualitative descriptions of IS sign forms used in international contact across a variety of discourse settings.

The notion of "sign" is often mentioned without elaboration of what constitutes a lexical item and without clear differentiation of sign types that constitute the stream of utterances in IS. Signs listed in IS glossaries propose the idea that there is a small, standardized IS vocabulary. However, in the research reviewed thus far, rich lexical material is observed in IS contact settings, but it is difficult to know which symbolic forms in IS are established lexical signs, and which are gestures, enactments, or depicting types. Lexical items are also described as being borrowed signs from native SLs (McKee & Napier, 2002; Rosenstock, 2004; Woll, 1990). Signs are lexical contributions from the interlocutors in the setting or signs established through conventional use or negotiated agreement.

Lexical signs in IS are described as simplified and small in number and are often the most transparent, iconic signs (Allsop et al., 1995; Moody, 2002; Rosenstock, 2008). Noted above, Allsop et al. describe the use of "strings of paraphrases" (p. 181) to expand on ideas where there is no equivalent sign in IS. In a later study, Rosenstock (2008) asserts that these types of expansions are not necessarily reflections of a lack of corresponding sign in IS, but indications of "discourse-pragmatic choices such as a suspected lack of knowledge of the topic or the IS interpreter's attempt to bridge cultural differences" (p. 141).

Adding to the lexical description of IS is evidence of phonological variation in a few of the most frequent IS signs. Lang (2012) shows that the highly frequent sign for DEAF exhibits four different phonological variations in her analysis of informational online IS videos. Supalla and Webb (1995) also uncover varied negation signs in their data: two gestures that serve to negate utterances, the borrowed ASL form, NOT, and an established *Gestuno* negation sign, IMPOSSIBLE. Phonological and lexical variation is thus evidenced in IS but perhaps for different reasons than in NSLs, owing to the fact that a larger number of existing forms are borrowed in to the contact situation where IS is used, rather than as a result of intergenerational usage settings and instances within a NSL-using community. NSLs typically exhibit considerable variation in vocabulary and grammar due to language external influences (age, gender, social networks, education) such as Northern versus Southern dialects of Auslan (Johnston & Schembri, 2010) and due to historically shaped, language internal forces (lexicalization and grammaticalization) (c.f. grammaticalization in ASL, see Janzen & Schaffer, 2002; Wilcox, 2004b).

Spontaneous international contact signing creates inconsistency and obvious challenges to pinpointing a static, established collection of sign forms in IS. However, iconic motivation behind lexical choices in IS is cited by many authors (Moody, 2002; Rosenstock 2004, 2008; Scott-Gibson & Ojala, 1994; Woll, 1995). Both imagistic iconicity (it looks/feels/sounds like what the form represents) and diagrammatic iconicity (expresses spatial relationships or metaphoric relationships) are seen in IS lexicon and grammar (Rosenstock, 2004, 2008). The lexicon is thus described as highly iconic, with iconicity prevailing at all linguistic levels. Such iconic motivation is assumed to aid in comprehension.

The Rosenstock study identified 162 sign forms that occurred more than five times in her data of interpreters' target IS. These frequent forms are reported in a table of English glosses but unfortunately video clips demonstrating each form are not included, and the study's glossing conventions make it difficult to identify the exact form, linguistic type, or semantic range of these signs in the dataset.

In order to determine whether frequent signs in IS are common across different SLs, Rosenstock showed these 162 signs to users of 15 different SLs. She reported that a large number (53%) of signs were similar across several Western SL families, while only 12% were loans from a single SL. Less than 2% are reportedly unique to IS. It is not indicated how many matching parameters were required to consider a sign form a cognate between different SLs. The method relied on judgments by these native users who were all living in the United States for some indeterminate time and may have already begun learning ASL and incorporating it in their daily lives. A criticism of the native user approach comes from what is known about interference and attrition in L1. People who live in a community of foreign language users are exposed to (and often learn) the foreign L2. Spoken and SL studies show that users of a new L2 are often confused about L1 lexical items when judging L2 and L1 forms, often demonstrating miscues and interference from L2 lexical items—even when they think they are using their L1 (Waas, 1996; Yoel, 2007).

Methods of comparative lexicostatistics applied to SLs are varied in the literature, with mixed endorsement for using the traditional 200 word Swadesh list, or Woodward's (1978) modified list of core words, or a more random selection of vocabulary items (McKee & Kennedy, 2000). One of the reasons given for a modified Swadesh list is the potential for overestimation of similarity between SL lexicons given iconic indexical signs (e.g., pronouns). Of the highly occurring signs used in IS by interpreters, 24% were shared across 10 out of the 15 SLs (e.g., HOUSE, TIME) (Rosenstock, 2004, p. 88) and were described by Rosenstock as iconic. It makes sense that the most transparent signs would be selected by IS interpreters in order to improve their recognition by audience members, and it appears that given the 53% reported similarity, many of the signs are likely transparent to some degree to varied SL users.

Rosenstock does not indicate whether the frequent IS signs are established lexical signs, or gestures, or grammatical function signs. Function signs that contribute to grammatical relations, such as points and transition markers, are not delineated in the list, and depictions are not identified as such, although some of this can be deduced from examples in her data. The English glosses she uses to name some of these forms suggest the presence of pointing signs (e.g., PRO-1 "first person pronoun" and POSS "possessive"), gestures (e.g., THUMBS-UP), gestures that act as transition markers (WELL), and depicting signs (e.g., HEAR-SHRINK). The example HEAR-SHRINK given in the research incorporates what she calls a metaphoric morpheme articulated at the ear location. In the framework of this current study, that example is best described as a depicting sign. The form engages a FLATBC handshape  that closes or opens to depict changing quantity of some referent, in this example the magnitude of sound available to the ear.

IS use in presentations during the past decade may exhibit an increasingly stabilized lexicon over the past 20 or 30 years, which can only be verified by historical study. Pidgins arrive at a "certain degree of conventionalization and thus have to be learned by non-members of the pidgin-using community," and this would not really apply to IS as "it is designated to be a system of universal accessibility" (Rosenstock, 2004, p. 46). This designation of IS as a universally accessible system is assumed but is not supported by evidence from these studies.

A standardized "WFD SIGN" contact variety is suggested to be the result of ongoing negotiation and use over time in 1:1 and larger group meetings of deaf leaders in international meetings (Supalla, 2008a). A full linguistic description of sign forms is not available, only public resources that suggest IS signs.

IS SIGN GLOSSARIES AND TRAINING

Preoccupation with learning the "vocabulary" of IS signs is evidenced by materials published and presented for public consumption. There are a handful of public resources on IS lexicon that serve as a response to public demand over the past few decades. Meanwhile, one of the intentions behind creation of dictionary-like sign language resources often is to standardize. Johnston (2003b) notes a difference between standardizing languages of deaf people versus documenting the languages (and their variations). There are inherent dangers unifying a language through dictionaries, which often promote the association of "standard" or "correct" varieties of signs with prestige and power. The natural variation inherent in the ongoing evolution of young sign languages (with contact effects being a developmental factor) is therefore suppressed. In these early days of a naturally occurring SL contact phenomenon such as expository IS, the availability of IS dictionaries has potential influence on the forms that may gradually become codified.

The creation of the *Gestuno* (BDA, 1975) publication created controversy, and the glossary of suggested IS signs eventually failed (cf., the artificially created language Esperanto). This was mainly due to the inaccessibility of the signs' meanings and an imbalance between signs that were arbitrarily borrowed from geographically diverse regions (Moody, 2002). Other publicly available IS "dictionaries" have become available in the past two decades.

Of these current resources, the first is a pictorial sign glossary originally published by the British Deaf Society for the WFD, *Gestuno: International Sign Language of the Deaf*. This publication is no longer in print, and most of the 1,500 signs in the volume are not observed in IS current usage. The few that are currently in IS usage are shared forms across several SLs (Rosenstock, 2004). There are recently available digital media products as well as intermittent community training endeavors that aim to provide more information to the interested deaf community public about IS lexicon. Currently there are five IS resources available,[9] all of which are collaborations by committee members or individuals creating materials for instruction about common lexical signs attributed to IS usage. Rather than true dictionaries, they are sign glossaries or digital media that document some vocabulary recommendations for communicating in IS. All of them show lexical forms labeled with an English or other language word gloss but do not elaborate on meaning or usage.

Contributing to IS usage are formal trainings evidenced in different communities. Regularly practiced preconference IS trainings are offered in advance of various international events such as WFD Congress in 2011, and the 2009 Summer Deaflympics (Taiwan). Examples of community training efforts that have been offered include a 4-week IS intensive series in Melbourne in 2011, an IS training workshop in Hong Kong in October 2011,[10] a 3-hour IS training by the Association of Sign Language Interpreters of Australia (ASLIA) in Melbourne prior to the October 2013 WFD conference in Sydney, among many others typically offered before each Deaflympics or WFD event. Last, short courses in IS have

9. These print and digital resources are (a) *Gestuno: International Sign Language of the Deaf* (WFD & British Deaf Society), no longer in print; (b) *Suggested International Signs for Use at the World Federation of the Deaf General Assembly*, DVD format (WFD); (c) *International Signs: An Introduction,* DVD format (Sign Forward Ltd.); (d) *WFD Sign Lexicon* (Spanish Association of the Deaf); and (e) *International Sign* (DeafPlus, Korea).

10. Personal communications with Jenny Lam, IS training presenter and research lecturer at Hong Kong University, August to September 2011.

been given in recent years at Gallaudet University and in the European Master in Sign Language Interpreting (EUMASLI) program.

Inconsistent description and rising interest in IS training and IS interpreter screening creates the need for systematic documentation of conventional signs that comprise the lexicon, as well as the quantity and types of depicting signs, gestures, and other rich semiotic elements contributing to effective IS. By capturing IS sign forms from typical usage events and describing them linguistically, continued evaluation can be made to characterize variations and changes occurring in the contact system. In this way, linguists, practitioners, and community members interested in IS contact signing will be better informed than simply going by intuition.

SUMMARY

Thus far I have described prior IS, outlining the emergence of the label "IS" as a term broadly (and ambiguously) used to refer to international cross-linguistic SL contact phenomena. Distinguishable complexities around IS-type phenomena ought to be considered (in both public and academic discourse) given the variety of sociological, economic, and political factors that create contact situations between SL users. A small, emergent lexicon and a variety of semiotic approaches resembling NSL lexical and grammatical forms appear to create meaning for audiences. An expository form of IS—whether by deaf presenters or by interpreters—merits further inquiry as this is a frequent type of IS contact used with some degree of regularity.

The bulk of research on IS focuses mostly on North American and European interpreters and some deaf signers. Studied examples of IS created by SL users from different geographic and linguistic origins is therefore needed, particularly looking at the way deaf internationals compose meaningful symbols for diverse audiences. Furthermore, a closer look at the sociolinguistic and demographic background of audience members who glean the most from IS may indicate that there are some who are optimally poised to understand IS but others who are not.

Answering the research questions posed herein addresses assumptions about "universal access" through the use of expository IS. The next chapter provides theoretical background to this study and consideration is given to the ways that SLs create meaning, many of which may be exploited in SL contact situations such as internationally targeted expository IS lectures.

Chapter 3

Meaning Making in International Sign

Signed languages (SLs) have been the subject of linguistic research for a shorter time than for spoken and written languages. Most of the research thus far is focused on Western SLs, with predominant numbers of published works on those in Europe and the United States. Descriptions of SL lexicons and grammars have frequently applied analytic approaches and meta-language used to describe spoken languages. Historically, this was serendipitous given the hopes that visual/spatial language might uncover universals and thus validate the theory of Universal Grammar (Supalla, 2008b, p. 576). Stokoe's (1960) American Sign Language (ASL) discoveries align in time with the emergence of this new formalist paradigm in the 1960s (Chomsky, 1965) and offered opportunities for linguistic validation and study of SLs in subsequent years (Battison, 2000).

As a result, SL research has typically been grounded in a formal theoretical framework, which (in the most general terms) poses a universal human system of language competence (Chomsky, 1965). However, it has become clear over time that an independent language system cannot solely be explained from looking at its internal parts (phonology, morphology, syntax, etc.). A number of linguistic ideas have led to research on external explanations for phenomena observed in language (e.g., functionalism, cognitivism).

In this study I assume a cognitivist lens and assess the effectiveness of the unique communication phenomena of expository IS. This viewpoint asserts that our human experiences shape cognitive structure and that the organization of our experience is inextricably embodied (Lakoff & Johnson, 1980, 1999), and the language we use in our discourses about such experiences is situated in usage settings (Langacker, 2001).

Language is the faculty by which we make sense of our experiences. As a result, language—as it resides in the mind—cannot be studied in isolation from human embodiment (Evans & Green, 2006, p. 44). In recent decades, cognitive approaches to the description of SLs have emerged, with emphasis on language as a human cognitive faculty that relies on mental representations or schemas. Cognitive theories of Mental Space (Fauconnier, 1985, 1997) and real space blending (Fauconnier & Turner, 1996) have been recently applied in the description of SL grammars (for ASL: Liddell, 2003; Dudis, 2011; for Auslan: Ferrara, 2012, and Johnston & Ferrara, 2012). Metaphoric blends and Idealized Cognitive Models (ICMs) (Lakoff, 1987) are other theories that have relevance to SL grammars (Taub, 2001; Wilcox, 2000, 2004a). These are important concepts that provide a backdrop in the current study.

Langacker's theory of language (1987, 1990, 1991) links human cognitive capacity with language capacity and uses terms such as figure/ground structure, viewpoint, and schematization, which align well in a discussion of visually grounded signed languages (and thus signed languages in contact such as IS). Figure/ground structures are observed in the way signed languages use depicting signs[1] to indicate a subject and its relationship to and or movement within an environment. Figure 1 gives an example of a figure/ground representation in Auslan (which may be similarly articulated in other signed languages).

The main premise of cognitive linguistics is that semantic structure is not universal but is language specific, based on conventional imagery and knowledge structures—that is, the images in our mind represent what we know about things we have experienced. Inner conceptualizations are meaningful (Langacker, 1987), and they are realized from our perceptions of words, signs, or other types of visual and/or auditory symbols.

Further, grammar constitutes symbols that are conventionalized meaning structures, and lexicon and grammar are symbolic structures that fall on a continuum that may be grouped and described arbitrarily; there is no distinction between lexicon and grammar (Langacker, 1987, p. 2). Meaningful symbols can be simple such as a word, a handshape, or a sign, or they can be complex such as a sentence or a string of signs.

In order to assess how well IS effectively conveys meaningful utterances that can be recognized, it is necessary to take a closer look at how SLs construct meaningful symbols for an observer, and particularly how IS appears to use similar ways of making meaning as NSLs.

1. Schembri (2003), following Liddell (2003), makes a case that the "classifier" may not be an applicable term for what Supalla (1986) and others have additionally referred to as "classifier structures" or "verbs of location and motion." Dudis (2011) describes how these signs participate in "depictions" of scene events.

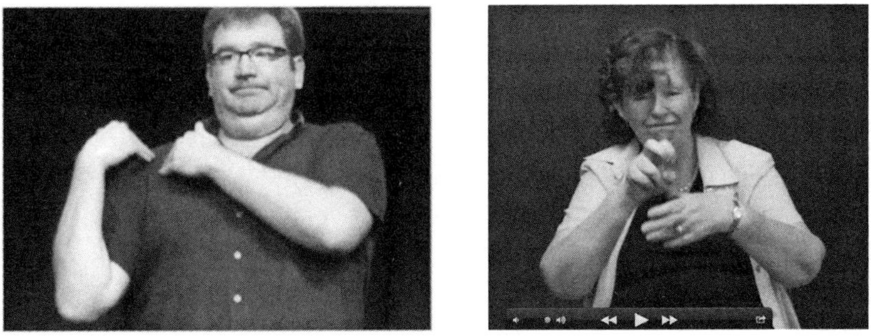

a) b)

FIGURE 1. *Figure/ground example:* ANIMAL-JUMPS-OUT *(From the Auslan Corpus, Endangered Languages Archive, URL: http://elar.soas.ac.uk/deposit/0001#q=%3Ffilters%3Dtype%253Abundle%2520im_og_gid%253A4%2520tid%253A6959%2520tid%253A3674).*

LANGUAGE USES MEANINGFUL SYMBOLS

Language and forms in language are modifiable to serve a number of functions in human interaction (Halliday, 1975; Hymes, 1974; Jakobson, 1964). One of the main functions is to refer to or inform about ideas or content that is external to interlocutors (Buhler, 1965, in Young, 1993). Language can be flexible, and one's social environment informs a language user about the language's system of use (Hymes, 1974, p. 75). However, Hymes refers to conventional language communities, not an ad hoc contact language. Deaf presenters who use IS as a contact strategy to address an audience of mixed SL users aim to communicate ideas, usually for the purpose of community building around a marginalized Deaf experience, or toward other political and educational purposes. The sign forms in expository IS that they select are what the signer believes to be salient, based on the assumption that the audience may recognize the symbols, based on features of SLs known to them. Presumably, the expectation is that meaning will be conveyed.

Meaning is influenced by several factors: (a) the knowledge an observer brings from life experiences, (b) the lexicon and other symbolic linguistic and nonlinguistic forms that the communicator uses to construct the message, (c) the observer's interpretation of the form of the message, and (d) the context in which the message is rendered and perceived.

For each of these factors, the successful perception of message meaning is dependent on the personal experiences and the symbolic expressions that a communicator uses, and whether the interlocutors share the same form-meaning relationship (conventionality) represented by these symbols. Context also provides support to meaning intended by the symbols people use to communicate. Additional external factors that shape an IS contact situation must be considered, such as the demographic profile of the community of users, cultural traditions, settings where a contact variety is used, and the sociopolitical systems of the interlocutors, deaf people.

Each language has identifiable patterns that are easily recognized by experienced users of those patterns; therefore, the mental ideas that are construed from these patterns are generally also shared. A language emerges from use of symbolic expressions that become abstracted and conventional (Langacker, 2001), within a geographically situated community of users.

For a contact sign system such as expository IS, the maintenance of conventional structuring of symbolic units seems untenable without stable contact. However some amount of regular contact would allow for creation of somewhat stable form-meaning symbols, which is shown to be the case in some regularized lexical forms in IS (used by WFD members, or other stakeholders in international deaf-related settings).

The more complex a symbolic unit (i.e., a clause or sentence, or string of signs), and the more regularly the symbol is used, the more abstracted and complex it may be. Languages may share some symbols, and even formational parts of the symbols (phonemes in spoken language or handshapes and movements, in signed languages), but they are used to represent meaning, and the ways they are put together are conventional within that language (and may not be understood by those who do not know how the conventions work).

MEANINGFUL SYMBOLS CAN BE SIMPLE OR COMPLEX

A Notion of Lexico-Grammar

Languages are typically studied with some degree of distinction between their two complementary mechanisms: their open and closed class elements (i.e., the lexicon and the grammar), both of which are responsible for specifying different portions of a cognitive representation or "an experiential complex" (Talmy, 2000, p. 21). Fauconnier (1985) explains how linguistic symbols, which have meaning *potential* in a given discourse context, prompt mental space representations (Fauconnier, 1997, p. 37). Mental spaces and the elements comprising their constructions come from knowledge and cognitive models (Lakoff, 1987) from our experiences and semantic frames (Fillmore, 1982). The lexicon provides content information, and grammatical constructions provide information about the way the cognitive representation is structured. The concept of "lexico-grammar" is based on the premise that symbolic units fall along a continuum where they vary in their size and schematic complexity (Langacker, 2005).

Symbolic units may be morphemes, conventional lexical items such as list-able words, or signs in a dictionary, as well as symbolically complex constructions, such as short multiple sign utterances or depicting sign sequences, which are schematic constructions of grammar (Langacker, 1987). A schema of symbolic complexity (Langacker, 2005, p. 108) is shown in Figure 2.

Recently, cognitive theories of construction grammar have been applied to ASL (Liddell, 2003), Chinese Sign Language (CSL), French Sign Language (LSF), and Italian Sign Language (LIS) (Wilcox, 2004), as well as Auslan (Ferrara, 2012; Johnston & Ferrara, 2012). These applications have relevance to this current study, because they are based on the premise that meaningful symbols in a language can be described along variable dimensions such as symbolic complexity, schematicity, and

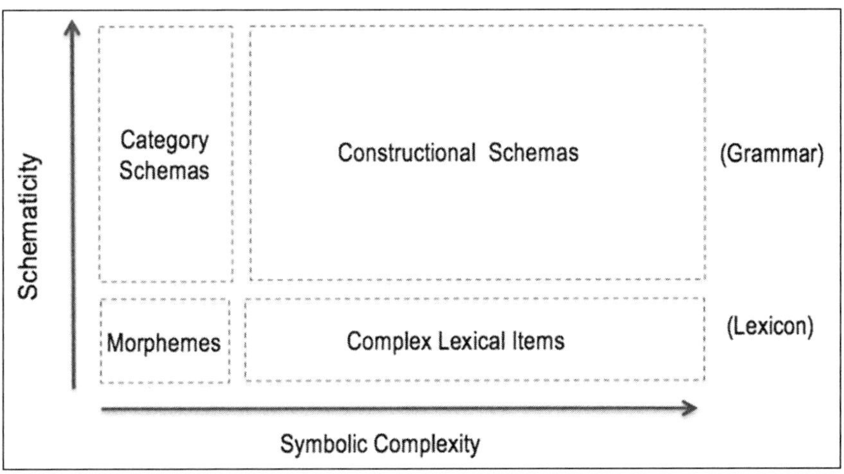

FIGURE 2. *Langacker's schema of symbolic complexity (Reproduced from Langacker, 2005, p. 108).*

conventionalization (among other dimensions). (For elaboration on these ideas in terms of SL grammars, see Wilcox, 2004.)

Meaningful symbols in IS are considered in light of these theories, that utterances in expository IS discourses are composites of simple to complex semiotic material, which vary in their conventionality and specificity. Symbolic units and complex constructions created by IS users have meaning potentials that are determined by the way that signs and more complex utterances are used by a group of signers in the contact setting. At times signs and other complex ways of creating meaning are shared or understood, much like conventional ways of communicating within one's language community. Other times symbolic expressions may not be shared or easily understood, given lesser conventionality and a need to negotiate meaning about simple signs or parts of signs and/or the way strings of signed utterances are put together and understood. Symbolic expressions include gestures as well as linguistic forms.

The point here is not to analyze or map out IS signs or utterances using this framework. However, the theory serves as a background to this study of meaning-making and comprehension of IS lecture. Providing examples from a native signed language (NSL) in terms of these ideas, Johnston and Ferrara (2012) map fully conventional sign language–Auslan constructions onto Langacker's schema of symbolic complexity. They note, for example, that conventional signs (e.g., SISTER, PAPER) are symbols that fall closer to points on the schema that represent smaller-sized and substantive, fully specified symbols (near "Morphemes" in Langacker's scale, Figure 2). These are fully lexical signs that, within the community of Auslan users, are conventional and rely very little on context for their meanings. Other symbolic units are more complex, such as depicting signs or grammatical clause utterances. These would fall somewhere in the area of "Constructional Schemas" on the scale. For example, a depicting sign in Auslan (e.g., DS[I]:PERSON-WALKS-AWAY-CASUALLY) is characterized further out on the scale, because it is a more complex grammatical construction that "depicts multiple blended elements and the relations between them" (p. 235).

In addition, the component parts to a lexical sign sometimes have more complex meaning that give it internal complexity; this comes from iconic or gestural origins. Johnston and Ferrara elaborate on the way that component parts of fully lexical signs are component symbolic units, whose parts acquire meaning when instantiated for participation in a real space blend (2012, pp. 237–239). Langacker's scale is thus adjusted (in Figure 3) for sublexical "atomic" components of signs (handshape, orientation, movement, etc.).

To illustrate the scale I offer, the ASL sign, CAMP, is a lexical sign that has entrenched structure and meaning, yet its sublexical parts have some complex parts that are iconic (Figure 4).

The handshape, orientation, and movement components depict quite iconically the erected poles and the outlined shape of a tent, although the form is strongly associated in ASL with specified meanings, [CAMP], [CAMPING], or [TENT]. A narrator, however, might tell a story where a tent became unstable and caved in on one side. By modifying the handshape, orientation, or movement of the sign, one could create a novel symbolic unit and the sign becomes de-lexicalized (Johnston & Schembri, 1999), a partly lexical depiction, and takes on an altered meaning, such as [TENT-COLLAPSE]. Johnston and Ferrara (2012) describe this as the "two faces" that a fully lexical sign has: (a) unit status (i.e., lexical sign as idiom) that may or may not have predictable meaning and (b) componential token meaning that is dependent on context and other signs in an utterance.

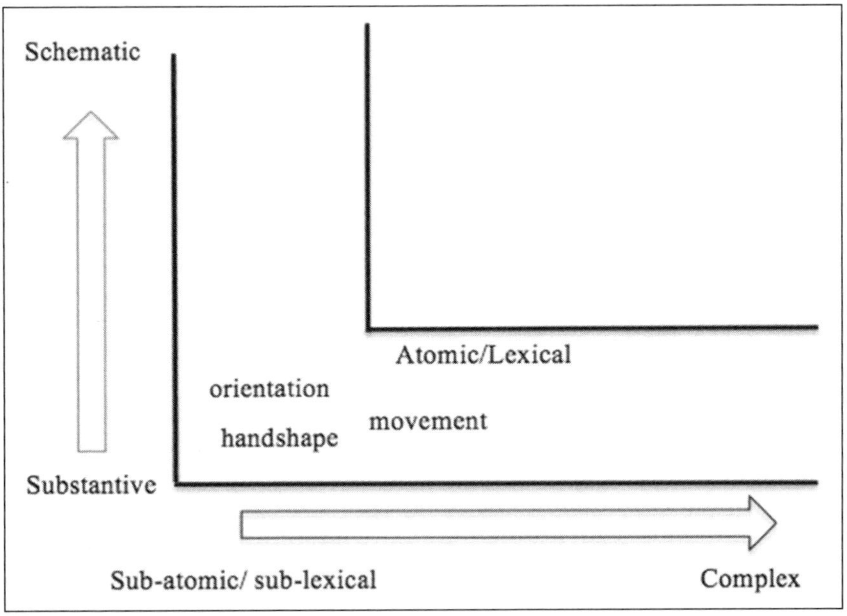

FIGURE 3. *Langacker's scales of size and content, with adjusted sublexical scale. (Reproduced from Johnston & Ferrara, 2012, p. 7).*

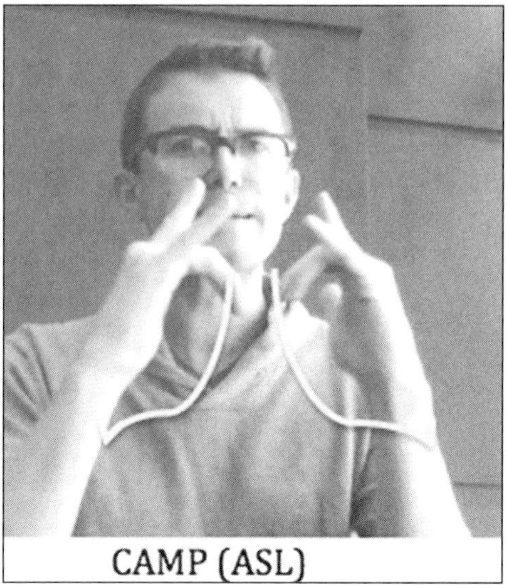

FIGURE 4. *The fully lexical ASL sign* CAMP.

Complex symbolic units in a SL can move from a more complex constructional schema to a symbolic lexical whole that is substantive and fully specified through conventional use and entrenchment by signers in a community (Johnston & Ferrara, 2012). This is how lexical signs (e.g., compound signs) are added to a SL from gestural and componential elements.

More complex examples along this thread would be seen in a string of ASL signs, or utterances, such as, THEY (BOY SCOUTS) GO ON CAMPING EXCURSIONS FAR INTO THE WILDERNESS, which is seen in Figure 5.

In Figure 6, the scale is shown with the ASL sign CAMP, the sublexical, phonologic parts (handshape, movement, orientation), as well as the complex utterance from Figure 5 accounted for on this scale of simple to complex meaningful symbols.

Ferrara extended this idea further and posited a three-dimensional (3D) model of language (adding a *Z*-axis) that integrates conventionality onto the two-dimensional scales pictured. In doing so she argued for a "grammar of depiction" to account for the nonlinguistic (gesture-type) forms and for hybrid forms (e.g., depicting signs) that occur in a given language (Ferrara, 2012, p. 289). This idea would explain the incidence of sign forms that are purely gestural (and perhaps somewhat recognizable although not conventional), such as physically enacting putting on a backpack, and trudging in place.

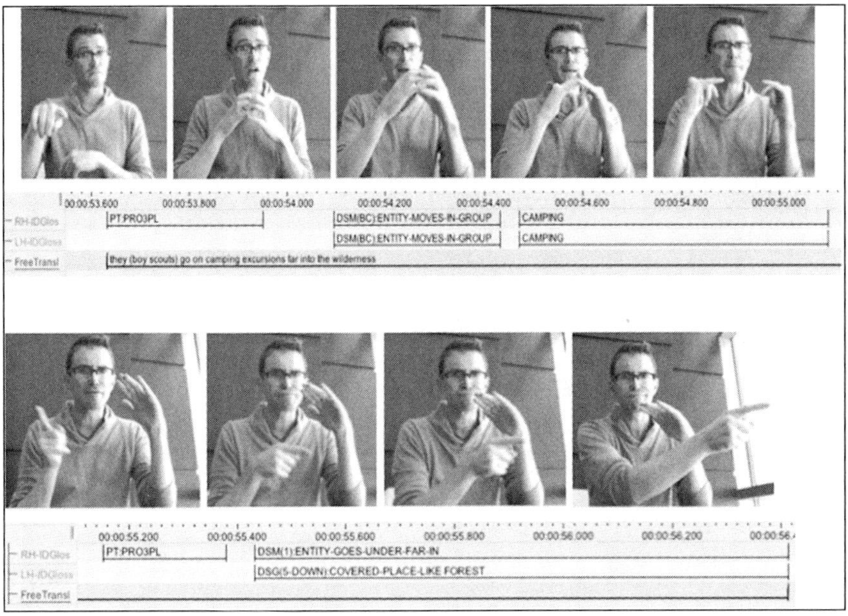

FIGURE 5. *ASL complex construction meaning:* [THEY (BOY SCOUTS) GO ON CAMPING EXCURSIONS FAR INTO THE WILDERNESS].

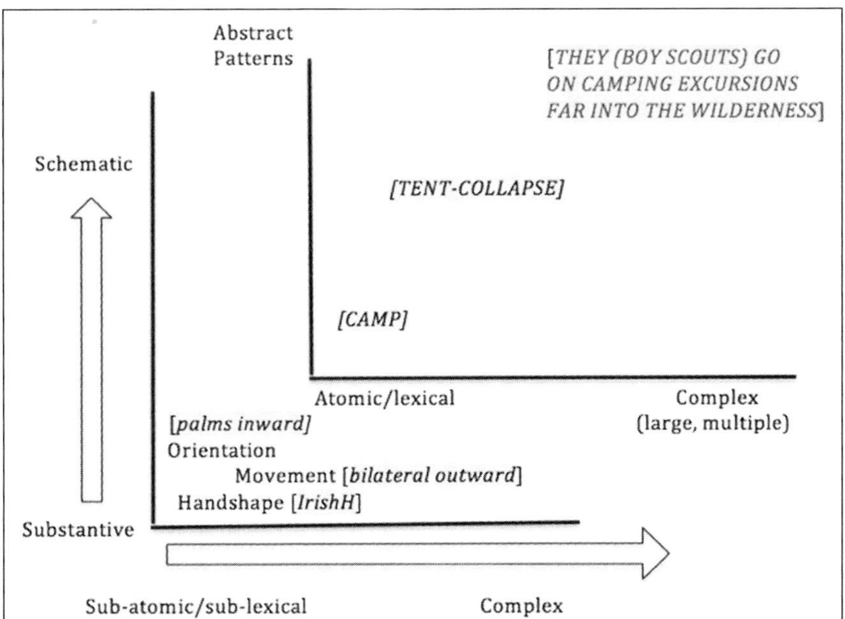

FIGURE 6. *Examples of simple to complex symbols in ASL (Adapted from Ferrara, 2012, and Langacker, 2005).*

So far, I have discussed the different kinds of symbolic forms that form a theoretical framework about an *established SL*. The scales shown in Figures 2, 3, and 6 refer to symbolic units in an established sign language—a NSL. These ideas have relevance to what happens when signers are in contact regularly and create symbolic expressions when mixing across SLs, some of which might be more or less conventional in the contact system.

In terms of expository IS and comprehension, the meaningful symbols that signers recruit arise from what they are accustomed to from their own NSLs. These are substantive lexical forms, subcomponents of lexical forms (inventory of handshapes, movements, and other parameters permissible in their SL), nonlinguistic manual gestures and enactments, as well as complex schematic constructions. Effective understanding of forms in IS, in the context of this schema, means that different SL users are able to recognize symbolic units and complex constructions and either set aside their own entrenched conventional meaning, or activate the iconic and gestural productive elements of these symbols.

Symbolic Units and Composite Utterances

Words, signs, or other forms of visual and/or auditory communicative symbols are perceived and have realized meaning. A listener interprets some auditory or visible signal, which may be linguistic and context independent, or it may be nonlinguistic and enriched by context. A "sign" in a semiotic sense refers to an object that signifies some meaning (Peirce, 1955). An example of a fully lexical symbolic unit in ASL is shown in the schematic in Figure 7. It refers to the symbolic correspondence between a phonological unit and a semantic unit. Linguistic signs are one kind of symbolic unit, and other symbols such as pictures, culturally recognizable emblems, and gestures also prompt meaning.

Symbolic units that are larger in size than single words or signs are sometimes referred to as sentences. IS has previously been analyzed by Supalla and Webb (1995) and Rosenstock (2004) in terms of "sentences." Yet, "whereas the sentence has been treated, traditionally and in modern theory, as the fundamental structural unit of grammar, such a unit does not exist in conversational language" (Biber, Johansson, Leech, Conrad, & Finegan, 1999, p. 1039). Like spoken conversation, IS and NLSs do not take written form. Moreover, the grammaticality of IS is not fully

Phonological pole	
Semantic pole	**[HELP]**

FIGURE 7. *Symbolic representation of ASL lexical sign* HELP.

known and is at best graded given any potential grammatical description of the contact system.

McKee and Napier take a discourse approach and describe characteristics of IS that illustrate strategies of interpreters who create IS target interpretations. "Utterance" is a term that best suits this project, rather than *sentence*, and I refer to *discourse* to mean segments of signed text that vary in size from several utterances to complete presentation texts.

A composite utterance is defined as "a communicative move that incorporates multiple signs of multiple types" (Enfield, 2009, p. 15). Enfield applies this notion to examples of visual images occurring with spoken language, or spoken language and co-speech gestures. The three main types of semiotic signs he identifies are conventional signs (e.g., words, gestural emblems), symbolic indexical signs (e.g., pronouns, pointing gestures), and nonconventional signs (e.g., representational gestures). Obviously, some can occur in the visual-gestural modality, and more than one can occur in the same utterance or move: hence, "composite utterances." Johnston (2013a) explicitly relates these semiotic categories to his own categories of fully lexical, partly lexical, and nonlexical signs in a SL. In this way, Enfield's notion of composite utterances can be used to describe complex constructions of multiple sign types, as it has been for Auslan (Ferrara, 2012; Hodge, 2013). Composite utterances can be analyzed as a turn in a communicative setting, while complex constructions are complex symbols that are created in conjunction with composite utterances.

The fully lexical symbolic units shown in Figure 7 and CAMP in Figure 4 are conventional examples, with an established and specified "given" meanings (Johnston & Schembri, 1999) in a specific language. SLs also incorporate productive lexicon characterized by not completely specified, "generated" meaning, depicting signs that arise from handshapes and movements. Depicting and pointing signs are not fully formational or semantically specified and rely on context to complete meaning. One thus invariably finds all three sign types outlined by Johnston (2013a) within composite utterances in SLs, partly because they are face-to-face languages, for the same reason one does in face-to-face spoken language: they interface with the context of utterance. In SLs, generally, the use of this type of contextual scaffolding is extremely frequent. An example of complex constructions used in a composite utterance in ASL is seen in Figure 8 (shown as a semantic symbolic unit).

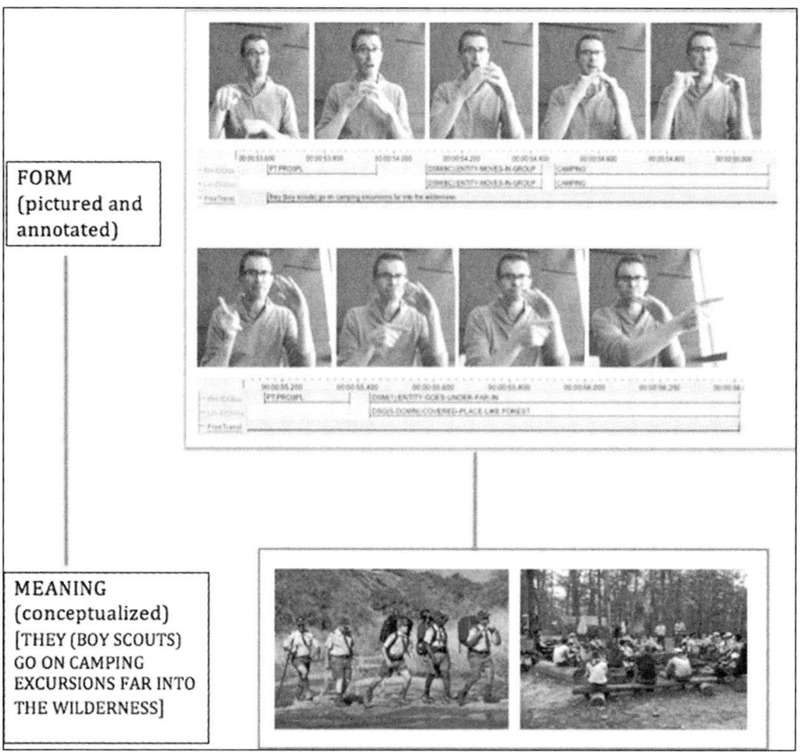

FIGURE 8. *Symbolic form-meaning representation of a complex construction in ASL.*

The utterance shown in Figure 8 is a form-meaning construction that is more complex than the ones in Figures 7 and 4. It is an excerpt from one of the translated ASL videos (Video E, "Boy Scouts") shown to U.S. participants in this study (Study Two). The example can be understood with the translation, "They (boy scouts) go on camping excursions far into the wilderness."

In this example, the observer of the utterance would rely on previously mentioned fully lexical and semantically specified topical signs, such as SCOUT, in combination with the initial PT:PRO3 pointing sign to the topic and subsequent depicting sequence about some entity moving as a group to a different location. The ASL sign CAMPING would also need to be understood in the composite utterance to realize the specification that DSM(1): ENTITY-GOES-FAR-IN/ DSG(5-DOWN):COVERED-PLACE-LIKE-FOREST refers to a trek into the wilderness. The elements of the sign CAMPING and the partly specified depicting verb prompt the idealized conceptual model and then complete the specific elements of camping. These are trees, picnic benches, forest, and campfires, among others. These symbolic units of varied size and complexity, lexical signs, pointing signs, and depicting signs, are all elements of the construction in ASL, and the utterance and its patterned meaning would be easily understood to an ASL user. Different types of signs are similarly shown to contribute to core argument and predicate elements in Auslan (Hodge & Johnston, 2014), yet it is not known whether the construction shown in Figure 8 would be as easily understood by an Auslan user (or other SL user for that matter). For expository IS, signers incorporate similar ways of constructing meaning using conventional resources from their own or other NSLs. Differences in the amount and patterning of conventional substantive, fully lexical symbols and those that are more complex and schematic may have an positive or detracting effect on IS comprehension.

Enfield describes multiple types comprising composite utterances, but they are categorized differently from the three sign types analyzed in this current study. The two taxonomies are similar in that they both make delineation between symbolic types that either (a) conventionally (linguistically) encode meaning for users or (b) are nonlinguistic tokens enriched by context. Because conventionally encoded symbols (fully lexical signs) appear to be fewer in IS contact, their meaning is even more dependent on the composite nature of utterances and the successful conveyance of meaning by complex constructions in IS discourses. The extent of meaning arising from complex symbolic constructions is applicable to the assessment of IS discourse comprehension in the current study.

MEANINGFUL SYMBOLS AND MEANING CONSTRUCTION IN IS

For a sign language contact system such as expository IS, the maintenance of shared, conventional meaning seems restricted given limitations to regular, ongoing contact and exchange. When a signer communicates a message in IS lecture, he or she brings form-meaning symbols from his or her first language (Woll, 1990) as well as other gestural or iconic strategies (Allsop et al., 1994; Moody, 1979; Rosenstock, 2008). Also, the IS perceiver's interpretation of the meaning is influenced by his or her own language's (NSL) linguistic conventions (Sasaki, 1991), which are based on entrenched "webs of significance" (Geertz, 1973, p. 5) that are spun from one's own cultural and communicative traditions. In cognitive linguistics, meaning comes from usage and culture shapes usage. Meaning arises from culture, which "consists of patterns, explicit and implicit, of and for behavior acquired and transmitted by symbols" (Kroeber and Kluckhohn, 1952, p. 181, cited by Berry, 2004, p. 168).

Therefore, symbolic units in IS may hold different conceptualized meaning for varied audience members, because although they use familiar phonology (handshapes, locations, movements, etc.), they are conventionalized differently in their own SL. To illustrate this point, I offer examples where two sign languages have the same sign forms but the meanings are different.

ASL users who come in contact with or attempt to learn a second SL, such as BSL or Auslan, will find that numerous lexical forms look similar, yet the meanings they reference are completely different. Figure 9 shows examples of these cross-linguistic form-meaning mismatches: CHAIR(ASL)-FATHER(AUSLAN), SAME(ASL)-WHICH(AUSLAN), PAPER(ASL)-HAPPY(AUSLAN), and SOCK(ASL)-LEARN(AUSLAN). The last example also is the LSM sign for HERMANOS or BROTHER (Quinto-Pozos, 2008) and resembles an older variant of the ASL sign meaning BROTHER.

Other signs are also recruited by signers communicating to a mixed language using audience. An example from the IS lecture data in this

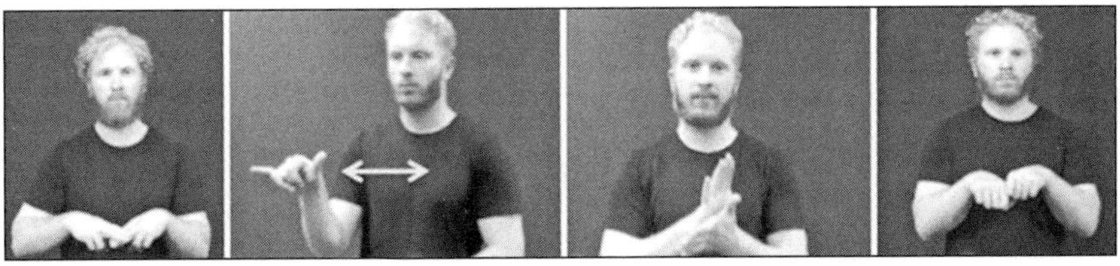

FIGURE 9. *Potential form-meaning mismatches across ASL and Auslan: (a)* CHAIR-FATHER, *(b)* SAME-WHICH, *(c)* PAPER-HAPPY, *and (d)* SOCK-LEARN *(Images credit: Auslan Signbank; Retrieved from http://www.auslan.org.au/dictionary/).*

study is a lexical form conventionally used in IS and listed in the 1975 *Gestuno* glossary, with a keyword "GOVERNMENT." The form (with movement variation) is also a conventional Auslan sign, MONARCH, pictured in Figure 10.

The sign is conventionally used to mean a person who is a member of royalty and in a variety of contexts it can mean the proper noun "queen," "princess," "king," and so on. In some utterance contexts, it is understood to mean a state of being royalty (adjective or verb), or in others, it acts as a homophone to mean "chef" or "Munich" (Auslan Signbank, 2014). It also happens to be a somewhat iconic sign, whose meaning might be realized outside of an Auslan-situated communication. In fact, a nonsigner may guess correctly or incorrectly at its meaning, purely on its enactment of a type of gesture: the putting on of a crown or a hat.

In IS, this sign form is articulated with a variation in movement, where the dominant hand starts at the head and moves upward, as if it is depicting the shape of a tall hat or crown. (Some signers, such as the one pictured, articulate it with a slightly lowered location at the temple side of the head, depending on the sign that occurs just before or after.) Auslan signers who see this sign in IS at an international conference may likely recognize it from the Auslan context, and may be able to guess or perhaps

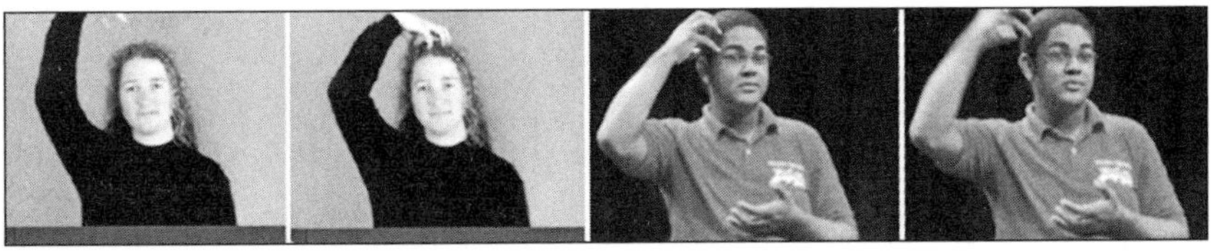

FIGURE 10. *Comparing Auslan* MONARCH *to IS sign* GOVERNMENT*: (a) Auslan* MONARCH *and (b) from IS dataset:* GOVERNMENT (Gestuno) *(Image a: retrieved from http://www.auslan.org.au/dictionary/words/queen-1.html).*

recognize its borrowed meaning in the IS usage setting. Knowing conventional use in both of these distinct contexts (in an Auslan setting, or an IS contact setting) would enable an audience member to comprehend the symbolic unit in the appropriate setting.

Meaning is thus constructed not only by linguistic parts of an utterance but also by other relevant aspects of the embodied communication and its context:

> Language is just a subset of the full resources necessary for recognizing others' communicative and informative intentions. (Enfield, 2009, p. 2)

Although Enfield is referring to the way conventionalized spoken languages incorporate images and gestures toward meaning construction, his work signals a recent shift in thinking about how, during face-to-face interactions, language incorporates other communicative material besides just lexical forms and morpho-syntax. When attempting to communicate in a contact situation with users of one or more distinctly different SLs, signers bring their own set of "full resources"—material from their own NSLs that is both linguistic and gestural, used in patterned way, which is informed by their linguistic and cultural backgrounds.

When people communicate in face-to-face interaction, they utilize any combination of three strategies: the use of description, pointing (to referents—real or imagined), and demonstration (Clark & Gerrig, 1990). Ferrara (2012) established relevance of Clark and Gerrig's ideas to clauses and composite utterances in Auslan. In doing so, she noted that signers are able to describe, or *tell* meaning, and demonstrate, or *show* meaning (p. 102). Telling meaning aligns with giving *specific* description with established (linguistic) signs that are fully lexical, whereas showing aligns with demonstration through the use of gestures, and to some extent pointing signs and depicting signs. Depicting signs are considered to be simultaneously linguistic and gestural (following Liddell, 2003; Schembri, 2001; Schembri, Jones, & Burnham, 2005). Later in this chapter, three types of signs are outlined, as they will be applied in the lexical analysis in Study One.

Users understand signs and utterances in NSLs because the form-meaning constructions in the system are symbolic, and they conventionally and specifically point to and elaborate concepts in discourse. Thus, users of the same language can (generally) understand one another. In the case of IS, where interlocutors do not share the same native SL, it is curious that anecdotal reports indicate IS to be "fairly effective" (Moody, 2002, p. 38).

It raises questions about the patterning of meaningful symbols in IS that might allow recognition and shared meaning in a contact situation.

This investigation of IS and its conveyance of meaning at the lexical level and the larger discourse level—to some extent in comparison to NSLs—devotes attention to a range of elements and form-meaning pairs that, together, tell and show meaning in IS discourses. Next, a discussion is devoted to several features of meaning-construction that are observed in NSLs, for the purpose of grounding the way shared features might contribute to meaning-conveyance in IS contact.

COMMON FEATURES OF SLs THAT INFLUENCE IS MEANING-MAKING

Prior studies report that IS borrows features from NSLs for creating meaningful symbols. It was suggested by Quinto-Pozos (2007) that cross-linguistic comprehension in SLs is attributed to the prevalence of iconicity, gestural resources, and the structural similarity of SLs. These three aspects are briefly discussed before outlining sign types that operate in SLs and are then analyzed in IS in this current study. Meaningful symbols in SLs and some of their features that appear to be similar across studied SLs are given as the reason for ease of recognition and shared meaning between users of different SLs.

Iconicity and Meaning in SLs

Iconicity in both spoken languages and SLs is discussed at length in the published literature, with iconic motivation a shared way all SLs use handshapes to create meaningful forms. An example of a sign that depicts an entity is the bent2 handshape , often used to denote a crouched human or animal. SLs exhibit varying degrees of transparency between signs and their referents, whereby a handshape can make an iconic reference to an object or it can point metonymically to a whole object. The 1-handshape  can denote an upright standing person, whereas only one part of an object is represented by the S (fist) handshape , which can depict a nodding or moving head on a person. In all documented SLs, certain handshapes appear to be selected systematically within the language (and at times shared across SLs), such as the 1-handshape to represent a human and the B handshape  to represent a motor vehicle (Brennan, 1992; Engberg-Pederson, 1993; Schembri, 2001; Wilcox, 2004a; among others).

On the lexical level, similarity between the lexicons of different, non-genetically related SLs arises from borrowing, or shared symbolism (particularly in language communities with similar or related cultures), as well as due to iconic motivation, or indexical signs that point to referents directly (Guerra Currie, Meier, & Walters, 2002; Kyle & Woll, 1988; Woll, 1984). Even a relatively low (in terms of SL comparisons) 23% lexical similarity is shown between Japanese Sign Language (NS) and Mexican Sign Language (LSM), which are unrelated SLs (Guerra Currie et al., 2002). Guerra Currie et al. attribute this percentage to a base, shared symbolism between SLs. The visual mode of SLs provides more opportunity for representing material iconically, as shown by the examples of the handshape parameter in sign phonology above. However, the iconic nature of some signs is not related to the way they are used, because each SL linguistic system has its own conventions for selecting features of a referent to map onto the hands, fingers, and body, thus forming and modifying symbols. Zeshan reminds us:

> All signs, whether iconic or not, have a conventional form and meaning, and it is not possible to modify the form of a sign at will, even if a different form might seem iconically more suitable. In fact, iconicity is irrelevant to communication between users of SLs most of the time; in fact, it is not necessary to be aware of the iconicity of a sign in order to use it. (Zeshan, 2004, p. 12)

In other words, the manner with which a NSL patterns and abstracts form-meaning pairs may be so entrenched, that when forms (or their parts) are borrowed into a contact situation, they may or may not prompt the intended meaning. With expository IS, deployment of iconically motivated forms may be a strategy that indeed impacts an audience's comprehension of these lectures, whether intended or not.

Common human embodiment provides universal experiences on which to build conceptualizations of one's surroundings (Lakoff, 1987). The experience of being deaf in any part of the world brings with it certain shared experiential frames; meanwhile, deaf people live in different, larger, spoken language communities, each with its own rich history and culture. There is evidence suggesting that the transparency of a sign, based on its iconic resemblance, is dependent upon symbols and concepts that are culturally familiar (Pizzuto, Boyes-Braem, & Volterra,

1996). In Pizzuto et al., Italian nonsigners—and not simply Italian (LIS) users—were able to guess meanings of a number of iconically transparent signs, which was explained by a shared Italian culture. In Japanese Sign Language, the formation of sign names is often influenced by written Japanese kanji characters (Nonaka, Mesch, & Sagara, 2015). Meaningful symbols, therefore, will be shaped by surrounding social and cultural norms, as well as shown in specific linguistic patterns of a local NSL.

For example, the concept of work may be an idea shared by human experiences across varied cultures, yet manifestations of work can take on different forms. Distinct compound signs for [WOMEN'S WORK] and [MEN'S WORK] in Central America iconically indicate types of work for each gender. The signs are iconic mimetic movements meant to convey the concept of work, even when the work is not related to these actions: COOKING (flipping tortilla dough from palm to palm), WEAVING (pulling a loom back strap), and WASHING (scrubbing clothing over a stone); or men's work—FARMING (raking a hoe), HAULING (tracing an imaginary trump line across one's forehead and shoulders), and CHOPPING (miming diagonal machete chops) (FoxTree, 2009, p. 340). People from the United Kingdom or the United States who use their local signs for WORK would be challenged to create a meaningful symbol for work for a signer from Central America who signs the compound sign for WORK in Meemul Tziij, a Central American sign language variety. It might take a large amount of circuitous gesturing and elaboration to convey the concept of work between such interlocutors. The point here is that ethnocentric assumptions in making iconic sign choices might impede communication (rather than aid it), even when the cross-linguistic sign choices are deliberately iconically motivated, purely as a result of culturally embedded differences.

Two-handed alphabets more iconically depict letters of the Roman alphabet than one-handed ones (Hohenberger, 2007). If iconicity is expected to play a role in a universally understood language system, then it would make sense that the two-handed alphabet system would be more prevalent in IS use. The opposite is true, however. The fact that IS incorporates a one-handed alphabet for fingerspelling of proper names and some initialized signs suggests the heavy borrowing from American and European sign languages that use one-handed fingerspelling, rather than simply employing iconically motivated forms. IS may construct meaning by establishing arbitrary forms (that are agreed upon by a community of users) that may be less transparent in their form-meaning connection.

Gestures and Meaning in SLs

Gestures are visible, nonlinguistic movements of the torso, head, hands, arms, and face that people engage to communicate, often (but not always) simultaneously with speech. Gestures are meaningful symbols that play an integral part in language and speech and are characterized as falling on a continuum (Goldin-Meadow, 2003; Kendon, 2004; McNeill, 1992, 2005). They are yet another type of semiotic material that has been attributed to the early forms of language in humans (Armstrong, Stokoe, & Wilcox, 1995). Gestures also provide substrate material for lexical and grammatical forms in sign languages (Janzen & Shaffer, 2002; Wilcox, 2004). Gesture is a communicative action that has a function in discourse, such as for marking discourse transitions, for example, G(5-UP):WELL. The sign G(5-UP):WELL is also observed in ASL and described as filled pauses (Winston & Monikowski, 2003) and is noted to serve as a boundary between discourse segments or footing shifts.

In addition to manual gestures, another kind of nonlinguistic element contributing to imagery in SL discourse comes from mimetic enactment, known as constructed action and constructed dialogue (Liddell & Metzger, 1998). Signers often switch between conventional lexical signs and constructed action or dialogue (Dudis, 2004; Roy, 1989; Winston, 1991) in addition to using emblems that are known by the wider spoken language communities in which they live, like the thumbs-up G(6-UP):GOOD gesture. The symbol "OK" or "thumbs up" is familiar in many (but not all) communities. The "thumbs-up" emblem is a high frequency conventional lexical form in IS and in Auslan, and is coded in this study as such—GOOD(AUS).

In a contact system such as IS, gesture and enactment via constructed action and dialogue are resources that signers already have in their repertoire; therefore, it makes sense that not only would iconic gestures be used in cross-linguistic contact, but an amount of enactment would be incorporated to enrich signs that might not be understood if they are not shared by users in contact with each other. Prior research reviewed in the previous chapter indicated that "mimed actions," "invented gestures" (Moody, 1979; Woll, 1990), and "strings of paraphrasing" (Allsop et al., 1994) complement the limited conventional lexicon of the IS contact system. Mentioned above, the strategy of demonstrating meaning by showing includes using gestures that prompt imagery.

In a cognitive-linguistic framework, both nonlinguistic gestures and linguistic units are considered a reflection of imagistic thinking. This can be via concrete, direct form–to-referent imagery or by analytical thinking that organizes referents in an abstract, hierarchical way (Okrent, 2002, p. 185, following McNeill, 1992). The main difference between gesture and linguistic unit pivots on degree of conventionalization, where and how the form is conventional, and the constraints on how gestures combine with linguistic elements (Okrent, 2002). For example, signers incorporate a restricted number of handshapes to depict varied objects in motion, which differs from the wide variety used by nonsigners (gesturers) to depict the same images and movements (Schembri, 2001). The fact that certain handshapes are similarly used by signers from different SL origins, such as the V (two legs) handshape  for human referents and beak-like GO> , BO>  handshapes for birds (Schembri, 2001), means that a direct connection to imagery is available to different SL users and is exploitable in IS contact.

Okrent (2002) suggests gestures can be determined in terms of whether (a) they express an imagistic aspect of a referent; (b) they are not regular, established forms; and (c) "the form of the gesture patterns meaning onto form in a gradient, as opposed to categorical, way" (p. 187). Gradient patterning on a form in spoken language is given as vowel lengthening (e.g., "a looooong time") or rising/falling pitch ("cliiiimbing/descennnnnding") (except where it has phonemic value as in Mandarin Chinese; p. 191). In a NSL and in IS, when a sign is more regularly used, it becomes aligned with a specific semantic structure. Gradient meaning is a vague sense that a form may carry, such as the gesture G(5-SHAKE):WOW-VERY shown in Figure 11. It is an example of a gesture, although it is used often by IS signers (and observed in NSLs such as Auslan and ASL). The form's meaning is not predictable; it can mean several different things that conjure the image of a physical reaction to an emotion. Depending on the context, other nonmanuals that accompany it, and aspect of movement, it may suggest something good or bad, or it can signify varying degrees of intensity (e.g., volume, quantity, badness, excitement). If a sign requires contextual support for understanding, it is considered to be gestural, given that "a conventional sign does not need much contextual support to have meaning" (Okrent, 2002, p. 179). Other signs involve both linguistic and gestural components, or may be established forms. A taxonomy of sign types—fully lexical, partly lexical, and nonlexical—considered in this study is described below.

FIGURE 11. *IS Gesture (5-SHAKE)WOW-VERY.*

Spatial Reference, Displacement, and Meaning in SLs

Many of the meaning-making constructions found in studied SLs, while different in their form and function, still show evidence of universally constructed visual-spatial elements. One of the features that all studied SLs have to date is the use of space to organize referents in discourse. Some researchers explain this in terms of verb agreement (Engberg-Pedersen, 1993; Sandler & Lillo-Martin, 2006; Supalla, 1982, 1990), while others describe the use of space modification to direct and locate (point to) the movement of referents (de Beuzeville, Johnston, & Schembri, 2009; Liddell, 2000, 2003).

In a cross-linguistic study of 15 different geographically distinct NSLs, Newport and Supalla (2000) identify "classifier structures in verbs of motion" contributing to the use of "location and movement through space in common ways to mark grammatical agreement with the subject and object" (p. 110). They claim that these common morphological structures in unrelated SLs allow users of unintelligible SLs to develop and communicate by IS (Supalla, 2008b, p. 580). In earlier work, Supalla notes the inherently iconic representation of objects being referred to in what he calls "visual-geometric classifiers," which depict the size and shape of referents (Supalla, 1982). Johnston identifies this "shape iconicity" as one type of iconicity that gives meaning in Auslan (and perhaps by extension to other SLs), but that "the displacement and behavior of a sign is an analogue of its meaning," distinguishing between shape-iconic signs and analogue-iconic signs (Johnston, 1991, p. 22). In these ways, NSLs make use of visual-spatial elements to make reference between subject—object role-play, physical relationships (next to, above, etc.), and structured use of space to build cohesion in the discourse (Winston 1991). Exploiting the signing space involves creating real space blends that are conceptualized from mental representations, or mental spaces (Ferrara, 2012, following Fauconnier, 1985, 1997; Liddell, 2003). Before mention of blending and its role in meaning-making in SLs (and its relevance to IS), a rudimentary discussion is made about Mental Space Theory as applied in this study.

DISCOURSES ARE MENTAL SPACE CONSTRUCTIONS THAT INVOLVE BLENDING

In a cognitive description of ASL grammar, Liddell (2003) elaborates on the application of mental space theory via real space blends to describe meaning-creation in ASL. The theory, proposed by Fauconnier (1985), explains how linguistic symbols, which have meaning *potential* in a given discourse context, prompt mental space representations (Fauconnier, 1997, p. 37). Mental space representations are highly abstract cognitive constructions, comprising knowledge and cognitive models (Lakoff, 1987) from our experiences and semantic frames (Fillmore, 1982). At the start of this chapter, I mentioned Idealized Cognitive Models—structures with which we organize knowledge (Lakoff, 1987). Our knowledge about things, such as *mothers,* is complex and includes prototypical ideas (birth, nurturer) that may be stereotypical (housewife) or cultural variations (unwed, adoptive, foster, stepmother; Lakoff, 1987, p. 75). These types of knowledge structures comprise the domains of information that are mental space constructions when discourses are expressed and understood.

A full elaboration on Mental Space Theory goes beyond the scope of this study; however, brief mention of it here provides some theoretical background to methods I use in the IS comprehension test in Study Two. It is assumed that expository IS discourses prompt meaning via cognitive processes that are involved in understanding SLs. Cognitive processing of semiotic symbols (signs and gestures) prompts conceptual representations and discourse structure. Figure 12 provides an example of a mental space construction created from utterances in a discourse. The discourse content is an excerpt from a content analysis and rubric for the IS source video D used in the comprehension test in Chapter 6 (Retell task). For ease of explanation of the figure, I use the English translation of the source IS discourse.

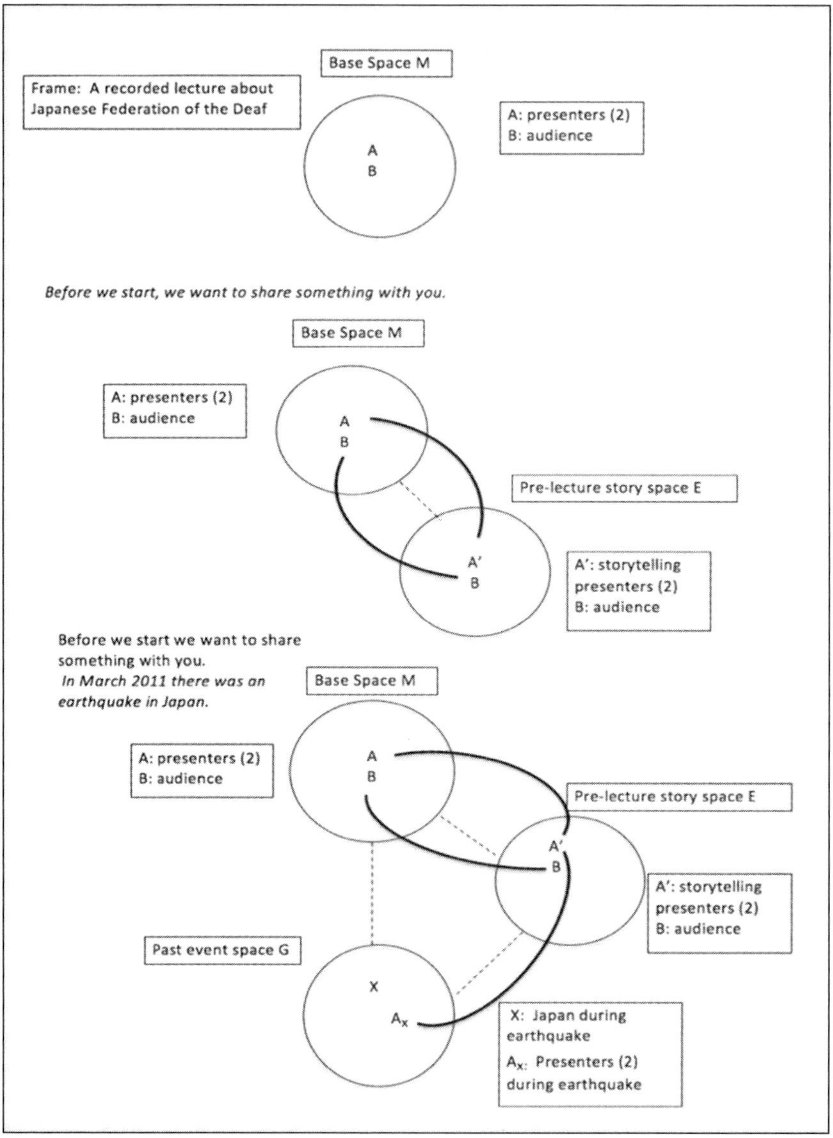

FIGURE 12. *Example of mental space construction from IS lecture discourse.*

In the illustrated example, the base mental space M establishes the cognitive configuration of a lecture by two Japanese deaf men to an audience. The mental representation includes all of the elements one might construe from the semantic domain of "lectures." In the base space M, the lecture begins, but a new mental space is also prompted with the opening statement, "Before we start, we want to share something with you."

The phrase "Before we start" is an expression that serves as a "space builder," which establishes a shift in focus to a new space (Fauconnier, 1997). A space builder can also prompt a shift back to a previously established space. Examples of space builders in English are "In 1947," or "however,". Specific elements in a mental space are known *things* that are part of our conventional lexicon and knowledge structures around *things* and topics. The "lecture" is a *thing* in the knowledge structure framing this particular discourse. A participant in this current study is informed that the recorded presentation is a lecture, and this prompts a knowledge structure in the mind of the participant about "lectures." Additional elements are built up in the mental spaces as new linguistic (and nonlinguistic) information is uttered. In the example given, the participant viewing the IS presenter perceives meaningful linguistic and nonlinguistic information and recognizes these symbolic forms (either through established lexicon or iconic reference). From this recognition of the signs' meaning [BEFORE WE START, WE WANT TO SHARE SOMETHING WITH YOU], participants arrive at a construal about a pre-lecture narrative, which then preempts the expectation of the lecture topic. The signed utterance meaning [IN MARCH 2011] is a space-building prompt informing observers that they are about to hear a story from the past. Recognition of varied symbols in the utterance (JAPAN, EARTHQUAKE, etc.) completes the mental space with more detail.

Symbolic expressions in discourse (signs, strings of signs, whole texts) instantiate mental space constructions and convey meaning. Most importantly, understanding utterances of a language (or a contact system like IS) involves successful prompting of intended mental space constructions.

In addition to discourse structuring through mental spaces, SLs create meaning through blending mental spaces and their elements. A central process of grammar is blending (or cognitive integration: Fauconnier & Turner, 1996), in which elements of one domain are mapped onto another. Liddell provides an example for the way people use real space anchors such as implementing a knife or a cup on a table to map out and discuss relationships between entities that are not present in the discussion (2003, pp. 149–150). Because mental spaces are cognitive conceptualizations, they are not grounded in reality; however, conceptualizations that become part of elements in signing space are grounded in real space, which are "current conceptualizations of the immediate environment" based on sensory input (Liddell, 2003, p. 82). Real space is the created conceptual "reality" that is conceived from visual input, such as an imagined keyboard that a person might gesture and tap away at in space (Liddell, 2003, p. 83). In SLs, real space is the created discourse "reality" that is mapped out and grounded in front of the signer by incorporating the hands, arms, torso, and face. Some of these conceptual entities resemble their referents iconically, and others are more opaque. In addition, real space blends incorporate locations in the signing space, which is seen in the way a signer directs verbs at representative placeholder tokens in space (2003, p. 188) (Figure 13).

In Figure 13, the signer creates a real space blend with which he interacts. With the nondominant hand, the signer articulates a token blend ||ballot|; it is a depicting sign (DS) that is a size and shape specifier (FLAT B is shaped like a piece of paper). (See Table 1 for annotation conventions.) The interacting behavior is also a blend, a surrogate, in which the signer is not just narrating or telling, but switches to become the actual voter enacting a selection (using the Auslan sign "SELECT"). A mental space is triggered by the physical shift in shoulders and eye gaze. The physical shift is one example of a space builder in Auslan (also seen in other SLs). With his dominant hand, he articulates the Auslan sign "SELECT" as if to pick something from the nondominant hand, which has been established previously in the discourse as a voting ballot, with names of candidates. This specific information is not transparent in the blend; however, the specific information comes from the signs earlier in the utterance, such as ELECTORATES, REPRESENTATIVE, NAMES, and VOTING FORM.

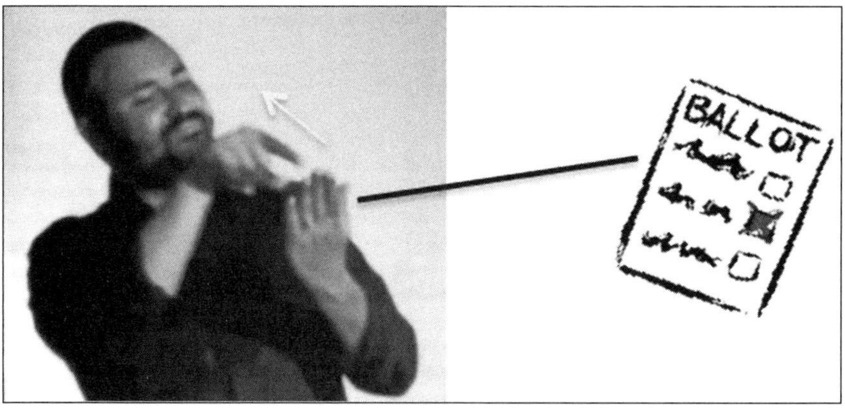

FIGURE 13. *Real-space blend in Auslan* SELECT-ITEM-FROM-LIST*: RH:* SELECT*; LH:* DSS(B):FLAT-SURFACE-LIKE-A-BALLOT *(Ballot selection [video image], 2012, retrieved from http://www.vec.vic.gov.au/Voting/AssistanceForVoters.html).*

The space builder noted in the utterance above is one of the ways that signers are also able to use gestural behavior (pantomime) to prompt mental space constructions in discourse. The signer becomes part of a surrogate blend by enacting behavior of a participant referred to in a discourse (Dudis, 2004, 2011). This is shown in the way signers express nonmanual markers and body postures separately from and simultaneously with signs (Liddell, 2003). The process of space blending is one of the strategies for meaning creation and is observed in SLs. Different SLs may exhibit a stable use of some forms over others, and there are forms that are so iconic and gestural that they might be understood across SLs in an expository IS contact setting. Whether IS discourses are understood depends to some extent on how well the symbolic material (signs and gestures) prompts conceptually integrated mental spaces.

METAPHOR AND MEANING IN SLs

Metaphor is a type of blend, a mechanism whereby the elements of one domain are mapped onto elements of another. In SLs, metaphoric blending means that iconic images are extended, and their meanings can reference abstract ideas (Brennan, 1990; Taub, 2001; Wilcox, 2000). Often, metaphors derived from human-embodied experience become ingrained in everyday language; our human conceptual system is by nature metaphoric (Lakoff & Johnson, 1980). One of the common spatial metaphors used in some spoken and SLs is the UP-IS-GOOD metaphor. Metaphors are types of cognitive blending that enable humans to understand and create links between symbols and ideas to convey meaning. In blending, through conceptual integration (Fauconnier & Turner, 1996), structure from two input spaces is projected to a third space, which then has its own unique semantic structure. A classic example of a metaphoric blend in English is the metaphor, LIFE IS A JOURNEY, where "bumps in the road" refer to and are understood to mean challenges or difficult periods in one's life. In the blend, elements of one conceptual domain are mapped onto those of another (Figure 15).

In metaphor and blending, the input spaces that contribute to the blend constitute domains of conceptualization. In these domains are ideas and construed information we have from experience. Domains are understandings about concrete artifacts in our surroundings, as well as basic human sensorimotor experiences, such as perception of

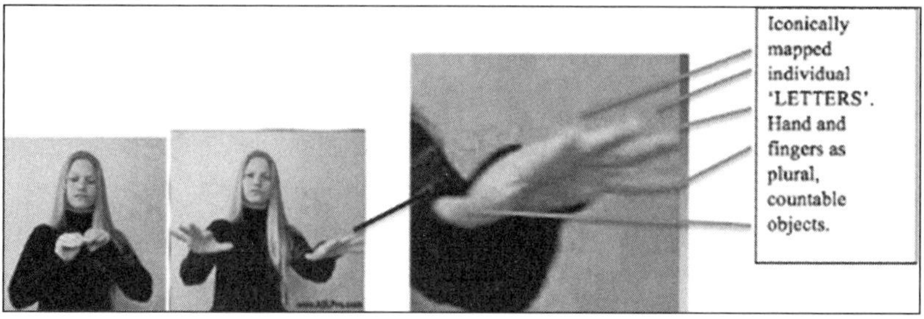

FIGURE 14. *Iconically mapped meaning of ASL sign* DISTRIBUTE *(Distribute [video image], 2011, retrieved from http://www.aslpro.com/cgi-bin/aslpro/aslpro.cgi).*

size, space, physical boundaries of vertical and horizontal orientation, bodily motion, and sense of touch and smell, particularly manipulation of objects (Grady, 1997; Lakoff & Johnson, 1999). Common ontological and spatial metaphors described in spoken (Lakoff, 1987) and in some SLs (Brennan, 1992; Taub, 2001; Wilcox, 2000) are considered in this study while assessing how depiction operates in IS.

A range of visual metaphors (blends) can be utilized in SLs to express abstract meanings, many of which are iconically represented in handshapes and locations in the signing space in front of a signer.

Consider, for example, the ASL sign DISTRIBUTE (Figure 14). The two-handed flat O handshape  begins with hands together in a hold and then opens up and moves outward into a two-handed 5 handshape sign . The extended 5 hands iconically represent individual items on each finger, and their spreading movement forward and outward maps the transfer of several countable entities (fingers) to some abstract target. This sign might be used in an utterance to convey the meaning of DISTRIBUTE LETTERS.

In this case, the iconic mapping does not resemble LETTERS, because letters are not shaped like long fingers. The blend involves fingers as countable items, and it is metaphoric in that each finger represents one or many items. In an utterance, the specified referential meaning would come from the context or a more specific sign before or after this one. For example, LETTERS DISTRIBUTE would allow the concept of letters to be mapped onto the fingers in the sign and convey the meaning. The meaning might be altered if the utterance were YESTERDAY RAIN, WATER DISTRIBUTE. In this case the fingers on the 5 handshape  are mapped not as individual water droplets, but as the shape of a spreading surface of water.

The sign DISTRIBUTE is a conventional lexical sign in ASL; however, in a contact situation, such as where IS is used, the iconic, metaphoric

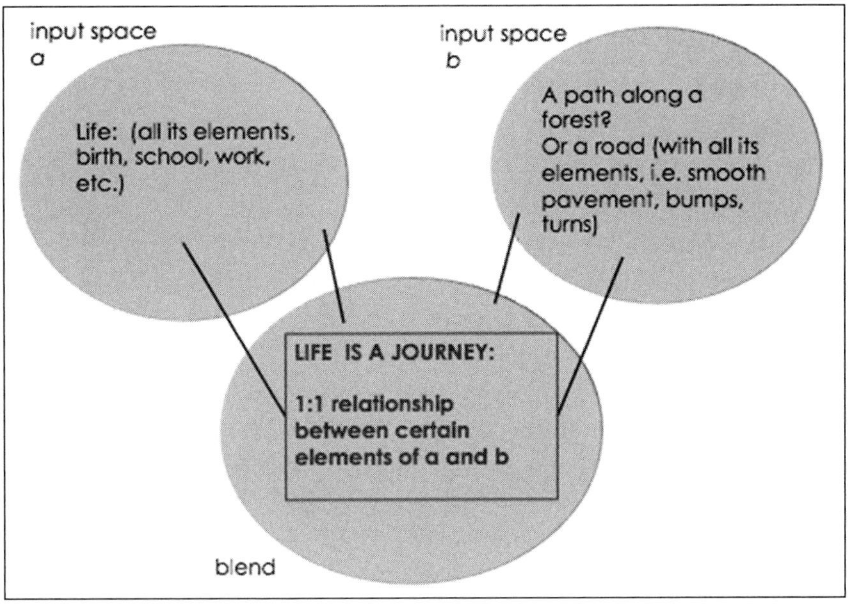

FIGURE 15. *Blended space from two input spaces.*

potential of this sign may be exploited to construct grounded real space blends in the same way the formational parameters of a depicting sign in a conventional sign language might be productively used (Johnston & Schembri, 1999). The conventional ASL is no longer read idiomatically but is de-lexicalized (Johnston & Ferrara, 2012).

The iconic imagery that is conjured by the articulators, and the way that they can be engaged in metaphoric blending in SLs, was illustrated above. This description is informed by Liddell's work on blending and grammar in ASL, and Taub's theory of analogue building (2001) in sign languages. Taub provides a model for how iconicity and metaphor operate in ASL. These common elements are found in varied NSLs, and their use in IS discourse may contribute to improved comprehension. An analysis from this framework is particularly relevant and applicable to the analysis of participants' understanding of six short depicting segments in the IS texts they watched (Findings, in Study Two).

Referring to metaphoric mappings between a concrete domain of experience to describe an abstract domain of experience, Taub describes *two* relationships that build up an analogue in the concrete and abstract domains. The concrete domain relationship is iconic, where the form (handshapes, movement, location, palm orientation, nonmanual signals) is iconically mapped onto meaning. One example that may be perceivable to a variety of SL users is the 5-handshape  as representative of the branches on a tree. Yet, there are building blocks in varied SLs for iconic forms. An example is the V (or 2) handshape  held upside down to depict a two-legged form in ASL (and in other SLs). While the form is not actually a set of legs, the iconic mapping is concretely made between the image of a standing person and the shape of the upside-down V handshape. Thus, the semantic structure of a person or entity standing on two legs is preserved and mapped onto the fingers (Taub, 2001, p. 22). These are real-world articulators that participate in a "structure preserving correspondences between our mental models of the two entities" (p. 22).

In the second relationship, an abstract domain is represented by an iconic concrete image. In the example above, with the depicted set of legs, once the image is mapped onto the handshape, the domain of everything we understand that can be done with a pair of legs—walking, crouching, jumping, kicking—can be metaphorically represented by movement of the upside-down V handshape. This type of meaning-making can occur with conventional signs as well as with productive depicting signs that comprise SL discourses.

I have outlined the ways meaning is created in SLs, and these same resources are brought into a contact sign language situation, like expository IS presentations. In IS, these mechanisms can be exploited to convey meaning to audience members, but their effective comprehension has yet to be shown, especially regarding whether all of the specific information is successfully conveyed to the audience. Insights can be gained about how well depicting signs and other elements contribute to participant understanding, particularly where conceptual metaphors are recruited by iconic, linguistic, and gestural structures observed in the IS discourse.

The varied types of signs that are present in NSLs are discussed in the next section, with examples in a NSL as well as those observed the IS lecture data described in Study One.

TYPES OF SIGNS IN SLs AND APPLICATION TO IS SIGN TYPES

The lexicons of established SLs are described by different terminology and taxonomies by varied researchers, noting that signs arise from different origins to become part of a given SL lexicon. In one view, these origins are labeled as foreign, core, and spatial (Brentari

& Padden, 2001). Signs are categorized into core lexicon and a non-core lexicon (Brentari, 2010). Distinctions are made between signs that are foreign or borrowed and those that are considered "core" given their adherence to nativization constraints of symmetry and dominance (Battison, 1978). The difficulty here arises from applying this framework when a contact language, as a system of borrowing from several languages, technically does not have a "core" lexicon. There are some forms, however, that operate as established signs (lexemes) in IS and some that are more productive, contributing to the grammar. The task is to ascertain which signs constitute the most regular ones used and lexicalized in IS, such as the forms borrowed from a NSL. As reviewed in Chapter 2, prior research indicates that IS exhibits some signs that are common to NSLs, such as BSL and ASL, among others (Rosenstock, 2004; Woll, 1990).

In another view, the core lexicon of a SL is made up of fully lexical signs (Johnston & Schembri, 1999), which are also referred to in the literature as fully specified signs (Johnson & Liddell, 1986), or monomorphemic signs (Engberg-Pedersen, 1993). Each of these models means slightly different things, but for the purpose of the lexical analysis in Study One, I adhere to the hierarchy of lexicalized forms first outlined by Johnston and Schembri (1999) and elaborate on three sign types—lexical, partly-lexical, and non-lexical, proposed by Johnston and Schembri (2010). All of these types of signs are semiotic symbols (in the Peircean sense, 1955) of varied complexity found in NSLs and can be employed in IS presentations.

Fully Lexical Signs

When people think about any particular language, what comes to mind is the basic unit of individual words, or the lexicon. Knowing minimal units of meaning in a language means that a person has the ability at some basic level to compose and to understand messages using these meaningful elements. The next degree of complexity is grammatical relations between meaningful elements. Identification of lexical signs in IS is central to the methods used in this research; therefore, some description is needed about what a lexical sign is, and what constitutes a lexical sign in expository IS. In this study, a distinction is made between "lexicalized" signs and those that are partly lexical or nonlexical as outlined by Johnston and Schembri (2007) and Johnston (2012).

FIGURE 16. *Lexical signs in IS from (a)* Gestuno *glossary, or NSLs such as (b) ASL or (c) Auslan (a, Approve [Image]; b,* IMPORTANT *(ASL); c,* DEAF *(Auslan), 1975, British Deaf Association; retrieved from http://www.bda.org.uk).*

Lexicalization in SLs essentially occurs when a signed unit acquires a clearly identifiable and replicable citation form that is regularly and strongly associated with a meaning that is more specific than the sign's componential meaning potential, even when cited out of context; cannot be predicted based on these components alone; or is quite unrelated to its componential meaning potential—that is, it may be arbitrary (Johnston, 2012, p. 166).

Fully lexical signs are those that are defined as conventional in their form and meaning, such as signs listed in a dictionary. In expository IS lecture, presenters recruit signs from their own SL lexicons and other established signs such as those from IS glossaries created by WFD or the out-of-print, *Gestuno* glossary (BDA, 1975). Examples of lexical signs seen in IS are in Figure 16.

As noted above, componential parts of fully lexical signs are also symbolic units with potential for constructing meaning. Johnston and Schembri (1999) distinguish fully lexical signs from partly lexical stating that a lexeme (word/sign) is "a linguistic unit with a 'given' rather than a 'generated' meaning" (p. 2). A sign may also be lexicalized instantaneously when a linguistic community establishes and accepts any form/meaning connection (Johnston & Ferrara, 2014, p. 236). The ability for sublexical components to become engaged in a new form and usage is one of the aspects of productivity and creation of new sign forms. Some of these productive, created forms are partly lexical depicting signs, which are outlined in the next section.

Partly Lexical Signs

Many NSLs exhibit complex forms that can be characterized as partly lexical. These complex signs have properties of gradation and category, rely on discourse context for meaning, and are not specified for usage in a conventional way. The specified aspects of these signs typically come from their handshape and orientation, and their movements are mapped in the signing space in any variety of constructions and discourse contexts to create gradations of meaning (Schembri, 2001). Parts of these complexes—handshape, orientation, location, and movement—often have their own meaning, although there is no consensus about their status as morphemes (Johnston & Schembri, 2007). There is also some debate around the movement parameter as an agreement morpheme (Okrent, 2002, p. 176).

Two kinds of partly lexical signs are points and depicting signs (Johnston & Schembri, 2007). Pointing signs are a type of deictic gesture that are meaningful. They have several functions in SLs, one of the most important of which is for reference tracking. They also serve an adverbial locating function, a determiner function, and a discourse cohesive function (buoys). Pointing signs indicate physical referents in space as well as imagined entities in the form of tokens or buoys in the signing space. Referents are established through deixis in signing space in front of the signer, and used when referring back (anaphora) to previously established referents (Lillo-Martin & Klima, 1990; McBurney, 2002). The imagined entities that points refer to are placeholders for conceptual real space referents in the signed discourse (Liddell, 2003, p. 192). Some researchers also analyze them with grammatical distinction between pronominal first person and non-first person (Engberg Pederson, 1993; Meier, 1990), or of first, second, and third person (Friedman, 1975). The pronominal status of points in SLs is questioned, and it has been defended that points participate in discourse as independent signs or blends to direct and indicate verbs (Johnston, 2013b; Liddell, 1995, 2000). Pointing signs are complex elements in SLs, and they have been characterized as hybrid forms (partly conventional, partly nonconventional), with features that are both gestural and pronomial (Cormier, Schembri, & Woll, 2013), and it is suggested that points are gestural, much like co-speech gestural pointing that occurs with spoken languages (Johnston, 2013a). It appears that these sign types are common among all SLs to (at the very least) indicate and locate, and are context-dependent for their meaning.

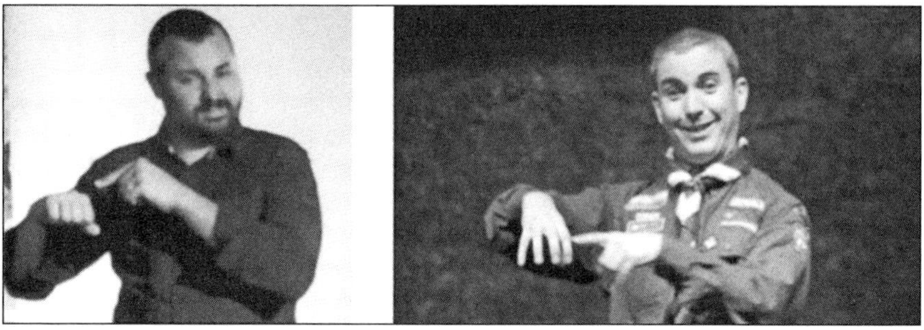

(a) (b)

FIGURE 17. *Partly lexical pointing sign with depicting sign in (a) Auslan lecture and in (b) IS lecture data (a, [video image], 2012, retrieved from http://www.vec.vic.gov.au/Voting/AssistanceForVoters.html).*

The pointing sign on both signers' left hands in Figure 17 does not have a stable meaning, although in the discourse it draws attention to a lexical sign in Figure 17a (the Auslan verb TAKE) or the depicting sign (the IS form DSL(Bent5-DOWN):OTHER-GROUP) that is being articulated. These partly lexical signs are types that are semiotic symbols but are not listable in the lexicon of a NSL.

Depicting signs are another type of partly lexical sign that are often engaged in real space blends, as illustrated by the concept of voting ballot in Figure 13. They depict a shape, location, or movement of a referent with sometimes iconic portrayal of the referent through productive, sublexical sign parameters of handshape, orientation, location, movement, and nonmanual signals. For example, the flat "B" hand  held palm down generally refers to a flat, horizontally oriented entity like a tabletop.

The handshape parameter is particularly salient, so it has been credited with prompting meaning (Brennan, 1992), mainly because it is easy to isolate this sublexical component of a sign (Johnston & Schembri, 1999). There is ongoing discussion in the literature about the status of location and movement components of signs. It is debated whether they are nonlinguistic gestural components (Liddell, 1995) or linguistic types of agreement marking (Supalla, 1982). The productive aspects of what are referred to here as depicting signs are discussed in the IS literature under different assumptions, just as they are in the general SL linguistic literature. In the SL literature, these are morphemic analyses (e.g., Schick, 1990; Supalla, 1978) or nonlinguistic, analogue analyses (e.g., DeMatteo, 1977). Recent works identify both linguistic and gestural elements in depicting signs (polycomponential verbs; Schembri, 2001). Some of the many references to these sign types in IS are "verbs of motion and location" (e.g., Supalla & Webb, 1995), "classifiers" (Allsop et al., 1994; McKee & Napier, 2002; Rosenstock, 2004), "agreement marking verb inflections" (McKee & Napier, 2002), "spatial verbs" and "classifier morphology" (Woll, 1990), and "depicting verbs" (Rosenstock, 2004). As noted earlier, the term "depicting signs" is used throughout this study and can be analyzed (as well as pointing signs) as comprising a combination of both linguistic and gestural components, following Liddell (2003), Schembri (2001), and Schembri, Jones, and Burnham (2005).

An example of a partly lexical depicting sign, DSM(1):PERSON-MOVES-FORWARD is juxtaposed with the Auslan fully lexical sign BUT in Table 5. The fully lexical image (and several others in this study) is listed in the *Auslan Signbank*, a corpus-based Auslan dictionary that served as a reference throughout this study.[2]

Nonlexical Signs

The third category of sign types is nonlexical signs, which are important to include in the comparisons of signs in NSLs and IS lectures, particularly given that they are assumed to be prevalent and important to meaning making in IS discourses, according to prior claims. Nonlexical signs are intentional bodily actions that convey meaning, and in this study two types are categorized, but they are not conventional in terms of their form or meaning. They are dependent upon context for their interpretation. These signs can appear to be gesture-like manual movements that are not conventional in their meaning but depend on context. The second type of nonlexical signs (or gestures) is elaborate pantomime and enacted behavior such as forms of constructed action or constructed dialogue. Some nonlexical signs provide a discourse pragmatic function as in the hand waving HEY gestural form (Hoza, 2011). Another function of some gestures is to mark prosodic boundaries between utterances in SLs (e.g., the form annotated as G(5-UP):WELL in this study and in work on the Auslan Corpus). In this way, nonlexical signs can also prompt new mental spaces in the buildup of discourse.

2. URL: http://www.auslan.org.au [Image] BUT: http://www.auslan.org.au/dictionary/words/but-5.html).

TABLE 5. *Comparing a Fully Lexical and Partly Lexical Sign in NSL, Auslan.*

	Fully lexical sign	Partly lexical depicting sign

Fully Lexical Meaning	Interactive 1. Used alone to tell someone to stop doing (which usually involves trying to get your attention) and to wait until you are ready to attend to them. English = "hold on!," "Hang on!," "Wait a sec!," and so on. As Modifier 1. Use to introduce a statement that contrasts with what you have just said. English = but, yet, although.	N/A
Partly Lexical Meaning	Upright tall object	An upright entity (animate) moves in a forward direction toward something.
Contextual meanings that complete partly lexical meaning	When context forces the abandonment of the conventional fully lexical meaning, context narrows it to: Utility pole, fence pole, long piece of wood, tall person standing-at-location...etc.	Only when the context narrows meaning to: Attend, travel, go, follow, approach, assert oneself... etc.
Gloss	BUT	DSM(1): PERSON-MOVES-FORWARD

Note. BUT [Image] (2012). Retrieved from http://www.auslan.org.au/dictionary/words/but-5.html. Depicting MOVE [Video image] (2012). Retrieved from http://www.vec.vic.gov.au/Voting/AssistanceForVoters.html.

FIGURE 18. *Nonlexical signs in (a) Auslan [G(5-DOWN):* AWW-FORGET-IT*] and (b, c) IS [(b) G (CA):*WIPE-SWEAT*; (c) G(F-2H):*ALL-OKAY*] (a, [video image], 2012, retrieved from http://www.vec.vic.gov.au/Voting/AssistanceForVoters.html).*

Gestures were discussed above as types of signs or symbolic bodily movements that are seen commonly across all SLs. They are observed in IS as well by researchers noted in the literature review. Through a lexical analysis of sign types in expository IS, identification of nonlexical forms such as gesture and enactment leads to an understanding about how prevalent they are in meaning construction in IS, and whether they contribute to comprehension. Figure 18 shows examples of nonlexical signs in an Auslan lecture: (a) a constructed action, (b) a gesture example, and (c) from the IS data in this study.

This taxonomy of three types of signs in a SL described above allows for an analysis of semiotic material that is present in a mixed SL system that employs a variety of resources, as alluded to in the quote that opened this chapter. Enfield's proposition that utterances are composites of both linguistic and nonlinguistic elements is particularly relevant here.

SUMMARY AND RELEVANCE TO MEANING-CONSTRUCTION IN INTERNATIONAL SIGN

In this chapter, cognitive descriptions of meaning-making applied to SLs were reviewed to ground several assumptions about meaning-making in IS. Prior research and what is known about languages in contact outlined in Chapter 2 identified that signers (and interpreters) incorporate a variety of symbolic resources from their own NSLs when communicating into IS. With NSLs, signers typically produce signals for showing meaning in nonlinguistic ways as well as telling meaning via conventionally established sign forms (Ferrara, 2012; Ferrara & Johnston, 2014;

Liddell, 2003). IS presents as a mixed system of symbolic expressions that can be understood from and compared to meaning-making strategies described in SLs. These include the engagement of gesture and linguistic resources in symbolic, meaningful ways, but perhaps with increased variation and less conventionality of form-meaning pairs (signs and complex constructions). The main difference between NSLs and IS likely arises from amounts of conventional form-meaning pairs at different levels of complexity—sublexical, lexical (substantive), and complex constructions (composites), which could have some impact on comprehension of IS compared to NSLs.

Through regular use, symbolic units are conventionalized. The entrenched meanings are then tapped by recognition of signs (in the Peircean sense) used between interlocutors. Conceptualizations are built up through bodily experience with objects and actions; so shared experiences create the potential for similar conceptualizations to be held in the minds of signers and audience observers.

In expository IS presentations, IS signers employ symbolic expressions of form-meaning pairs that are constructed to profile objects (things, topics, actions, relations) and ideally tap into the audience's semantic structures, construct mental spaces, and fill these spaces with conceptual ideas about those objects. When different SL users see the communicated symbolic expressions, what is of interest here is whether meaning is successfully conveyed, or if part or all of the symbolic linguistic expression is so entrenched with its own language-specific symbolic value that it profiles something different in the mind of the perceiver.

Quantitative analysis of the lexical patterns in IS can yield a detailed understanding of signs that are most regularly used in the studied context. Similar kinds of constructions described in NSLs are likely to be observed in an IS contact strategy, but there may be no guarantee that they are exhaustive or universally applicable.

Chapter 4

An Analysis of the Lexical Frequency of Expository IS

This chapter outlines the first part of this research project, which is a small-scale lexical frequency analysis of expository International Sign (IS). It provides a quantitative description of the IS lexicon from the collected IS lecture data, and a comparison is made to lexical frequency studies on conventional native signed languages (NSLs) such as Auslan, American Sign Language (ASL), and British Sign Language (BSL). Results from the analysis report sign types and their distribution in IS and uncover high-frequency signs used in the context of lecture IS at international conferences (e.g., World Federation of the Deaf [WFD] and World Association of Sign Language Interpreters [WASLI]). High frequency signs resulting from the analysis are also provided in a DVD supplement to this book, for the reader's reference.

High-frequency lexical signs and longer segments of the collected IS data were used to later create a comprehension test, described in Study Two (see Chapter 6). Because previous research suggests shared lexical signs, gestural elements, and depicting signs are important elements that could impact IS comprehension, Study One quantified sign forms recruited by deaf IS lecturers and used them in a comprehension assessment across different signers. This first study contributes added detail to earlier findings about IS linguistic and gestural features.

RESEARCH DESIGN

Quantitative evaluation of source IS lecture data was made using digitized media annotation software and a method of annotation following those outlined for the Auslan Corpus (Johnston, 2014). The first part of this research (Study One) is an analysis and description of the lexicon of expository IS from a collection of 13 IS lecture samples. The second part of the research (Study Two) applies quantitative methods (as well as some degree of interpretive text analysis) and qualitative approaches to ascertain

IS comprehension by geographically and linguistically diverse participants. The use of interpretive qualitative research methods, combined with quantitative measures, offer differentiated data (Saldahna & O'Brien, 2013) about factors influencing IS comprehension by demographically different signers.

Given the mixed methods applied in this research, different types of data provide a slightly different view about the degrees of success that receivers of messages in expository IS have toward understanding aspects of the text information. The approach allows quantitative and qualitative information to be gathered at the same time and compared in order to create a richer understanding of the research questions posed (Ivankova & Creswell, 2009). Triangulation design is a widely used mixed methods approach. The results are reported separately, and then interpretation and discussion are presented, where the cross-comparison of different types of results can be elaborated.

Data Collection

This investigation captures authentic[1] expository IS lecture in a typical usage setting and includes deaf people from varied countries. A first step involved collecting situated use of IS lecture by Deaf presenters. Data were collected at an international conference pertaining to deaf people and their aim to improve quality of life and human rights. Audiences were composed of 300 to 2,000 mixed deaf and hearing attendees, representing as many as 25 different countries. Since expository IS is used in a conference discourse setting every 2 to 4 years, the 2011 Conference of the WFD and the 2011 WASLI Conference were the chosen venues for capturing IS in use. The historical longevity of WFD conferences provides a consistent, stable forum for expository IS use. One earlier study used this same discourse example of IS lecture data from two deaf, European signers to describe grammatical devices (Supalla & Webb, 1995). Two others analyzed IS target messages produced by North American and European interpreters (McKee & Napier, 2002; Rosenstock, 2004). This research collection is different in that it includes 13 deaf signers from Asian, African, North, West, and Central European, Oceanic, South American, and North American countries.

1. Authentic data corpora is material that "is gathered from genuine communications of people going about their normal business." This differs from experimental data collected in conditions that are artificial (Sinclair, 1996, cited by Granger et al., 2002, p. 8).

Filming took place over the course of several days during the 2 weeks of both conferences. Presentations were video recorded using a high-definition digital video camera for analysis and use in assessing audience comprehension. All source IS video samples were labeled to de-identify the presenting participant, backed up and stored on a digital storage device, and kept in a secure place in the researcher's home office.

Study One Participants

Participants were recruited after direct contact with the organizing committees of the 2011 WFD Congress and the 2011 WASLI conference. The request to recruit participants was approved by the president and board of the WFD and by the WASLI conference organizers. Initial contact with prospective participants was made via email prior to the conference or on site, with face-to-face follow-up in person on site. All completed an informed consent form and a demographic questionnaire, with which sociolinguistic and educational variables were collected.

Participating deaf, IS presenters are from a variety of geographic origins and native signed language backgrounds. Table 6 lists the countries of origin of the 16 participants, as well as information about their first and other SLs. Most (12) have used their native SL since birth or before age 6, and the other four used home signs and learned their local SL during their teenage or young adult school years. Fourteen (14) of the 16 read and write English in addition to communicating fluently in their first sign language. All presenters are well traveled, having met other deaf people in their travels. Notably, for those whose first language is not ASL, most report knowing some amount of ASL and/or BSL.

The Dataset and Selections for Two Studies

In total, 21 IS samples of varied length were collected and available for analysis. Of the 21 expository presentation samples, 13 were included in the linguistic analysis in Study One of this project. The schema in Figure 19 depicts how the study dataset was refined from an initial source IS collection to balanced selections for the analysis and testing in Studies One and Two. A total of 283 minutes of IS video samples was collected. Of these, a majority of the data (160 minutes) came from Western signers from Europe, Australia, and North America. The

TABLE 6. *Source IS Signers.*

Participant number	Presenter(s)' country of origin	First SL	Other SLs	Parents D or H	Age	Number of countries traveled to and met other Deaf people
1	Australia	Auslan	ASL, ISL, KAL, German SL	D	35–55	30
2	Finland	Finnish SL	ASL	D	33–55	60
3	United States	ASL	Norwegian SL, Swiss-German SL, Danish SL	H	33–55	50
4	Japan	JSL	ASL, Philippino SL, Indian SL, Myanmar SL	H	33–55	19
5	Japan	JSL	ASL	H	33–55	42
6	Togo	Francophone ASL	Signed Exact French	H	33–55	15
7	Canada	ASL	NZSL, KSL, Franco-phone ASL, LSQ, BSL	H	33–55	40
8	Brazil	LIBRAS	ASL	H	20–35	3
9	Brail	LIBRAS	ASL, Portuguese SL	H	20–35	2
10	Ireland	ISL	BSL	D	20–35	10
11	Czech Republic	Signed Czech/CZSL	RSL, BSL	H	20–35	18
12	Hong Kong	ASL	HKSL	H	35–55	17
13	Uganda	UGL	Kenyan SL	Mixed	20–35	14
14	Nigeria	Nigerian SL	LSF	H	35–55	10
15	Australia	Auslan	BSL, ASL, AlbSL, KAL, Serbian SL, Cambodian SL	D	35–55	60
16	Canada	ASL	BSL, JSL, LSF, Portuguese SL	H	33–55	75

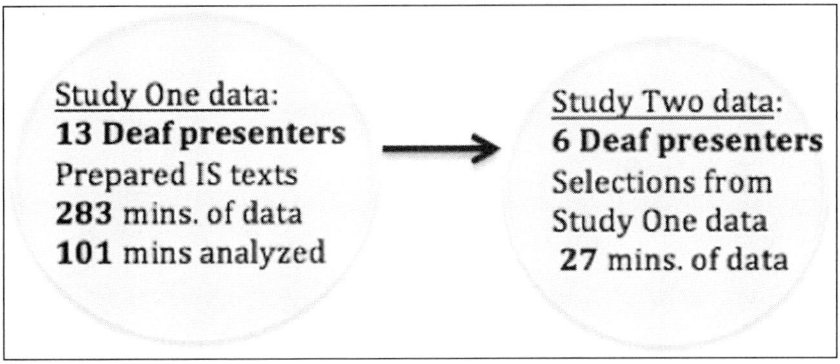

FIGURE 19. *Data collection and selection for both studies.*

remaining data were evenly elicited from signers from northeast Asia (48 minutes), South America (33 minutes), and Africa (41 minutes).

Due to time constraints, the large amount of data collected, and the scope of this research project, it was not feasible to annotate all 283 minutes. Mori (2011) points out that much of the research on IS has not included signers of Asian or other non-Western SL backgrounds. In an effort to balance the heavy percentage of Western samples, two long presentations were eliminated, and I included a larger percentage of the Asian, African, and South American signers. Poor video quality or barriers to clear video capture, such as insufficient lighting or less-than-optimal positioning in the venue also excluded some other videos in the collection. This first refinement yielded 212 minutes of source IS in the collection. One hundred and one (101) minutes of source IS are analyzed in Study One, roughly half of the balanced collection of IS data. For videos longer than 10 minutes, the first 3 minutes, the middle 3 minutes, and the final 3 minutes were annotated rather than the entire lecture. This was to ensure that opening, middle, and closing lecture discourse would be captured, rather than only the opening parts of the lectures. Table 7 shows the overall distribution by different continents or regions, the total source expository IS text gathered, and the amount analyzed in this first lexical frequency study.

The data that were selected for lexical analysis are therefore representative of varied international users of IS giving prepared expository conference presentations to a large, mixed, deaf group. Deaf signers rendered these addresses in South Africa to a diverse audience from different countries. The 101 minutes chosen for this first study are listed

TABLE 7. *Overview of IS Data Collected by Signer Regions*

Signer origin	Total minutes of data	Minutes analyzed
Europe	55	19
Australia	63	10
Asia	48	31
North America	43	10
South America	33	11
Africa	41	20
Totals	**283**	**101**

in Table 8, with video clips and total time segments from each noted. These are henceforth referred to as the "IS Lexical Frequency Dataset."

Noted in highlight in Table 8, a subset of this data was selected and used in the second study, a comprehension test. These are henceforth referred to as the "IS Comprehension Dataset." The Comprehension Dataset selection criteria and procedures for Study Two are elaborated on later in the Study Two chapter.

Two expository Auslan texts (public information available on DVD) were also included in the analysis to augment the discussion about how IS lecture compares to lecture in a NSL. The few available NSL lexical studies lack similar expository genre material for a fair comparison. Text genre is known to affect distribution of sign types, and vocabulary can be influenced by a smaller corpus with a narrower range of topics (Johnston, 2012; Morford and MacFarlane, 2003). Because the IS contact examples in this study are a collection of a specific discourse genre—expository conference lecture—it was important to compare similar text types to understand differences between NSL lectures and IS lectures in terms of sign type distribution.

Including the two Auslan expository presentations, although limited by sample size, enriches the genre-specific comparisons between international contact signing and a NSL. The Auslan presentation topics were comparable expository texts: "Negotiating the Politics of Language and Access"[2] and "Voter Registration,"[3] totaling 14 minutes of data—6 minutes and 8 minutes, respectively.

2. Conference presentation from the 2011 ASLIA National Conference (ANC), Sydney, NSW. DVD produced by the Australian Sign Language Interpreter Association (ASLIA).

3. Video URL: http://www.vec.vic.gov.au/Voting/AssistanceForVoters.html

TABLE 8. *IS Lexical Frequency Dataset*

Video sample number	Total data collected	Origin of presenter	Comprehension test data set (clip length)	Topic
1	21m 13s	Australia		Deaf Interpreters
2	5m 21s	Finland	5:21	Health issues for Deaf people
3	3m 56s	United States	3:56	WFD Election speech
4	17m 54s	Japan		Int'l Sign Research
5	43m 40s	Japan	5:00	Japanese Federation of the Deaf collaborative work
6	6m 0s	Togo, Africa	4:03	Plenary on developing countries; Part 1
7	14m 50s	Canada	2:00	Plenary on developing countries; Part 2
8	22m 14s	Brazil		HIV education: Part 1
9	10m 20s	Brazil		HIV education: Part 2
10	17m 24s	Ireland	6:05	Boy Scouts International
11	6m 20s	Czech Republic		Real-time speech to text transcription
12	2m 46s	Hong Kong		Asia-Pacific meeting—Representative report
13	33m 55s	Uganda		Human Rights for Women
14	2m 58s	Nigeria		Deaf Women in West Africa (final minutes of presentation)
Totals	212 mins		26 mins	*Highlight = inclusion in Comprehension Test*

Ethics

The Macquarie University Human Research Ethics Committee reviewed and approved this research project in May 2011, with annual reports submitted as required (Ref. 5201100310).

Due to the identifying nature of video recording, which compromises anonymity for participants, the consent form included a separate video recording consent section. It allowed participants to determine the use of material captured in video recordings of them beyond the purpose of research analysis.

One of the IS source participants requested that the video capture not be used as a clip in the comprehension testing. Accordingly, that data were included only in the frequency analysis of the 13 IS source samples. Although it was a desired IS clip by a diverse signer for the Study Two comprehension testing, it was not one of the selected texts.

ANALYSIS

Lexical analysis of the dataset allowed for a closer assessment of comprehension of sign types that comprise expository IS discourses, and was completed using similar methods exercised in NSL frequency studies (Fenlon, Schembri, Rentelis, Vinson, & Cormier, 2014; Johnston, 2012).

Digitized video material provides access to review sign language forms, but the creation of horizontal, linear transcription of sign language is not necessarily valuable. This is because SL patterning is typically simultaneous (Johnston, 2010). (For elaboration on rationale and methods of documenting and describing SLs, see Johnston, 2010.) The digital video annotation software ELAN[4] (Crasborn & Sloetjes, 2008) was used in order to make time-aligned annotations of signed language (IS) video source text. ELAN allows users to define and analyze visual-gestural language on a number of linguistic parameters and empowers the researcher to create, edit, visualize, and search annotations of video data.

The investigation was informed by corpus linguistic methods to make a detailed description of lexical distribution and frequency in IS expository discourse.

A Corpus-Informed Approach to Annotating IS texts Using ELAN Tiers

Corpus methods of linguistic description, as applied in the documentation of the Auslan Corpus (Johnston, 2014), involve a methodological process of analyzing representative language data for machine readable analysis. A corpus is a collection of language media that is linked to

4. Eudico Linguistic Annotator (ELAN)(Version 4.7.2). Nijmegen, Netherlands: Max Plank Institute for Psycholinguistics: Technical Group (Language Archiving Technology). Retrieved from http://www.lat-mpi.eu/tools/elan/

annotation files and metadata files. The researcher can annotate the sign stream to unlimited simultaneous parameters on custom-created annotation tiers, which are vertical, and time-aligned to the visible video capture of the sign language utterances being analyzed. The annotations are then analyzed within the ELAN program using search functions that can view, count, compare, sort, and order results according to multiple criteria. (See Appendix E.) The IS data in this project were recorded with a high-definition camera, and the digital files were transferred into iMovie (v.8.0.6) then converted and archived in digitized QuickTime Player (v.10.3) video format. This allowed for easy import into ELAN (v. 4.5) and creation of ELAN annotation files (EAFs).

A linguistic corpus can be specific to a particular genre, among other characteristics for the purpose of cross-corpus comparison (Gries, 2009, p. 1232). In this study, the corpus is monologic, expository IS source video, which is taken as a snapshot in time, and which may be expanded later or enriched further for additional types of analysis. One of the most basic levels of corpus annotation is lemmatization (Gries, 2009), where words (or, in this case, signs) are identified and annotated based on their form, rather than their meaning. Once this level is completed, additional annotation passes can be made for additional interpretations of the form, such as its grammatical class tagging and clause-level analyses. These more complex levels are typically informed by the theoretical approach of the researcher. Two glossing tiers (one each for the dominant and the nondominant hand) and a written free translation tier are the three minimally required annotation levels in order to create a basic machine-readable SL corpus according to Johnston (2014, p. 11). I have adopted this practice in this research dataset. In the gloss-based multitier annotation environment exemplified in the Auslan Corpus, one assigns glosses for signs on one tier and makes annotations on other tiers about the sign's form (e.g., repetition for aspect, nonmanual feature for intensification or adverbial modification) or any supplementary annotation regarding its meaning-in-context, its grammatical role, and so on.

Study One in this project creates a basic corpus as described by Johnston with additional study-specific tiers in order to answer some of the research questions posed in the introductory chapter. The ELAN tiers used are shown in Table 9.

During the analysis, fully lexical, partly lexical, and nonlexical sign types were identified, glossed, and annotated on the dominant and nondominant hand tiers. This taxonomy of sign types was described in the

TABLE 9. *Annotation Tiers Used for Lexical Analysis and Depicting Sign Clusters*

Annotation tier name	Description
Dom ID gloss	Unique English gloss (dominant hand)
Non-Dom ID gloss	Unique English gloss (nondominant hand)
Free Translation	English translation
CA	Constructed Action or Constructed Dialogue
Mouthing	Mouthing of spoken English words
DS Cluster	A short utterance with at least one depicting sign; used in comprehension test
DS Cluster Meaning	Meaning of the short utterance
Metaphor1	Simple metaphor within DS cluster (e.g., UP-IS-GOOD)
Source Domain1	Source domain of Metaphor1 (e.g., low and high locations)
Target Domain1	Target domain of Metaphor1 (e.g., negative and positive)
Metaphor2	Secondary simultaneous metaphor within DS Cluster (e.g., BODY-IS-A-CONTAINER-OF-EMOTIONS)
Source Domain2	Source domain of Metaphor2 (e.g., heart circulation)
Target Domain2	Target domain of Metaphor2 (e.g., sensation of emotion)

previous chapter, and examples of each from the IS Lexical Frequency Dataset are shown in Table 10, including their glossing conventions. Dominant and nondominant hand annotations were made because some signs are two handed, some are one handed, and constructions include both hands articulating different forms, such as in a figure-ground relationship observed in depicting signs. A free translation was also initially made to align contextual meaning to the signs that are documented. In additional annotation passes, on the mouthing tier, concurrent English words (or parts of words that were visible on the signer's mouth) were also annotated. Although several IS presenters reported their written first language to be other than English (e.g., French, Portuguese, Japanese, or Czech), these other spoken language mouthings were observed but not rigorously documented.

Periods of constructed action and constructed dialogue were annotated on the dominant and nondominant tiers when they occurred as part

TABLE 10. *Examples of Sign Types in IS*

Lexical category	Example of type	Note
Fully lexical sign	 **701** Approve Approuver	Used regularly in expository IS to mean "ratify, or approve a document, a policy, or law." Seen here listed as an entry in the 1975 BDA *Gestuno* glossary (reprinted with permission). Glossed as: APPROVE(GEST) ***Approve*** **[Image] (1975) British Deaf Association. URL: http://www.bda.org.uk**
Partly lexical sign Depicting sign		A depicting sign glossed here as: DSM (Bent5): ENTITY-EXPANDS-INCREASE-IN-NUMBER-OF-MEMBERS.
Partly lexical sign Pointing sign		A pointing sign that aids in referencing in IS discourse. This example is glossed as: PT:DET (determiner)
Nonlexical sign Gesture		A gesture, fully depending on context, movement, and facial features, which is glossed here as: G(5-UP): WELL, or G(5-UP):HUH, G(5-UP):SO (other glosses are also possible).
Nonlexical sign Constructed Action		A gesture, where the signer enacts or expresses action that selectively imitates a character/referent: RH tier: G(CA):WIPE-BROW CA tier: CA:WORKER (wiping sweat from her brow)

of a gesture sign, and they were also annotated on their own separate tier—the CA tier. This is because constructed action is known to occur simultaneously with fully lexical signs and depicting signs, and not only gestures, particularly in partitioned surrogate blends (Dudis, 2004). One can therefore capture periods of enactment that occur simultaneously with different types of manual signs.

Additional annotations were made about selected IS utterances that incorporated depicting signs (what I call DS clusters). Depicting signs were of particular interest, because they are incorporated in complex constructions in SLs and IS in utterances that use blending to create discourse meaning. Although depicting signs were glossed individually and annotated on the dominant and nondominant hand tiers (along with other sign types—points, fully lexical signs, gestures), additional tiers were created to note blending between source and target domains that were metaphoric or iconic. Discussed in the previous chapter, mental space theory and blending (metaphoric and conceptual) in SLs serve as the framework in reporting comprehension of these DS clusters in Study Two.

Once the annotation process was completed, multiple queries were made (using a structured search of multiple and individual files, see Appendix E documenting each search type). The queries investigated the number and distribution of sign annotations by token count (including by origin by lexifier SL), sign type (e.g., fully lexical or partly lexical) or subtype (e.g., fingerspelling, numbers), and so on.

A sample screen shot is given in Figure 20 of the annotations on all tiers used in this study, as shown from one IS Lexical Frequency Dataset file section.

Categorizing and Naming Lexical Elements of IS

The taxonomy of sign types applied in the analysis of the IS source data includes these categories: (a) fully lexical, (b) partly lexical, and (c) nonlexical. Examples of each sign type in the IS dataset are shown in Table 10, with a description and example of how each type was named with a gloss. See Table 1 on p. xi for a list of glossing and annotation conventions used for the dataset. Fully lexical signs were glossed with an English word and a tag denoting its apparent origin, which is further discussed below (e.g., NOW(ASL); HAVE(AUS), COUNTRY(WFD)).

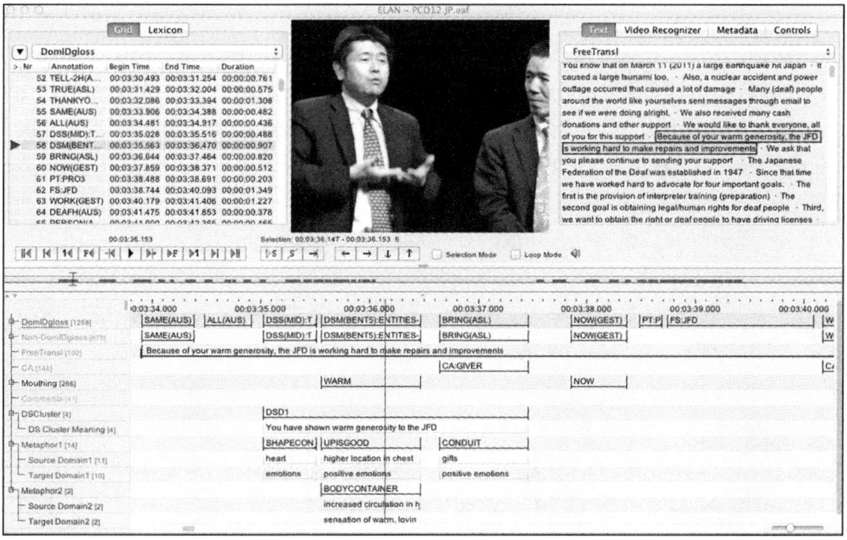

FIGURE 20. *Screen shot of IS annotation tiers in ELAN annotation file (.eaf).*

Partly lexical depicting signs were glossed with DS (depicting sign), and a letter denoting subtype of depicting sign (S for size and shape specifier, H for handling of entity, M for movement of entity, L for location of entity, and G often for nondominant hand that backgrounds the entity). Depicting signs were glossed in the following manner: DSS/H/L/M/G(HANDSHAPE):BRIEF-DESCRIPTION-OF-MEANING-OF-SIGN.

Partly lexical pointing signs were glossed with PT and the apparent type of point—PRO1 for first person, PRO2 for second person, etc., or POSS, if it appeared to be a point indicating possession. Some points were directed at entities, such as list buoys or fragments, and were noted as PT:LBUOY(4), for example.

Nonlexical signs glossed with G and additional information about the handshape if it was a manual gesture (see Table 10 for annotation example) and also glossed with meaning information. Other gestures that were nonmanual, bodily enactments or facial expressions were glossed with G and the tag CA (for constructed action) (e.g., G(CA): CROSS-ARMS). Additional information about periods of constructed action and constructed dialogue were noted on the separate CA tier as well.

While analyzing the IS dataset for this project, the most challenging aspect was to identify sign forms and use consistent glosses for them while making annotations. It is difficult to know which forms have been borrowed, and from where, because there has not been any study of IS lexicon or its evolution. Some of the signs are mimetic or iconic gestures, some have emerged from international contact signing phenomena over the years, whether documented by public resources or not, and others appear to be borrowed from natively occurring sign languages such as BSL, Auslan, LSF, and ASL, among others. The next sections elaborate on factors that guided the naming of lexical signs in the dataset.

It is not possible to point to a single reference to aid in naming the fully lexical, established forms observed in the dataset. Productive depicting signs and iconically motivated forms are part of regular meaning construction in IS, which at times confounds the decision whether a sign is best categorized as a fully lexical sign or a partly lexical depicting sign. This arises from the previously mentioned two faces of fully lexical signs (Johnston & Ferrara, 2012). A sign in the source IS that is used regularly and points to a consistent meaning was therefore determined to be a symbolic unit (fully lexical) rather than a partly lexical construction. At times these were recognized ASL, Auslan, or established IS (WFD and *Gestuno*) signs. Others appeared to be novel "created" forms with meaning arising from each of the component parts of the sign rather than as a symbolic whole. Component parts of these forms seemed to exploit gesture in their movement and location, and iconicity in handshape. The partly lexical depicting sign in Table 10 provides general semantic sense of [EXPANDING OR GROWING OBJECT OR OBJECTS]. Novel complex utterances such as partly lexical signs are characterized as fully analyzable, and the componential parts are noticed and integrated into the form's meaning (Johnston & Ferrara, 2012, following Langacker, 1987). Determining sign type and ID glosses for some forms required the repeated review of the data and checking against dictionaries, researcher knowledge of NSL and IS forms, and observation of the form in its composite utterance to determine the form's dependence on context.

For the purpose of assessing nonlexical signs, or gesture, sign forms in the collected IS source dataset were considered following Okrent (2002) in terms of whether (a) they express an imagistic aspect of a referent; (b) they are not regular, established forms; and (c) "the form of the gesture patterns meaning onto form in a gradient, as opposed to categorical, way" (p. 187). Nonlexical signs were recognized by their manual and facial actions that were not easily categorized as a conventional language-specific sign, or were emblems, and had gradient meaning dependent on context. These were gesticulations, mime, or enactment.

Naming an IS Sign: Glossing During Transcription

IS and native SLs operate in the visual-spatial mode and do not have a codified written form; however, they can and have been transcribed using complex notation systems such as the Stokoe Notation system and the Hamburg Notation System (HamNoSys) (Prillwitz & Zienert, 1990). The convention of glossing signs with English words with transcription symbols is also a common practice in SL research. English glosses are often relied on for organizing entries in many SL dictionaries, and this is true particularly in publicly available sign resources for IS.

Before continuing, it is important to distinguish between the ordinary use of a word or the dictionary entry of a word in any language, and a word of one language that is used to gloss a lexical unit in another language. The gloss is simply a rough approximation of the meaning of a unit, both with respect to its semantic range and perhaps its grammatical function. This is true even when the language being glossed is an established and stable spoken (or signed) language. Issues with consistency arise and complexities multiply when we attempt to gloss the signs of a contact sign variety, such as IS, which is by its very nature unstable. Finally, a gloss is not a phonetic or phonemic notation or transcription—it gives no indication of the form of the lexical unit that has been glossed.

Glossing, therefore, does not capture well the meaning of a sign, and it does not usually give any reliable information on its formational parameters or even how it can be used (e.g., its grammatical function). With respect to the glossing of IS signs in published resources, Figures 21 and 22 show excerpts from two IS glossaries that give a picture of a sign form, and an English gloss word (and Korean or French as well in the examples). Where dictionaries give information about definitions and permissible parameters for usage, this is not the case for documented IS glossaries.

The sign in Figure 22 for PRESIDENT is often seen in expository IS; however, the sign above it in Figure 21, glossed BRING, is a form that is not established, nor is it fully specified. It looks like a gesture and does not appear in the IS source data—even by Asian IS presenters. It may be one regularly used by people in Asian countries given the publication is from Korea, but it was not apparent in this study's data collection. If a person with experience using IS in international conferences was shown the sign PRESIDENT, it would most likely be recognized out of context. Upon showing the form here named BRING to the same experienced user

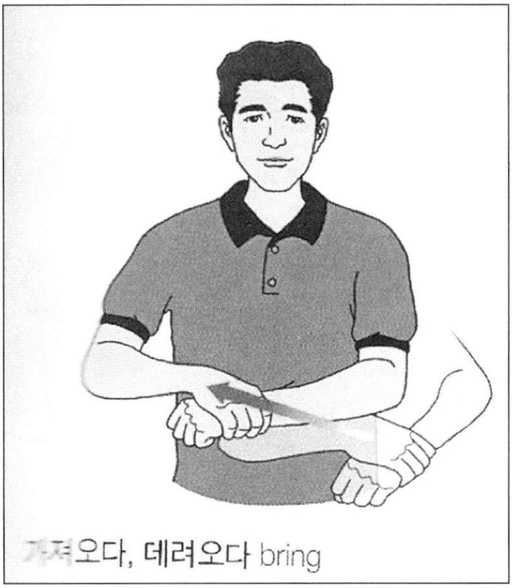

FIGURE 21. *BRING as listed in IS glossary (SignBooks, 2012).*

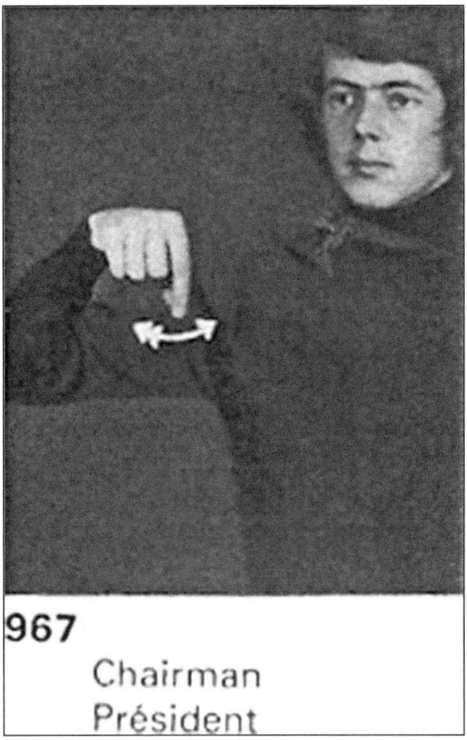

FIGURE 22. *CHAIRMAN (PRESIDENT) as listed in* Gestuno *glossary (Chairman [Image], 1975, British Deaf Association, retrieved from http://www.bda.org.uk).*

of IS, it is likely that several possible meanings might be guessed, one being [BRING], and another potentially being [GRAB], or [PULL] or some other semantic sense might be triggered by seeing the form in different utterances.

The point here is that published sign lists often merely suggest iconic visual options for conveying a concept—they are not attested examples of usage. Therefore, it is only through sign forms *actually observed and counted from varied usage settings* by IS signers that one can reliably describe the lexicon. Documentation of relatively established forms in authentic IS usage settings is not available or consistent. However, in this study it was important to rely on available resources in order to look for common signs that were perhaps previously identified or borrowed from a NSL, and attested to in the data.

There are challenges to identifying and naming signs in a contact sign system such as expository IS (or any evolving SL for that matter). Many sign forms are still in the process of being lexicalized so a principled and systematic method is needed.

The practice of "ID glossing" to identify fully lexical signs in SL corpora was therefore adapted in the creation of the IS dataset used in this study. ID glossing differs from conventional SL glossing practice in that it is intended to uniquely identify sign lemmas in a machine-readable corpus, rather than use one language (English) to provide a gloss to stand for a sign (Johnston, 2010, 2014). In the latter situation, a sign is given an English name, based on one of its possible meanings. Yet, the same lexical unit may be given a different gloss depending on the context in which it is used. ID glosses, according to Johnston (2010, 2014), are stable: the same gloss word is used for the same sign form or similar form.

In other words, the ID gloss identifies lemmas. A lemma is essentially the headword form one finds in a dictionary of any language. ID glossing in a SL corpus is thus like identifying headwords to put in a dictionary and to the simplification ("lemmatization") of words in a corpus of a spoken language that has been written down using transcription or a standard orthography.[5] During annotation and subsequent creation of the online

5. The handful of publicly available IS dictionaries resemble basic word lists, rather than true dictionaries. This research project is not a dictionary project, aimed at providing a full, linguistic analysis and documentation of the IS lexicon and signs' grammatical usage and meanings; however, methods used here are suggested for the continued study of lexicon of this contact sign variety.

BSL dictionary, the process of lemmatization, of naming of the headwords for each sign in the BSL dictionary, required methodical analysis of each sign form and nuances of meaning to determine an inventory of lexical signs in the language (Cormier, Fenlon, Rentelis, & Schembri, 2011).

An ID gloss may or may not point to one of the varied meanings of the sign; it is meant to uniquely identify a sign from another as a distinct form (see Johnston, 2010, 2014). In this research, ID glosses are denoted by a capitalized English word, which is taken from a dictionary entry from an online or print publication. Given the example of a sign meaning NOTHING, I offer a corpus-based dictionary example of a lexical sign form that varies and may have different meanings. If the same English gloss is used to gloss both signs, this could be misleading.

The *Auslan Signbank* corpus-based online dictionary lists several different sign forms when querying matches for the English word "run." Although the English word RUN is associated with the different sign forms, each of these forms is denoted by a distinct ID gloss.[6] Others have also pointed out that there are potential illusions created about a sign and its functions, and therefore there is an inherent risk to transcribing a sign language using English (or any other spoken/written language) (Slobin, 2005). This indicates the importance of using a unique ID gloss to identify lemmas.

Sometimes two signs in a SL (and in the IS data) can be almost identical but differ slightly in their phonology. The actual instance of a sign named by an ID gloss in the corpus can vary phonologically if this creates no new lexical item. These minor changes in form are reflected in the ID gloss if the researcher wishes to investigate such variety. In other words, variations of the sign that arise from inflections for directionality, number, manner, or aspect, are ignored when assigning an ID gloss to a lexical unit. If, however, a difference of phonological or morphological characteristics in a sign form identifies a distinct lemma, it is assigned its own unique ID gloss. Table 11 exemplifies this procedure with Auslan signs.

The first three sign forms in Table 11 are all considered to be the same lemma. The one-handed form is considered to be the citation form and the other two to be simply variants of that lemma: they do not constitute separate lemmas so they have the same ID gloss.

6. See Auslan "RUN-MOTOR" and "RUN1" at http://www.auslan.org.au/dictionary/words/run-4.html and http://www.auslan.org.au/dictionary/words/run-3.html

TABLE 11. *Documenting a Sign Form by ID Gloss, Usage, and Meaning*

Lemma → variant	ID gloss	Possible ID gloss suffix (used in corpus for research purposes only)	Meaning (using keywords only)	Usage
	NOTHING	n/a	nothing, no, not, trivial, trifle, insignificant	noun, verb or adjective, interactive (for denial of something)
→ 		-2H (for "two-handed")		
→ 		(O) (for "made with 0 handshape")		
	NOTHING-LOCATED	n/a	empty, bare, nothing, vacant	verb or adjective
	ISLAND	n/a	island, locale	noun

Note. NOTHING [Image] (2013). Retrieved from file://localhost/ http/::www.auslan.org .au:dictionary:words:nothing-1.html

The fourth image constitutes a *separate* lemma, NOTHING-LOCATED, because it has additional, specific meaning and has a different pattern of use, even though it shares an element in common, (the "zero" handshape). The fifth sign form is yet another lemma, ISLAND, because it has a completely unrelated and separate meaning, despite having the same form. The fourth and fifth images are homonyms.

In this study there is no lemmatization, per se, given the difficulty in distinguishing whether a form is a substantive conventional sign in IS, or a modification of a substantive sign, or whether it is a nonce creation that exploits sublexical components of a fully lexical sign borrowed from an NSL Nonetheless, I attempt to make a more rigorous description of the lexicon in keeping with complexities discussed in this section regarding sign type identification.

In order to clearly document the forms of many of the signs used in the IS dataset and then run a frequency analysis on the lexicon, each apparently established or conventional fully lexical sign was annotated using unique ID glosses in this manner, with some additional suffixation to identify different lexifier SLs. The partly lexical (pointing and depicting) signs and the gestural (enactment) signs were also glossed in a systematic manner to aid in analysis. Again, mentioned above, depicting signs, gestures, and points were annotated.

Identifying IS Sign Origins and Creating Unique ID Glosses

It was expected that a large number of signs appearing in expository IS would be sourced from widely used SLs, especially ASL and BSL. BSL was not, however, directly used as a referential lexifier language for this study; rather, it was referenced indirectly through the surrogate SL, Auslan. It was decided to use Auslan as the second major reference SL for two reasons. First, it is possible to do so because Auslan is very closely related to BSL, with both SLs, together with New Zealand Sign Language, having been described as dialects of a larger language, named BANZSL (Johnston, 2003a).[7] The larger language, or family of SLs, has been shown to be very closely related with more than 80% lexical similarity between each variety or dialect. Second, this PhD project was supported by an Australian Research Council grant that funds research on the Auslan Corpus. Since use of data from the Auslan Corpus was mandated by the project, it was a happy coincidence that Auslan could be used as a surrogate for overall BSL (or BANZSL) influence on IS.

Recall that one aspect of the analysis was to verify percentages of NSL signs used by deaf presenters lecturing in IS and to what extent this impacts discourse comprehension by audience members. The fourth research question asks: "Does increased intelligibility of IS correlate with increased use

7. Henceforth in this study, references to Auslan also imply BSL. When BSL alone is intended, "BSL" will be used. When there is a need to reinforce reference to the whole language family, "BANZSL" will be used.

of lexical signs sourced from a NSL (e.g., ASL)?" During annotation, each sign was given a unique name and noted on the dominant hand and non-dominant hand ID gloss tiers. These were annotated according to the sign's match to a lexical item from print and digital resources or the researcher's recognition of the sign as conventional in international contact signing.

Distinct gloss names chosen for each sign were informed by several resources: the *Gestuno* resource (British Deaf Association, 1975), the online *Auslan Signbank* dictionary, the ASLLRP searchable ASL database (URL: http://www.bu.edu/asllrp/), the "aslpro.com" online ASL resource, an IS DVD dictionary (WFD, 2008), and an IS dictionary published in Korea (DeafPlus, 2012).

My personal language background and the above resources aided the recognition of many of these signs and informed decisions about varied sign forms in the analysis. As a bilingual user of both ASL and English, I am a native English speaker and have been a L2 ASL signer for 30 years. Also, I hold professional-level national qualifications awarded by the U.S. Registry of Interpreters for the Deaf (RID) as an ASL-English interpreter. My other work using IS contact strategies spans the past 9 years; I have lived in foreign deaf communities for months at a time and have interpreted and communicated intermittently on many occasions with international deaf people, at conferences and in local communities. Finally, I am a second-language learner of Auslan, qualified at an entry level to interpret with it, and currently live in a community of Auslan users, but I lack native, intuitive use of the language. Verification of sign forms occurring in the data was made by consultation with native Auslan users and *Signbank* (2009), the Auslan Corpus–based dictionary.

The following process of analysis was applied for determining consistent naming sign forms in the dataset.

If a sign was first recognized as a conventional ASL sign, it was glossed as such with an ASL tag after the gloss, for example, NOW(ASL). As needed, it was verified with two online ASL lexical resources. The first, the American Sign Language Linguistic Research Project (ASLLRP), hosts the American Sign Language Lexicon Video Dataset (ASLLVD). The ASLLVD is an online, searchable research database created and maintained by a Boston University SL linguistic research group. It is a project within the National Center for Sign Language and Gesture Resources (NCSLGR) Corpus (Neidle & Vogler, 2012).[8]

8. URL: http://secrets.rutgers.edu/dai/queryPages/

A secondary source was referred to at times—an online ASL video glossary, http://www.aslpro.com. Both resources served as an aid to creating unique, consistent ID glossing. It is important to note that at the writing of this research, there is no lemmatized ASL lexicon online or in print. The ASLLRP provided the most consistent linguistic lexical resource. Although there were recognized ASL forms in the IS data, some were difficult to find in the searchable ASLLRP corpus. The second source (http://www.aslpro.com) filled some of these gaps, although it had limitations. ASL signs on the site are entered under more than one English keyword or typically a semantic gloss. Only one English gloss was chosen from the corresponding English options available as the unique identifier for that ASL sign form appearing in the data.

For example, the sign RESPONSIBLE is an ASL sign, shown in Figure 23. It was not listed in the ASLLRP under several related keywords. The keyword under which it is listed at the aslpro website glosses the sign with the English word, "responsible." The form, with slight modification, appears in the same online glossary under a different keyword, BURDEN (shown also in Figure 23). Both forms are the same sign with slight modification. BURDEN is the modified form of RESPONSIBLE, showing the signer lowering her shoulder as if carrying a heavy object. This example shows how problematic it can be to document sign language forms when they are identified based on meaning only, rather than on the form. When this sign form appeared in the IS dataset, I gave it the unique ID gloss (regardless of how slightly modified it was articulated) as RESPONSIBLE(ASL).

This form appeared in the IS data 24 times, with the phonological variant occurring once with the (signed English) ASL "R" handshape (Figure 24). Historical contact with written English creates signs that incorporate the first letter of the English word that closely relates to the meaning of the sign. These signed English forms are prevalent as variations in ASL, which arise from contact effects with the spoken language (Lucas & Valli, 1992). The fact that it appears in this dataset shows evidence of spoken language contact effects that are observable in IS contact.

To illustrate the glossing methods used in the IS data, examples of this same ASL sign form that appeared in the data—with two variants—are shown in Figure 24. Both are glossed as RESPONSIBLE(ASL). If interested in the variant forms, the researcher can note handshape variations such as this on a separate ELAN tier, and quantify them.

When a sign was recognized as a possible Auslan sign, it was verified as such and glossed with an additional tag—that is, HAVE(AUS). Verification

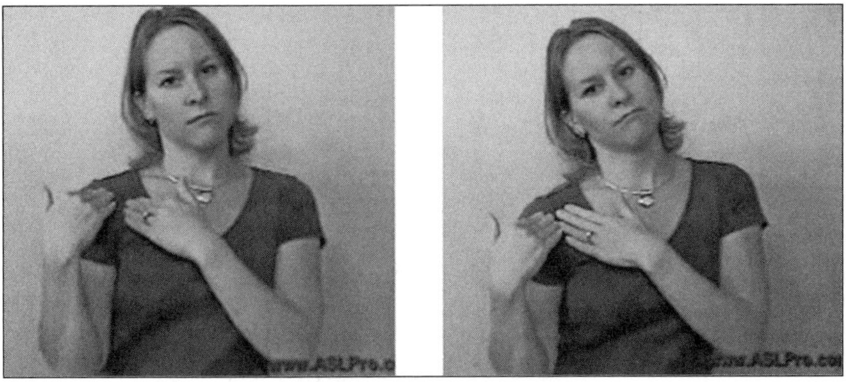

FIGURE 23. *ASL listed sign form: (a)* RESPONSIBLE *and (b)* BURDEN *(Images retrieved from http://www.aslpro.com/cgi-bin/aslpro/aslpro.cgi).*

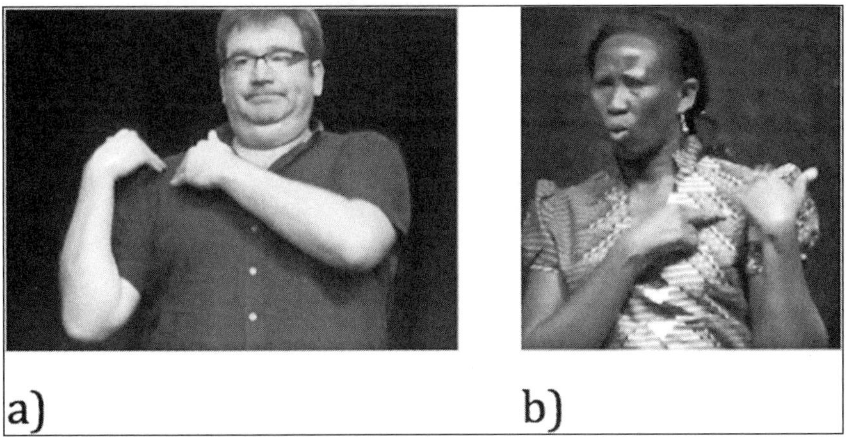

FIGURE 24. *IS data example signs.(a)* RESPONSIBLE*(ASL) and (b)* RESPONSIBLE*(ASL) with Modified (R-handshape).*

was usually made by consulting *Auslan Signbank*, but on a few occasions verifications were made by consulting a native Auslan signer.

Recurrent signs unique to IS were annotated according to the researcher's experience as a regular user and interpreter of IS. These signs were also checked against existing IS word lists and glossed with a (GEST) or (WFD) tag. The BDA publication of *Gestuno: International Sign Language of the Deaf* was consulted for some sign forms recognized in the IS dataset. Additional video resources from the WFD (a DVD with suggested IS signs for use at the WFD Assembly) and the Korean publication *International Sign* by SignBooks (DeafPlus, 2012) were consulted to cross-check regularly used IS sign forms observed in the data; however, it was not used for sign naming.

FIGURE 25. UNIVERSITY1 *(AUS) (Images retrieved from http://www.auslan.org.au/dictionary/words/university-1.html).*

Sign forms in the dataset at times appeared to be conventional in both ASL and Auslan. A number of signs were determined to be not only an ASL or an Auslan conventional sign, and were also typical to IS used at international deaf conferences, according to researcher recognition as such. These forms were first annotated with the ASL tag and a separate Excel database of ID glosses, and their corresponding sign form video clip was created. When the form appeared to be the same across different NSLs and IS resources, a notation was made in the database. For example, the sign denoting [HIGHER EDUCATION] or [COLLEGE] has been observed in expository IS. It is articulated with the two index fingers tracing the outer edge of a graduation mortarboard as listed in the *Gestuno* glossary (Figure 25). This form is listed in both the Korean International Sign dictionary as UNIVERSITY(a) (not shown) and is listed in the *Auslan Signbank* with the ID gloss UNIVERSITY1 (in Figure 26). In this case, the sign was ID glossed as UNIVERSITY1(AUS).

FIGURE 26. COLLEGE *(BDA, 1975) (College [Image], 1975, British Deaf Association, retrieved from http://www.bda.org.uk).*

After completion of annotating right-hand and left-hand tiers with ID glossing, a free translation into English utterance equivalents was also made of each presentation. This helped to identify high-frequency sign meanings. A free translation captures in English the idiomatic ways of expressing the ideas conveyed in the referenced signed utterance (Napier, McKee, & Goswell, 2006). Translations were made at the English sentence level, in clusters of utterances at their prosodic boundaries, such as pauses or lowering of presenter hands. I was present at each lecture, had access to, and captured the English interpretation and the intent of each presenter, and I had numerous hours to analyze each signed text. An equivalent translation into English was rendered for the free translation tier, and high-frequency sign meaning became apparent from its use in the IS utterance.

Additional forms in the data were also annotated, including presence of spoken language (English) mouthing. When the signer simultaneously made mouth movements that followed the lip patterns of English words, an annotation was made on the "mouthing" tier. Several French mouthings were also noticed, as were other spoken-language influences in mouth pattern, but these were not systematically counted—only the English mouthing tally.

Annotating Enactment and Depicting Sign Clusters

Constructed action (Winston, 1991) is gesture-type behavior that signers use in discourse. NSL users enact the "physical actions or behaviour of a character" when they selectively re-enact a referent's actions (Johnston, 2014, p. 51). Periods of constructed action and constructed dialogue were identified in the IS data by recognizing shifts in eye gaze or body posturing observed in the texts. They were annotated and counted to gauge the extent to which these NSL elements are also productive in the IS lectures. Moreover, the role of constructed action and constructed dialogue in assisting IS comprehension was sought.

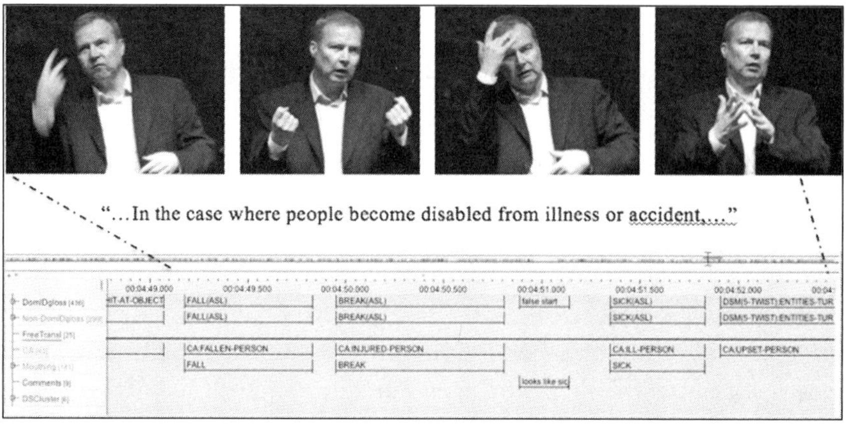

FIGURE 27. *Examples of co-occurring lexical signs and depicting signs with CA in expository IS.*

Depicting signs were annotated as I have previously described. Periods of constructed action and dialogue were annotated on their own separate tier—the CA tier.

Figure 27 shows an example from the IS data, where several successive examples of constructed action co-occur with other sign types, in this case three times with lexical signs FALL(ASL), BREAK(ASL), and SICK(ASL) and once with a depicting sign—DSM(5-TWIST):ENTITIES-TURN-UPSIDE-DOWN. By annotating such instances of constructed action as well as those that occur independently, it was possible to quantify how much enactment occurs in expository IS. Constructed action and constructed dialogue were treated as a measure of gestural material that could be counted along with quantity of nonlexical signs in the dataset.

Several short depicting sign clusters selected from the data were shown to participants in Study Two. Nine (9) of these were annotated on the DS cluster–related tiers shown in Table 9. Individual depicting signs were ID glossed on the dominant and nondominant hand tiers, but the depicting cluster was annotated on the DS tiers to note its meaning and the blended domains that were operating in the cluster metaphorically and iconically. The nine clusters were analyzed and used in Study Two to determine whether text meaning is gleaned from these complex constructions.

An example of a DS cluster is provided in Figure 28. The utterance incorporates not only depicting signs, but also a lexical sign HIT(ASL) and pointing signs with a list buoy, and two instances of constructed action. The constructed action, annotated as CA:BUILDER, is a sequence where the signer makes several depictions of moving entities on top of

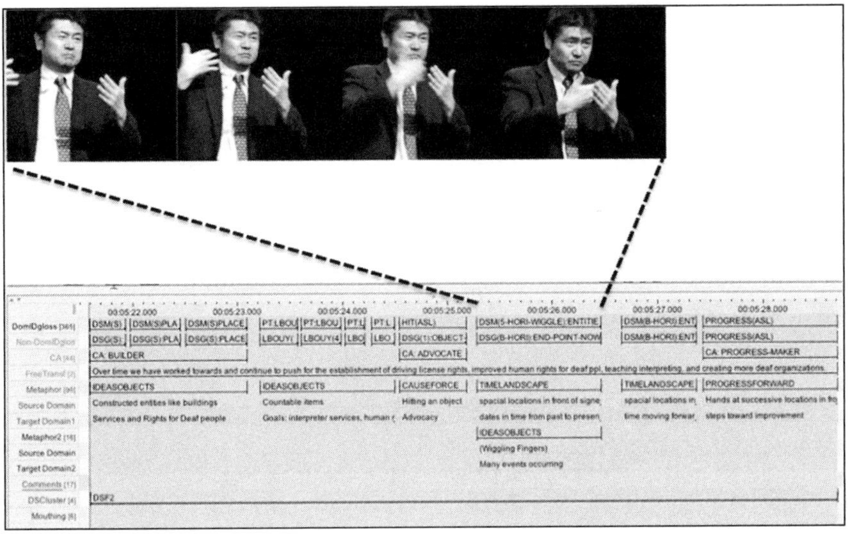

FIGURE 28. *Example annotations on depicting sign cluster tiers.*

one another, and he shifts his shoulders to place both S-handshape hands in different spaces in front of him. The DS is repeated three times and annotated as

> DomIDGloss: DSH(S):PLACE-ENTITY-ON-TOP-OF-OTHER-LIKE-FOUNDATION;
>
> NonDomIDGloss: DSG(S): ENTITY-UNDERNEATH-LIKE-FOUNDATION

The presenter also maintains an effortful facial expression and makes torso movements that demonstrate the action of "building." This DS is a partly lexical sign in that it uses several different linguistic and non-linguistic elements to create meaning. In the comprehension test, it was anticipated that participants would be able to understand varied elements of the meaning that was constructed from these complex utterances.

Pictured in the figure, the depicting sign cluster also contains the depicting sign, DSM(5-WIGGLE):ENTITIES-PASS-THROUGH-TIME. A metaphoric blend operates in this depiction, and the domains of the metaphor are annotated on the Metaphor 1 and 2 tiers. Taub's analogue building model was applied to the domains for both levels of mapping—the metaphor of IDEAS-ARE-OBJECTS is mapped iconically onto the wiggling fingers of the 5 handshape (Taub, 2001). Each finger represents separate objects or events, and as a whole depicting entity, the wiggling fingers refer to plural things or events that occurred through time. In this case, those events are ongoing advocacy work toward four aims that the signer introduces earlier in the text, referencing them with a list buoy (4). The forward movement of the hand in the signing space closest to the signer toward space further in front of the signer indicates another metaphoric level, the TIME-IS-A-LANDSCAPE-WE-MOVE-THROUGH, back-to-front time-line that is often seen in NSLs (Taub, 2001; Wilcox, 2000). Meaning in this piece of the depicting segment is constructed on several levels, and this annotation method captured these elements for comprehension analysis in Chapter 6.

A Reference Database for Shared Cross-Linguistic Form/Meaning Pairs

The ID glossing approach and related glossing and annotation conventions allowed for a referential list of forms to be created in a database. For high-frequency forms, a basic semantic description of the form-meaning pairs was added to this database. This could be used for referencing during analysis and annotation. As already explained, when a sign form was recognized to be an IS sign and a sign from an established NSL, this was noted in the database (and in the gloss).

In cases when signs were unable to be identified by source language, but nonetheless appeared to be lexical borrowings from the IS signer's NSL and not a depicting sign or gesture, the sign was given the ID gloss UNKNOWN and the additional tag, "OTHER." Although there are resources such as the BSL corpus (Schembri, Fenlon, Rentelis, & Cormier, 2011) and LSF-French dictionaries available to the researcher to verify sign types recognized from these other major SLs, an exhaustive comparison of sign origins in the IS dataset was not made here.

Database entry notations were made when sign forms and meanings shared several sign parameters in more than one SL. Future enrichment of this information could come from further study and offers a starting point for additional corpus-driven inquiry into shared form/meaning pairs across NSLs and their usage in the IS contact system.

STUDY ONE INTER-RATER RELIABILITY

In Study One, I made all annotations with verification of a representative sampling of the data by a second annotator. There are inherent complexities with determining sign types in a contact SL rather than a conventional language, mainly due to the lack of conventions and community of users. Therefore, to check intuitions about IS forms and their types—fully lexical, partly lexical, and nonlexical signs—a second coder provided a reliability check on a random sampling of 10% of the 1,753 unique sign tokens. These sign-type judgments were later compared to how they had been separately coded and annotated by the researcher. The second coder is a qualified professional Auslan interpreter, works sometimes with IS, and is familiar with ASL. The second coder independently assessed 175 sign forms and determined, according to their fit, one of the three types applied in this study. An inter-rater reliability analysis was made using the Kappa (k) statistic to determine consistency between coders. The result was an agreement of 94%, with $k = 0.91$ and a 95% confidence interval (90.46, 97.62). Kappa values below 0.59 are considered moderate, 0.60 to 0.79 are considered substantial, and 0.80 to 1.0 are considered outstanding (Geertzen, 2012; Landis & Koch, 1977). This is interpreted to mean that the sign types and their distribution in IS reported in Study One are based on separate coders' high level of agreement.

FINDINGS FROM IS LEXICAL FREQUENCY ANALYSIS

High-Frequency Signs in IS

A frequency count of the annotated IS data yielded 7,033 tokens comprising 1,751 different sign forms. The top 50 most frequent signs are shown in Table 12. These account for 43.5% of all tokens in the annotated collection, with pointing signs figuring prominently. Within the top 50 signs, 80% of all the pointing signs in the dataset occur—824 out of 1,017 total pointing signs. The top four most frequent sign types are pointing signs that, when combined with all of the subtypes of points in the data, total 1,017, comprising 14.5% of the signs in expository IS. Lexical frequency studies of Auslan, ASL, BSL, and NZSL also report points are the highest frequency signs. (See comparative discussion below.)

The topics covered in sampled texts will impact vocabulary, which is especially notable in a smaller corpus. Presentation topics in the 13 different texts were central to civic life and education of deaf people in varied countries. Often at international deaf conferences, presentations report on the efforts of local and national deaf organizations toward sign

TABLE 12. *The 50 Most Frequent Signs in Expository IS* (n = 7,033)

Rank	ID gloss	Total	% of n	% Cumul	Rank	ID gloss	Total	% of n	% Cumul
1	PT:PR03	193	2.7%	2.7%	26	CONNECT(ASL)	42	0.6%	32.0%
2	PT:PR01	182	2.6%	5.3%	27	CAN(ASL)	41	0.6%	32.5%
3	PT:DET	163	2.3%	7.7%	28	PT:PR03PL	39	0.6%	33.1%
4	PT:LOC	141	2.0%	9.7%	29	NOW(GEST)	38	0.5%	33.6%
5	DEAFH(AUS)	126	1.8%	11.5%	30	KNOW(ASL)	37	0.5%	34.2%
6	G(5-UP):WELL	110	1.6%	13.0%	31	GOVERNMENT(GEST)	35	0.5%	34.7%
7	WHAT(ASL)	99	1.4%	14.4%	32	PT:POSS3	33	0.5%	35.1%
8	DEAF1(ASL)	98	1.4%	15.8%	33	ANALYZE(ASL)	32	0.5%	35.6%
9	SAME(AUS)	96	1.4%	17.2%	34	FINISH(ASL)	32	0.5%	36.0%
10	HAVE(AUS)	94	1.3%	18.5%	35	NS:JAPAN	32	0.5%	36.5%
11	PERSON(GEST)	85	1.2%	19.7%	36	THINK(ASL)	32	0.5%	37.0%
12	SIGN(AUS)	87	1.2%	21.0%	37	COUNTRY(WFD)	31	0.4%	37.4%
13	PT:PRO2PL	75	1.1%	22.0%	38	EXPLAIN(WFD)	31	0.4%	37.8%
14	G(6-UP):GOOD	62	0.9%	22.9%	39	GROUP-TOGETHER(ASL)	30	0.4%	38.3%
15	TEACH(ASL)	61	0.9%	23.8%	40	PROGRESS(ASL)	30	0.4%	38.7%
16	WORK(GEST)	59	0.8%	24.6%	41	YEAR(ASL)	29	0.4%	39.1%
17	DIFFERENT(ASL)	56	0.8%	25.4%	42	DISABLED(WFD)	28	0.4%	39.5%

18	G(5-UP):HUH	56	0.8%	26.2%	43	NINE(WFD)	27	0.4%	39.9%
19	ONE(ASL)	56	0.8%	27.0%	44	TWO(ASL)	27	0.4%	40.3%
20	IMPORTANT(ASL)	55	0.8%	27.8%	45	WRITE(ASL)	27	0.4%	40.7%
21	ASSOCIATION(GEST)	54	0.8%	28.6%	46	GIVE(ASL)	26	0.4%	41.0%
22	G(5-UP):SO	51	0.7%	29.3%	47	HOW(ASL)	26	0.4%	41.4%
23	INTERPRETER(WFD)	50	0.7%	30.0%	48	WANT(AUS)	26	0.4%	41.8%
24	HELP(ASL)	49	0.7%	30.7%	49	WOMANB(WFD)	26	0.4%	42.1%
25	WORLD(GEST)	47	0.7%	31.4%	50	HEARING(WFD)	25	0.4%	42.5%

language recognition and access issues that deaf people face around the world. It is not surprising that the most frequent signs used by IS presenters are DEAF, SIGN (language), TEACH, WORK, IMPORTANT, ASSOCIATION, INTERPRETER, HELP, PROGRESS, COUNTRY, and WORLD. There are also many signs that are easily understood as ASL citation forms and Auslan citation forms.

After separating out lexical signs from partly lexical and nonlexical signs, the distribution of lexical signs from the rest (n = 4,383) comprise 62.3% of all tokens. The top 50 most frequent *lexical* signs (N = 4,383) are listed in Table 13. These 50 high-frequency signs make up to one half (49.4%) of the lexical signs in the data.

The resulting ID gloss database with corresponding video clips includes 200 of the most frequent fully lexical signs in the source IS data. These were extracted and compiled as a reference database of lexical signs in expository IS. Appendix A lists these 200 (lexical) signs, as well as the most frequent gestures and depicting signs. Video clips of these signs are viewable on the Gallaudet University Press YouTube channel at the URL goo.gl/RfhvdT.

The 100 most frequent signs (all types) comprise 55.6% (3,910) of all of the sign tokens (7,033) in the full 13-file dataset, with a large variety of different sign forms appearing. In addition, 1,162 signs occur only once in the corpus. More than half of these hapax legomena are depicting signs (n = 462) and gestures (n = 230). The other half are varied singly occurring forms from presenters' NSLs, variations of these, as well as numbers, fingerspelled words, or low-incidence signs that are listed in the *Gestuno* glossary or the WFD video materials. With this large number of varied sign forms and the relatively small number of highly occurring signs (shown in the list of the top 50 most frequent lexical forms), the data empirically support intuitions about the "limited" conventional lexicon in this international sign contact system. The conference context where IS presentation is used shows conventional form-meaning pairs with a small number of highly occurring signs, and a large amount of depicting signs and gestures contributing to meaning-making in these discourses.

DISTRIBUTION OF SIGN TYPES

The analysis of sign types in expository IS indicates lexical signs comprise 63.6% of the lexicon, with partly lexical pointing signs and depicting signs constituting the next largest type at 14.5% and 10.2%, respectively (Table 14). Gesture signs and the embodied enactment of

TABLE 13. *The 50 Most Frequent Fully Lexical Signs in Expository IS (n = 4,383)*

Rank	ID gloss	Total	% of n	% Cumul	Rank	ID gloss	Total	% of n	% Cumul
1	DEAFH(AUS)	126	2.9%	2.9%	26	COUNTRY(WFD)	31	0.7%	35.5%
2	WHAT(ASL)	99	2.3%	5.1%	27	EXPLAIN(WFD)	31	0.7%	36.2%
3	DEAF1(ASL)	98	2.2%	7.4%	28	GROUP-TOGETHER(ASL)	30	0.7%	36.9%
4	SAME(AUS)	96	2.2%	9.6%	29	PROGRESS(ASL)	30	0.7%	37.6%
5	HAVE(AUS)	94	2.1%	11.7%	30	YEAR(ASL)	29	0.7%	38.2%
6	PERSON(GEST)	85	1.9%	13.6%	31	DISABLED(WFD)	28	0.6%	38.9%
7	SIGN(AUS)	87	2.0%	15.6%	32	NINE(WFD)	27	0.6%	39.5%
8	TEACH(ASL)	61	1.4%	17.0%	33	TWO(ASL)	27	0.6%	40.1%
9	WORK(GEST)	59	1.3%	18.4%	34	WRITE(ASL)	27	0.6%	40.7%
10	DIFFERENT(ASL)	56	1.3%	19.6%	35	GIVE(ASL)	26	0.6%	41.3%
11	ONE(ASL)	56	1.3%	20.9%	36	HOW(ASL)	26	0.6%	41.9%
12	IMPORTANT(ASL)	55	1.3%	22.2%	37	WANT(AUS)	26	0.6%	42.5%
13	ASSOCIATION(GEST)	54	1.2%	23.4%	38	WOMANB(WFD)	26	0.6%	43.1%
14	INTERPRETER(WFD)	50	1.1%	24.5%	39	HEARING(WFD)	25	0.6%	43.6%
15	HELP(ASL)	49	1.1%	25.7%	40	ZERO(ASL)	25	0.6%	44.2%
16	WORLD(GEST)	47	1.1%	26.7%	41	BUT(AUS)	24	0.5%	44.8%
17	CONNECT(ASL)	42	1.0%	27.7%	42	INTERNATIONAL(WFD)	24	0.5%	45.3%

(Continued)

TABLE 13. (*Continued*)

Rank	ID gloss	Total	% of n	% Cumul	Rank	ID gloss	Total	% of n	% Cumul
18	CAN(ASL)	41	0.9%	28.6%	43	RESPONSIBLE(ASL)	24	0.5%	45.9%
19	NOW(GEST)	38	0.9%	29.5%	44	BRING(ASL)	23	0.5%	46.4%
20	KNOW(ASL)	37	0.8%	30.3%	45	NONE(ASL)	23	0.5%	46.9%
21	GOVERNMENT(GEST)	35	0.8%	31.1%	46	UNKNOWN	23	0.5%	47.4%
22	ANALYZE(ASL)	32	0.7%	31.9%	47	CRPD(WFD)	22	0.5%	47.9%
23	FINISH(ASL)	32	0.7%	32.6%	48	INDECIPHERABLE	22	0.5%	48.4%
24	NS:JAPAN	32	0.7%	33.3%	49	PROBLEM(ASL)	22	0.5%	48.9%
25	THINK(ASL)	32	0.7%	34.1%	50	CHILDREN(ASL)	21	0.5%	49.4%

TABLE 14. *Distribution of Sign Types in IS*

	IS lectures (n = 7,033)	Tokens
Lexical signs	63.6%	4,474
Fingerspelling	1.7%	123
Name signs	1.7%	122
Depicting signs	10.2%	721
Pointing signs	14.5%	1,018
Gesture	9.0%	645
Constructed action (CA)[a]	1:12	572

[a]CA was tallied on a separate ELAN tier; ratio of CA for every sign token.

constructed action (CA) and constructed dialogue (CD) make up the non-lexical material in expository IS, although only a few instances of CD occurred in the IS full dataset. Gesture signs make up 8.8% of the tokens. Constructed action (and dialogue, if it had been observed) was annotated on a separate CA tier in ELAN and was therefore tallied separately from gesture signs. There were 572 periods of CA in the dataset, which means that for every 12 signs (on average), a period of CA occurs. Many gestures occurred within a period of CA (206 out of 645). Last, there are low-incidence equal percentages of fingerspelling and name signs, each distributed in expository IS at 1.7%.

Lexical Signs in IS and Their Origins

Findings indicate that 63.6% of sign types in expository IS created by Deaf presenters are lexical forms with some degree of conventional use in the international conference setting. Many of these forms appear to be recognizable from ASL and Auslan. Because many lexical forms in IS have been shown previously to belong to more than one SL or SL group (Rosenstock, 2004), one cannot say for certain that the sign forms observed in this dataset are *only* ASL or BANZSL signs. It is reasonable, however, to say that given these forms and their membership in the established lexicons of ASL or Auslan (or both at times), users of these NSLs are able to recognize them and are therefore aided in comprehending an IS discourse wherever they appear. Given these two NSL distributions in the IS dataset, the resulting amounts of fully lexical signs by origin are

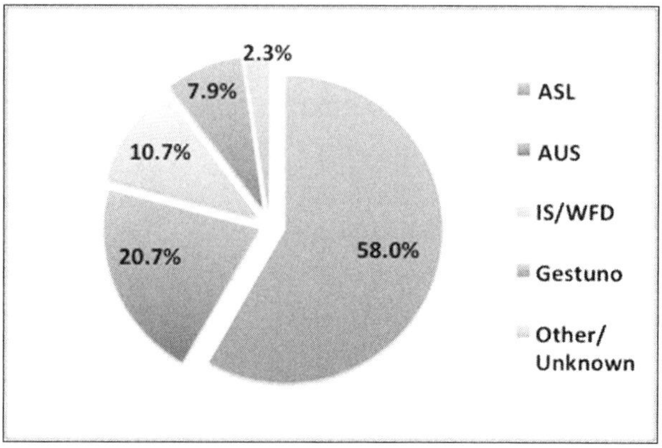

FIGURE 29. *Origins of lexical signs in expository IS.*

FIGURE 30. *IS sign* SCHOOL.

therefore limited by only these viewpoints. Findings about fully lexical signs by contributing origins are indicated by the pie chart in Figure 29.

A majority of lexical signs, 58%, in IS are recognized citation forms in ASL, with the second most prevalent forms, 20.7%, recognizable forms in Auslan. Many signs listed in WFD resources or known IS forms from conferences and activities of the WFD are also frequent, comprising 10.7% of the forms in the dataset. Signs that are listed in the *Gestuno* glossary comprise 7.9% of tokens. This report about *Gestuno* listed forms is not exhaustive, because some signs identified as ASL or Auslan are also listed in the *Gestuno* glossary. The remaining 2.3% sign forms are unknown, likely sourced from other SLs.

To illustrate some of the varied and shared origins of expository IS sign forms, I offer the example in Figure 30, which is ID glossed in this research as STUDY(AUS). It is a sign that is listed as a conventional Auslan sign in the *Auslan Signbank* online dictionary. It occurs as a lexicalized sign regularly in the IS data, and it is used in the collected data to mean "education, school, study(ies)."

In Auslan this form can function as a noun, verb, or adjective. Documented meanings are as follows: "The period of time spent learning about a particular subject or the effort you put into it," "A person who studies (e.g., student)," "to spend time learning about a particular subject, often by reading books," and "to read a book" (*Auslan Signbank*, 2014).[9] The form is also found in LIBRAS, as well as in Japanese Sign Language (JSL), although the movement is outward from the face and not in a circle or side-to-side movement. It is also iconic and might be perceived by a nonsigning person as a gesture to mean "reading a book or paper."

For observers who have a similar form-meaning pair in their NSLs, this IS sign might be easily recognized and will aid understanding of the utterance in which it occurs. Lexical items have semantic sense to the "listener," and when the item has a more conventional use, then the possible meanings are limited or extended to what convention tells us is permissible about the meaning of the word, as well as the contexts in which it operates.

ASL Signs in IS

One of the hypotheses in this project is that IS frequently employs signs common to ASL. The data presented confirm this. It has been posited that there may be differences between IS used in an international context in Asia and the IS used in international conferences historically occurring in European and North American contexts (Mori, 2011). Although this may prove to be true in future inquiry, there seems to be some influence from ASL even in the IS used by Asia-Pacific region signers, when they are in contact with Western SL users. Annual conferences have been taking place in the Asia-Pacific region for more than a decade, and frequent IS training (heavily influenced by ASL) is given to aid communication among deaf signers from varied countries in the region.

During data collection with participants in the Japanese cohort, I was made aware of ASL teaching efforts in Japan[10] as well as a published glossary of IS signs. This resource, published in Korea and distributed

9. *Signbank*, URL: http://www.auslan.org.au/dictionary/words/study-2.html

10. Deaf Japan is an organization in Osaka that offers ongoing second SL training, ASL, to JSL users. I personally do not take issue with deaf people learning additional SLs, but also believe in the importance of ongoing recognition and promotion of their native, local L1 SLs.

throughout Asia, titled *International Sign* (DeafPlus, 2012), lists 851 signs used in IS. Upon closer examination, it is notable that 375 (44%) of the forms in the SignBooks resource are the same form-meaning pairs that occur in ASL. Of these 375 lexical entries, 305 (36%) are conventional lexical items used in ASL and 68 (8%) are recognizable phonological variants of ASL, differing only by one or two parameters.

It is evident that the contact effect of ASL continues to influence forms in IS through varied media, not only through Internet and social media, but also through quasi-promotion via modern published IS sign glossaries.

Auslan (BANZSL) Signs in IS

ASL signs are not the only lexical forms seen in expository IS. Results from this frequency study indicate that BANZSL signs are also observable in the lexicon. Recall that Auslan is a secondary reference lexifier language in this analysis of IS presentations, with the rationale noted in Chapter 3 (essentially a surrogate for BSL). Several NSLs in countries other than England are historically related to BSL, just as countries in Africa and South east Asia have historical contact-related ties to ASL. International conferences pertaining to deaf persons have taken place over several decades of activity described in Chapter 1. A large number of international Deaf events have occurred in Western European countries, and attendees may have had exposure to BSL due to close geography and opportunities for contact across Western Europe and activities of the European Union of the Deaf. BSL is also reported as a second language for many world-traveled Deaf people, as noted in the demographic profiles of IS source data participants in Table 7. Many of the international deaf leaders attending conferences where IS is used report knowing BSL and/or ASL as a first or second language.

It is also possible that BSL forms may be appearing via Auslan as a result of numerous civic and humanitarian contact situations in Asia, given geographic proximity between Australia and Southeast and Northeast Asian countries.[11]

11. Activities in the WFD's Asia-Pacific regional secretariat include Australian delegates; disability social program links are strong between Australian and Southeast Asian countries, and Australian interpreter educators provide trainings to Fiji, Solomon Islands, and Tuvalu.

CONVENTIONAL IS SIGNS, WFD SIGNS, AND *GESTUNO* SIGNS

Many of the established signs in expository IS are conventional due to activities of the WFD or are agreed-upon signs that are conventional in international settings. Some are form-meaning pairs that continue to be used in international contact signing and are listed in the 1975 *Gestuno* dictionary (BDA, 1975). A handful of these signs have been maintained in IS usage for more than three decades, and some are also signs in NSLs, such as BSL, LSF, or ASL. Several frequent "X(GEST)" signs and "X(WFD)" signs ones from the dataset in this study are shown in Table 15.

TABLE 15. *Established IS Signs from* Gestuno *and WFD Sources*

ID Gloss	Form	Meaning
WORK(GEST)		Any kind of work -manual or non-manual labor. (This sign is articulated with different orientation and/or handshape than similar forms in ASL and other SLs.)
PRESIDENT(GEST)		The head of a political or business organization. Typically in the context of a national association of the Deaf.
ASSOCIATION (GEST)		Organization(s) of Deaf people, to associate, the national association of the deaf in a given country or countries.
WORLD(GEST)		World, global, international.

(*Continued*)

TABLE 15. (*Continued*)

ID Gloss	Form	Meaning
GOVERNMENT (GEST)		The ruling body of a nation or region. Also the capital city of a country in some contexts.
CONGRESS(GEST)		The official meeting of the WFD that occurs every 4 years.
INTERPRETER(WFD)		To interpret, an interpreter, to translate.
EXPLAIN(WFD)		To convey information, explain something(s).
DISABLED(WFD)		Person(s)with a disability, disability

Note. [Images] (1975). British Deaf Association. Retrieved from http://www.bda.org.uk

DISCUSSION ABOUT INTERESTING IS SIGN FORMS IN THE DATASET

Numerous examples of signs in the data were sufficiently highly frequent and stable in form and meaning that they can be said to be lexical, established forms. Some of these were modified to express related meanings. Earlier, I discussed the process of ID glossing and lemmatization. It was established that lemmatization is not easy with an unstable contact sign variety, due to the difficulty in distinguishing whether a form is a substantive conventional sign in IS, or a modification of a substantive sign, or whether it is a nonce creation that exploits sublexical components of a fully lexical sign borrowed from an NSL. In this section I present a few examples of signs that were ID glossed with the same name, although it

FIGURE 31. ASSOCIATION(*GEST)—as a noun.*

FIGURE 32. ASSOCIATION(*GEST)—modified as a verb.*

is evident that some of these regular forms were also modified in some of the discourse contexts. Modifications of signs were not methodically analyzed, but further investigation of the forms would provide some empirical evidence and patterns of how these signs are used in IS utterances.

The ID gloss "ASSOCIATION(GEST)," listed in the *Gestuno* glossary, is applied in each instance where this form occurs in the data (Figure 31). When this form is used, it typically refers to national or local deaf associations or organizations, yet in a few instances it was seen modified, by movement and location in space, in a way that employs the form to mean [TO ASSOCIATE WITH AND COLLABORATE TOGETHER] (Figure 32).

Another example of a sign in IS that was modified by a signer comes from Video D, where the presenter uses ACCEPT(ASL) and modifies it slightly. He articulates it very slowly, with the two-handed 5 hands  moving in toward the chest and simultaneously closing into two flat-O handshapes  on the upper chest, but stopping just before the last hold of the flat-O hands on the chest. In most cases, the citation form occurs in the IS dataset (more quickly articulated start to finish, and without facial NMS to alter meaning). In this one case described above, the meaning the signer attempts to convey is [IN THE PROCESS OF BEING ACCEPTED].

There is also variability in signs denoting the same concepts used by different lecturers. More than one sign is even seen used by the same signer, in the case of WOMANB, WOMAN.EAR, and the ASL sign for WOMAN. WOMANB articulates a Bent-B handshape  over the rise of the breast, whereas WOMAN.EAR is expressed with the thumb and index finger tugging at the earlobe. Table 16 shows this and another example of form variation for the sign, WORLD. Not only do IS presenters use more than one sign for the same concept at different times in their discourse, for example, MONEY(ASL) and MONEY(GEST), often a signer will use two different signs consecutively for the same concept. Typically, a sign from ASL and an established WFD sign might be used consecutively, or at times an Auslan and an ASL sign.

Findings in this lexical analysis show similar evidence of phonological variation in IS, which was also illustrated in a small, unpublished study of online website IS presentation videos (Lang, 2012). Mentioned in the literature review, Lang identified that the signs DEAF, WHAT, and HAVE exhibit two to four phonological variations by IS presenters. The wide variation of lexical forms observed in expository IS suggests complexities

TABLE 16. *Variation in IS Sign Forms*

WOMAN.B (WFD)		WORLD (WFD)	
WOMAN.EAR (WFD)		WORLD (ASL)	
WOMAN (ASL)	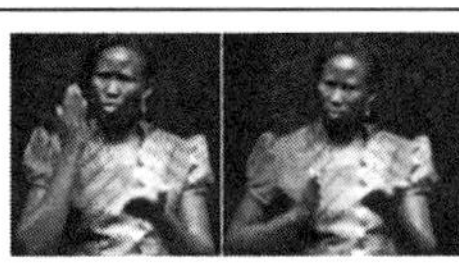	WORLD.B (WFD)	

that need further investigation. Slight variations in phonemes of similar signs may impact their meanings across different SL users. As with spoken language dialects and accents, at some point the articulation of a word will trigger perception by the listener that the word is a completely different one from the speaker's intent, a mistaken minimal pair rather than an articulatory "accent."

Fully lexical signs in expository IS may resemble too closely a lexicalized sign in the observer's native SL, hence presence of certain aspects of native SLs in IS discourse may hinder comprehension for some audience members. High-frequency signs in IS may share phonetically similar forms across SLs, but the impact on comprehension needs closer examination. Testing high-frequency signs with diverse participants in Study Two probes this question as a factor that potentially could impact comprehension of IS discourse.

Polysemy in Lexical Examples

The high-frequency sign form glossed as DIFFERENT(ASL) is used in two semantically different ways in IS as it is in ASL. The meaning is often literally the adjective [different] or the noun [difference], but on 15 out of the 64 instances, the signer uses DIFFERENT(ASL) to mean "but." Typically, ASL users distinguish this sign form when they mean [but] as opposed to [different] by altering the nonmanual feature of facial expression and sometimes including English mouthing. Mouthings and nonmanual features were highly varied with this form across IS presenters. Some mouthed "BUT," while others mouthed "different," an Asian signer regularly expressed neutral facial, nonmanual features, and an African signer mouthed the French word "mais," which means [but]. One Asian signer used the form in his IS presentation as a one-handed sign and always means "but." However, for most instances where the signer intended to mean "but," the data show a predominant reliance on the Auslan or BSL form of BUT, which occurs 26 times in the data. The appearance of both of these sign forms—one from ASL and the other from BSL and Auslan (BANZSL)—and their usage for similar purposes in IS from these two languages is evidence of both widely used SLs on this international type of contact language. The variations in mouthings suggest the signer brings his or her native SL mouthing patterns into the contact setting to communicate. Additional study of these phenomena is warranted to support this general observation from the data.

FIGURE 33. *(a) ASL sign* WHAT *and (b) IS sign G(5-UP):*WELL.

The sign ID glossed WHAT(ASL) appeared frequently as the citation form of the ASL sign meaning [WHAT?] (Figure 33a). The two open 5 handshapes  are held palm up, given a slight side-to-side shake, and accompanied by either furrowed eyebrows or sometimes raised eyebrows.

This form was consistently equated with a conventional meaning [WHAT] and was used (as it is in Auslan) to mean [WHERE] on a few occasions. With the example of WHAT(ASL), it becomes unclear whether the form is truly lexicalized, or if contact between BANZSL and ASL in IS is creating a semantically extended meaning in IS to this form that is distinctly different in the lexicon of ASL and Auslan. The form may also be an interesting example where a specified form-meaning pair in a lexifier language is instantiated with some gestural qualities in IS.

Other times the form appeared in a modified way by movement and/or with nonmanual signals that simultaneously prompted a contextual meaning that did not mean [WHAT] or [WHERE]. Although the gestural forms appear similar, their meanings could not be predicted if taken out of the context. Occurrences of these nonlexical forms were glossed according to the context as "G(5-UP):WELL," "G(5-UP):SO," and "G(5-UP):HUH." In many cases, these gestures served as prosodic functions or as transition markers between discourse segments or utterances.

Novel Arbitrary Lexical Signs

The analysis reveals examples of lexical signs that are arbitrary and appear to be novel forms that are used in a regularized way. Iconic motivation often prompts creation of new signs in IS, yet some signs may be potentially iconically misleading. The best example of this comes from

FIGURE 34. *IS sign* PROJECT*(WFD).*

an emerging recurring form in expository IS—the sign PROJECT(WFD) (Figure 34). This sign occurs 11 times in the full data, with several presenters using it in their lecture. The articulation appears to mimic the movement of grasping a handle and cranking it alongside an upheld flat-B nondominant hand; much in the way one might handle a movie projector. A majority of Study Two participants did not understand the signs's meaning. The four participants who *did* recognize it reported some familiarity with IS. The sign is an interesting example of an arbitrary sign that is lexicalized in expository IS. Its origins are speculated here.

The original *Gestuno* glossary cites the sign PROJECT [PROJECT] with movement of an index finger tracing a square on the upheld flat palm of the nondominant hand (Figure 34). The sign appears to have undergone a slight handshape change and is articulated in expository IS with a more concise circular movement that may fit constraints of economized movement. Ironically, the sign form pictured next to this one in the 1975 *Gestuno* glossary is the sign labeled PROJECTOR, which illustrates the dominant hand grasping a crank handle and turning it. This is the current movement of PROJECT(WFD) seen in Figure 34. It is unknown whether this is an example of phonological reduction of the BSL and Auslan sign PROJECT (initialized P-J) or a reduction of the form PROJECT originally pictured in the *Gestuno* glossary (Figure 35). Otherwise, it could be a random loan translation or intrusion blend from the two English words labeling the two sign forms in the glossary, given the simplified movement from PROJECTOR rather than the 1-handshape tracing an outline on the upright hand. Last, it could be a new borrowing from an NSL not considered in this study. English forms in SLs have been documented, and the juxtaposition of two sign forms in the *Gestuno* glossary is somewhat ironic.

A second novel form that appears in the data relates to a relatively new concept in international deaf discourses. It is the sign for the UN Convention on the Rights of Disabled People (UNCRPD), ID glossed

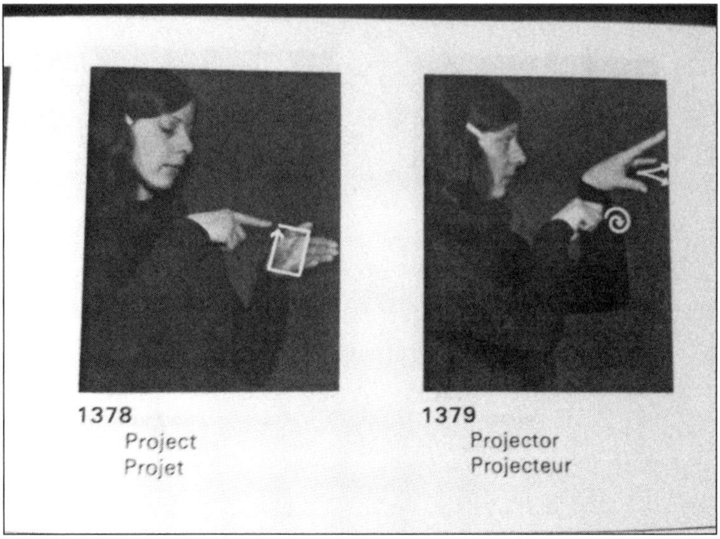

FIGURE 35. *Side-by-side entries* PROJECT *and* PROJECTOR *([Image], 1975, British Deaf Association, retrieved from http://www.bda.org.uk).*

FIGURE 36. *IS sign for the* UNCRPD *(WFD).*

in the data as CRPD and shown in Figure 36. The form resembles the ASL sign SIGNATURE but incorporates a Z-shaped movement of an H handshape across the flat upturned nondominant B or 5 handshape. It may be an approximated action of signing or ratifying a document, and it is unknown where the form originated. However, it is a conventional lexical sign that appears in several presentations in the dataset, and it is

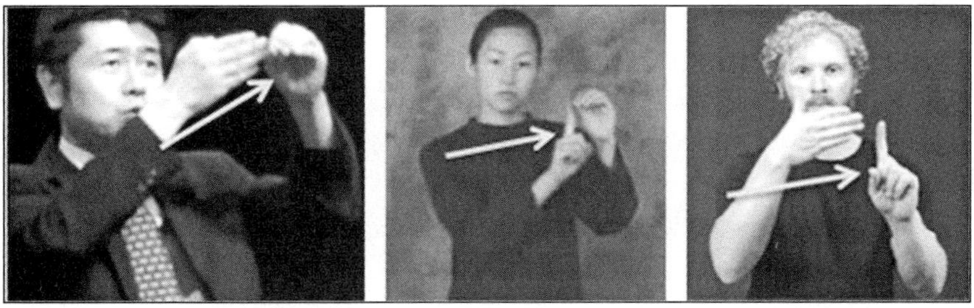

FIGURE 37. *(a) [AIM] IS depicting sign; (b) OBJECTIVE (JSL); and (c) Auslan [AIM] (Objective [Image], retrieved from http://www.spreadthesign.com; Aim [Image], retrieved from http://www.auslan.org.au/dictionary/gloss/aim1a.html).*

visible in online materials from the WFD promoting the human rights document and raising awareness of its legislative powers for deaf people in nations worldwide.

Last, at times the data revealed interesting examples where a sign form resembled a borrowed fully lexical sign from an NSL, but one of the parameters was altered that matched a phonological parameter of another SL, from the contact setting. The sign in Figure 37 was used by one of the native JSL signers, which looked like the Auslan sign AIM meaning [OBJECTIVE] but with the nondominant hand in the shape of the JSL sign meaning [OBJECTIVE]. Both the Auslan and JSL sign are also shown as a comparison to the IS form used.

The form occurred once in the presentation and was annotated as a movement-depicting sign (in a two-handed figure–ground relationship):

DomID gloss: DSM(B):OBJECT-MOVES-FORWARD-AT

NonDomID gloss: DSG(O):ENTITY-OBJECT-MOVES-TO

It is difficult to know if the form is a loan blend, mixing two parameters from two different SLs, or if the presenter intends to initialize the targeted O handshape to mean "objective," thus borrowing from English. It may also be interference from the sublexical (O handshape) component of the signer's NSL. It is one example of a few interesting forms that posed a challenge in annotating sign types in the mixed IS contact system. A partly lexical sign, it exploits gesture and metaphoric reference in the way the movement and location parameters are articulated, and the form may be a close enough approximation for the meaning [AIM] in several other SLs, and thus a lexical sign that is easy to understand. If used regularly in the dataset, and by other presenters, it would have been reasonable to consider it an established lexicalized form; however, it is an ad hoc construction that appears to be motivated by gesture and conventional linguistic components.

PARTLY LEXICAL SIGNS IN IS

Signs that are partly lexical and rely to a high degree on the context of the utterance are also observed in expository IS. These two types are pointing signs and depicting signs, described in the previous chapter.

Pointing Signs

The most frequent signs in IS are pointing signs, comprising 14.5% of all tokens in the data, as shown in Table 12. The top four frequent sign types are points (PT:PRO3, PT:PRO1, PT:DET, and PT:LOC, respectively), and they make up 9.7% (824) of the 1,017 tokens. Points on the dominant hand that overlap with a list buoy or a fragment buoy on the nondominant hand were counted, and the result uncovered a variety of points (61 in total) directed at list buoys (PT:LBUOY-FIRST, etc.). In addition, the data reveal 80 tokens of points that were directed at fragment buoys. This supports the intuition that IS relies on points in organizing discourse, and given their prevalence in IS and in NSLs, their function may be similar in both.

As discussed previously, pointing signs have several functions in SLs, one of the most important of which is for reference tracking. Others include an adverbial locating function, a determiner function, and a discourse cohesive function (via buoys). Figure 38 shows an excerpt from one presentation where the IS signer uses as many as nine pointing signs of varied subtype in the 12-second span, underlying their importance in the discourse.

In the segment pictured, points are directed at list buoys, which tokenize objects of discourse or topics not physically present. They are also aimed at fragment buoys, which are nondominant handshape holds at the end of a sign. Points are included here as referential indexes to the signer himself, but may not specify the pronoun I, as in this example the PT:PRO1 appears to preface the sign JAPAN. He establishes "I, pretend I am Japan," before making a comment about the programs that Japan

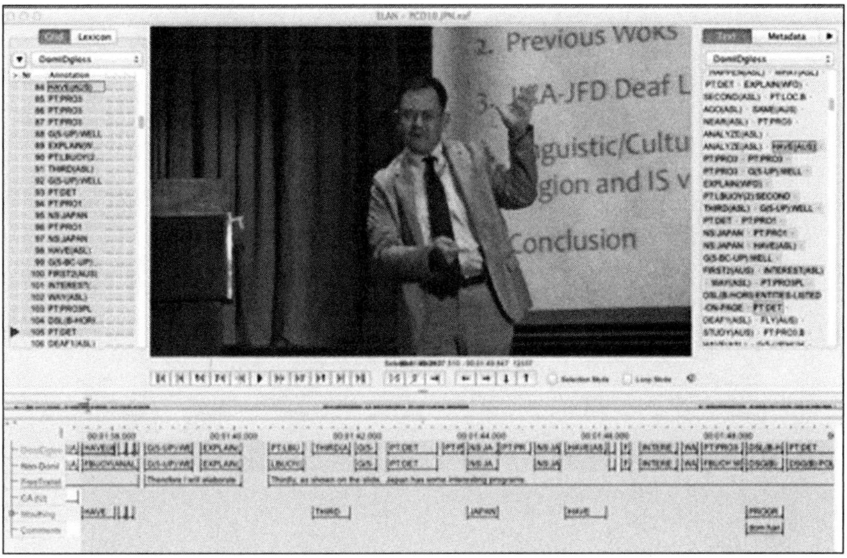

FIGURE 38. *Prevalence of pointing signs in IS.*

offers in training. Points also direct the audience to physical entities in space that are real, such as the presentation slide behind the presenter.

In the IS data, pointing signs may be exploiting the gestural aspect of these signs, or they may be recruited for some linguistic role that might be pronominal or contributing to argument (subjects/objects) structure. There is continued discussion in the literature about pointing signs and their function, with recent evidence suggesting some SLs (e.g., Auslan) lack pronouns (Johnston, 2013a, 2013b). Without additional study of the patterning of pointing signs in IS and other semiotic material that occurs with them (e.g., eye gaze)—especially in comparison to NSLs—it is difficult to make claims about them in IS, except that the data reveal a large variety of pointing signs and a similar percent distribution to what is reported in NSL lexical frequency studies.

Depicting Signs

In the expository IS dataset there were 721 distinct depicting signs, most of which occur once, a few recurring two, three, or as many as six times. Two depicting signs stand out as relatively established, recurring 14 times and 17 times, respectively, in the data.

FIGURE 39. *DSS(GS)*:SMALL-AMOUNT.

The first sign, annotated as DSS(GC):SMALL-AMOUNT (Figure 39) occurs 14 times and is a depiction that is used to mean "a small amount of something." In the data, it quantifies abstract, intangible things such as information as proficiency with signing skill, as well as physical entities such as students, distance, and money. The form is gestural and somewhat emblematic, and it occurs in different NSLs such as ASL and Auslan. In this study, it fits the criteria for a depicting, "classifier"-type sign, because the same depicting handshape is also used 10 other times with varied movement (DSM) to show the shape of a long, thin, or flat object, such as a banner, title, or tie. This sign is partially specified depending on the context.

The second most common depicting sign was glossed and annotated as DSS(BENTB):ENTITIES-LISTED-ON-PAGE and the form is seen in Figure 40. The sign appeared in the WFD *Suggested International Signs* DVD, glossed as REGULATIONS, and is also listed in the SignBooks *International Sign* glossary under the entry PRINCIPLE. It is suggested by these resources that the form is an IS lexical sign, and it is also lexicalized in Auslan to mean [RULE], or [LIST, PROGRAM, AGENDA, CATALOGUE]. The sign presents an example that posed a challenge for ID glossing during lexical analysis, given possible "two faces" (Johnston & Ferrara, 2012) of signs in a NSL (discussed in Chapter 3), and given an uncertainty regarding its conventionalization. It was difficult to discern whether the form should be described as a partly lexical depicting sign or a fully lexical sign, with the tag (WFD) or (AUS). The decision to label it a depicting sign was originally made based on the understanding of it as a complex

FIGURE 40. *DSS(BENTB):ENTITIES-LISTED-ON-PAGE.*

construction that appeared to show compositional meanings of its parts. I documented it as a partly lexical sign, which is a real-space blend that depicts the visual image of long, thin rows of text located on and filling the length of a page.

Fifteen (15) out of the 17 occurrences of the form in Figure 40 are used by one presenter, and the other two occurrences are used once by two other IS presenters. There were additional variations of this depicting construction, all of which used the same backgrounding nondominant handshape, but there were varied dominant hand configurations (e.g., B-UP handshape, G handshape, and a pointing gesture aimed at dot-point items on the B-UP palm). In all cases, the sign exploited iconicity, and meaning was dependent on the utterance context in which it was used. Several intended meanings were [PROGRAM], [LAW], [REGULATIONS], [REPORT], [POLICY], [DOCUMENTATION], and one IS presenter used it for two of these meanings in the same lecture. In general, it was used to show a type of written documentation, or a planned sequence of actions. However, given the number of occurrences of the form (by one signer) and several phonologic variations on the construction, it may be an example of a form that is in the process of becoming lexicalized within a community of IS presenters. The presenter who used the depicting sign 15 times may have been lexicalizing it instantaneously, but whether or not the form/meaning link is conventionalized to mean something more than the predictable value of its components is unclear.

Recall the discussion about lexico-grammar and the image from Johnston and Ferrara (2012) in which Auslan signs were mapped onto scales of lexical size and content. With this framework in mind, formational aspects of the sign, DSS(BENTB):ENTITIES-LISTED-ON-PAGE bear iconic resemblance to figure and ground referents that the subatomic components (the handshapes, orientation, and movement parameters) are depicting. It was unclear whether or not the form-meaning relationship was stable enough to be called a fully lexical, symbolic unit in expository IS lectures (as it is in Auslan for the similar sign RULES).[12] However, it is clear that IS signers exploit the components of signs to show what they mean through depicting signs in IS discourse.

The productive nature of depicting structures, along with metaphor, is a potentially rich area of inquiry in cross-linguistic contact signing. Simple metaphor in SLs maps the linguistic form to a source domain, exploiting visual iconicity such that the linguistic form (i.e., handshape, movement, etc.) resembles the referent or a part of the referent in a metonymic relationship (Brennan, 1990; Taub, 2001; Wilcox, 2000). Often these metaphors are simple, orientational, and ontological, enabling an observer to estimate the meaning based on the iconic relationship between the articulator and the visual or embodied experience of the referent.

The fact that a majority of depicting signs occurred only once in the dataset is further evidence of signers' recruitment of formational elements of NSLs in IS. The large number of novel constructions compensate for reduced established lexical signs, yet some qualification must be made about depicting sign documentation and analysis. Depending on how an annotator glosses depicting signs, the resulting count of unique types could be misrepresented (Johnston, 2012, p. 183). Depicting signs can be annotated with more general descriptive information, such as their handshape and other, more specific descriptive characteristics that enable subtype categorization and meaning information. (See Johnston, 2014, and Table 1, "Annotation Conventions" in this book.) The DS tokens totaled 721, but the data require further analysis to report confidently the exact number of unique tokens. It is possible to have slightly different glosses for identical depicting forms, such as DSS(BENT5):GROUP-OF-PEOPLE-STUDENTS and DSS(BENT5):GROUP-OF-ANIMALS-SHEEP, or "regularized and simplified" (Johnston, 2012, p. 184) to DSS(BENT5):GROUP-OF-ENTITIES. In general, depicting signs were characterized in this study by five broad types and then further glossed with additional, more specific glossing for meaning. Table 17 lists the distribution of general depicting types from the IS source dataset.

12. *Auslan Signbank* URL: http://www.auslan.org.au/dictionary/gloss/4867

TABLE 17. *Depicting Signs by Subtype*

Depicting signs (DS) $n = 721$	Dominant hand (Top three handshapes)	Nondominant hand (Top three handshapes)
DSM	337 (B, 5, 1)	196 (5, 1, B)
DSS	182 (B, 1, GC)	122 (B, 1, Bent5)
DSL	69 (B, 5, Bent5)	36 (B, Bent5, 1)
DSH	48 (FlatO, S, BC)	20 (BC, B, FlatO)
DSG	3 (B, 5, BentB)	180 (B, 5, BC)

The majority of depicting signs in IS represent movement (or displacement) of entities (DSM), and others depict size and shape (DSS), or are entity locating (DSL), and some are handling entities (DSH). In most cases, handling entity depicting signs (DSH) co-occurred with constructed action, because enactment often involves the handling and manipulation of entities. DSH signs were not easily distinguished from gesture signs, and if they had been glossed as gestures, the number would increase the percentage of gestures in IS by 0.5%. Last, there were depicting signs that backgrounded an entity represented by the dominant hand (as seen by the high percentage of DSG sign types observed for the nondominant hand). Most of the DS signs occurred on both hands, often in coordination, but also in a figure-ground relationship.

A variety of handshapes and movements were recruited by IS presenters for creating these complex sign constructions, presumably to maximize iconicity, movement that has similar meaning across SLs, and use of space blends often seen in NSLs. Each subtype (DSM, DSL, DSS, DSG, DSH) exhibited a number of different handshapes and orientations, with different qualities of movement and additional nonmanual information. The resulting effect was a large number of different depicting sign forms that were dependent on their utterance context for meaning, rather than prompting specific meaning (as a fully lexical sign would do). The summary Table 17 that shows the most frequent handshapes observed within each depicting sign subtype provides a picture about the variety of productive forms in expository IS. Table 18 however, reports all of the twenty-four (24) different handshapes observed in the DS data, with a majority of tokens one of the top five most frequent forms. Four of the five are noted to be some of the widely acknowledged seven basic handshapes (B, A, S, C, O, 1, 5) (Battison, 1978).

TABLE 18. *Distribution of Handshapes in IS Depicting Signs*

Handshape	Image	Percent distribution	% Cumulative	Handshape	Image	Percent distribution	% Cumulative
B		29.2%	29.2%	4		1.0%	96.1%
5		18.2%	47.4%	FLATBC		0.8%	96.9%
1		11.8%	59.2%	BENT2		0.68%	97.6%
BENT5		10.5%	69.7%	IRISHT		0.60%	98.2%
BC (or C)		9.3%	79.0%	MID		0.51%	98.7%
BENTB		3.7%	82.7%	H		0.30%	99.0%
FLATO		3.0%	85.7%	2		0.30%	99.3%

GC		2.8%	88.5%	O		0.26%	99.5%
S		2.8%	91.3%	L		0.17%	99.7%
6		1.3%	92.6%	F		0.17%	99.9%
GCFLAT		1.3%	93.9%	Y		0.01%	100%
BABYO		1.2%	95.1%	IRISHK		0.01%	100%

FIGURE 41. *Depicting the concept of [DECREASE]/[INCREASE] in IS.*

Another example of a depicting sign from this study that exploits iconic and gestural features of formational parts of signs is shown in Figure 41. Sign forms that involve a handshape movement from a lower position to an upper position convey a meaning of an "increase" of some kind. Rosenstock (2004) mentions this as one example of effective metaphoric reference that was observed in her IS data. If the semantic domain of "increasing entities" is effectively mapped onto the form—the articulating hands and arms—as long as the lexical argument is understood, the observer will know what "thing" is increasing as well as the manner of the increase. The signer in Figure 41 refers to the increased interest and number of attendees at HIV training, after previous ones were not conducted in the local SL. The image created is one of a declining then increasing slope, as if a line on a chart, quantifying a numerical increase. The second half of the sign also resembles the ASL sign DEVELOP; however, the presenter de-lexicalized the sign by initially constructing a downward sloping movement that pivoted at the lowest point and then sloped upward.

Given that 10.2% of the signs in expository IS are depicting types, the use of depiction to convey complex meanings is assessed in the comprehension in Study Two. Of the total number of depicting signs (721), the top five comprise 7.7% of all tokens (Table 19).

One of the selected depicting sign clusters in the IS comprehension test is shown in Figure 42. The co-presenter in *video* B (segment B2) describes how collaboration from Deaf associations from other countries has influenced improved access for deaf people in English-speaking East African countries, yet those in French-speaking West African countries experience great disparity in access to education and civic life.

The presenter used a depicting sign, DSM(5-DOWN):ENTITIES-FLY-IN, at the end of this utterance to indicate the varied collaborators who have flown in to the area to aid in their development. She established discourse referents in the signing space via token blends |Foreign associations| and |local association|. The discourse referents of overseas Deaf associations

TABLE 19. *The Five Most Frequent Depicting Signs in IS*

Rank	Depicting signs (n = 721)	Total
1	DSS(BENTB):ENTITIES-IN-A-LINE-LISTED-ON-PAGE	17
2	DSS(GCFLAT):SMALL-AMOUNT	14
3	DSM(1):ENTITY-GOES-FAR-IN-DEEP	11
4	DSM(5):ENTITIES-GATHER-TOGETHER	8
5	DSL(BENT5):AREA-THERE	6
		56

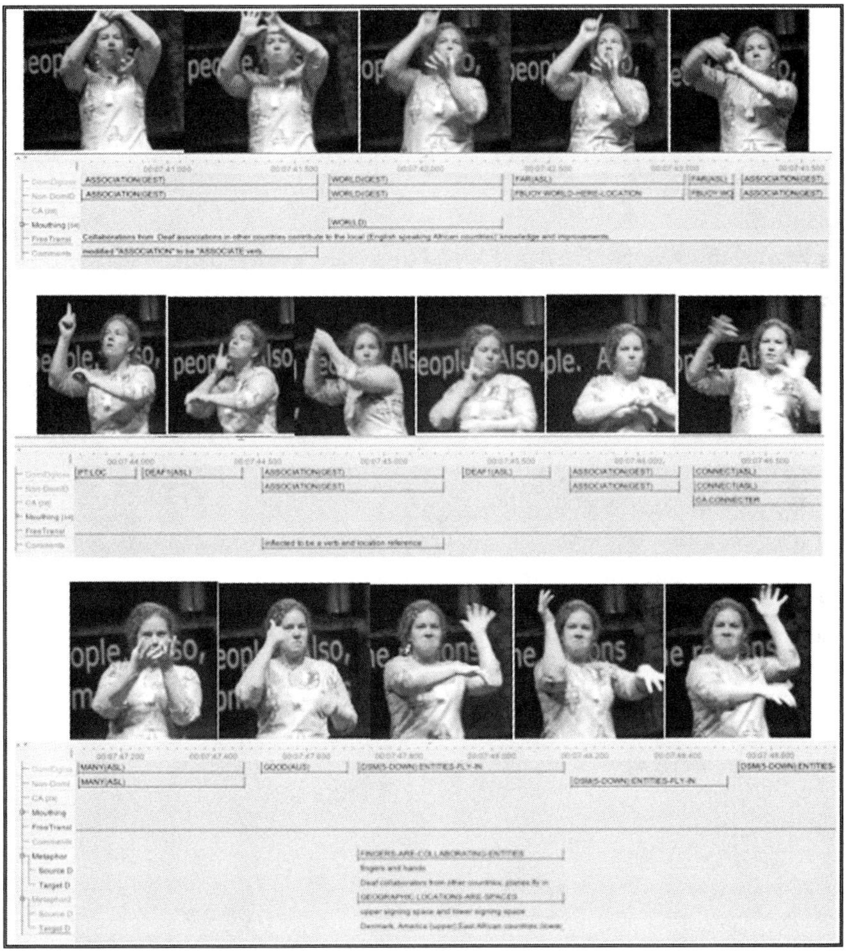

FIGURE 42. *Depicting segment DSB5 (Free Translation: Collaborations from Deaf associations in other countries contribute to the local [English-speaking African countries] knowledge and improvements).*

and their geographic distance are set up in the signing space with fully lexical signs, ASSOCIATION(GEST) WORLD(GEST) FAR(ASL) FAR(ASL). A pointing sign PT:LOC DEAF1(ASL) ASSOCIATION(GEST) establishes the token |Foreign (English-speaking community) associations| and a lexical sign articulated in a lowered, different space establishes the second token |local (English-speaking community) association|. In the utterance, the IS signer even articulated the sign ASSOCIATION (GEST) in each token location she established. The utterance is a good example of a complex construction that includes varied sign types (lexical signs, points, and depicting signs) and one instance of constructed action and uses signing space to map out references and build up the discourse main point. This sequence provides the answer for one of the content questions (see Appendix C: Content Questions Rubric), but also depicting segments like these are shown and participants are asked about the meaning they understood from the depicting signs in the utterance context.

Nonlexical Signs: Gesture and Constructed Action

The amount of gesture incorporated into the studied IS presentations ranged from 5% to as high as 20% by some IS signers. Gestures (n = 645) comprised 9% of signs in the 13 IS source files, and the most frequent seven comprise 50% of all gesture signs in the dataset (Table 20). There were 399 different gesture forms, most occurring once and 34 occurring twice. The three most common gestures—G(5-UP): WELL/SO/HUH—are typically seen in NSLs as cohesive, discourse-marking devices, and they appear to be functioning similarly in IS.

TABLE 20. *The Seven Most Frequent Gestures in IS*

Rank	Most frequent GESTURES (n = 645)	Total
1	G(5-UP):WELL	125
2	G(5-UP):HUH	72
3	G(5-UP):SO	61
4	G(5-SHAKE):WOW-VERY	23
5	G(1-SHAKE):NO-NO	20
6	G(5-WAVE):NO-NO	10
7	G(F):ALL-OK	9
	Total	320

Presenters used gestures to create meaningful symbols in IS utterances, such as a hand-waving gesture, G:HEY-YOU, or in the expression of enactment and emotional responses via nonmanual markers and torso movements, for example, G(5-2H):FIGURE-IT-OUT (Figure 43).

Gestures that serve to negate utterances such as G(1-SHAKE):NO-NO were frequent, and align with other studies' reports of manual negation in IS (Supalla & Webb, 1995; Woll, 1990). One of the more common forms that most IS signers incorporated into their lectures, was the gesture glossed as G(5-SHAKE):WOW (shown in Figure 43). It operates as a modifying form and in many cases means [VERY] or intensifies some aspect of what is being discussed.

In this analysis, gesture also includes the mimetic enacting behaviors known as constructed action (CA) and constructed dialogue (CD). Enactments were annotated on the CA tier as instances of nonlinguistic behavior, facial expressions, and bodily movements that are mimed emotions and actions. In total, there were 572 periods of CA enactment. These enactments were coded separately on the CA tier and overlapped (were time-aligned) with gestures, depicting signs, and/or fully lexical signs on the dominant and nondominant ID gloss tiers. Because of these concurrences and separate treatment of the two, the amount of CA is discussed as a separate finding and is not reported in terms of percentages of the total 7,033 sign tokens. The frequency of CA enactment ranged on average from 1 enactment every 33 signs, to as high as 1 enactment every 7 signs, depending on the presenter.

McNeill (2005) describes gestural viewpoints of "observer" and "character" for co-speech gestures, with gestures often acting as a "material carrier" (p. 98). The "material" in constructed action and dialogue in IS enacts a visual story about a referent's described activity. CA occurs not only simultaneously with gesture signs, but also with other types of signs.

FIGURE 43. *Gesture: G(5-2H):FIGURE-IT-OUT.*

FIGURE 44. *Constructed action with depicting sign in multiple blend.*

A clausal analysis was not made here; however, Ferrara showed that in Auslan, CA overlaps in clauses with sole depicting signs and in most cases CA serves as the argument in the clause (Ferrara, 2012). These varied frequencies of CA occurrence are suggested to be a narrative device (Ferrara & Johnston, 2014) as opposed to obligatory (Quinto-Pozos, 2007). The prevalent occurrence of periods of CA in the IS data suggests that this form of semantically coordinated gestural material aids depicting signs and lexical signs to convey meaningful utterances, similar to the way it is in NSLs (e.g., Auslan).

In the IS data, the way that CA co-occurred with manual signs (ID gloss tiers) varied. The co-occurrences ranged from a single sign token in a period of CA to as many as 11 sign tokens in a period of CA. Lexical signs were at times aligned 1:1 with CA and thus offered additional gestural material to fully lexical signs. During many examples of CA in the IS dataset, the co-occurring signs and the CA elements (nonmanual signals, body posturing, eye gaze) constructed complex utterances that resembled what Dudis (2004) describes as partitioned blends. With partitioned blends, the signer used a two-handed DS to depict discourse material from the observer point of view, and at the same time created a second blend from the point of view of the character. For example the IS presenter in Figure 44 created a partitioned blend by depicting DSM(1):ENTITY-GOES-FAR-IN-DEEP to mean [women located in rural community], while also enacting with body posture, head, and nonmanual features a character point of view of ducking under something and moving into a remote area.

DS signs co-occurred with CA 152 times, gestures co-occurred with CA 206 times, and fully lexical signs were accompanied by CA 182 times. A follow-up clausal analysis of this IS data would enable one to draw more conclusions about how CA and gesture (as two kinds of gestural material

FIGURE 45. *LOOK(ASL) co-occurring with CA.*

in IS utterances) are distributed and participate with depicting signs and fully lexical signs. Intuitions can be proposed from some of the findings.

It seems the co-occurrence of CA with fully lexical signs in IS serves as a complementary way of conveying composite utterance meaning. Fully lexical signs are forms that are typically strongly associated with specified meanings, without need for much contextual information. Yet in IS, the presenters supplement fully lexical signs with gestural material, perhaps due to the contact setting and a potential for some audience members to not be regular users of the lexical sign in IS. In Figure 45, the example LOOK(ASL) is given; although fully lexicalized in IS, it co-occurs with CA in the example (but not always). It is possible that the lexical signs in IS that are aligned with CA behavior are being semantically supported by the enactment. A future comparison of this feature in IS and how the patterning of CA operates with lexical signs in NSLs would offer insights about the function of co-occurring CA with lexical signs in signed language contact.

COMPARING IS TO NSL FREQUENCY STUDIES

The analysis reveals suggestive findings about high-frequency sign types in IS as compared to NSLs. Results from quantitative analysis of the 7,033 tokens indicate similarities as well as differences in the type

TABLE 21. *Comparing IS Sign Type Distribution to NSL Sign Type Distribution*

Sign types	IS lectures (*n* = 7,033)	Auslan Corpus[a] (*n* = 54,506)	ASL[b] (*n* = 4,111)	BSL[c] (*N* = 24,823)
Fully lexical signs (including numbers)	63.6%	64.8%	73.1%	60.3%
Fully lexical fingerspelling	1.74%	5.0%	6.4%	3.0%
Fully lexical name signs	1.74%	0.25%	2.3%	n/a
Partly lexical pointing signs	14.5%	12.0%	13.8%	23.0%
Partly lexical depicting signs	10.2%	11.0%	4.2%	2.3%
Nonlexical gesture	9.0%	6.5%	0.2%	8.9%

[a]Data from Johnston, 2012a.
[b]Data from Morford and MacFarlane (2003).
[c]Data from Fenlon, Schembri, Rentelis, Vinson, & Cormier (2014).
Note. Depicting signs are called classifier signs in (b) and (c).

of signs distributed in the lexicon of expository IS compared to NSLs. Quantitative results of expository IS sign types were compared to what is reported in Auslan, ASL, and BSL to ascertain any unique type characteristics of IS expository discourses. These comparative data are shown in Table 21.

The sample sizes of the IS source data and the other NSL datasets differ. It is recognized that one must take care when generalizing from small datasets. Also, the effect of text genre in the collections in these reported studies, as well as different glossing and transcription practices, will impact the comparability of data. Gesture occurs almost as much in BSL as in the IS data, with Auslan showing more gesture than ASL. In the ASL study, gestures are not mentioned, but results for "fragments" are given (Morford & MacFarlane, 2003, p. 220). Johnston (2012) and Cormier et al. (2011) consider the ASL reports of fragments as nonlinguistic sign types; hence, they are compared with their nonlinguistic types (gestures). Coding differences between researchers are noted by Cormier et al. (2011) and Johnston (2012); some researchers may or may not annotate several types of gestures the same way. Many gestures include discourse cohesion markers like G(5-UP):WELL or those that fill utterance space (e.g., UM) as well as CA and CD (Cormier et al., 2011, p. 5). While pointing sign distributions vary across these reported results, in all datasets they are the most prevalent types. Later in the next section, with a focus on the subsets of *formal* Auslan and ASL, some comparison can be made, keeping in mind mentioned limitations.

The amount of fully lexical signs are similar, if not slightly lower in IS than in other NSL distribution results. Lexicalized signs comprise a lower percentage of the total in IS, at 63.6% when compared to ASL (73.1%), but are similar when compared to Auslan (64.8%) and BSL (60.3%). Pointing signs in each NSL and IS are distributed relatively similarly, with BSL showing significantly more pointing signs—roughly 10% more than ASL, Auslan, and IS. The largest differences in distribution occur with fingerspelling, depiction, and, to some extent, gesture. IS exhibits much less fingerspelling than the NSLs, but overall much more depiction and gesture than ASL, BSL. These differences are more pronounced when comparing data from similar text genre and register (below). Fingerspelling occurs less frequently in IS lectures, presumably given that not all SL users are familiar with the one-handed system in IS. Presenters aim to make their IS utterances understandable to a wide variety of SL using audience members, so reducing fingerspelled forms reduces chances for misunderstanding. These results are similar to what is shown in studies on IS interpreted text (McKee & Napier, 2002), and only 55 instances (2%) of fingerspelling were observed (Rosenstock, 2004).

Auslan's use of depicting signs is relatively high compared to ASL and BSL at 11%, which comes close to the 10.2% observed in the IS data. The Auslan Corpus comprises a few different text genres, with a heavy representation of narrative texts (retelling stories from visual picture book *Frog Where Are You*; Mayer, 1969). There are no expository lectures or presentations in the corpus (Johnston, 2012). This may explain the slightly higher percentage of depicting signs in the Auslan full corpus than in IS lectures. The BSL study also reports a relatively high amount of gesture—8.9% of sign types—which is almost as much observed in the 9% gesture in expository IS. The BSL text genre is all spontaneous conversational data, a less formal type of discourse. The formality differences between prepared formal IS lecture data and the spontaneous informal BSL conversational data likely influence the amount of gesture in each, and may not be a valid comparison. This is because the genre of a text is shown to have some effect on the distribution of sign types (Cormier et al., 2011). A comparative analysis of datasets that comprise similar genre texts is made in the next section.

Mentioned in the methodology, a lack of lecture-type expository texts in the Auslan Corpus prompted the consideration for a likewise comparison of the same genre texts. Hence, two 5-minute Auslan lecture segments (publicly available) were also annotated for sign types, constructed action, and spoken language mouthings, using the same glossing and annotation method as the IS source dataset. The two Auslan expository lecture samples are included in a comparison of IS to NSLs in terms of their composition of sign types.

Comparison to Similar Text Genres and Auslan Expository Text

There are reportedly text genre differences that impact frequency distributions in the larger Auslan Corpus, when comparing the full corpus to what Johnston identifies as a subset of formal Auslan data (Johnston, 2012). Formal Auslan texts have more fully lexical signs (69.4% versus 64.75%) and more nonlinguistic gesture signs (8.8% versus 6.5%) than shown in the full corpus, but much less depicting types (1.6% in contrast to 11%). Table 22 illustrates some of the differences in distribution of fully lexical signs, partly lexical pointing and depicting signs, and nonlexical gesture signs across comparable text genres of different datasets. The data in the first two columns are reported from this current study, and the latter two columns indicate data from the Auslan and ASL lexical

TABLE 22. *Comparing Sign Types in IS and Similar NSL Genres*

Sign type	IS lectures (n = 7,033)	Auslan lectures (n = 1,137)	Auslan Corpus formal (n = 22,100)[a]	ASL formal (n = 1,363)[b]
Fully lexical	63.6%	71.3%	69.4%	80.2%
Fingerspelling	1.7%	8.3%	4.7%	4.8%
Name signs	1.7%	0.1%	0.5%	0.7%
Pointing	14.5%	15.0%	15.0%	13.4%
Depicting	10.2%	3.9%	1.6%	0.9%
Gesture	9.0%	2.8%	8.8%	0.1%

[a] Formal texts only from Johnston (2012a).
[b] Formal texts only from Morford and MacFarlane (2003).

frequency studies. In a smaller subset of ASL formal texts, "frozen" (fully) lexical signs comprise 80.2% versus 73.1% of the lexicon. Reported depicting signs are less in the latter as well—2.3% as opposed to 0.1%. Comparative information about BSL formal or expository texts was not available given that spontaneous conversational data was the text genre in that lexical frequency study.

These frequency results provide some insight into unique characteristics of expository IS that enrich the description of IS and supplement what has been observed in other studies. Intuitions about increased depiction and gesture in IS are verified.

Including two samples of Auslan expository presentations in the analysis allows for making genre-specific comparisons between international contact signing and a NSL. Although limited by sample size (n = 1,137), they augment the comparison to Auslan formal texts (interviews). Because Auslan is a conventional language and not a contact mix of languages, lexical signs annotated in the data were not tagged with origin information (e.g., THINK(ASL), WORLD(GEST), etc.). Only the sign types were analyzed, and a free translation was made by the researcher and two graduate students, and checked by a professional Auslan-English interpreter. The two videos totaled 20 minutes of expository Auslan, but the annotated segments total 14 minutes, resulting in 1,137 sign tokens available for comparative analysis. Text "Negotiating the Politics of Language and Access" was a prepared Auslan lecture rendered to a live audience of several hundred interpreters and deaf people who use Auslan. The topic was about language access and the politics of language in the Australian Deaf Community. The second text, "Voter Registration," is a prepared presentation available online and on DVD that serves as a public information resource about voting in the state of Victoria.

In genre-specific comparisons, results show that expository IS has a smaller established lexicon than formal Auslan, formal ASL, and expository Auslan. In fact, the figures in Table 22 indicate 5.8% to as much as 16.6% *more* fully lexical forms than those in expository IS. In addition, it appears that an NSL expository lecture recruits much more fingerspelling than IS, for reasons discussed previously. Once again, pointing signs are consistently similar across these datasets. Although there are limitations to generalizing from small collections, there are, nonetheless, suggestive differences in type distribution.

According to the data, there are at least 10% less established, lexical materials in IS than in the same genre NSL texts. Even if only approximate, these numbers support prior claims that there is a smaller number of lexicalized forms in IS than in NSLs. Although not unexpected, what this implies for expository IS discourse is that limited conventional, fully lexical signs used in IS presentations potentially impact the information gleaned. The semantic economy and specificity provided by conventional lexical forms would therefore be lacking, and patterning and usage of conventional forms may differ from that of the NSL from which they were recruited. A presenter's messages would need to be grounded in additional meaning-making elements in the discourse through depiction and gesture.

Turning to other potential meaning-making elements in IS, one can see differences in the distribution of partly lexical and nonlexical components in expository IS when compared to comparable text genres in NSLs, except for pointing signs. It is notable that the frequency distribution of pointing sign types is remarkably similar to their distribution in NSLs; in particular, prototypical indexing types are the most frequent sign types in IS as they are in Auslan, ASL, and NZSL (Johnston, 2012). However, it cannot be assumed that points function with any universality in NSLs (and therefore in IS) as pronominal linguistic types or deictic gestural types (Johnston, 2013b) without further study of their form and function in a variety of NSLs (and in IS).

The largest difference is that expository IS exhibits a higher amount of both depiction and gesture than Auslan (formal and lecture) and ASL formal texts. The distribution of depicting signs in IS is 10.2%; this is more than double what was measured in the expository Auslan lectures (3.9%), nearly six times more than the Auslan Corpus formal texts, and 10 times more frequent than the ASL formal data. Depicting signs (described in 3.3.3) are productive signs with categorical and gradient properties and in NSLs combine meaningful units (handshapes, movements, locations, etc.) to create new forms (Brennan, 1992; Johnston & Schembri, 2007). In IS, the need to create nonce and new forms to supplement limited established signs is more pronounced, given the lack of conventional fully lexical forms available for discourse. Moreover, borrowed lexical signs from NSLs into IS might undergo modification, to exploit subatomic parts of signs and prompt meaning for the IS context. This productive capacity of NSLs is assumed to be a contributing benefit for communicating across NSLs in a contact sign such as expository IS.

The differences in gesture distributions are not easily compared. The ASL study does not elaborate on coding of gesture, and the Auslan data were based on formal interviews, not monologic lecture. Johnston notes that in the interview texts, there appeared to be many gestures due to the interactive nature of the data, such as cues for turn taking. Neither the ASL nor the Auslan study reports on the amount of the gesture categorized as constructed action (Johnston, 2012, p. 14). A recent study on depicting signs in Auslan grammar showed that constructed action (CA) is exploited in narrative text clauses (37.2%) rather than in the interactive conversations (6.1%) (Ferrara, 2012).

CA is another type of gestural material in IS and NSLs, which is of interest. The CA analyzed in expository IS was annotated on a separate tier, and periods of CA overlap with gestures and the other sign types observed. As reported in the lexical frequency results, there were 645 gesture signs and 572 CA instances. Only 153 of these co-occurred. Extrapolating these numbers, one arrives at 1,027 total nonlexical gestures (CA and gesture combined) that occurred in the expository IS data. This suggests that gestural material is much higher in expository IS than in any of the other datasets in similar genre comparisons.

Selections for Comprehension Testing

The IS contact examples in this study are a specific type—expository lecture at an international human rights–themed conference—and therefore, the most recurrent lexical signs reflect this theme. A subset of this Study One data, which comprises six video clip presentation segments, is used in Study Two and referred to as the Comprehension Test Dataset (see Table 15). Lexical frequency information about the Study One full dataset and Study Two Comprehension Test dataset is juxtaposed in Table 23.

The most frequent sign forms in both sets of data were identified, as well as the meaning for 45 signs selected from the top 100. These 45 signs were used in the comprehension testing in Study Two, as they were key signs occurring in the IS dataset. Information about sign meanings is reported in the findings here, as it helped to determine whether participants in Study Two understood these 45 signs, keeping in mind their given textual context. Rank frequency information is also noted about these signs in the full IS dataset (13 files) and in the subset comprehension test dataset (six files).

TABLE 23. *Lexical Identifications 45 High-Frequency IS Signs*

Sign #	ID Gloss	Meaning	Frequency in Full Dataset (per 1000) N=7030	Frequency in Test Dataset (per 1000) N=2045	Rank in Full dataset	Rank in Test dataset
1	DEAF1(ASL)	Deaf	13.9	20.5	3	1
2	HAVE(AUS)	have, possess, own	13.4	19.6	5	2
3	WHAT(ASL)	what	14.1	15.6	2	3
4	ASSOCIATION(GEST)	Deaf association, organization, collaborate	7.7	13.2	12	4
5	SAME(AUS)	also, same as	13.7	13.2	4	5
6	PERSON(AUS)	person, (also pluralized "people")	12.1	12.2	6	6
7	DIFFERENT(ASL)	different, varied	8.7	11.2	10	8
8	WORLD(AUS)	world, global	6.7	8.8	15	9
9	GOOD(AUS)	Good, alright, high quality	8.8	8.3	14	9
10	BODY(AUS)	health (care, physical care)	2.4	7.8	36	10
11	ANALYZE(ASL)	research, analysis	4.6	6.4	32	12
12	KNOW (ASL)	know, aware, knowledge	5.3	6.4	19	12
13	SCOUT(ASL)	boy scouts, scouting organization	2.3	6.4	37	12
14	CRPD(WFD)	The UNCRPD- Legal document giving rights to ppl. with disabilities/ Deaf	3.1	5.9	31	13

15	NOW(ASL)	now, today, immediate time	5.4	5.9	18	13
16	STUDY(AUS)	education, school, study	3.0	5.9	31	13
17	DISABLED(WFD)	person with disabilities, disability	4.0	5.4	25	14
18	HELP(ASL)	help, assistance	7.0	4.9	14	15
19	WORK(GEST)	work	8.4	5.4	9	16
20	DSS(GC):SMALL-AMOUNT	a small amount of something, a little	2.1	5.4	52	14
21	THINK(ASL)	think, realize, idea	4.6	4.9	21	15
22	FINISH(ASL)	finish, completed	4.6	4.4	21	16
23	IMPORTANT(ASL)	important	7.8	4.4	11	16
24	PROGRESS(ASL)	progress, move forward/on, advance	4.3	4.4	23	16
25	YEAR(ASL)	year	4.1	3.9	24	16
26	CONNECT(ASL)	connection, relate, connect	6.0	3.9	16	17
27	GOVERNMENT(GEST)	government	5.0	3.9	20	17
28	SIGN(GEST)	sign language	12.4	3.9	7	17
29	COUNTRY(WFD)	country, region	4.4	3.4	22	18
30	WANT(AUS)	want	3.7	3.4	27	18
31	CAN(ASL)	able, can	5.8	2.9	17	19
32	CHILDREN(ASL)	children (plural)	3.0	2.9	32	19
33	APPROVE(WFD)	approve, ratify, legalize	0.9	2.4	47	20

(Continued)

TABLE 23. (*Continued*)

Sign #	ID Gloss	Meaning	Frequency in Full Dataset (per 1000) N=7030	Frequency in Test Dataset (per 1000) N=2045	Rank in Full dataset	Rank in Test dataset
34	BOY(ASL)	male person; man or boy	2.0	2.4	14	20
35	INTERPRETER(WFD)	interpret, interpreter, translate	7.1	2.0	13	20
36	PROBLEM(ASL)	problem, difficult	3.1	2.4	41	20
37	HEARING(WFD)	hearing, able to hear	3.6	2.0	28	21
38	CONGRESS(GEST)	congress, conference	0.9	1.5	47	22
39	SEE-2H(ASL)	see, look, view	3.0	1.5	32	22
40	BRING(ASL)	bring, carry, deliver	3.3	1.0	30	23
41	INTERNATIONAL(WFD)	international, WFD	3.4	1.0	29	23
42	NS:ASIAPACIFIC	asia-pacific region	3.0	1.0	37	23
43	ACCEPT(ASL)	accept	1.7	0.5	41	24
44	LANGUAGE3(WFD)	grammar, language, text information	3.0	0.5	32	24
45	PROJECT(WFD)	project	1.3	0.5	44	24

High-Frequency Signs—Lexical IDs

Table 23 shows 45 high-frequency IS signs selected for inclusion in the comprehension test. This part of the comprehension test measured lexical semantic identification; participants' responses were totaled into a percentage score. It is suggested that once high-frequency terms are learned, then lower frequency words should be learned—less frequent or unknown words could possibly be guessed from context (Mehrpour & Rahimi, 2010).

The 45 lexical forms used in this measurement occur in the larger dataset and in the subset of test videos, although with slightly different frequency due to the effect of topic content on lexical frequency, especially a smaller corpus. Highly frequent signs from the analysis of the larger, 13-sample data, were checked to see if they also occurred regularly in the IS test video passages. The fully lexical signs used in this measurement come directly from frequent signs in the full database, and also appear in the 3- to 5-minute IS videos viewed.

Distribution of Lexical, Partly Lexical, and Nonlexical Signs in IS Test Videos

Lexical sign type information about the Comprehension Test Dataset was also determined and is shown in Table 24. Presenters incorporate more or less of some sign types in their expository IS, with varying amounts of lexical, partly lexical, and nonlexical signs. The two presenters in Video B employ the most gesture and constructed action with the least amount of lexicalized signs. A large amount of English word mouthings is also observed in these IS presentations, except for the signers in Videos B1 and D. Both are from countries whose surrounding spoken language is not English.

In terms of origins of the lexical signs expressed in expository IS, videotexts A through E all are representatively similar to the full lexical frequency dataset in Study One. The amount of lexical signs in this subset is similarly balanced between a predominance of ASL and Auslan forms, and shows evidence of conventional IS signs seen in the 1975 *Gestuno* glossary and WFD and IS sign lists. A small number of other or unknown sign forms also make up some of the lexical signs, which were not identified but suspected to be forms from the presenter's NSL. The 13 source IS presenters agreed to have their presentations filmed for this study, but

TABLE 24. *Distribution of Sign Types in Test Videos A Through E*

Test Video	Lexical	Depiction	PT	Gesture	Ratio of CA	English Mouthing	IS/WFD	GEST	ASL	AUS
A	61%	13%	16%	11%	1:11	42%	5%	11%	56%	18%
B1	64%	8%	10%	15%	1:7	28%	6%	3%	61%	16%
B2	45%	14%	18%	20%	1:7	16%	10%	12%	45%	26%
C	61%	12%	12%	11%	1:10	52%	12%	9%	60%	17%
D	66%	15%	10%	4%	1:8	24%	9%	11%	59%	21%
E	65%	15%	9%	9%	1:11	56%	7%	1%	65%	14%
AVG	**60%**	**13%**	**13%**	**11%**	**1:9**	**36%**	**8%**	**8%**	**58%**	**19%**

they were not contacted about their presentation after data collection was competed; therefore, unknown sign forms were not verified with presenters directly.

Elements of the test stimulus texts are presented here for later analysis in the results discussion. Linguistic features of these texts are of interest, in particular whether these distributions correlate with participant ratings about the texts' comprehensibility. It will also be relevant to the research questions to consider how participants perform on other comprehension measures vis-à-vis some of these linguistic characteristics of the test videos.

SUMMARY

This chapter reported the results from a lexical analysis of the collected expository IS dataset. The distribution of sign types was categorized by lexical, partly lexical, and nonlexical (gestural) token and type qualities. IS presentations incorporate a similar amount of pointing signs; however, there are fewer conventional lexical, specified forms and fewer fingerspelled borrowings in IS than in NSLs. The amount of fully lexical signs in IS is, on average, 10% less than what is noted in similar genre data of NSLs. The fully lexical material in expository IS includes signs recognized from ASL (58%), Auslan (20%), and signs observed in regular use through activities of the WFD (10.7%) as well as signs in use that originally were listed in the *Gestuno* glossary (7.9%). The reduction in lexical signs is offset by an increase in IS signers' use of depicting signs and gesture. Given lesser numbers of fully lexical, conventional forms, it is suspected that an increase in these depicting and gesture sign types serves to supplement semiotic material that composes IS utterances, and helps to convey information in this contact sign system. Comprehension tests are elaborated on in the next chapter, in order to assess whether varied deaf NSL users understand expository IS discourses. Several video presentations and segments from the source IS dataset and a selection of fully lexical and depicting, semiotic elements are put to use in assessing comprehension.

Chapter 5

Assessing IS Comprehension

This chapter reports and discusses results from Study Two, an assessment of comprehension of expository International Sign (IS) by 32 linguistically diverse deaf participants in five different continents. An assessment protocol that uses several measurements was created for this study from a subset of the source IS data analyzed in the first study (Chapter 4). From the 13 IS lectures analyzed in Study One, five short presentation discourses (six presenters) were selected as stimulus testing material. In the next section, I review what the literature offers regarding measuring comprehension of signed language discourse, particularly lecture-type texts, before elaborating on creating and administering the comprehension test elements in this study.

Study Two focuses on the communicative effectiveness of IS lexicon and discourse, and a comparison is made to comprehension of the same content in participants' national signed language. The research augments prior work (Rosenstock, 2004) by contributing new findings about IS comprehension, particularly IS created by deaf presenters.

DISCOURSE AND COMPREHENSION

Throughout this work I refer to IS presentations given by deaf people as discourses comprising mixed linguistic and gestural material, creating an expository type of contact language. Volumes are written about the nature of spoken language discourse (see Schiffrin, 1994; Van Dijk 1985, 2008, 2011), and SLs have also been described by discourse analysis (Metzger & Bahan, 2001; Roy 2000, 2011). Discourse refers to language organization above the sentence level, "utterances" that can be analyzed by their structure as well as their function or use (Schiffrin, 1994). This study considers discourse "as it is actually expressed and understood by people engaged in a social interaction to accomplish a goal" (Roy, 2011, xvi). Discourse "utterances" are chunks or idea units that may or may not be grammatically whole or formed according to what one considers a "sentence" (Chafe, 1980, cited in Roy, 2000). Discourse (and its analysis) "has as a central goal to discover and demonstrate how participants in a conversation make sense of what is going on within the social and cultural context of face-to-face interaction" (Roy, 2011, p. xvi). IS discourse expression and understanding is central to this study:

> Understanding discourse is related to the way people more generally **understand situations** and represent their **experiences** in mental models, typically consisting of a Setting (Time, Place), Participants (and their Identities, Roles and Relations), one or more Events and Actions, as well as the Intentions/Goals and the Knowledge of the participants. [author's emphasis] (van Dijk, 2011, p. 164)

Context informs all language use, as does the knowledge base of participants. Contextual knowledge pertains to properties of the communicative situation and the presence of certain objects (van Dijk, 2008). For IS conference lectures, participants know that there are typically podiums, large presentation screens, a stage or platform, interpreters, and live captioning, and that presenter language use will be more formal in its characteristics. General knowledge comes from world knowledge and conventional ideas about objects or concepts. Therefore, interlocutors bring to the communication setting, from their experience, a set of ideas and knowledge frames as well as expectations for the rules of behavior, turn-taking, and roles.

Discourse comprehension involves the ability to parse pieces of text that are incoming to the listener, and regardless of visual or auditory modality, continuous input is segmented into discrete lexical items (Orifanidou, Adam, Morgan, & McQueen, 2010). Additional types of semiotic material such as gesture, imagery, and contextual clues contribute to the prompting of meaning, as has been discussed by other researchers (Enfield, 2009; Goldwin-Meadow, 2003; Kendon, 1980; McNeill, 1992, 2005). From discourse information a mental representation is built up about concepts, and the organization of propositional ideas and a text base are created in the mind of the perceiver (Kintsch & van Dijk, 1978; van Dijk & Kintsch, 1983).

Effective comprehension may be described best by the interconnectivity between language (symbols), perception, and cognition. Comprehension involves perceiving the real world then conceptualizing these perceptions in a cognitive model of the world. Therefore, the language (or semiotic) input has certain features that are recognized and prompt meanings in cognitive semantic representations, conceptual mappings, and idealized conceptual models (ICMs) (Lakoff, 1987). Idealized conceptual models are structured wholes or gestalts that organize the way we think about a concept. Lakoff (1987, p. 68) points to the idea of a 7-day week as an example of an ICM (which may be different from others who organize their calendars using a different, culturally salient model).

Language enables "one person to have another's experience of the world by proxy"; "the listener constructs a model of the state of affairs based on a speaker's remarks," irrespective of the degree to which an experience accurately represents reality (Johnson-Laird, 1981, p. 139). In the process of comprehending, the listener creates mental models, and judgments of truth come after a mental model is created. Mental models are conceptual models of the world, which provide semantic material in the partial assembly of mental spaces that unfold in a discourse, but they are different from mental spaces (Fauconnier, 1985). Mental spaces are conceptual constructs that are built up in a discourse, prompted by the symbolic expressions being uttered. They are "small conceptual packets constructed as we think and talk, for purposes of local understanding and action" (Fauconnier & Turner, 1996, p. 113). This theory of discourse construal applied to SL meaning-construction was described in the chapter on meaning-making in IS. I apply it in the next section when I describe methods for quantifying the retell task used in the five-part IS comprehension assessment.

Measuring discourse comprehension thus tests how well the communicative intentions of the text—in this case the expository IS text—are aligned with what has been construed by the audience. There are several instruments in education and research that measure comprehension, and these are discussed next.

METHODOLOGICAL CONSIDERATIONS FOR ASSESSING IS COMPREHENSION

A great deal of literature is available on (spoken) language comprehension, typically comprising studies on L1 and L2 learners. These primarily focus on one of two general areas: reading comprehension and listening comprehension. However, there is much less research reported on comprehension of SLs. It naturally follows that there is no available assessment tool to measure comprehension of a contact language such as IS.

Comprehension tests measure whether ideas or propositional information are understood, using instruments designed to assess receptive and expressive language competence and linguistic features of both. Methods employ different discourse situations and use interviews, videotext stimuli, picture interactions, and elicitation tasks to measure comprehension of sign language (SL) discourse. Typically, tested elements include morphological and syntactic structures and lexical knowledge, as well as expressive communicative competencies and formation of grammatically appropriate utterances (according to grammatical description of the target language).

Many of the available studies and instruments for assessing production and comprehension of a native signed language (NSL) are aimed toward monitoring language developmental progression in children, or as educational tools, such as checklists of language features for L1 or L2 sign language learners (Johnston, 2004). Haug (2005) reviews SL assessment instruments used for educational assessment, language acquisition in deaf children, and for linguistic research. There are only a few; all of them differ somewhat in the kinds of linguistic information measured, and they are often designed toward a specific target group. Adaptation of existing SL comprehension tests for other SL testing is problematic (Haug, 2011), as most tests focus on SL expressive ability as opposed to reception and comprehension.

Although many SL assessment tools are used with children, the *Test Battery for ASL Morphology and Syntax* (Maller, Singleton, Supalla, & Wix, 1999) and the Australian version, *Test Battery for Australian Sign Language Morphology and Syntax* (Schembri, Wigglesworth, Johnston, Leigh, Adam, & Baker, 2002) have also been used in linguistic research with adults (Haug, 2005). Except for these latter two, it should be noted that most tests are not publicly available.

Some assessments include a vocabulary recognition section, which has methodological relevance to this current research. Formats such as the British Sign Language (BSL) Receptive Skills Test focus on selected aspects of morphology and syntax of BSL, comprising a picture-naming vocabulary task and a 40-item, video-based receptive skills test. The latter assesses spatial verb morphology, number and distribution, negation, size and shape specifiers (SASS), noun-verb distinction, and handling classifiers (Haug, 2011).

An assessment of lexicon in the form of a receptive vocabulary task is one element in the *Assessment of Sign Language of the Netherlands*

(Jansma, Knoors, & Baker, 1997). The use of picture-naming tasks to elicit lexical data is also utilized in studies of language contact and attrition in immigrants (Waas, 1996; Yoel, 2007). Understanding of IS lexicon has not been tested, and the Rosenstock study identified the need for more research in this area. In the "Methods" section below, the lexical recognition task is described for this research.

A description of "normal" language phenomena in typical usage settings is the foundation on which instruments are devised to measure comprehension and expression of a language. Only a few of the available assessment tests of established SLs are based on normative data and a comprehensive linguistic description of them. However, the very notion of normative data for IS is problematic. "Normal" IS for the purpose of testing is difficult to delineate, but capturing IS from actual usage events and in the form of typical expository IS discourses can offer representative stimulus to measure degrees of understanding, or effective comprehension of diverse audiences.

The question of *effective* IS comprehension prompts a consideration for how communication can be measured in L1 users and L2 learners. The determination of competency in a language—whether for a person's L1 or L2—is measured by educational assessments of language proficiency. Language proficiency assessments provide insight about "effectiveness" and how it could be established for participants' IS comprehension performances in this current study.

There are several available tests of English proficiency, such as the English Language Proficiency Exam (ELPE) and the Test of English as a Foreign Language (TOEFL). Perhaps more relevant to communicating from an international point of view are tests such as the International English Language Testing System (IELTS) and the Test of English for International Communication (TOEIC).[1] These provide quantitative scores for different areas of language such as reading, writing, speaking, and listening, as well as vocabulary and grammar. Typically, organizations define a benchmark level of proficiency for academic or general employment purposes. Tests such as the IELTS and the TOEIC do not

1. Information about these tests: IELTS URL: http://www.ielts.org/ (accessed November 4, 2011); TOEIC URL: https://www.ets.org/toeic (accessed January 17, 2012); ELPE URL: http://www.un.org/depts/OHRM/sds/lcp/English/elpe_resources.html (accessed May 20, 2012); TOEFL URL: http://www.ets.org/toefl?WT.ac=toeflhome_why_121127 (accessed May 20, 2012).

establish a pass or fail score; however, various institutions establish proficiency standards. For example, universities often require a minimum score of 70% on all test areas for undergraduate students, and 80% on all test areas for graduate students. All of these measures are indications of competency, but effective comprehension implies a slightly different evaluation.

Assessing proficient understanding of a contact language must consider the function of the communication. "Effectiveness" can be measured by how well information is communicated and understood given the aims, intent, and consequences of the communication setting. Effectiveness can also be considered from an efficacy framework, whereby effectiveness of some approach is judged by its ability to achieve a target outcome, or one that can be compared to an alternate treatment condition. Rosenstock did not establish criteria around effective IS comprehension but discussed the "very limited" comprehensibility of IS (2004, p. 272). She demonstrated that IS—whether signed directly by a deaf person and interpreted IS—is more understandable to a perceiver than a foreign, established NSL (ASL). In this sense, she established that IS is more efficacious as an alternate universal communication system than provision of information in a *foreign* NSL that is unknown to an interlocutor. The Rosenstock study did not include stimulus text that was rendered in participants' NSL for comparison. Therefore, the information gap between receiving a lecture in one's NSL or a contact language such as IS has not yet been evaluated.

Researchers and authors of standards for efficacy testing distinguish between *efficacy* and *effectiveness*: "*Efficacy* refers to the beneficial effects of a program or policy under optimal conditions of delivery, whereas *effectiveness* refers to effects of a program or policy under more real-world conditions" (Flay et al., 2005, p. 153). A criterion proposes including a statement of efficacy such that "Program or policy X is efficacious for producing Y outcomes for Z population" (p. 154). Standards also require naming an outcome that is reliable, and it is recommended that the construct be measured by multiple sources to increase the robustness of findings. These issues are considered in the design of the current study, which includes several measures to assess understanding of expository IS lectures by different audience groups.

Test format is a factor that influences the performance of varied kinds of test takers with different abilities as well as different linguistic and cultural backgrounds (Zheng, Cheng, & Klinger, 2007). Written language–based assessment tools are inappropriate for assessing verbal measurements with users of signed (unwritten) languages (Pollard, 2002). This is because natural SLs are distinct from the surrounding spoken, written languages of the communities in which they co-exist. The visual-spatial modality of SLs lends them to a composition of three-dimensional, simultaneous constructions with nonlinear organization of grammatical material. (e.g., for ASL, Lawrence, 1994). Written test stimuli are therefore not likely to prompt content information as effectively as visual stimuli in a participant's NSL.

Multiple-choice formats are shown to produce higher scores and in some cases performances are higher than chance (Cheng & Gao, 2002). This is because test takers are tasked with selecting their response as opposed to answering structured content questions and producing their responses (Zheng et al., 2007). Researchers and practitioners prefer the latter format as it can get at dynamic cognitive processes and may represent more systemic validity. When a test taker answers a multiple-choice question (MCQ) about a text in his or her own language, the surface form of the target answer is often familiar and recognizable from the limited answer options. The way that the MCQ is framed may trigger source text information that was stored in episodic memory (Graesser, Ozuru, & Sullins, 2010; Magliano, Millis, Ozuru, & McNamara, 2007). This may or may not accurately point to full understanding but merely to the ability to recognize surface form. On the other hand, open-ended questions are more sensitive to measuring quality in the processing of relevant and accurate ideas from a text at the time of integrating the message than multiple-choice questions; performance on MCQs is related to the amount of prior knowledge of text content (Ozuru, Briner, Kurby, & McNamara, 2013).

Several studies on the comprehension of interpreted sign language relied on MCQs to determine degree of understanding of lecture content (Marschark, Sapere, Convertino, Seewagen, & Maltzen, 2004; Marschark, Sapere, Convertino, & Seewagen, 2005a, 2005b; Marschark, Pelz, Convertino, Sapere, Arndt, & Seewagan, 2005). Marschark, Sapere, Convertino, Seewagen, and Maltzen (2004) created a nine-question multiple-choice questionnaire from a 5-minute video presentation that had been interpreted and transliterated (English-like signing). They used a written evaluation (MCQ) in two tests and a signed MCQ evaluation in the third test. Although there was no difference in comprehension performance between the two groups, deaf students in all three experiments performed 10 to 13 points lower than hearing peers. The fact that participants were tested bimodally—watching a stimulus in SL (presumably their L1) then responding in written English (presumably their L2)—may have had some effect on results.

Rosenstock created a pictorial MCQ test to reduce English literacy bias. She adapted her instrument from a spoken listening comprehension test, creating nonverbal responses to verbal (signed IS, ASL, and Interpreted IS) stimuli. The test was computerized and aimed to reduce bias in literacy differences or non-L1 language skill of her diverse SL using participants. She suggested that other methods be applied in future research on IS comprehension, particularly lexical identifications and quantifiable measures to assess understood discourse content.

Rodriguez Ortiz (2007) also showed the importance of using varied types of assessment in sign language comprehension testing. These may include readability scales, text recall tasks, lexical identification, and free summaries, among others. Some of these assessment types are noted in discussion about comprehension studies on SL lectures in the next section.

Comprehension of a Sign Language Lecture

The literature on comprehension of SL is small, but a handful of studies have assessed deaf students' comprehension of classroom lectures, almost all of which were interpreted texts rather than direct lecture by a NSL signer. In addition, many studies compare deaf students' comprehension with that of hearing colleagues or late-deafened colleagues. Fleischer (1975) found that deaf students understood slightly more from an ASL interpreted lecture (73%) than one that was transliterated (English-like sign order) (67%). Mixed evidence of this difference has been presented by a series of other similar studies as detailed by Rodriguez Ortiz (2007) (Livingston, Signer, & Abramson, 1994; Marschark, Pelz, et al., 2005; Marschark et al., 2004; Marschark et al., 2005a; Murphy & Fleischer, 1977). In all of these studies it was shown that deaf students extract less information from interpreted lectures than hearing colleagues, whether they were viewed live or on video, and that performances are not impacted by demographics, age of exposure to SL, or communication preferences (ASL or English-like signing).

Often it was reported that none of the students scored 100% on comprehension tests, and in fact performance scores are quite low (42% to 73%). This appears to be a common finding across several studies of *interpreted* SL lectures (Murphy & Fleischer, 1977; Rodriguez Ortiz & Mora Roche, 2008), and is even self-reported by students in their own assessments of interpreted lecture comprehension (Napier & Barker, 2004). In another study by Jacobs (1977) deaf participants performed at 69% versus their hearing counterparts' average score of 84%. In these studies, students watched a lecture rendered in SL and were then asked to respond to different types of test questions. Written MCQs were utilized in a majority of these studies (Fleischer, 1975; Jacobs, 1977; Marschark et al., 2004, 2005a).

It is suggested that the use of different methods (other than MCQs) in testing comprehension has benefits, given that one measurement can only provide limited insight into the communicative potential of a SL and its comprehension (Rodriguez Ortiz, 2007). In a study by Rodriguez Ortiz (2007), the researcher used recorded lectures that were translations into LSE. Participants were asked a variety of open-ended questions and several global content questions, in true/false format. Participants were also asked to make a subjective evaluation of their own performance.

Other methods of assessing SL comprehension are discussed in the literature, such as the use of recall tasks in testing. An ASL story recall protocol was one of several tools for measuring verbal ability in deaf persons (Pollard, DeMatteo, Lenz, & Rediess, 2007; Pollard, Rediess, & DeMatteo, 2005). In addition, researchers judged literacy-related behaviors of deaf students who watched ASL videos and were given tasks related to the video stimuli. Methods included story recall, signing, and fingerspelling target vocabulary. These behaviors indicate engagement with a signed ASL educational text and influence comprehension of the text (Golos, 2010).

ASSESSING IS COMPREHENSION

Not much is known about IS comprehension and factors related to its communicative effectiveness. The Rosenstock study is the only one to pursue this question. Comprehension of lexical forms in IS has not yet been studied, nor has the relationship of lexical comprehension on overall IS discourse comprehension performance. How IS comprehension compares to NSL comprehension is also underexamined. Rosenstock showed that participants understood interpreted expository IS better than a foreign, conventional SL (ASL), comparing both in terms of second language comprehension. Although SL users from Western countries appear to understand IS better, it is not known if country of origin alone or other sociolinguistic factors affect this comprehension. Participants performed better on MCQs that targeted depicting verb tokens and fingerspelling (Rosenstock, 2004) but not as well on surrogates and indicating verbs. It is surprising that fingerspelled signs were better understood, because fingerspelling systems vary in many different SLs. This may have been indicative of Rosenstock's participants, all of whom were internationals living in the United States and exposed regularly to the ASL one-handed fingerspelling system. IS utilizes the same one-handed fingerspelling system except for the letter "T." Improved performance on IS (that uses many ASL signs) rather than ASL stimulus, and the relative success with fingerspelled signs for Rosenstock's participants may be a result of interlanguage interference—L1 attrition and L2 sign forms replacing L1 forms (Grosjean, 1989).

Rosenstock noted depicting verbs[2] were understood better than other sign types (79% average not including nonsigners). In the author's discussion about the three questions targeting depicting signs, a connection to the depicting verbs and targeted correct responses was not transparent. It is possible that other semiotic elements contributed to comprehension. Participants' reduced comprehension of surrogates and indicating verbs conflict with intuitions about gestural forms in IS being better understood, because these sign types incorporate gestural elements (enactment and directional movement at referents). Established lexical IS signs and gestural forms have yet to be definitively linked to IS comprehension, although it is proposed that presence of NSL structures—including gesture and depicting components—makes for more easily understood IS (McKee & Napier, 2002). It is unknown what mix of these structures is most effective for different audience members relying on IS and whether "universal access" is possible.

Signs that are shared by several sign languages or are iconic, resembling their referent, are also attributed to successful comprehension of IS discourse (Rosenstock, 2004). Although many of the high-frequency signs identified in the 2004 study are shared across different SLs, these forms were not isolated and shown to comprehension test participants to ascertain their understanding. Thus, very little is known about the way lexicon and depiction influence IS comprehension.

2. Rosenstock does not make a distinction between handling, movement, locating, or entity (SASS) depicting "verbs."

Frequency effects are important to consider when assessing how people recognize and process words (or in this case signs) in discourse. If knowing the most frequent words or signs in a second language aids in that L2 comprehension, then participants' ability to recognize the most common signs in IS text becomes one measure of audience comprehension. However, it is established that L2 listeners may be able to understand and decode all of the words but may not be able to comprehend the main goal or argument of the speaker (Hu, 2009; van Dijk & Kintsch, 1983). For the design of the comprehension assessment in this study, both lexical identifications as well as text content questions are measured in order to capture whether the IS audience understand the signs as well as discourse goal and content.

Study Two Design

From the source IS data collection and lexical frequency and distribution analysis, selections were chosen to create the Study Two comprehension assessment protocol. Lecture segments, highly frequent fully lexical signs, and depicting segments identified from the first study were used in the testing. The test protocol was administered in five geographically diverse test locations: the Czech Republic, Brazil, Japan, Australia, and the United States.

It was suggested from studies on SL comprehension (Rodriguez Ortiz et al., 2008) that different methods for testing comprehension allow a broader view of the way participants understand a discourse. Varied measurements were chosen in order to get a richer understanding about IS comprehension based on diversified methods for eliciting data, and to meet the needs of varied kinds of test takers with different abilities as well as linguistic and cultural backgrounds (Zheng et al., 2007). The Rosenstock study of IS comprehension recommended additional types of measures in future investigations other than multiple-choice questions.

Measuring Comprehension

In this study, five methods measure IS comprehension—four quantitative and one qualitative. Several of these assessment types were used in prior studies to assess SL discourse comprehension (Marschark et al., 2005; Pollard et al., 2007; Rodriguez Ortiz & Mora Roche, 2008). Self-assessment about comprehension (Napier & Barker, 2004) also is a noted method for comparison against other comprehension measures. The four quantitative scores result from the following testing tasks: (1) subjective comprehension ratings of video clips, (2) correct meaning identification of high-frequency lexical signs in the data, (3) answers to content questions about a viewed IS lecture passage in a structured interview format, and (4) quantifiable discourse idea information conveyed in a retell task. In addition, qualitative information about IS comprehension was gathered by using nine short depicting sign (DS) clusters. These were complex utterances and specific depicting signs taken from the lecture context; participants' responses to them were collected and analyzed. It enabled me to qualitatively assess whether lecture information was partially or more richly understood from metaphor and space blends evident in depicting signs and in the DS clusters overall.

The Rosenstock study primarily used a computerized multiple-choice test using pictorial, nonverbal question prompts. She determined a score for participants' comprehension of a 1-minute IS segment they had viewed immediately before. For this current study, a multiple-choice question format was not used, and other suggestions from the 2004 study were chosen instead. This decision was also informed by reported benefits in the use of recall tasks (Rodriguez Ortiz, 2008), vocabulary identifications (Haug, 2011), and open-ended content questions (Ozuru et al., 2013) in SL comprehension testing.

Comprehension of IS discourse passages is determined by several measures that required participants to recognize lexical signs from presentations they viewed, and to reproduce realized content. Participants were asked direct content questions about the stimulus video information in a structured interview procedure and for one video, they were given a retell task. The assessment also included one measure to elicit general, subjective understandability ratings about each video segment.

Participants were asked broad and specific questions about larger texts in order to determine global understanding, main points, and details understood from the IS lecture passages. They were also tasked to recognize lexical signs from the text viewed, as well as numbers and fingerspelled words. At the same time, the limits of working memory are considered in determining utterance length for the retell task. Constraints in working memory are known to impact higher cognitive tasks such as comprehension, learning, and reasoning (Baddeley, 1986). The retelling task is outlined in the next section along with the other test sections.

For lexical identifications and content questions, a threshold of successful comprehension was established at a minimum score of 75% each and combined. The benchmark was established based on the fact that many tests of language proficiency and/or comprehension identify a threshold of "competence" to be roughly between 75% and 80% or better (TOEFL, ELPE, and TOEIC).

Participants' performances on lexical identifications, content questions, and the retell task are measured by rubrics that are created from a content analysis of the textual information in each of the stimulus IS video clips shown. "Correct" responses about the meaning of frequent IS lexicon and textual content were quantified, allowing for comprehension scores for each participant to be determined. Finally, a qualitative analysis of participants' understanding of short depicting sign clusters was made.

Collaboration with Cultural Liaisons and Interpreters/Translators

In each of the five countries from where participants were recruited, comprehension tests were administered in the community with assistance from a local cultural liaison and/or qualified interpreter. At least one interpreter, and in some cases a cultural liaison, was present to assist with the administration of comprehension tests.

Working with interpreters to aid in cross-cultural research projects is not a new concept, given the need to elicit accurate data and ensure that the meanings of questions are understood by participants (Harkness, Pennell, & Schoua-Glusberg, 2004). It is important to develop research partnerships between investigators both within and outside the sociocultural situation under investigation to help guard against researcher bias (Davis, 1995; p. 437). To obtain valid and reliable data, it is important that quantitative measures use a culturally appropriate instrument (Brislin, 1970). Reliance on skilled translation in cross-cultural research is a methodological issue and procedures used for interpreting quantitative instruments in cross-cultural research can be complex, but appropriately utilized translation can reduce the impact of cross-linguistic misunderstandings and avoid inaccurate conclusions (Willgerodt, Kataoka-Yahiro, Kim, & Ceria, 2005). The local interpreters and liaisons served as cultural "insiders" to ensure that culturally sensitive approaches are used when including participants who do not share the researcher's culture and language.

Local SL interpreters were relied upon in order to provide a translation of IS video clips into the local NSL and be available during testing. Translation of lecture video was done using an adapted translation approach proposed by Brislin (1970, 1980). This included development of an idiom-free English version of the IS videos D and E, which corresponds to short utterance segments in the source IS videos. The interpreter created a local NSL translation of the retell stimulus videos, and a backtranslation was used to review the content and semantic equivalence of the translation. Videos D and D′ were both used for the retell task. For the translated video D′, the local interpreter was relied upon for verification of participants' responses after being trained in use of the retell rubric.

Assessment Elements

IS comprehension was assessed by five different test elements (four quantitative and one qualitative) as noted earlier. A summary of two test sequences is shown in Table 25. Participants were randomly assigned one sequence or the other. The tasks are coded in the table by the following numbers: (1) a quantitative Likert-type judgment scale used to rate comprehension of each IS videotext, (2) direct content questioning via a structured interview procedure, (3) a lexical semantic identification task that was quantitatively scored, (4) elicitation and quantitative analysis of a propositional retell task, and (5) qualitative analysis of meanings understood from reviewing short segments of depicting signs in the texts.

TABLE 25. *Comprehension Test Sequences 1 and 2*

Test Sequence #1	Tasks	Test Sequence #2	Tasks
Video A	1,2,3,5	Video A	1,2,3,5
Video B1	1,2	Video B1	1,2
Video B2	1,2,3,5	Video B2	1,2,3,5
Video C	1,2,3,5	Video C	1,2,3,5
Video D	4,1,2,3,5	Video E	1,2,3,5
Video *E'*	1,2,3,5	Video *D'*	4,1,2,3,5

Note. Comprehension Tasks Key: (1) rating about video understanding, (2) content questions, (3) lexical identification, (4) text recall/retell task, and (5) meaning identification of depicting sequences.

Five short presentation video clips were shown to each participant—four IS lectures and one locally translated lecture—each with subsequent queries to ascertain aspects of comprehension of the video just watched. For example, participants first viewed video A, then made a judgment about how well they understood it and then answered a series of questions about the content. Next, they were shown several high-frequency signs that occurred in the video and asked to identify their meaning, and last they were shown two to four short depicting sequences from the video and asked to explain what they meant given the context. Comprehension tasks for videos A, B, C, and E were the same—view the signer's full segment, rate one's comprehension of it, answer content questions, and identify lexical signs and short depicting segments. The task for video D was different. Rather than watch the entire segment, the text was paused intermittently to allow participants to give a retell of the content. Then the other four comprehension tasks were given as they were with the other videotexts.

The test was designed with two different sequences, both starting with videos A, B, and C, but with slightly different sequencing of videos D and E. Participants from each country test site were randomly assigned one or the other. The design allowed for half of the participants to be tested on the original IS version of video D or E or the local NSL version of them (D′ or E′). The aim was to also see if there are potential differences in comprehension of IS versus the same content in a NSL. One of the inquiries of this study is, "How does comprehension of IS compare to comprehension of NSLs?" The first method for answering this comes from participants' subjective judgments about how well or not they understood each videotext and signer they viewed. In each test sequence (#1 or #2), participants view four IS videos and one video in their NSL, and thus a comparison can be made. A second measurement to address this inquiry comes from the retell task, which assesses the amount of discourse conveyed between participants who see the IS version D or their local NSL version D′.

The amount of discourse information conveyed in the retell was quantified by a content analysis and from this, a rubric was created to measure discourse content retold. The rubric for this measurement is seen in Appendix C. The total idea unit information conveyed for those who saw the IS text was compared to what was conveyed by those who viewed the local SL version.

TABLE 26. *Comprehension Test Video Segment Information*

Test Video Clip	Segment Time	Topic
A	0:00–5:21	Health issues for Deaf people
B1	0:00–4:03	Plenary on Developing countries; Part 1
B2	4:03–5:33, 7:29–8:38	Plenary on Developing countries; Part 2
C	0:00–3:56	WFD Election speech
D	2:55–3:50, 4:55–5:45, 6:40–7:35, 29:32–30:13, 30:44–31:14, 31:35–31:50, 32:11–32:41	Japanese Federation of the Deaf collaborative work
E	0:0–4:39, 5:54–6:37	Boy Scouts International
D′	5:00 mins	JFD collaborative work (local SL version)
E′	6:30 mins	Boy Scouts International (local SL version)

Information about each presentation video segment is indicated in Table 26. Note that video D included two presenters, alternating between IS and JSL. The IS segments from the original were edited and spliced together as a continuous text, with pauses for retelling. The same was done for the JSL version of video, which served as the local NSL version for the Japanese test site.

Rationale for Selections

These test videos were chosen based on several considerations: text length, familiarity with lecture topic, and diversity of IS presenter. Signer pace and video quality were additional considerations. First, it was important to show one or two cohesive, complete discourses rather than short 1-minute clips (as was done in the Rosenstock study). The size of the chunk used for testing stimuli was an important consideration. From the 13 presentations in the full dataset (see Study One), only two IS source videos were complete presentations with an opening, a body, and a closing. Videos A and C met this criteria, and they capture two different deaf presenters with many years of experience using IS to large groups of linguistically and culturally diverse audiences. One is from Northern Europe and the other is from North America. The other texts fulfilled other criteria sought for the IS stimuli: inclusion of broadly familiar topics and diversity of presenter native language and country of origin.

When deciding on the length of the segment of text to show participants, care needed to be taken that enough input could allow a participant to watch and construct the meaning of the text. Context, as explained in Chapter 3 ("Meaning Making in International Sign"), is essential for meaning, both in its creation and interpretation. The decision was therefore made to show participants full passages of IS text and then give them tasks to measure different levels of comprehension.

Video clip selections were also based on the potential for varied deaf people to be familiar with the topic or interested in the presentation subject. Background knowledge or prior experience with content of a text has been shown to aid in listening comprehension (Long, 1990). Comprehension is aided by observers' familiarity with the topic, as they bring knowledge and experience to decoding a text (van den Broek & Kremer, 2000). In addition, interest in the topic of an expository text also aids comprehension, and receivers of the text process it for deeper meaning than those without initial interest in the subject (Schiefele, 1996). Interest in the discourse topic also is shown to increase recall of text information (Ramsay & Sperling, 2010).

Video B is a lecture segment about a topic familiar and important to many deaf people and Deaf education. The clip was taken from the first part of a shared presentation given by two co-presenters. It is separated into two consecutive sections, B1 and B2, because each captured two different signers, one of whom is from West Africa and the other from Canada. Video segment B1 and video D met the goal of including diverse IS presenters whose language and country origins are not solely European or American.

Video D is the beginning and middle excerpt of a presentation given by two Japanese co-presenters, one using JSL and the other using IS, presenting the same information in consecutive fashion. Only the IS portion is captured for video D; however, the JSL version was also used as the local NSL version when it is shown to participants in Japan. The other four lecture texts were shown in full, with comprehension tasks given after each, but use of this text is different. Video D was chosen for propositional retell task at all test sites. Half of the participants at each site are shown the original IS video, while others are shown a version in their local SL. The original IS text of this presentation is used for the comprehension test at all test sites but translated into the local SL in the other four test sites. In the Japanese test site, the JSL segment was reviewed for equivalence by the local interpreter and shown as the local SL version, instead of having the IS text translated into JSL.

The fifth selection, video E, was included due to topic familiarity and its clear video quality and the slow, even signing pace of the presenter. Also, the presentation topic was expected to be somewhat familiar to deaf people in different countries due to the international presence of organized Boy and Girl Scout activities in many continents. Video E is the beginning segment of a presentation by a signer from Western Europe. The selection was chosen for the topic (Boy Scouts International), as well as to assess comprehension about the numeric and fingerspelled details given in the text about different scout age groups and names. Like video D, this text was translated and shown to half of the participants in each country test site to determine how much detailed information is gleaned from IS versus the same information in one's NSL.

The aim was to create a mixed testing protocol, recognizing the need to balance several factors. It was important to include IS presenters from diverse backgrounds yet limit the time of the testing tasks to reduce potential for fatigue that could arise. Eliciting responses to the content from different measures after participants viewed videos A, B, C, D, and E served to capture various aspects of comprehension. Furthermore, by presenting different content topics in different selections, the intent was to offer enough diversity of topic with which all participants, regardless of country of test site, might have some prior experiential awareness and/or interest.

Test Element 1: Comprehensibility Ratings

The initial measurement of comprehension was a subjective understandability rating, asked of participants immediately after viewing each short IS presentation text. Judgments were made about the overall comprehensibility of each video clip text using a nonverbal, pictorial rating scale. The numerical scale indicates values between 1 and 5, with 1 being difficult to understand and 5 being very easy to understand. Each of these

FIGURE 46. *Subjective Comprehension Rating Scale.*

icons was further explained at the start of the test so that participants knew the scale and their options for making a judgment. An icon corresponding with each numeric value allowed participants to circle their subjective rating of the preceding IS text they viewed. Figure 46 shows the pictorial rating scale.

Test Element 2: Structured Questions Interview

The second measurement of comprehension is determined by answers to content questions asked after the participant viewed each IS text. Some of the questions were meant to elicit information about inferences and interpretations participants made regarding the goal of the signer, the composition and size of the audience, as well as the type of presentation. Other information was sought about what was understood about the main points as well as details in the text. An overall score was calculated for participants' responses, as well as a breakdown of what kind of information was understood from the IS videotexts viewed. Thirty questions measured the conveyance of several kinds of information from the lectures: discourse pragmatics and goal, main points, and details. The full list of questions and their types are noted in Appendix C within the rubric created to score this part of the comprehension assessment.

Content questions about what was viewed were interpreted into participants' NSL, which would not likely resemble the IS lecture surface form. Discussed in methodological considerations above, open-ended questions require the participant to generate meaningful and accurate ideas from the input text (Ozuru et al., 2013). Therefore, participants must actively recollect information from the source text that would show they were able to comprehend and integrate the material via memory and a conceptual mental representation of what they perceived the IS text meant. By providing the opportunity to respond to content questions in their NSL, it aimed to elicit a more realistic measurement of the amount and the specific text information that had been retrieved and understood.

Pragmatics is related to how people use language in different contexts. The questions, "What type of presentation is this?" "Who do you think the audience is, and where might this lecture be taking place?" and "Tell me about the audience you think s/he is talking to?" were asked to ascertain what the participant thought regarding the size and makeup of the audience.

Questions about the goal of the discourse in videos A, B, and C were asked to ascertain whether or not participants understood the purpose and overarching goal of the presenters. Examples were "Why is he giving this lecture?" and "What is she talking about and why?" Anticipated target answers were broad, such as "To give background on a project and introduce the main speaker," or "To inspire the audience and/or to get elected," and "To describe the educational situation for deaf people in developing countries." It was also predicted that participants might give ideas about general points made by the speaker, almost in a summary style, which would match target answers to the subsequent questions about main points.

Questions about speakers' main points and details conveyed in the IS presentations were asked in all five clips. Main point questions sought key points conveyed in the IS presentation about comparisons being made, problems the signer describes, and causal relationships. "What did the presenter and that other person do together?" "What are the two presenters comparing?" and "What are some of the education problems in her country?" are examples of questions that targeted main points conveyed in the video. Detailed questions sought names, places, numbers, and specific, listed examples given in the IS lectures. Example questions about details were, "Who is the person to the left of the speaker?" "How many Deaf people attended the 1991 World Federation of the Deaf (WFD) conference?" "Name four activities that Boy Scouts participate in" and "What are the five different age groups in the Boy Scouts called?"

Immediately after responding to questions about the IS lecture segment just viewed, participants were then shown individual high-frequency IS signs that had occurred in the text. The next section elaborates on the lexical identification task.

Test Element 3: Lexical Identifications

In this second measure of comprehension, a series of IS signs appearing in the lecture text just viewed, are subsequently shown to participants in order to ascertain their understanding.

Forty-five (45) high-frequency fully lexical signs were identified in the first study (Table 23). Six to thirteen signs were shown to the participants *twice* consecutively before they were then asked to give an answer about the IS sign meaning. Sign meaning was documented on the scoring sheet. A tally of all correctly identified lexical signs, fingerspelled words, and numbers was made and each participant was given a score for lexical identifications, numbers, and fingerspelled words.

Test Element 4: Video D Retell Task

A retell task of Video D evaluated comprehension by asking participants to restate discourse information from an IS presentation. This measure assessed the understanding of discourse idea units from an IS presentation text or from a NSL version of the same presentation information. An IS presentation ("JFD Collaborations"—Video D) to participants in each country cohort. Half of them were asked to retell from the original IS text (Video D), and the other half from a translation of the same IS lecture into the local NSL (Video D′).

The stimulus videos D and D′ were shown in short a series of consecutive, 10- to 20-second segments with pauses that allowed participants to retell immediately after seeing each segment. Pauses were inserted at intuitive prosodic boundaries of the IS utterances, typically cued by phrase-final lengthening of sign hold, blinks, or head nods. Varied SLs exhibit phrase final cues via these types of articulations (Fenlon, Denmark, Campbell, & Woll, 2007; Wilbur, 1994). Furthermore, short utterances can be segmented, each contributing to the build-up of discourse. A text base is built up over the course of the retelling task, and at the end of the retell, using the comprehensibility rating scale, participants could make a judgment about comprehension.

Size of chunk selected for the recall task is informed by prior studies on working memory for spoken lecture listening. The very few studies on sign language working memory to date often use sign item recall lists rather than immediate retell or summaries (Wang & Napier, 2013). While listening to lectures, attendees simultaneously or in overlapping manner activate a knowledge base, and then, through recognition and analysis of utterances, interpret possible pragmatic meaning and store an organized mental representation in long-term memory (Rost, 1994). The number of propositions in a sentence also influences retention for readers (Kintsch & Keenan, 1973). It has been shown that two to four propositions are optimal for integrating new information into working memory and making coherent the immediate text information (Rickheit, Schnotz, & Strohner, 1985). Deaf native signers' ASL working memory capacity is similar to native English speakers' English working memory capacity (Boutla, Supalla, Newport, & Bavelier, 2004). Keeping in mind these facts of working memory that would impact the participants' retell task, segments were paused after between 30 and 80 seconds and comprised between two and six ideas contributing to the discourse construction.

A content analysis of IS video D resulted in the identification of 58 idea units for the scoring rubric (excerpt shown in Figure 47). This was verified by a second researcher who works regularly with IS, and had been present during the live presentation. When the NSL translated version (D′) did not equivalently align with all 58 propositions in the source text, the rubric was adjusted. It was also expected that a participant would not obtain a perfect score retelling all of the propositional idea information from the source video, due to test fatigue and potential working memory differences in participants. Of interest in this assessment is the difference in the average amount of content retold between those who viewed the IS lecture and those who retold from the same content in their NSL.

Video segment	Idea Units	1 point each	Participant #
1a	Before we start, want to share something	1	
1b	There was an earthquake in Japan	1	
1c	It happened March 2011	1	
1d	It caused a large tsunami	1	
1e	The damage was terrible	1	
1f	A nuclear accident and power outtage occurred.	1	
2a	The world Deaf communities (you) sent messages	1	
2b	Asked if we were ok	1	
2c	Money and donations were sent	1	
2d	We want to thank you for your generosity.	1	
2e	This supports the work of the JFD	1	
3a	The JFD is working hard to help Deaf people affected	1	
3b	We are making repairs	1	
3c	Please continue to send donations.	1	
4a	The JFD started in 1947	1	
4b	Since then we work towards 4 aims	1	
5a	One is interpreter training	1	
5b	The second is obtaining legal/human rights for deaf people	1	
5c	Thirdly attainment of Drivers licenses for Deaf persons	1	
5d	Fourth, establishing more deaf (community service) organizations	1	
6a	Soon Japanese government will pass a law recognizing JSL as a language	1	
6b	We are both very excited about this.	1	

FIGURE 47. *Excerpt of Video D retell rubric.*

Contextual information was given about the presentation at the start of the retell task. It was important to ensure the text could be situated in a context for the observer, to enable each successive clip (if understood) to construct a large enough chunk of discourse to generate mental representation of ideas that could be realized.

Test Element 5: Depicting Sign Clusters

The fifth assessment in the comprehension test results in qualitative information about what participants understood by short utterances that appeared within the video clip just viewed. The utterance units from the stimulus video use at least one depicting sign and another SL sign type. The purpose of including depicting sign segments in the stimulus material for IS comprehension testing is to determine the extent of meaning-creation in short utterances that combine common sign language elements in real space blends. These depicting segments are composite utterances because they employ at least one depicting sign and other types of semiotic signs.

The inventive power of depiction as constituents within complex utterances is a potentially rich area of inquiry in this international contact signing system. The DS clusters that were selected for this level of analysis provide main point information in the text in which it appears. Participants were shown a few of these short sequences after each video, and nine were selected for analysis and are reported in the results.

Demographic Questionnaire

Demographic information was collected by administration of a short questionnaire to all participants. Data of interest included their country of origin, education, first SL, whether raised by deaf or hearing parents, frequency of IS use, knowledge of ASL, knowledge of English, as well as questions about SLs with which they were familiar and their travel experience and contact with foreign deaf people. These data were elicited so that certain sociolinguistic characteristics of participants could be analyzed against comprehension measures.

Study Two Participants

Participants were recruited for this second study with the assistance of a local cultural liaison or interpreter. Initial contact was made with potential liaisons during the international conference where expository IS was collected for the first study. A follow-up letter was emailed to several interested contacts in eight different countries. Due to funding and time constraints and response rates from potential local liaisons, I was unable to enlist a liaison or participants from an African or a Middle Eastern community as hoped. The five test sites eventually chosen were in diverse geographic regions, each with unrelated sign language origins. Northern Asia, South America, Central Europe, and from two regions where the NSL may share some signs with IS—North America and Australia.

The criteria for participants were clearly outlined, with the aim of recruiting deaf people between the ages of 18 and 65, preferably who had begun learning sign language before the age of 6, and had completed a minimum of a 12-year, high school education. The aim was to locate deaf participants who had been using their NSL since childhood. Soliciting for participants with an early exposure to language aimed to control for potential deficits in cognitive development that might impact performance on language processing, such as lexical identification (Emmorey & Corina, 1990). Deaf individuals who are exposed to language earlier in life perform better than those with delayed exposure on sign language processing and knowledge tests (Morford & Mayberry, 2000), recall tests, and comprehension of shadowed sign language material (Mayberry, 1993). By including participants with a solid first language foundation, it is assumed that this would potentially maximize their cognitive skills and better position them to recognize and understand aspects of a mix SL system presented in the comprehension test video clips.

Five different country locations were selected for participant recruitment. A total of 32 deaf participants were recruited, six to eight from each country. Their first sign languages are JSL, LIBRAS, Auslan, CZSL, and ASL. Some participants reported their first written or spoken language (speech and lip-reading) to be their national spoken language—Japanese, Portuguese, (Australian) English, (American) English, and Czech. A few also reported second or third language familiarity with English, or other SLs. Seventeen (17) of the 32 were monolingual SL users, and 15 had varying knowledge of two to five other SLs.

Demographic information was collected to ascertain factors that correlate with comprehension of IS information. Data of interest for analysis include country of origin, first SL, whether raised by deaf parents,

TABLE 27. *Study Two Participant Demographics*

Demographics	Men	Women
Participants (n = 32)	11	21
Age (mean and std. dev.)	43 (±15 years)	34 (±9.8 years)
Age acquisition 1st SL (mean)	3 (±4 years)	4.6 (±6 years)
Deaf parents	5	6
Monolingual SL user	6	11
Bilingual SL user	5	10
Education:		
High school diploma	5	5
Some university	3	7
University degree	3	9
Travel experience:		
None	2	4
1–5 countries	6	8
6–14 countries	2	7
>15 countries	1	2
Use of IS		
Never	1	3
Rare	5	6
Sometimes	3	7
Regular	2	5

frequency of IS use, knowledge of ASL, knowledge of English, and amount of travel experience and contact with foreign deaf people. Table 27 summarizes demographic groupings of the participants in this study.

Out of the 32 total participants, there were 21 women and 11 men of varied age groups. Eight were between 19 and 29 years of age, 13 were between 30 and 39, five were between ages 40 and 49, three people were in their 50s, and three were between 60 and 65 years of age.

All participants met the minimum educational criteria: 10 were high school graduates, 10 had completed some college or higher education, and 12 had completed a university degree or higher qualification. Eleven participants had been raised by one or both deaf parents and the majority (21) were raised by hearing parents. Twenty-eight had begun learning their native SL before the age of 6 years old at home or in preschool, and the remaining four had some exposure to their NSL by peers in first and second grade, although not in the classroom.

The range of participants' travel experience and contact with other deaf foreigners was highly varied but balanced across all participants. Six (6) had no foreign travel experience, 14 people had traveled to up to five different countries where they met foreign deaf people, 9 participants had been to 6 to 14 countries, and 3 had travel experience in more than 15 countries, one of whom had traveled and met deaf people in more than 30 different countries.

Another important variable of interest is how often participants had used some form of international sign contact. In each country cohort group, there were varied degrees of exposure and experience using IS to communicate. Four (4) people had never seen or used IS before, 11 people stated rare usage—less than one to two times per year, 10 reported using it sometimes (every few months), 5 participants reported use of IS often (one to five times per month), and 2 stated they use IS one to three times per week.

The profile of participants in the study is a sociological mix, which is a fairly representative picture about the variation one finds in deaf community members who would come into contact with each other and rely on expository IS via conference attendance or online information.

Comprehension Data Collection and Analysis

Each participant was scheduled for 2 hours of individual testing, at a location that was accessible from his or her home. All testing sessions were conducted in a quiet room, free from distractions. The participant sat at a table facing a computer laptop with the video stimulus clips queued, and the researcher sat at a 90-degree angle to the participant. A qualified interpreter and assistant were seated near the researcher, within the sight line of the participant. The interpreters were encouraged to use sufficient processing time before rendering the target interpretation, and often the interpreting was done consecutively. It is shown that more processing time between receiving a source message and rendering a target increases the accuracy of the target message. Interpreters who use more processing time make fewer errors and omissions (Cokely, 1992a).

Before the start of the assessment, an orientation to the study was provided and consent and demographic information were collected through the local interpreter. In some cases, consent and initial paperwork were completed directly by the local cultural liaison, who was trained and collaborated with the researcher. Participants were encouraged to ask questions before signing the consent and before the start of the assessment.

The sessions were video and audio recorded with a high-definition video camera situated to capture the participant's signed responses to the researcher's questions, as well as to record the interpreter's translations of responses. This ensured that interpreted responses could be reviewed during data coding, scoring, and analysis.

After receiving instructions about the assessment and signing consent, participants were given some contextual information about the videos they would be viewing. To adjust for the fact that participants were not viewing the presentation in its original setting, some basic contextual information was given to aid their schema building.

Audiences at international conferences where expository IS is used often have access to a conference handbook written in English. These materials include presentation titles, a short description, or perhaps information about an overarching theme in a series of presentations. Often, conference program books note the names and biographies of the presenters, and include anywhere from a limited or more detailed description of the actual presentations and their goal. Audience members can usually determine the formality of the presentation and the goal of a speaker, as well as the main points and details, soon after a presentation begins. Pragmatic discourse cues prompt meaning, and the observer is expected to make inferences and coherent sense of the presentation setting, goals, and addressed audience.

Participants in this study were given the information that was available on site where the presentations took place. This was taken from the conference program book, which was printed in English and included the title of the presentation; no other information was available in the conference program book about the lecture. Participants were told that they would be viewing an IS presentation lecture by a deaf person on a given theme, and prior to viewing each video segment they were told the title of the presentation, which suggested the general topic. This information was interpreted through the sign language interpreter. The title of each presentation was also shown in English at the start of each of the five video clips used.

Participants were randomly placed in either test sequence 1 or 2 (see Table 25). After viewing each video clip, participants made an initial judgment rating about ease of understanding. Then several structured questions about content were asked. Next, a selection of high-frequency IS signs taken from the text just watched were shown. Participants gave the meaning of each sign if they knew it (using their own SL); if not, they were asked to guess the meaning. Finally, short depicting segments from the text were shown, and participants were asked to describe what they believed the short utterances meant or referred to in the text.

For test sequence 1, participants viewed IS video D in short segments with pauses for participants to retell (in their own SL) the content and work through the whole text. At the end of this retell task, the same assessments were given: make a comprehensibility judgment, answer three content questions, make nine lexical identifications, and identify four depiction cluster meanings. Finally, they viewed video E′ (duration 6:00), which was in their NSL, and made comprehensibility judgments, answered seven content questions, watched and identified five lexical signs from the original IS text, and viewed two depicting clusters and identified their meaning.

For test sequence 2, participants viewed IS video E and made comprehensibility judgments, answered seven content questions, watched and identified five lexical signs from the original IS text, and viewed two depicting clusters and identified their meaning. Finally, they viewed local SL video D′ (duration 5:00), which was in their NSL. They were shown the text in short segments with pauses to retell the content and work through the whole text. At the end of the retell task, the usual assessments were given: comprehensibility judgment, three content questions, nine lexical identifications, and four depiction cluster meaning identifications.

SCORING AND RUBRICS

The participants' comprehension judgments of each lecture text yielded a numeric value (1 to 5). For the lexical identifications, a score sheet was used to mark whether the participant correctly identified the sign's meaning (see Appendix B). The score sheet was based on the lexical frequency analysis in chapter 4, which identified conventional meanings of the 45 highly occurring signs. Participants were given one point for each response that matched any of the meanings associated with the sign. If the response was a semantic equivalent, they were scored a point. Depending on which test sequence the person viewed, the score for lexical identifications was adjusted, to account for four IS lexical items that were not seen by half of the participants. Only the sign forms occurring in the viewed IS clips were included in the final calculations of this comprehension measurement.

A rubric (see Appendix C) was created to quantify responses to content questions, and the researcher used it to give points for correct answers. The interpreters assisting in each test site were consulted during a review of their video recorded interpretations of participant responses to content questions. This allowed for verification of responses before determining a final score on questions. As long as participants responded with the elements of the expected answers noted in the answer key in the rubric, they were given full or partial points. For example, after IS presentation video A, one detailed question asks, "Who is the person to the presenter's left side (to whom does he point while signing)?" The answer (worth two points) is the person's name, and one or both replies, "a colleague" or "a doctor." The fingerspelled name of the person was difficult to decipher for those who do not use a one-handed fingerspelling system, and it included the abbreviated honorific letters, D-R. It was also difficult for those who do use a one-handed fingerspelling system because it was articulated very quickly. If the participant replied with, "a research partner" or "his colleague," then one point was granted. If they replied that the person was also a doctor, and a colleague or work partner, then the full two points were scored for that question. As participants gave their responses, the researcher asked questions in a semistructured way, rephrased if needed, and, with the help of the interpreter and research assistant, made a determination about whether or not the question was answered satisfactorily. All participants were given one chance to elaborate on their reply if their initial response was vague or insufficient. A follow-up question was asked to allow the researcher and interpreter to reframe the question in a way that would elicit a response to determine whether or not the target information was understood.

Video D Retell Task Scoring and Analysis

The analysis of the retelling task for video D or D′ (depending on which test the participant was assigned) required the completion of a content analysis of this expository IS presentation segment. The researcher is an interpreter who works from and into IS and rendered a text content analysis, which resulted in a sequence of 58 propositional idea units built up during the 6 minutes of the presentation clip. Also, a second experienced practitioner of expository IS, who rendered the live interpretation of video D, was asked to review and check the resulting main idea units identified from video D. The idea units were used to measure text retell information. The resulting idea unit list was used as a scoring rubric to score the amount of information retold in a recall task (see Appendix D: Main Idea Unit Scoring Sheet for Video D/D′). The content of the English version of IS videos D and E was also checked by an experienced, skilled IS interpreter to verify that the English version captured information in the IS lectures.

Participants were shown one of two versions of the presentation in video D—the original IS or a translation into participants' native SLs. After each local SL version of video D (named D′) was created, the cultural liaison and/or the interpreter in each test site reviewed the propositional scoring sheet and assessed it to be sure that the translated version contained the same propositional information as the original. Any discrepancies were either corrected before administering the retell task, or if realized afterward, adjustments in scoring were made to reflect the correct expected number of propositional idea units. For example, in one of the local NSL translations, it was recognized that only 54 of the 58 idea units were clearly rendered in video D′. Therefore, participants retelling performances in that cohort group were measured against an expected 54 propositions rather than 58.

After the testing was complete, the researcher collaborated with the local interpreter liaisons to review participants' test data and their own interpretations of participant responses, which had been captured on video. Interpreter liaisons were trained in the aims of the retell and the use of the rubric during this collaborative process. This was to ensure the researcher appropriately scored whether or not the participant had retold the idea unit in each line of the rubric. Shortly thereafter, the local interpreters were asked to independently score participants' retelling of video D or D′ (depending on which test the participant had been assigned).

Analyses

Several types of data were collected in this study, and some qualitative data are quantified by use of inferential text analysis, such as the video D content analysis and content questions. "Content analysis is a research technique for making replicable and valid inferences from texts (or other meaningful matter) to the contexts of their use" (Krippendorf, 2004, p. 18). Assessing an IS text for idea units involved a degree of interpretive analysis, which is unavoidably influenced by researcher subjectivity (Croker, 2009).

In Study Two, varied methods of comprehension testing lend the data to qualitative and quantitative analysis. Quantitative Likert scale information from participants' text comprehensibility judgments was calculated, and a comparison of numeric mean ratings is reported in the results; however, responses to the lexical identifications, the content questions interview, and the text retell task resulted from transforming qualitative information into quantifiable performance scores. Rubrics were created for these quantitative data analyses and applied to scoring participants' comprehension results. Participant responses to seven depicting sign segments—composite utterances taken from the test videos—are presented in a qualitative discussion about composite elements that create meaning and the role of depicting signs in IS.

The collection of varied types of data provides different perspectives on the researched phenomenon. Test scores on lexical identifications and content questions, as well as quantitative information from retell performances, are discussed in comparison with qualitative information collected from depicting segment questioning. These results are compared with performance scores as part of the discussion of the findings in Chapter 7.

Linguistic and sociolinguistic factors for the comprehension of expository IS presentations are of interest, so quantitative results from both studies are assessed by several types of analyses between factors and/or measures. A correlation analysis using Pearson's product-moment correlation coefficient allows one to determine the strength and direction (positive or negative) of the linear relationship between variables, and offers a simple starting point for assessing complex relationships between variables (Kraska-Miller, 2014). A Pearson's r is used initially to correlate participants' scores on the lexical identifications and performance on the content questions and retell task (Table 28). This tests the hypothesis that knowledge of high-frequency lexical items in IS correlates with improved comprehension performance. In order to see if the mean comprehension scores of different groups is significantly different, one can run several t-tests between groups (such as scores of participants who viewed specific users of ASL). This tells something about the data, but when there are several factors to be considered, running an analysis of variance (ANOVA) or regression is the better option to avoid a type 1 error (Alreck & Settle, 1995). ANOVA was applied to determine if there are any main effects that certain linguistic factors and sociolinguistic factors have on performance measures. Regression modeling and analysis

TABLE 28. *Performance Variables*

Independent variables performance scores	Dependent variables (significance at $p \leq .05$)	Test used
Lexical IDs score	Content questions	Pearson's *r*
Lexical IDs score (on Video D)	Retell task	Pearson's *r*
Combined score (Video D lexical IDs + content questions)	Retell task	Pearson's *r*
Subjective IS comprehension ratings	Content questions	Pearson's *r*
Subjective IS comprehension ratings	Retell task	Pearson's *r*

TABLE 29. *Linguistic Factors: Independent and Dependent Variables*

Independent variables	Dependent variables
Amount of gesture signs (Hi, Med, Low)	Subjective comprehension ratings Content questions score
Amount of CA enactment (Hi, Low)	Subjective comprehension ratings Content questions score
English mouthing (Hi, Low) Ling (Eng, nonEng) SocLing	Ratings by English L2 participants Ratings by Non-English participants Content question scores of English L2 Content question scores of Non-English
Sign origins ASL, Auslan, WFD, *Gestuno*	Ratings by all Ratings by ASL/Auslan native users Content question scores all Content question scores ASL/Auslan native users

also indicate what factors more or less predicted a response, such as comprehension test measure.

Participant's performances on comprehension tests were first correlated across tests, with variables shown in Table 28. Linguistic features of IS video data used in comprehension testing were considered for their correlation with higher mean performance on content questions. In Table 29 main effects between groups were primarily sought, given hypotheses about linguistic characteristics of the stimulus video correlating strongly or not with participant performance scores. Last, participants' sociolinguistic profiles were analyzed against their performances on comprehension measures in order to predict whether certain factors favor

TABLE 30. *Sociolinguistic Factors: Matrix for Regressions Analysis*

Independent variables Sociolinguistic (sample groups)	Dependent variables (Significance at $p \leq .05$)
Travel experience (zero, less than 5, less than 15, extensive)	Lexical IDs score Content questions Lex IDs + content questions combined score
Knowledge of ASL (native, non-native)	Lexical IDs score Content questions Lex IDs + content questions combined score
Knowledge of English (zero, some, L2)	Lexical IDs score Content questions Lex IDs + content questions combined score
Experience with use of IS (zero, sometimes, regular, often, weekly)	Lexical IDs score Content questions Lex IDs + content questions combined score
Education level (Yr12, some university, degree)	Lexical IDs score Lexical IDs score Content questions Lex IDs + content questions combined score
Native SL user/Deaf Parent(s) (1 or both, neither)	Lexical IDs score Content questions Lex IDs + content questions combined score

better comprehension of expository IS lectures (Table 30). ANOVAs and regression analyses were made across several dependent and independent variables to test if correlations emerge about factors in IS comprehension. Correlations, main effects, and interactions between sociolinguistic factors were analyzed through multivariate analyses using tools in the statistical program Minitab 17.[3] The relationships between performance measurements, linguistic characteristics of test videos, and sociodemographic information of participants were assessed between groups.

Tables 28, 29, and 30 show the design of experiments applied for each hypothesis. In addition to assessing whether knowledge of lexical items in IS correlates with improved comprehension performance, subjective comprehension ratings were compared to actual performance on questions and the results of the retell task with Video D. A correlation was

3. Minitab 17 is a statistical package available from Macquarie University's iLab remote desktop interface.

made to determine if one's rating of their perceived comprehension correlates with actual performance on comprehension measures.

The linguistic makeup of expository IS and its relationship to comprehension is another area of inquiry in this study. Each of the videotexts in the comprehension test exhibits different amounts of linguistic features, reported in Table 25 on p. 173. Analyses were made about whether any observed features correlated with participants' comprehension ratings and performances on content questions (Table 28). Because intuitions suggest that more effective expository IS incorporates a large amount of gestural elements, depiction, and a reduced amount of lexical forms, it was important to test these hypotheses.

A series of *t*-tests were used to determine if participants performed significantly different on performance measures when the video stimuli featured more or less of a linguistic variable (such as amount of gesture, English mouthing, or amount of ASL). These independent and dependent variables are shown in Table 29.

Independent variables of video stimulus percent distribution of gesture, CA, English mouthing, and signs by origins were correlated with the participants' comprehension ratings of those videos. The same groupings for each independent variable were correlated with content question scores for those videos.

Finally, other than SL and country origin, several sociolinguistic factors are explored by assessing participants divided across demographic groups. Independent variables, such as an audience member's travel experience and knowledge of ASL, are noted in Table 30. Several ANOVAS and regression analyses were run for these variables, with a focus on main effects between groups.

STUDY TWO VERIFICATIONS AND INTER-RATER RELIABILITY

Scores on the comprehension test questions and also the propositional retelling task were checked and verified before final conclusions were made about participants' comprehension of the IS video clips. The researcher's scoring on the content questions and propositional retelling responses were discussed with the local interpreter and assistant, at times reviewing the video capture of the testing and live interpreted response. The aim was to ascertain an accurate assessment of the interpretation and the content of participants' responses. A few discrepancies were discussed with the interpreter, and the video clip was reviewed so that a determination could be made about whether the response matched or did not match the correct, anticipated answer.

Several months after testing, interpreter assistants in the local test sites were asked to independently view and score a percentage (25%) of participant performances, which were randomly selected. The interpreter's assistant scored these performances on the content questions and propositional information retell separately. Then scores were compared across the coder's and the researcher's itemized tally. A statistical analysis was made using Minitab to determine three measurements of inter-rater reliability (IRR). Although agreement between coders is frequently reported in terms of percentages, the approach has been criticized as inadequate due to the inability to account for chance agreement; other assessments are also suggested such as Cohen's Kappa and/or Krippendorff's alpha (Hallgren, 2012).

The average percent agreement between coders was 92.7%, ranging between 83% and 98.3%. Corresponding average Cohen's Kappa and Krippendorff's alpha were 0.831 and 0.832, respectively. This can be interpreted to mean that because these two values are above 0.8, the instrument is sufficiently reliable so that conclusions can be made from the scored results of the content questions and the retell task.

FINDINGS FROM STUDY TWO

Results from each part of the comprehension assessment administered in all test sites are reported below in the form of grand means. In subsequent sections, outcomes from each quantified element of testing are first reported generally and across the five country cohort groups. Additional comparative results of interest are also discussed with each section. The data across all participants are then summarized at the end of each section before presenting results for the next element of the test.

Table 31 indicates overall performance statistics on comprehension measures; however, these results provide only a partial story about participants' comprehension of expository IS presentations. The range of performance scores is wide on each measure, as evidenced by the large standard deviations in all measures (except for the retell task). Varied sociolinguistic factors of participants and linguistic elements in each stimulus text are considered, with a discussion about their correlation with higher or lower results.

TABLE 31. *Summary of Quantitative Results*

Performance variable (N = 32)	Mean (%)	StDev	Minimum	Median
Comprehension ratings (IS only)[a]	3.52	0.54	2.17	3.54
Lexical IDs	73.9	17.3	39.0	75.0
Content questions	61.5	14.1	39.0	63.0
Fingerspelling	43.4	23.2	0.0	43.0
Numbers	49.6	26.7	10.0	50.0
Retell task (IS only)	52.9	0.21	23.0	45.0

[a] Ratings based on scale from 1 to 5 rather than percentage score.

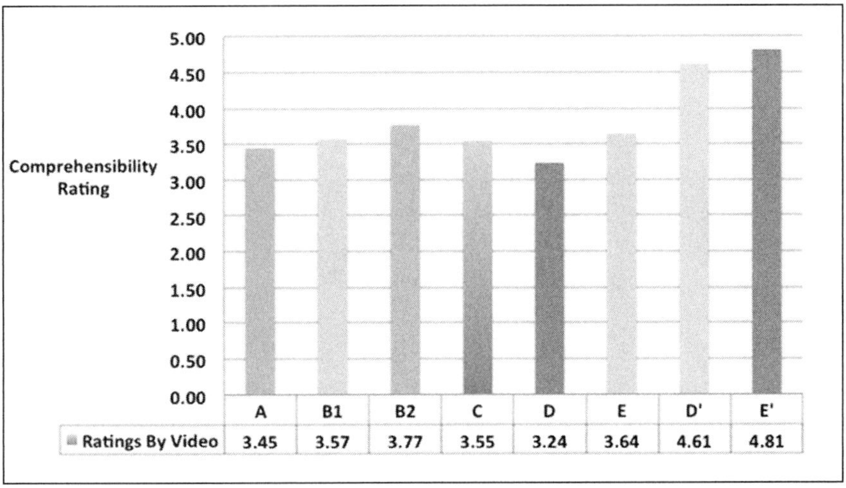

FIGURE 48. *Comprehension ratings of IS and NSL videos A through E′.*

Subjective Comprehension Ratings

Immediately after viewing each short IS presentation text, participants judged its comprehensibility using a nonverbal, pictorial rating scale. The numerical scale indicated values between 1 and 5, with 1 being difficult to understand and 5 being easy to understand. The scale was introduced in the methods above (Figure 46).

Comparing Comprehension Ratings across All IS Stimulus Texts

The average rating for each IS text across each country cohort ranged between 3.24 and 3.77 out of 5, as indicated in Figure 48. At first glance, one immediately notices the difference between comprehension ratings from IS videos A through E and the NSL videos D′ and E′. These differences are statistically significant and are discussed later in these results. Of the five IS presentation texts, video B (both parts B1 and B2) and video E were rated slightly more understandable on average by all participants. Both presentation topics are broadly familiar. Video B was about deaf education in developing countries and video E was about the deaf international Boy Scouts movement.

The *t*-test results indicated that the differences in participant ratings between the videos viewed in one's own sign language (NSL) and those viewed in IS were significant, but the rating differences across IS videos (A through E) were not significant (threshold $p \leq .05$). A closer examination of ratings made by demographically grouped cohorts is made next.

IS Comprehension by Country Cohort

While all participants rated presentations in their NSL to be more understandable than those in expository IS, there were some slight differences in how different country cohort groups rated certain IS presentation texts. This section looks at results by reporting on how cohort participants rated each IS video stimulus. Linguistic features in each IS presentation text are discussed later in these results as well.

Average ratings about the comprehensibility of each IS presentation video clip across all groups are shown in summary Table 32. Results indicate that audience understanding (their subject rating of it) is indeed varied. These differences are more pronounced for some cohort groups

TABLE 32. *Average Comprehension Ratings by Country Cohort and by Video/Presenter*

Group AVG Ratings	Rate A	Rate B1	Rate B2	Rate C	Rate D	Rate E	A-E AVG
JPN	2.33	3.00	3.25	2.25	3.00	2.17	**2.68**
BZ	3.25	3.50	3.33	3.50	2.67	2.50	**3.32**
CZ	3.31	3.85	4.19	4.08	3.38	3.83	**3.81**
AUS	4.00	3.58	3.67	3.82	3.77	4.50	**3.74**
US	4.33	3.92	4.25	3.92	2.50	4.33	**4.05**
Grand Mean	**3.45**	**3.57**	**3.74**	**3.51**	**3.06**	**3.47**	**3.52**
Std Deviation	**0.77**	**0.36**	**0.47**	**0.74**	**0.52**	**1.07**	**0.54**

for some IS presentation videos than others. The largest variation across groups is seen in videos A and E, with video C being similarly understood across all participants except the Japanese cohort. Videos A, C, and E feature presenters from European or U.S. origins, and their IS constructions may have been influenced by lexical borrowings or some other feature that made it difficult for signers from Brazil and Japan to understand. This aligns with findings in the Rosenstock (2004) study that non-European SL users performed lower on comprehension testing; however, videos B1, B2, and D are rated more consistently across the five country participant groups, with B1 showing the smallest standard deviation (0.36).

The Japanese cohort understood the IS video clips on average much lower than the other groups, except video B (B1 and B2) and video D. Video B—both presenters—discussed the widely appealing topic of "Deaf Education." The signer in video D was a native JSL signer presenting in expository IS, so participants from Japan perhaps connected better with him and recognized other features of his signing to be less "foreign." The topic was also about activities of the Japanese Federation of the Deaf (JFD); therefore, it was perhaps a more familiar topic. The Brazilian cohort exhibited similar ratings across the first four videos but rated videos D and E much lower. It is not clear whether the content or signing style of the last two presenters was difficult to glean for them, or if test fatigue influenced their subject ratings of understanding. The Australian, Czech, and U.S. participants rated expository IS texts consistently higher across all stimulus videos shown, with average subjective ratings not falling below 3.3, with one exception. The U.S. participants rated the JSL signer in video D as much less understandable than all of the other presentations, as did the Brazilian participants. Both the Brazilian group and the Japanese group experienced the Irish SL signer in video E as difficult to understand.

On average, videos B1 and B2 were rated more understandable than the others. The relatively higher rating of video B by observers may be attributed to the topic of the presentation. The debated topic of deaf education is arguably a commonly understood domain for deaf people from all corners of the globe. Much of this debate centers on the long-held controversies between oralist methods in deaf education and SL-based, bilingual approaches. Inequitable deaf education that does not include the most readily accessible, naturally occurring, visual language of the local deaf community for teaching is a long-standing topic of discussion among deaf people.

Audience members experience IS presentations as more understandable when there is familiarity with topic and themes of a presentation and when the IS presenter's NSL is shared by the audience member; however, one's *experience* (i.e., self-reporting by subjective comprehension ratings) of expository IS as more or less comprehensible may be different from actual *performance* on comprehension measurements.

Comprehension Ratings by Distribution of Sign Origins in IS Test Videos

The lexical frequency study reported the distribution of signs by varied origins in IS presentations. A query was also made to determine the frequency of lexical signs in the IS testing videos A through E, and these distributions are first reported in Table 24 on p. 158 in Study One. The lexifier SL origins analyzed in this study are shown in Figure 49. Signs that are recognizable ASL forms feature prominently in expository IS presentations, comprising between 45% and 65% of all lexical signs. In addition, signs from Auslan are regularly occurring, comprising 14% to 26% of lexical signs in IS presentations.

One would predict that prominently occurring NSL signs would influence participants' subjective comprehension ratings, particularly for videos B2 and E, which had the most Auslan and ASL forms, respectively;

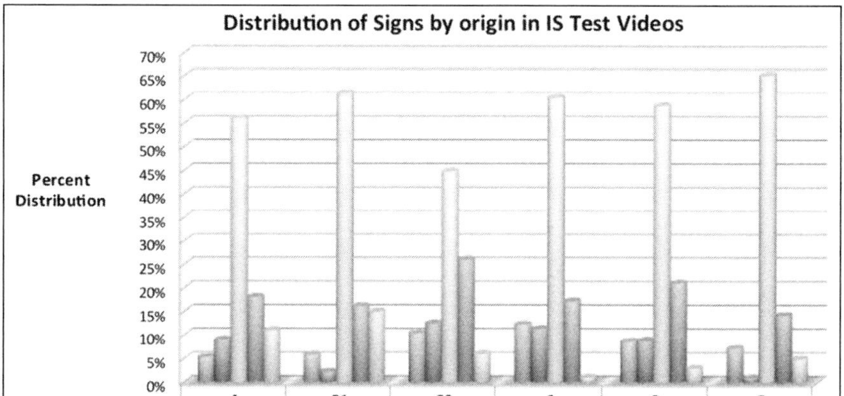

	A	B1	B2	C	D	E
IS/WFD	5%	6%	10%	12%	9%	7%
GEST	9%	2%	13%	11%	9%	1%
ASL	56%	61%	45%	60%	59%	65%
AUS	18%	16%	26%	17%	21%	14%
OTHER	11%	15%	6%	1%	3%	5%

FIGURE 49. *Distribution of signs by origin in IS test videos A through E.*

however, the U.S. and Australian participants did not rate them higher compared to other videos in the array. Native ASL signers rated video E comparatively higher, yet video segment B2 employs the least amount of ASL signs, and U.S. participants (as well as other cohorts) experienced it to be quite highly comprehensible. The B2 presenter employs the most gesture of all five videos, and this may have contributed to the subjective experience of better understanding. The only significant difference across ratings comes from ASL first language users, who rated video A significantly higher than those who know some ASL or do not know ASL at all; however, the video A presenter employs only an average amount of ASL signs, but discusses a current topic in the United States (health care).

Conversely, the Japanese presenter in video D employs a high number of ASL signs and Auslan signs, yet Australian participants stated they understood it better than only two others, and U.S. participants rated this text much lower by comparison. Brazilian cohort members also rated their understanding of video D as low compared to the other videos.

Auslan L1 signers rated video E significantly higher than the other cohorts did, with their understanding of video A second best. The IS presenters in videos A and E are White, European, and utilized a relatively large amount of both ASL and Auslan, with video E featuring a presenter whose first SL is Irish Sign Language (IrishSL). The co-presenter in video B2 is a White native ASL user who incorporates fewer ASL signs and the most Auslan signs in her section of the presentation. Yet, the Australian cohort does not rate this video segment as highly as video E. The video E presenter may have appeared the least "foreign" for the Australian cohort for several reasons. His NSL origins—IrishSL—might share some lexical signs with Auslan, given historical contact between Ireland and Australian deaf communities in some Catholic schools (Fitzgerald, 1999, cited in Johnston & Schembri, 2007), and also given BSL's influence on Auslan and Ireland's close geographic proximity to Great Britain, and BSL signers.

It appears, therefore, that sharing NSL sign origins with those that are borrowed into IS presentations appears to be a small factor in experienced comprehension; however, it is not consistently the only factor, and it is not always predictable. Familiarity with presentation topic and recognizable forms from one's NSL were other factors for improved understandability ratings by participants.

IS Comprehension Ratings and Type Distribution

Besides observer familiarity with presentation topic, other potential comprehension factors such as the amount and distribution of lexical signs, depiction, and gestural elements are of interest. Table 33 shows the distribution of these types for each IS video in the test array, which is an excerpt from Table 24 on p. 158.

Both signers in Video B use the most amount of gesture and constructed action in their expository IS, compared to the other IS texts. The co-presenter in video B, that is segment video B2, also was rated one of the highest consistently across all cohort groups. Both presenters utilize different amounts of conventional fully lexical signs, with the B2 segment incorporating the least amount of them. The A and B2 presenters both employ the most number of pointing signs, and a noticeably smaller amount of fully lexical forms. The increased frequency of pointing signs means that indicating referents and directing attention to discourse elements are more prevalent in this segment of the presentation. Recall in chapter 3 that points aid in focusing attention on real entities and real space blended entities, prompting varied mental spaces, and act as space holders in SL discourses. Points serve to "glue" the discourse together, and there is notably increased pointing in IS lectures where less specified fully lexical signs are observed (e.g., videos A and B2 compared with videos E and B1). Participants reported lesser understanding of video A, however. One explanation may be that this was the first IS text in the assessment and participants required adjustment to the "foreign" nature of the presentation.

Depicting signs appear to be relatively uniform in all test videos, except in the B1 segment. The B1 signer does use more gesture and CA and a higher than average amount of fully lexical signs. Gesture and prevalence of CA were other sign types featuring predominantly in B1 and B2, but

TABLE 33. *Average Scores (in percentages) on Content Questions by Cohort*

Avg Scores Total and Individual Range	JPN	BZ	CZ	USA	AUS	Overall Avg (%)
Avg IS (Videos A, B, C, D & E)	52	57	72	71	60	62
Range of Individual Scores	39–66	39–68	62–89	45–80	43–91	39–91
Std Deviation	11.3	8.7	9.8	12.2	17.7	14.1

not as much so for the other videos. Both signers in video B use the highest amount of gesture and constructed action. As noted above, the co-presenter in segment B2 was rated as the most understood consistently across all cohort groups. In addition, the large amount of pointing signs contributes to the gestural material in the presentation. Pointing signs are characterized in the framework of this study as comprising both linguistic and gestural parts, so the visible indexing provided by these signs may have increased judgments of understanding. Points, and the implementation of gesture and CA in this video likely provided content specificity (by demonstrating and indicating), because the ability to *tell* content was lacking due to the very low (45%) amount of fully lexical signs.

Impact of English Mouthing on IS Comprehensibility

A result from Study One revealed the presence of English mouthings in expository IS. Figure 50 shows the prevalence of English mouthings in each of the five IS videos shown to participants.

Video D, which captures a Japanese IS presenter, is on average considered the least comprehensible across four of the five cohort groups, with the Japanese participants being the exception. Not only does this signer use the smallest amount of gesture signs, but he also uses IS composed of 65% lexical signs, and less than half the amount of English word mouthings as signers in videos A, C, and E. There are likely signing and mouthing characteristics that the Japanese IS presenter uses which

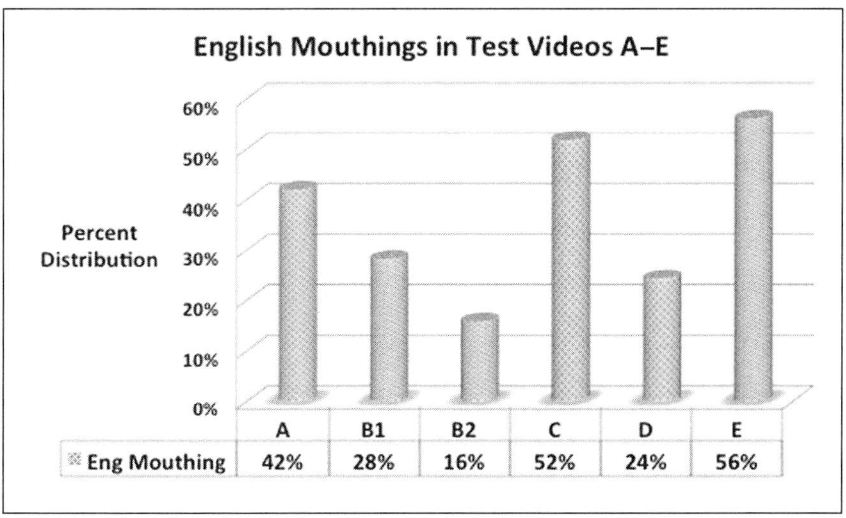

FIGURE 50. *English word mouthings in Expository IS videos A through E.*

are recognizable or more easily understood by participants in the Japan cohort. This could be investigated further in follow-up study. His mouthings are English words, but at times the articulation appeared to exhibit Japanese phonological features in these English mouthings. Additional examination of pronunciation features of varied SL signers would verify the extent of such occurrences for signers whose national spoken language is not English. Mori (2011) notes that there are qualities of IS used by Asian signers which are different from those used by IS rendered by Western signers. This was not specifically queried in this study; however, mouthings appear to have some effect on IS comprehension.

The Japanese IS presenter in video D uses a similarly large amount of depiction and constructed action as the North American presenter in B2, and a relatively small amount of English mouthings. He incorporates a higher percentage of lexicalized signs (ASL and Auslan borrowings) than the other IS a video clip. The fact that ASL native signers rated the presentation in video D as less understandable suggests that the lack of English mouthings in this presentation hindered their comprehension. In a contact situation where the signing system is not fully conventional for all audience members, the combination of mixed elements, including mouth patterns, appears to aid in understanding. Several participants who are familiar with English admitted to relying on the English mouth patterns of the IS signer in some presentations to understand some signs.

English mouthings occur frequently in videos A (42%), C (52%), and E (56%), and, not surprisingly, participants from the English-speaking countries of Australia and the United States rated these IS videos relatively high (range 3.64 to 4.33). It was noted earlier that Australian and U.S. participants, who share the same surrounding spoken language, rated Video E as the most understandable. Video E captures an IS presenter from Ireland, and the distribution of lexical signs by origin indicates more ASL (63%) than all the videos in the test sequence. He also uses a moderate amount of Auslan (14%) and some of the largest amount of depicting signs (15%) among the test videos. The ASL signs used by this presenter included a high number of shared Auslan cognates in the 15 most frequent signs.

Previously mentioned, deaf communities are situated within surrounding spoken language communities, which create contact effects on SLs. Spoken language mouthings are common, as evidenced among other contact phenomena in sign languages; these are shown to be artifacts of simultaneous language code mixing with spoken languages (Brentari, 2001; Crasborn, van der Kooij, Waters, Woll, & Mesch, 2008; Lucas &

Valli, 1992; Quinto-Pozos, 2002). The results described above, in combination with recognizable lexicon and depicting signs, propose that spoken language mouth patterns also have influence on comprehension when sign languages are in contact.

If the power of mouth patterns in contact signing is still doubted, it should also be noted that the presenter in Video section B1 is from a French-speaking African country and the researcher noticed qualitatively (yet not methodically annotated) that many of her mouth patterns produced simultaneously with signs were French words or pronunciations. Considering the large amount of ASL signs in her presentation segment, it is an interesting finding that U.S. participants understood this presenter second lowest, after video D. It therefore appears that reliance on reading lip patterns in a contact situation plays some important semiotic role for participants watching expository IS presentations.

Summary of Comprehensibility Ratings

Subjective ratings about the comprehension of varied IS presentation texts indicate that expository IS texts are experienced as more understandable by participants who have background knowledge of the presentation topic, and when the IS signer incorporates a large percentage of gestural elements. Audience members who share the same surrounding spoken language and culture of the IS presenter also experience those IS presentations as more understandable. This was observed in the higher ratings given by the Japanese participants watching the IS presenter from Japan (video D), and by the Australian and American participants watching the IS presenter from Ireland (video E), who also uses a large number of ASL signs in his lecture. It is suspected this is related to shared linguistic and gestural conventions, which includes recognition of familiar surrounding spoken language mouthings appearing in the IS lecture material. Interesting differences are observed between cohort group judgments about the five selected expository IS presentation stimuli. Findings reported in the following few sections address whether subjective claims of understanding hold true for participants in their actual performance on additional comprehension measures.

Structured Interview: Answering Content Questions

In the next part of the comprehension test, participants were asked content questions about the video clip they just viewed. Questions sought information in a range from global to detailed (see Content Questions Rubric, in Appendix C). Participants' scores in this section indicate mixed degrees of comprehension about content conveyed in the IS source videos as well as in the translated versions viewed in this section of testing. Only the questions asked of all IS videotexts are discussed here; comparison of performances on questions asked of videos D/D′ and E/E′—the IS and NSL versions—is made later in this chapter.

Comprehension of Content Questions by Level of Discourse Information Detail

Table 33 indicates the average score by each country cohort group for content questions from all IS videos. On average, participants scored 62% correct on questions posed about information presented by the IS signers. As will be seen the Czech Republic and U.S. cohorts scored above the average—at 72% and 71%, respectively. The Australians performed closer to the average at 60%, and the Brazilian and Japanese participants overall scored lower on the content questions, with scores of 57% and 52%, respectively. This is consistent with the comprehensibility judgment ratings that each cohort group gave about the IS videos overall. Participants from the Czech Republic and the United States as well as half of the Australian group answered a higher percentage of content questions correctly than did the participants from Brazil and Japan; however, the range of performances on this measure, and the standard deviations from the means, indicates wide variability.

Variation from the mean ranges from 8.7 to 17.7 percentage points, and although the sample size is small, the results show several trends. The largest spread is seen in the Australian cohort at 48 percentage points, with the lowest score 43% and the highest 91%. The participant scoring the highest on content questions also scored the highest on all other comprehension measures, an outlier among all participants. The smallest range is seen in the Brazilian cohort at 20 points and scores falling between 48% and 68%. The 39% to 68% range occurring with the Japanese participants represents the lowest, although separated by 26 percentage points at most. A scatter plot of participants' raw content question scores is shown in Figure 51 where individual performance across the cohort is seen.

Participants from the United States and the Czech Republic showed more success in answering content questions than did the other groups,

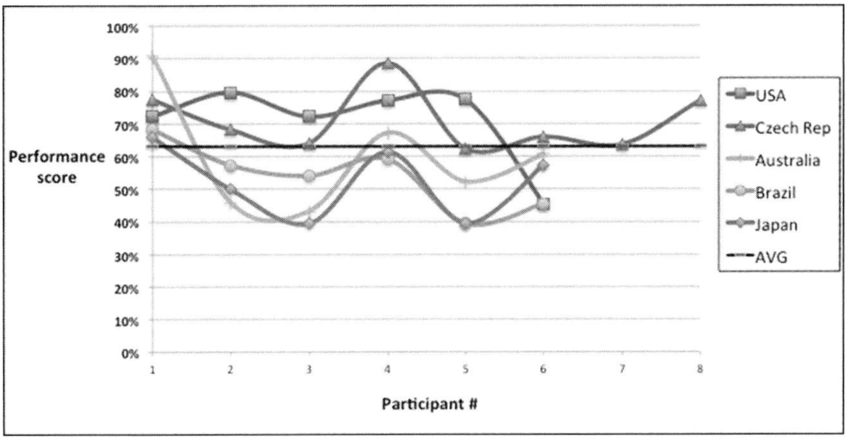

FIGURE 51. *Participant content question performance by cohort group.*

TABLE 34. *Average Understanding of Content Questions by Level of Detail and by Cohort*

	JPN	BZ	CZ	USA	AUS	Overall Avg
Discourse Pragmatics and Goal	79%	78%	81%	74%	80%	**78%**
Main Points	47%	49%	74%	68%	46%	**57%**
Details	29%	37%	51%	64%	51%	**46%**

with only one U.S. participant scoring below the average. The wide variability of correct response rates in each group suggests that additional variables other than country of origin contribute to an audience member's understanding of IS. An analysis and discussion of these other variables is undertaken further on in this chapter. A comparative discussion takes place about characteristics of participants who performed the best across comprehension measurements and those who had the hardest time understanding IS and performed in the lowest quartile.

While overall understanding of content questions gives general impressions about comprehension of expository IS presentation content, a closer look at the kind of information understood uncovers trends about the level of detail understood from IS. Table 34 displays the content question results by level of discourse detail.

Responses to content questions by question type indicate that participants were generally able to understand broader pragmatic and goal information conveyed by the IS text, with average scores ranging between 74% and 81% across all groups. The average score was 78% for correctly answered global content questions. These scores are significantly higher than participants' scores on questions about the texts' main points and details, with average scores of 57% and 46%, respectively for main points and detailed content questions. Scores greatly decrease as the questions attempt to solicit more detailed information from the IS texts viewed. In addition, the gap between different levels of detail is much less pronounced for the U.S. and Czech Republic participants. Other cohort members saw a much larger drop in comprehension of main point and detailed questions. The Australians showed better slightly better understanding of details over main points (51% and 46%, respectively). However, many of the detailed questions came from Video E, an IS presenter whose language origin is IrishSL. IrishSL is a language that developed in a country with historical, political, and economic ties to Great Britain, and the two countries are in close geographic proximity to one another. The relationship between BSL and Auslan has already been previously mentioned. Therefore, some sign cognates may be shared or more readily recognized between Auslan audience members and an ISL origin presenter of an IS lecture. It appears that IS main points and content details are more readily understood by U.S. and Czech Republic participants compared to the other groups; however, the very low performance across all participants shows clearly that details and main points in the IS presentations are not always realized by audience members.

The global comprehension average of 78% meets a 75% threshold in the consideration of "effective" comprehension laid out in the methodology. These questions were aided to some extent by the provision of some contextual clues that were given in the comprehension test instructions. Before viewing each stimulus IS discourse, all participants were given a general context and presentation title in English as well as in their local SL through the interpreter. Based on answers to questions such as, "What type of presentation is this?" "Who do you think the audience is?" "To whom is s/he giving it?" and "Why is he giving it? What is his/her aim?," participants often correctly identified information about discourse register and audience size and participation. At times, some nuances about the makeup of the audience and degree of formality of the presentation were missed, because study participants were not actually at the conference and were merely observing a video recording of the conference context. Nonetheless, pragmatic information from the video was readily understood and aided by the presenter's eye gaze, size and manner of signing, and other visual cues such as a lectern and large screen with captioning partly visible in several video clips.

Participants were not as successful correctly identifying main discourse points, scoring on average 57% correct, with average scores ranging between 46% and 74% across the five cohort groups. Main point questions sought key ideas conveyed in the IS presentation such as comparisons being made, problems the signer describes, and causal relationships. Examples of questions that targeted main points conveyed were, "What did the presenter and that other person do together?" "What are the presenters comparing?" "What are some of the education problems in her country?" and "What does the presenter say about ways that deaf people improve their communities?"

Finally, several questions sought detailed information from the IS presentations; these included the participants' ability to have understood and remembered certain facts, as well as specific numbers or dates. All participants were told before each video that they would be asked to remember a few details such as numbers and dates. It is true that working memory has an impact on a person's ability to store and recall such details, so it is expected that there would be some variability to performance on these types of questions and that the percentage scores would be somewhat lower. The much lower performance on these detailed questions overall, however, shows that the information was not integrated into participants' cognitive representation of the lecture content sufficiently enough for it to be retrieved.

Performance on Content Questions by Video and by Cohort

As reported above, participants believed IS presentations to be more understandable when they show evidence of a combination of several qualities: familiar lexical forms and mouth patterns, increased use of depicting signs and gestural elements and known shared NSL background (with the observer).

TABLE 35. *Average Content Question Performances by Video and Cohort (percentage score)*

Video Segment	JP	BZ	CZ	AU	US	Mean
A	60.0	58.3	66.3	51.7	60.0	59.3
B1	91.7	83.3	92.2	87.5	81.3	87.2
B2	43.3	41.7	76.3	48.3	70.0	55.9
C	58.3	52.8	72.6	66.7	75.0	65.1
D	16.7	58.3	31.3	58.3	50.0	42.9
E	19.0	36.5	61.9	50.8	76.2	48.9

In Table 35, results from performances across cohort groups on each IS video stimulus are reported, with mean performances on each video segment (in percentages). Upon closer inspection of each group's comprehension score from content questions, one notices that the Japanese cohort understood the presenter in Video B1 just as well as the Czech Republic cohort did. Both groups performed the best over other groups on these content questions. This is evidence that some factors other than country of origin and SL origin influence IS comprehension.

Signers from English-speaking surrounding communities rely on English mouthings (lip-reading) to aid comprehension of contact signing in IS lecture material, given notably higher ratings of subjective comprehension of IS texts with more English mouthings and more signs borrowed from their NSLs. The effect of this lip-reading reliance was seen in performance on content questions as well. Both the Australian and U.S. participants performed lower on questions about texts that incorporated fewer English mouthings, despite the high amount of ASL and Auslan forms in the text.

In video segments B1 and B2 (which were both rated most understandable by many participants), gesture and constructed action in both were highly prevalent. Many performed quite well on Video B1 questions. Although participants across all groups experienced the presentation segment B2 as the most understandable, their performance on content questions was notably lower than would be expected. The reduced amount of lexical signs and much higher amount of depicting signs in B2 may have some relationship to the dropped lower average performance on content questions from this segment across groups. This is an interesting finding that suggests participants believe certain highly visual characteristics of an IS lecture make it easy to understand, yet measures of content understanding can contradict this subjective experience. A similar effect occurred for the Japanese participants. They scored quite low on content questions for video D, which featured the IS presenter who shares the same NSL. Japanese cohort members rated this video as the most understandable in the ratings, but the performance on these questions is contrary to this rating. Notably, the questions from videos D and E are proportionately more detailed compared to the other three videos' questions. Relatively lower scores across all cohorts demonstrate the difficulty with comprehending more detailed information from IS lectures. Moreover, both IS signers employ many ASL and Auslan borrowed signs, which may have aided the Australian and American participants, and in combination with the lowest amounts of gesture (4% and 9%), there may not have been enough recognizable, sufficiently specified, and conventional information for the Brazilian, Czech Republic, and Japanese participants on those content questions.

The influence of English is evident in contact signing and comprehension, where the Australian and U.S. participants perform better on video questions with higher amounts of English mouth patterns. After separating participants into two groups—those with native or L2 English skill and those with none—a comparison was made in average performance on content questions.

In Figure 52, a comparison of question scores between participants who know English, and those who do not, provides evidence that knowing

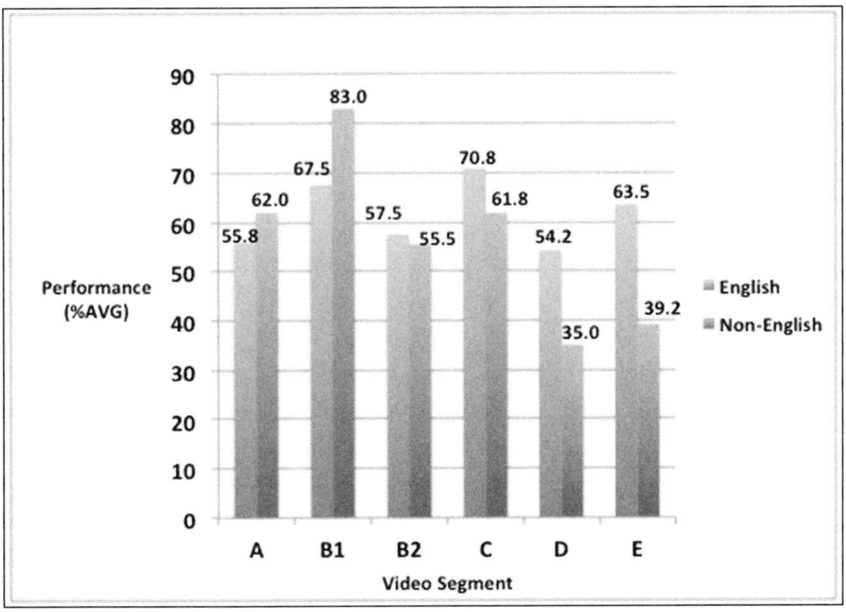

FIGURE 52. *Content questions scores by video for participants from English- and Non-English-speaking countries.*

some English (mouth patterning) and ASL or a BSL variant provides an advantage in comprehension of certain IS presentations. Participants from non-English-speaking countries performed the same or better for videotexts A and B, where the topic (deaf education) is known and there is less English mouthing, and where either more depiction or more gestural signs is evident. IS signers employ a large amount of English mouthing in C and E, and the presenters in C, D, and E incorporate the most ASL recognizable signs.

Summary of Structured Content Questions

Results from participants' answers to content questions about each presentation demonstrate an average performance of 62% across all participants, with Czech Republic and U.S. participants scoring above the average, Australians scoring at the average, and Brazilian and Japanese participants scoring below the average. There are also significant differences in the type of information understood from expository IS presentations. Findings indicate that the 62% average comprehension is heavily weighted in more global information rather than in the lecturer's points and details.

Although global comprehension of discourse goal and pragmatics (formality, setting, audience) are somewhat successful (78%), evidence shows that audience members glean a reduced amount of main point information (57%) and a substantially limited realization of discourse details (48%). In addition, when participants rate their comprehension of different IS presentations, their actual performance on this measure of comprehension does not always align with their subjective ratings. Many participants rated their understanding of video segment B2 (with increased amount of nonlinguistic, gestural sign types) higher than other presentation videos, yet average performance on content questions was only 54.9%. Participants performed better on questions from presentations where they have familiarity with the topic. This suggests participants believe certain highly visual characteristics of an IS lecture make it easy to understand, but measures of content understanding can contradict this subjective experience. Audience members who attend a presentation may expect to understand nearly 100% of content and even if not all of the information is fully understood, at the very least nobody expects to glean only 62% of the lecture material. Findings are significant here because when attendees watch an IS lecture they may *think* they are comprehending more than they actually are, because understanding global information and some main points may create the illusion of fuller comprehension.

Varied linguistic and sociolinguistic factors beyond country cohort group appear to impact understanding of IS lecture content. Knowledge of fully lexical signs in IS is another measure of comprehension discussed in the next section.

Lexical Identification Task

After answering content questions for each video, participants were asked to identify lexical signs and give what they believed to be a semantic equivalent in their own language. This part of the comprehension test measured lexical semantic identification, and participants' responses were totaled into a percentage score. In addition, from content questions and retell task, participants were tasked with identifying fingerspelled words and numbers from IS presentations. This section reports on overall scores for lexical, fingerspelling, and number identifications.

Forty-five (45) high-frequency IS signs that appear in the video clips were shown, including the recurrent conventional gesture of "thumbs up." This is an emblem that would be recognizable to people who do not know a SL, and at the same time is listed as a conventional Auslan sign. Also included is the most recurrent depicting sign, DSS(GC):SMALL-AMOUNT. Both of these signs are quite regular in the expository IS data, and were therefore included in the lexical identification task.

In addition, 12 fingerspelled words or acronyms were extracted from the IS video samples for participants to identify, six after immediate reviewing and six after several minutes in delayed recall. Seventeen (17) number identifications were also included in this lexical identification task; these were dispersed among the content questions (delayed recall) or in the video D text retell task (immediate recall).

Results for lexicon, number, and fingerspelling comprehension performances are shown in Figure 53. Average scores on the identification of numbers and fingerspelled words includes immediate recall and delayed recall. Lexical identification scores across all participants averaged 74%; numbers averaged 50%, and fingerspelling 43%.

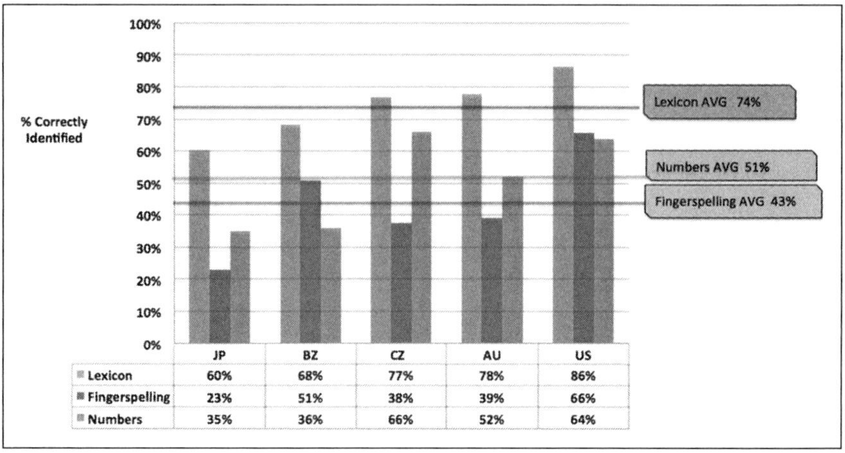

FIGURE 53. *Lexicon, fingerspelling, and numbers: Average comprehension across cohorts.*

Lexical Identifications by Cohort and Item

In terms of understanding individual lexical signs, both the Brazilian and Japanese participants' mean scores resulted below the average, at 68% and 60%, respectively. The U.S. mean score was the highest at 86%, with Australian and the Czech Republic participants slightly less, averaging 78% and 77%, respectively.

Average lexical comprehension for each country cohort is shown, and the range of scores within and across each cohort indicates varied success. Japanese participants exhibited 39% to 84% (range = 45) understanding of IS lexical signs, Brazilian participants ranged from 50% to 86% (range = 36), the Czech Republic group range was 50% to 100% (range = 50), Australian lexical ID scores fell between 61% and 100% (range = 39), and the U.S. cohort scores were between 77% and 95% (range = 18).

Twenty-two out of the 45 high-frequency lexical items in expository IS are recognizable citation ASL forms. This would explain the narrower range of scores by U.S. participants, and deviations that are mostly higher than for all groups. Since ASL users would understand almost half of the signs, a stable base of correct responses was the foundation to a smaller number of lexical identifications to be successfully made. Two participants (one from Australia and one from the Czech Republic) identified all 45 signs correctly. They were among the top six participants who demonstrated the greatest understanding of expository IS lectures.

Variation in comprehension of the remaining lexical IS signs warrants further discussion, considering other factors across language groups. Some of the comprehension test participants are familiar with ASL or BSL (or Auslan) to some degree. L2 knowledge of contributing foreign forms in expository IS likely influenced improved comprehension on content question scores.

Many of the signs in this assessment are also listed as conventional IS lexical items in one or more publicly available IS resource dictionaries. Participants' average scores for each of the 45 IS signs are shown in Table 36. The sign number in the first column is associated with the form's comparative rank frequency of all signs in this list. Highlighted scores indicate where the frequently occurring IS sign is also a shared citation form-meaning pair in the country cohort's NSL.

Each of the signs had been seen in the IS usage context, having been used regularly by several presenters. There were a number of factors behind whether or not the meaning of some signs were correctly identified, besides simply knowing its usage in IS. At times, a sign was correctly identified because (a) it has a shared cognate in the participant's SL or (b) iconic features of the sign make the referent and thus the meaning transparent to the observer. Otherwise, a sign was simply not known or it was incorrectly identified because (a) the sign has an exact shared form in the participant's SL but the meaning is not shared or (b) one parameter of the IS sign is slightly different from an otherwise similar form in one's NSL and the meanings are different. In the latter case, the IS sign is sometimes mistaken for the NSL sign.

Because there are a large number of IS forms that are the same in ASL and Auslan, participants from these sign language origins easily identified them; however, there were times that these were doubtfully realized. As participants knew they were watching presentations in IS, they were aware of the "foreign" nature of the signing system. When signs from their own NSL were shown in the context of the IS segment, a few times the response was tentative. For example, an Australian participant did not immediately recognize the Auslan sign HAVE when first shown. He was doubtful, weighing two possible meanings: "to have" or "to grab" and eventually chose the correct response. Participants were actively looking for iconic cues with unrecognized forms by ascribing them gestural features and even questioning forms that, in their own NSL, would be easily recognizable. The context of the symbolic unit confounded what otherwise would be a relatively straightforward understanding of the symbol

TABLE 36. *Lexical Identification Scores: Grand Mean by Lexical Item and Cohort*

Sign #	IDGloss	Meaning(s)	Score by Lex Item	Japan Avg	Brazil Avg	Czech Avg	US Avg	AUS Avg
43	**ACCEPT(ASL)**	accept	**42%**	★ 0%	33%	★ 75%	33%	100%
11	**ANALYZE(ASL)**	research, analysis	**87%**	67%	67%	100%	100%	100%
33	**APPROVE(WFD)**	approve, ratify, legalize	**57%**	17%	50%	88%	★ 100%	67%
4	**ASSOCIATION(GEST)** ★	Deaf association, organization, collaborate	**59%**	50%	83%	63%	67%	50%
10	**BODY(AUS)**	health (care, physical care)	**58%**	67%	0%	38%	83%	83%
34	**BOY(ASL)**	male person -man or boy	**87%**	58%	67%	100%	100%	75%
40	**BRING(ASL)**	bring, carry, deliver	**62%**	33%	0%	75%	100%	100%
31	**CAN(ASL)**	able, can	**84%**	67%	83%	38%	100%	83%
32	**CHILDREN(ASL)**	children, kids, young people	**83%**	100%	100%	100%	67%	83%
38	**CONGRESS(GEST)**	congress, converence	**38%**	50%	33%	100%	33%	50%
26	**CONNECT(ASL)**	connection, relate, connect	**97%**	100%	★ 100%	75%	100%	83%
29	**COUNTRY(WFD)**	country, region	**62%**	33%	17%	63%	50%	50%
14	**CRPD(WFD)**	Legal document giving rights to ppl with Disabilities/Deaf	**48%**	17%	33%	50%	50%	25%
1	**DEAF1(ASL)**	Deaf	**100%**	100%	100%	★ 100%	100%	100%
7	**DIFFERENT(ASL)**	different, varied	**84%**	★ 83%	83%	88%	100%	★ 67%

17	DISABLED(WFD)	person with disabilities, disability	**80%**	100%	50%	100%	83%	67%
20	DSS(GC):SMALL-AMOUNT	a small amount, little, not enough	**97%**	100%	100%	100%	83%	100%
22	FINISH(ASL)	finish, completed	**73%**	83%	33%	50%	100%	100%
9	GOOD(AUS)	good, all right, high quality	**82%**	83%	83%	75%	100%	83%
27	GOVERNMENT(GEST)	government	**82%**	50%	50%	50%	100%	83%
2	HAVE(AUS)	have, possess, own	**73%**	★ 67%	17%	88%	83%	100%
37	HEARING(WFD)	able to hear, not deaf	**77%**	33%	83%	★ 100%	83%	83%
18	HELP(ASL)	help, assistance	**81%**	67%	100%	100%	100%	100%
23	IMPORTANT(ASL)	important	**67%**	50%	67%	50%	100%	67%
41	INTERNATIONAL(WFD)	international (adjective)	**83%**	33%	83%	100%	100%	100%
35	INTERPRETER(WFD)	interpreter, translator	**80%**	83%	100%	100%	50%	67%
12	KNOW (ASL)	know, aware, knowledge	**97%**	83%	100%	★ 75%	100%	100%
44	LANGUAGE3(WFD)	grammar or text information	**58%**	17%	33%	88%	83%	83%
15	NOW(ASL) ★	now, today, immediate time	**73%**	★ 50%	33%	100%	100%	83%
42	NS:ASIAPACIFIC	Asia- Pacific (region)	**53%**	100%	33%	0%	67%	67%
6	PERSON(GEST)	person(s)	**83%**	67%	100%	100%	100%	100%
36	PROBLEM(ASL)	problem	**71%**	33%	67%	100%	100%	100%
24	PROGRESS(ASL) ★	progress, move forward/on, advance	**91%**	67%	★ 100%	75%	100%	100%

(Continued)

TABLE 36. (*Continued*)

Sign #	IDGloss	Meaning(s)	Score by Lex Item	Japan AVG	Brazil AVG	Czech AVG	US AVG	AUS AVG
45	**PROJECT (WFD)**	project, initiative	**18%**	0%	33%	38%	0%	17%
5	**SAME(AUS)**	also, same as	**73%**	50%	100%	63%	83%	67%
13	**SCOUT(ASL)**	boy scouts, scouting organization	**100%**	67%	★ 100%	★ 100%	100%	100%
39	**SEE-2H(ASL)**	see, look, view	**94%**	100%	100%	88%	100%	83%
28	**SIGN(GEST)**	sign language	**97%**	★ 83%	100%	100%	100%	100%
16	**STUDY(AUS)**	education, school, study	**87%**	100%	100%	88%	83%	100%
21	**THINK(ASL)**	think, realize, idea	**70%**	17%	83%	88%	100%	100%
30	**WANT(AUS)**	want	**72%**	33%	17%	38%	67%	83%
3	**WHAT(ASL)**	what	**80%**	83%	67%	50%	100%	50%
19	**WORK(GEST)**	work	**93%**	83%	83%	100%	100%	83%
8	**WORLD(GEST) ★**	world, global, international	**79%**	★ 33%	100%	88%	100%	100%
25	**YEAR(ASL)**	year	**80%**	50%	100%	88%	100%	83%

Note. ★ = variation on parameter and/or homophone to another sign with related meaning. **Highlight** = cohorts' NSL sign is a shared citation form-meaning pair.

in one's own NSL. Another example of this arose when an Auslan native signer viewed the IS sign CONNECT, which is the same sign in Auslan. The participant struggled to identify the sign, stating, "I would need to see the signs that came before and after that one." Participants observing IS presentations seem to integrate the forms differently from how they process discourse in their NSL, mainly from the contextual knowledge that they are attending to a mixed language system. Additional research on processing differences between NSL reception, and IS or other contact language reception is needed to verify this intuition.

In several cases, an IS sign resembled a similar form in the participant's NSL, but the semantic structure associated with the form in IS form was wrongly identified for the semantic structure of the form known in one's NSL. Examples of this misunderstanding occurred with the IS sign BOY (which is a borrowed ASL sign). For the Japanese cohort members, BOY resembles the JSL sign [COPY]. Also the IS sign WORLD(GEST) resembles the JSL sign meaning "everything." The IS sign NOW(ASL) was at times mistaken for the JSL sign "study" or "school." This type of misunderstanding occurred for participants in all country cohorts. The IS sign for INTERPRETER(WFD) was mistaken by a U.S. participant for the ASL sign COOK, and the Auslan sign HAVE was thought to be the LIBRAS sign meaning "accept." In JSL the sign UNDERSTAND is the same form for the IS (and Auslan) sign WANT (Figure 54). Four of the Japanese participants miscued on this sign, three of whom gave the JSL meaning for it. The fourth guessed it to mean "body," going on gestural instincts and knowing she was watching a foreign type of signing.

FIGURE 54. *IS sign* WANT/ *JSL sign* UNDERSTAND.

FIGURE 55. *COUNTRY(WFD).*

An example that illustrates misunderstanding from a parameter difference between IS sign and a similar NSL sign is the IS fully lexical sign, COUNTRY(WFD). It is conventionally used in IS and is listed in WFD International Sign resources (Figure 55). Its form is a BENT5 handshape articulated in one-to-three different spaces in front of the signer to indicate one country or plural countries. This sign prompted the meaning "group" for more than half of the Czech Republic participants. They did not specify its meaning as "country" or "countries." The Czech Republic SL sign for GROUP uses the same dominant handshape, but it is articulated onto the back of the upheld flat palm of the nondominant hand (similar to the Auslan sign CAKE).

These examples underline how the productive nature of SL lexicons permits the same symbolic form to be a substantive lexical item for one SL user (a conventional sign with established meaning in their NSL), while for others it remains complex and more schematic, prompting a much wider range of meanings, but nonetheless potentially similarly motivated. For the example shown in Figure 55, the sign may be an established form among IS users but it also is a depiction that could prompt other meanings to IS audience members.

Although the sign COUNTRY(WFD) is conventionally used to mean [COUNTRY] or [GEO-POLITICAL GROUP] among deaf people who know and use IS, the form is also one that might be used as a depiction in any number of NSLs. The productive placement or movement of the sign's handshape, BENT5, allows for numerous less-specified referents. The depicting sign DS(BENT5) is more schematic and might indicate a size or amount of some object(s), or a location of such object(s). Although the semantics of "group" is related in some sense to the semantics of "country," a group is a collection of people or things—a slightly different semantic concept than a group defined by national borders. Such depicting forms allow for rich meaning construction across SLs that use these productive forms, yet convention and context impact their effectiveness because the more specific meaning is intended; however, only a vague meaning is construed.

Another interesting example is the ASL sign CAN, which occurs often in expository IS at all times meaning "able" or "can." Not only does the sign look like the Auslan sign CONFIRM[4] [OFFICIAL APPROVAL], it resembles another ASL sign, YES. There are nuanced differences between the two forms, but they share partial conceptual semantic structure such as "positive" and "affirming," but the form CAN in IS is used the same way as its lexifier language, ASL. Several participants from the Czech Republic, Brazil, Australia, and Japan viewed the sign CAN and gave the meaning as YES or CONFIRM. For native users of ASL, the signs CAN and YES employ the same handshape but are differentiated in two ways. CAN is a two-handed S-handshape  sign (citation version) and moves strongly downward one time, where YES is typically one-handed "S" articulation with single or repeated movement (resembling a head nodding). The iconic "head-nodding" image may prompt meaning, and if not, for a nonnative, the phonological miscue can lead to misunderstanding of a sign or word. This miscue in a contact situation is easy to make, much like when an American hears an Australian English user pronounce a word with a different-sounding vowel or consonant and miscues the entire word.

Results in Chapter 4 described two examples of IS signs that occurred several times in the dataset and had the potential to be iconically misleading forms to which some participants incorrectly ascribed iconic properties. The sign PROJECT(WFD) (Figure 34) is a fully lexical sign in IS that was used by all presenters in the dataset. It appears to mimic the movement of grasping a handle and cranking it alongside an upheld flat nondominant hand; much in the way one might handle a movie projector. A majority of people did not correctly identify the sign, with an average of only 18% of participants correctly doing so. The few who did recognize it reported some familiarity with IS. The sign is an interesting

4. URL: http://www.auslan.org.au/dictionary/words/confirm-1.html

example of an arbitrary sign that is lexicalized in expository IS. It appears to be a phonologically reduced BSL sign from the fingerspelled P-J movement seen in the BSL sign.

In other lexical examples, the forms looked less specified to participants and the meaning is guessed at, using iconic interpretation. Returning to the example IS sign COUNTRY-PL, a Czech Republic participant commented that it looked like a depicting sign that handles some entity, where someone might be turning different knobs, like water taps, but she knew it didn't mean this. This is another example where iconic motivation causes confusion in this mixed language contact system. Other depiction-like sublexical features hinted that it might represent a series of groups, such as deaf associations. The usage and meaning of this sign is quite conventional in the IS data, where it means either "country" or "countries" or at times "regions," when articulated with repetition and slight location modification. Audience members who are not familiar with some of the conventional lexical signs in IS would struggle to understand specific meaning, with iconic interpretation not necessarily providing sufficient or correct information.

Fingerspelling Comprehension by Item and Cohort

Understanding of fingerspelling and numbers in IS was also mixed, with much less success by all participants. Poor comprehension of these elements is not surprising and is already alluded to in a study of interpreted IS (McKee & Napier, 2002); however, Rosenstock found that fingerspelled items were understood at a rate of 73% accuracy in her test items that targeted fingerspelled words (2004). Findings here indicate otherwise: fingerspelled items were recognized with much less success, ranging from 23% to 66%. The average scores for all cohort groups are summarized in Table 37. Results indicate that immediate response to fingerspelled targets was, on average, 56% correct, and delayed recall of fingerspelled words averaged 24%.

Fingerspelled word identifications were asked in two formats—immediate and delayed recall. The immediate identifications were made either after being shown the fingerspelled word during the lexical identification section of the comprehension test, or as they appeared in the main idea retell task for video D. Delayed identifications were asked in a delayed recall during the interview questions about details from videos E and E′. These were the name of the colleague mentioned by the IS presenter in

TABLE 37. *Results of Fingerspelled Word Identifications*

Immediate Retell Fingerspellings		Grand Avg	AUS	US	CZ	BZ	JPN
FS1	I-N-C-L-U-S-I-V-E	39%	17%	83%	13%	83%	0%
FS2	S-E-C-O-N-D-A-R-Y	33%	17%	83%	13%	50%	0%
FS3	W-F-D	79%	100%	100%	63%	83%	50%
FS4	J-I-C-A	78%	50%	100%	75%	100%	67%
FS5	T-O-K-Y-O	37%	33%	0%	100%	33%	17%
FS6	J-F-D	69%	33%	100%	63%	100%	50%
	AVERAGES	**56%**	42%	78%	54%	75%	31%
Delayed Recall Fingerspellings							
FS7	D-R F-E-L-L-I-N-G-E-R	0%	0%	0%	0%	0%	0%
FS8	BEARS/BEAVERS	13%	0%	67%	0%	0%	0%
FS9	CUBS	38%	67%	100%	25%	0%	0%
FS10	SCOUTS	38%	67%	67%	25%	33%	0%
FS11	ROVERS	20%	33%	33%	0%	33%	0%
FS12	VENTURERS	32%	33%	67%	25%	33%	0%
	AVERAGES	**24%**	33%	56%	13%	17%	0%

video A, and a list of English-based names of Boy Scout age groups given in video E.

Due to a difference in the load on working memory in discourse processing for these different comprehension tasks, the results are separated under the headings "immediate" and "delayed," recall fingerspelling. Recall comprehension of these five fingerspelled words was unsuccessful for all but one U.S. participant, although one of the Australian participants correctly identified four out of the five. Several participants from Japan, Australia, and the Czech Republic commented on the challenge to recognize fingerspelled words that were borrowed from English and using a spelling system that is different from their NSL fingerspelling system.

U.S. and Brazilian participants had more success understanding the fingerspelled words in the test content, because both of their NSLs use a similar, one-handed fingerspelling system prevailing in expository IS. Also, all of the fingerspelled words were loan words from English; therefore, participants with little to no knowledge of written English were at

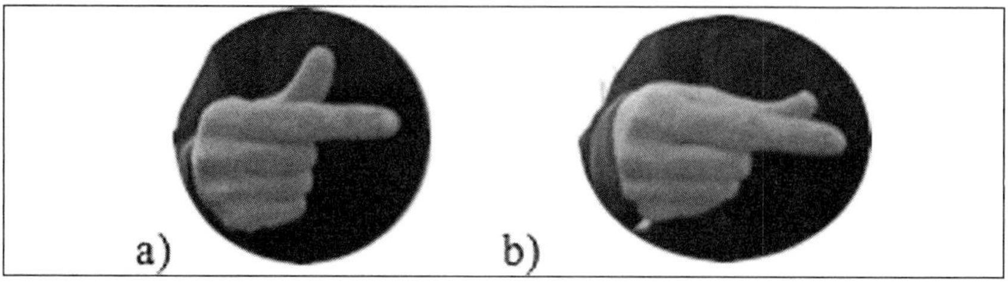

FIGURE 56. *(a) IS letter* T *(from DGS) and (b) ASL letter* G.

a disadvantage with comprehending fingerspelling. In IS, the letter T is the form seen in DGS and resembles the letter G in ASL (Figure 56). This caused a misunderstanding for the U.S. participants and several others who are familiar with the U.S. one-handed fingerspelling system. These participants were unable to recognize the fingerspelled word, T-O-K-Y-O; several of them guessed a nonsense word "G-O-K-Y," or "G-O-K-Y-O." All of the Czech Republic participants and a few from other cohorts recognized the IS "T" letter and were successful in using closure to recognize the fingerspelled city name, Tokyo. Several identified the word, being accustomed to the IS fingerspelling system form from experience. Interestingly only one Japanese cohort member recognized the fingerspelled word for their capital city. In addition to the fact of JSL's vastly different fingerspelling system from the one-handed IS system, this is likely due to the fact that JSL has a conventional sign for TOKYO, which was also used in the IS videotext viewed.

Participants had more success in recognizing shorter fingerspelled words, whether they knew what they meant or not, such as the acronyms for W-F-D, and J-I-C-A. Most everyone identified the acronym for World Federation of the Deaf; however, only a few of the Japanese cohort participants knew the full words represented by the acronym for Japan International Cooperative Agency (JICA). The sign for WFD for some time has been the lexical sign INTERNATIONAL(WFD) (Figure 57), but the influence of English contact seems to have introduced the fingerspelled variant by using the English initialized acronym for the organization. The sign in Figure 57 is included in the 45 lexical identifications.

Other trends in the fingerspelling results are seen in all participants' inability to catch the name of a person introduced in video A. A colleague by the name of Dr. Fellinger is mentioned by the IS presenter, but the fingerspelled name was articulated very quickly such that even the native ASL signers, who might have been able to catch the name, were unable

FIGURE 57. *Sign meaning* WFD *or* INTERNATIONAL.

to do so. There was no other available contextual knowledge (e.g., being at the conference, or having access to written supplemental materials) to provide cues to the doctor's name. Speed of fingerspelling in IS presentations, as well as length of the fingerspelled word are, therefore, factors in comprehension by audience members, especially when context is not sufficient to support understanding.

Last, participants' responses to delayed questions about fingerspelled information (delayed recall from content questioning) were less accurate, most likely due to working memory and short-term memory limitations. Words or acronyms may not have been fully processed in cognition, especially if the word was unfamiliar. Participants who viewed NSL versions of videos D (JFD Collaborations, D′) and E (Boy Scouts, E′), in most cases performed much better on fingerspelled identifications.

Number Comprehension in IS

As with fingerspelled items, number identifications were elicited from two formats: immediate recall as they appeared in the main idea retell task for video D and also in a delayed recall during the interview questions. Immediate number recognition was on average similarly low (range 33% to 61%). The trend here is shown by results in Table 38. Single-handed, iconic numbers such as four (FOUR) and twenty-two (TWO-TWO) thousand were more easily recognized than other complex numeric forms that appear in IS discourses.

Number signs are varied across different SLs, and this impacts comprehension of IS numeric forms. This is because as a developing SL becomes more conventional, the numeric representation system changes from being iconic to more complex and abstract (e.g., the development

TABLE 38. *Results of Number Identifications*

Immediate Retell Nbrs		Grand Avg	AUS	US	CZ	BZ	JPN
NBR 1	Mar-11	25%	33%	67%	0%	0%	33%
NBR 2	1947 (year founded)	44%	33%	33%	100%	33%	0%
NBR 3	4 (goals)	81%	100%	100%	100%	0%	100%
NBR 4	22,000 (Deaf members)	88%	100%	100%	100%	100%	33%
NBR 5	7,000 (attendees)	44%	33%	33%	75%	67%	0%
NBR 6	1991 (date of WFD)	56%	33%	33%	100%	67%	33%
	AVERAGES	**51%**	56%	61%	58%	44%	33%
Delayed Recall Nbrs Q & A							
NBR 8	(ARTICLE) #25	28%	33%	50%	38%	0%	17%
NBR 9	132 (associations)	63%	67%	67%	100%	50%	33%
NBR 10	1907 (year founded)	60%	100%	67%	100%	33%	0%
NBR 11	41 million (population)	30%	0%	100%	50%	0%	0%
NBR 12	(age) 6–8	40%	0%	67%	100%	0%	33%
NBR 13	(age) 8–11	35%	33%	67%	75%	0%	0%
NBR 14	(age) 11–15	50%	33%	100%	50%	67%	0%
NBR 15	(age) 16–18	37%	67%	33%	50%	33%	0%
NBR 16	(age) 18+	68%	67%	100%	75%	33%	67%
NBR 17	22,000	73%	100%	67%	100%	100%	0%
NBR 18	7,000	25%	33%	33%	25%	33%	0%
	AVERAGES	**46%**	49%	62%	69%	34%	18%

of Nicaraguan SL; Katseff, 2004, cited in Rosenstock, 2004). In addition, the more iconic approach to holding up fingers to symbolize numeric information in IS requires at times some quick mathematical calculation. For example, the sign for 8 typically involves holding up five fingers on one hand and three on the nondominant hand. Numbers more than 10 involve flashing all 10 fingers then following quickly with the next several fingers (e.g., TEN + FIVE, or TEN + EIGHT). The number signs that presenters use in IS show some variety as well, with incidental NSL influence appearing in an IS presenter's lecture, such as with the number 3 (thumb, index, and middle finger) as opposed to the 3 (index, middle, and ring fingers). The former looks like 8 in Auslan/BSL. In some Asian SLs the

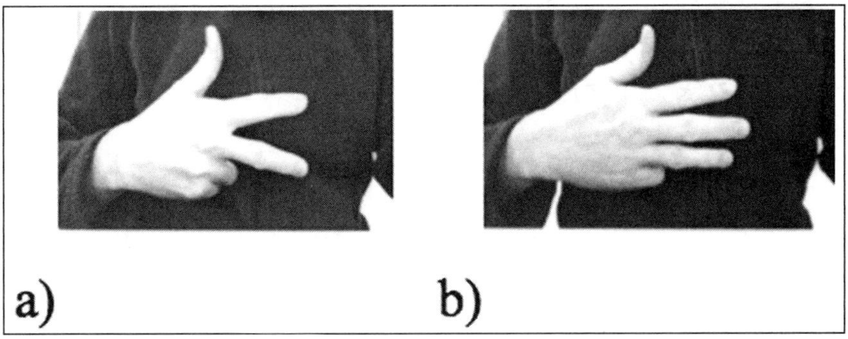

FIGURE 58. *Examples of numeric signs not always transparent across SLs: (a) three handshapes in ASL; (b) eight in JSL; eight in Auslan/BSL/CZSL; seven in JSL; nine in BSL/Auslan.*

numerical handshapes are different from what are seen in the American numeric handshape system and in IS conventions. In fact, the JSL number 7 is the same form as Auslan/BSL 8 and ASL 3. The JSL number 8 is the same form as Auslan/BSL 9. This added to some of the misunderstandings with numerical identifications (Figure 58a, b).

Results of number recognition in IS discourse are slightly lower for recalled numbers than for immediate retell (from video D). Again, this is likely due to cognitive processing effects and working memory. Correctly recalling the five Boy Scout age groups given in video E was problematic for many participants, even when these details were articulated slowly. Those who viewed the NSL versions, videos D′ (JFD Collaborations) and E′ (Boy Scouts), in most cases were better able to recall the number details given in their own NSL.

Summary of Lexical Identification Task

Results from the lexical identification section of the IS comprehension assessment indicate that lexical understanding by different IS audience observers is borderline successful, with average comprehension on this measure at 70.8%. The lowest score was 35%, and the median 72%. Comprehension of IS lexicon is mainly due to the observer's familiarity with the IS conventional lexical form. Otherwise, the sign may be a cognate from the observer's own NSL, or a transparent, iconic form. Unfortunately, iconicity does not always aid comprehension of a lexical sign, and there are some forms that are opaque to people who are not accustomed to using this IS contact system.

Differences across SLs number and fingerspelling systems impact what is understandable in expository IS lectures. Findings show that, contrary to Rosenstock's results, fingerspelled loan words (often English based) are not well understood by diverse observers. For immediate recall, fingerspelled words are correctly identified 56% of the time, and even less so after a short delay—24%. Only participants who share a similar one-handed fingerspelling system performed relatively successfully on these identifications. Numbers are similarly difficult to identify, with an average performance score of 51% (immediate) and 48% (delayed recall) across all participants. Shorter fingerspelled words and only iconic one-handed counting numbers are more easily understood by a variety of potential audience observers of an IS lecture.

Retell Task Performances

The next comprehension test element involved a retell task of video D (JFD Collaborations), which evaluated comprehension by asking participants to restate discourse information from an IS presentation. This measure assesses the understanding of discourse idea units from an IS presentation text and compares retelling performances from NSL versions of the same presentation information. This was done by showing a series of consecutive, 10- to 20-second segments of the IS presentation (video D) to half of the participants in each country cohort. The other half of the participants watched a NSL version (video D′).

A content analysis of IS video D resulted in the identification of 58 idea units for the scoring rubric. When the NSL translated version (D′) did not equivalently align with all 58 propositions in the source text, the rubric was adjusted. It was also expected that a participant would not obtain a perfect score retelling all of the propositional idea information from the source video, due to test fatigue and potential working memory differences in participants. Of interest in this assessment was the difference in the average amount of content retold between those who viewed the IS lecture and those who retold from the same content in their NSL.

Table 39 reports results of this comparison, and outlines participant performances by country cohort group. Across all participants, the average number of discourse idea units retold from the IS presentation text is 29 out of an average 55 idea units (53%). The number of units retold from the NSL versions is 42 (78%). With an average of 14 more idea units retold for those viewing the NSL text, the mean difference is 24%.

TABLE 39. *Comparing Amount of Retell Information from IS and NSL*

Country cohort (total idea units)	Average idea units IS (%)	Average idea units NSL (%)	Difference	Diff. %
Japan (51)	30 (59%)	39 (76%)	9	18%
Brazil (55)	24 (44%)	33 (60%)	9	16%
Czech Republic (56)	27 (48%)	45 (80%)	18	32%
Australia (57)	32 (56%)	45 (79%)	13	23%
United States (57)	34 (60%)	52 (91%)	18	31%
Average (55)	29 (53%)	42 (78%)	14	24%

Some cohorts retold as much as 32% more information from their NSL text than from the IS text, while the smallest differences are seen in the Brazilian and Japanese cohorts at 16% and 18%, respectively. The Brazilian cohort performed lower than other groups on both IS and NSL retells. It is unclear whether the smaller gap means the group on average understood more IS content or that they did not understand the NSL version as well as other groups. It is possible that the quality of an NSL interpretation varied between country cohorts, since the interpreter was not consistent across all NSL versions. In fact, the subjective rating of the video D′ NSL (LIBRAS) version was the lowest (avg = 4) among the other NSL versions. This suggests that they did not understand the NSL version as well as the other groups did.[5] At the very least, the cohort results indicate only that there is some improvement in understanding as demonstrated by more idea units retold, which is consistent with results seen in the other four cohorts.

Also, recall that the NSL version of video D for the Japan cohort was the only one that was not a translation and that the IS was rendered by a JSL native signer (as noted in the methodology). It is likely one reason that Japanese participants retold more than the average number of idea units (59%) from IS and the gap between NSL and IS retell scores is smaller. All other groups viewed a translated version created by a professional interpreter.

Besides the unique translation available for and used for this group, the reader is reminded that Japanese participants rated the IS text

5. During the time allotted to the research, the Brazilian interpreter was also quite ill with a severe cold, so this may have had some impact on the translations.

presenter in video D higher on average than other cohort participants. In other comprehension measures, the Japanese participants were at a disadvantage and had the lowest average results (lexical identifications, numbers, fingerspelling, and content questions). In the retell task, despite experiencing the IS presentation as slightly more understandable, this moderate difference in content retell performance between IS and NSL for the participants suggests that it was an advantage for Japanese participants to view IS presented by a JSL native signer. The advantage, however, merely levels the IS comprehension playing field, and still only an overall average of 53% of information was retold from IS versus 78% from one's NSL.

Upon closer analysis of participants individually, there were several strikingly different performances within each cohort. The results were polarized in that the participants showed much better comprehension or they did not understand IS much at all. In each cohort group there were participants who had traveled to a few other countries and met other deaf people; some participants reported they use IS regularly, and some not much or not at all. These participants were spread across the two treatment groups (IS versus NSL retell) and were randomly placed in a way that may have skewed these retell results. In the Japanese and Australian cohort, the two participants most experienced with IS were randomly assigned the IS retell—thus raising the average performance for their cohort on the IS retell. The two least experienced were both assigned the NSL retell. It is possible that these sociolinguistic factors on these performances balanced out the differences between the two treatment groups and make the gap appear smaller than in actuality. Given these results, it is reasonable to conclude *conservatively* that 24% less content is gleaned from expository IS texts than from NSL texts. Average scores for each group shown in Table 40 indicates that the 24% gap is typically the difference between successful and relatively unsuccessful comprehension of the discourse information, considering a benchmark of 75%.

The retell task required participants to restate idea information from the viewed segment of the presentation after each pause. A closer analysis of the average response scores on each idea unit in the rubric lends insight about types of information that was retold. In Appendix D, a comparison between the IS text retell and NSL text retell scores is listed for each idea

TABLE 40. *Average Detailed and Main Point Question Scores for IS Versus NSL Videos*

	JPN	BZ	CZ	US	AUS	Grand Mean
IS Video D & E	18%	44%	47%	55%	54%	**43%**
NSL Videos *D′* & *E′*	64%	68%	86%	86%	78%	**76%**

Video segment	Idea Units	Avg IS	Avg NSL
1a	Before we start, want to share something	31	44
1b	There was an earthquake in Japan	88	100
1c	It happened March 2011	25	75
1d	It caused a large tsunami	75	94
1e	The damage was terrible	50	94
1f	A nuclear accident and power outage occurred.	56	94
2a	The world Deaf communities (you) sent messages	81	94
2b	Asked if we were ok	69	63
2c	Money and donations were sent	94	88
2d	We want to thank you for your generosity.	94	94
2e	This supports the work of the JFD	19	50
3a	The JFD is working hard to help Deaf people affected	63	75
3b	We are making repairs	31	38
3c	Please continue to send donations.	38	88
4a	The JFD started in 1947	25	88
4b	Since then we work towards 4 aims	75	100
5a	One is interpreter training	56	75
5b	The second is obtaining legal/human rights for deaf people	38	75
5c	Thirdly attainment of Drivers licenses for Deaf persons	81	81
5d	Fourth, establishing more deaf (community service) organizations	38	69

FIGURE 59. *Selected results of IS and NSL idea unit retell (average) scores (% accuracy).*

unit. Figure 59 features an excerpt of the first five segments with average retell scores.

For participants who retold from the same text in their NSL, more of the discourse ideas were included in their retell than for their colleagues who viewed the IS original version. It also appears that more details are conveyed from one's NSL given the large differences in segments 1c, 3c, 4a, 5b, and 5d. Several segments of these retells are discussed next, along with discrepancies in participant responses.

In the first discourse segment, the presenter opens the lecture with a side narrative that is not related to his presentation. Earlier, mental space theory was mentioned as one of the frames assumed in this study, and an

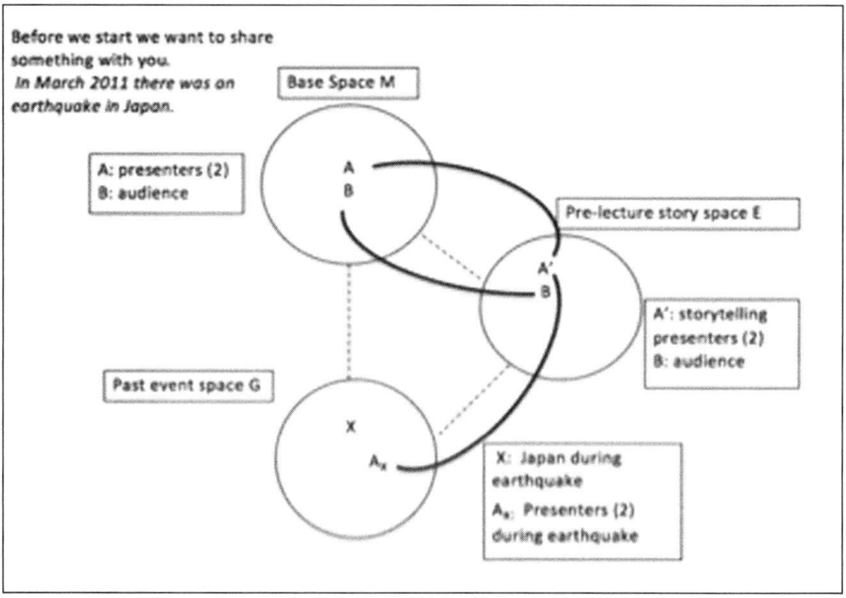

FIGURE 60. *Mental space construction of video D segments 1a to 1b.*

example from video D (JFD Collaborations) was given where discourse is built up via the prompting of different mental spaces (Figure 12 on p. 72, Chapter 3). The example is shown in Figure 60 again. The first segment in the idea unit rubric establishes a new mental space, diverting slightly from what is construed in the initial base space, 'M'. Initially, the aim of the presentation is to discuss the JFD and collaborative work (as given by the title of the video D), which prompts the audience to construe semantic information (idealized models) about lectures, types of audiences, and prior knowledge about the JFD, deaf associations, and the idea of collaborating with others.

Segments 1a–d provide more specific information (signs and semantic material) to complete the past event space G. The depicting signs and constructed action in the IS version prompt the understanding of the earthquake and tsunami. Because the differences between IS and NSL retell are small, this suggests that the signs aided understanding of segments 1b and 1d. The Japan earthquake was widely known from prior information that had been reported in the media for many months. The differences in IS and NSL performance is shown in the mention of the nuclear reactor accident (1f), which was indicated by a complex construction using depicting signs. The other, more detailed, discourse elements (1c, 1e, and 1f) were not fully realized or at least not conceptually integrated enough to be retold; however, they were retold more often by participants viewing their NSL version. The time-aligned sequence of annotations (File video D; time 2:51–3:14) for these segments is shown below (shaded bottom line denotes the nondominant hand simultaneous articulation):

1a PT:LOC BEFORE(ASL) LECTURE(ASL) START(WFD) PT:PRO3 WANT(AUS) INFORM(ASL) WHAT(ASL)

1c PT:PRO2PL KNOW(ASL) THREE-MONTH(WFD) G:ONE-ONE

1b NS: JAPAN G(5-SHAKE):WOW
DSM(5-DOWN):FLAT-ENTITIES-SHAKE-LIKE-EARTHQUAKE
DSM(5-DOWN):FLAT-ENTITIES-SHAKE-LIKE-EARTHQUAKE

1d SAME(AUS)
DSM(BENT5):CURVED-ENTITY-SWEEPS-AWAY-LIKE-TSUNAMI
DSG(B-DOWN):FLAT-ENTITY-EARTH-GROUND

1f SAME(AUS)ELECTRIC(ASL)DSS(BENT5):ENTITY-OVERHEAD-LIKE-LAMP
DSS(S):CYLINDRICAL-SHAPED-ENTITY-NUCLEAR-REACTOR
DSG(S):CYLINDRICAL-SHAPED-ENTITY-NUCLEAR-REACTOR

DSS(B):FLAT-TALL-BOXLIKE-ENTITY EXPLODE(ASL)
DSS(B):FLAT-TALL-BOXLIKE-ENTITY

DSM(5-WIGGLE):ENTITIES-MOVED-SPREAD-OUTWARD
FBUOY:REACTOR

1e DSM(5-WIGGLE):ENTITIES-SPREAD-OUT-RADIATE G(5-SHAKE):WOW
DSM(5-WIGGLE):ENTITIES-SPREAD-OUT-RADIATE

The results in Figure 59 suggest that the use of depicting signs to prompt the concept of the earthquake and tsunami (1b and 1d) may have been relatively effective for those viewing the IS presentation. Yet the established WFD signs THREE-MONTH may not have been understood by participants not accustomed to the form-meaning pair. Most participants who understood part of the date only retold the number 11 or 2011. Additional fully lexical signs construct the message, and some are more iconic than others, for example, EXPLODE(ASL) as opposed to ELECTRICAL(ASL). One gesture provides a visual number ONE and ONE (to denote 11), and another, G(5-SHAKE):WOW is a highly occurring gesture in IS that acts as a modifier. Uttered alongside the

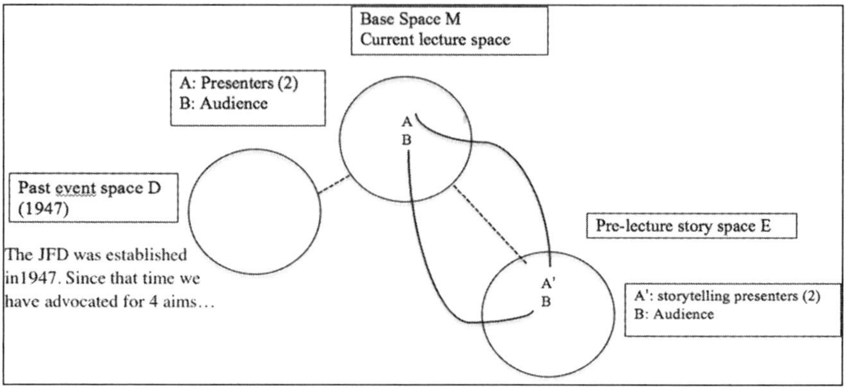

FIGURE 61. *Video D past event space.*

depicting signs before it, the construction was translated to mean [THE DAMAGE WAS TERRIBLE]. This is a less explicit piece of discourse, yet most participants who viewed the NSL version did retell this idea unit.

In segments 4a–5d, the presenter signs an utterance that shifts discourse focus back to the base space M (the original departure point of the presentation). He utters NS:JAPAN DEAF(AUS) ASSOCIATION(GEST) DSM(S)PLACE-ENTITY-ON-TOP-OF-OTHER-LIKE-FOUNDATION YEAR(ASL) ONE(ASL) NINE(WFD) FOUR(ASL) SEVEN (WFD). This utterance prompts a new mental space (continuing from the base space M with the main lecture aims and topic) with the space builder that means [THE JFD WAS ESTABLISHED IN 1947]. It also instantiates a new current discourse space: the past event of the JFD founding in 1947 (see Figure 61). Next, he prompts the meaning [SINCE THAT TIME WE HAVE ADVOCATED FOR] with the depicting sign and three fully lexical signs: DSM(5-WIGGLE):OBJECTS-MOVING-FORWARD-PAST-TO-NOW HIT(ASL) WHAT(ASL) IMPORTANT(ASL). He then introduces several aims of the JFD with the use of a list buoy (4) held up in the nondominant hand. (See Figure 62.) The signer points to each buoy (finger) to establish token blends for the four aims. The buoy refers to discourse (and mental space) elements including (1) interpreter training programs, (2) improved human rights legislation, (3) driving licenses for deaf people, and (4) more organizations by and/or for deaf people.

Several symbolic units (signs and constructions) that are semantically profiled and recognized provide specific detailed elements to the

FIGURE 62. *List buoy (4) aims of the organization.*

discourse and complete the new mental space. When participants do not completely understand symbols such as fully lexical signs from an NSL, they are left with gaps in understanding all of the points or details in the presentation.

Many participants who retold from IS did not understand the numeric founding year of the JFD; only those who retold from the NSL version demonstrated better understanding of this detail. Although the rubric does not distinctly measure the idea of the past establishment of the organization, responses by participants indicate they did understand (75%) the list buoy (4) (Figure 62) and the elements of the new mental space, which are *broadly,* four aims. The next series of signs provides more detail about what the four aims are, and require the participant to recognize several borrowed ASL, Auslan, and established WFD lexical items, as well as several depicting signs.

Results from the IS retell and NSL retell (excerpt in Figure 59 and full results in Appendix D) show that some of the discourse elements were realized for both treatment groups (81% for both), such as the third aim toward granting driver licenses to deaf people. The IS signer articulates an iconic sign STEER-CAR(AUS) and the ASL sign LICENSE, immediately followed by a depicting sign, DSS(GC):SHAPE-FLAT-RECTANGULAR-ENTITY. If participants did not know the ASL sign, the depicting sign provided a description of the object (license) referred to by the fully lexical form. The iconic Auslan sign, which enacts the behavior of driving, is also similar in ASL and other SLs, and might be commonly recognized as a gesture to nonsigners. The form provides context to the depiction of the flat rectangular entity describing the shape of the license.

The other three aims are understood with mixed success from the IS lecture and more successfully so from NSL versions. Semantically specific signs in a person's NSL provide familiar form-meaning pairs and enable profiled things and actions to be integrated into their cognitive representation and fill mental spaces that are constructed in lecture discourses. Shifts of discourse focus were sometimes missed, leading participants to misunderstand main points when this occurred. In the example above, where the presenter shifts away from the past event space of the prior earthquake to begin discussing the JFD's work, one participant did not make the shift and for the duration of the retell thought that the presenter was still discussing the repair efforts after the earthquake, rather than the ongoing development toward the four aims and additional text information about leadership training.

The full summary results (Appendix D) show that several other gaps in information between IS and one's NSL occurred for participants. Findings from this retell task for video D/D′ demonstrate that IS comprehension pivots on effective recognition of a multiplicity of semiotic symbols, and without sufficient conventional forms (as there are in established SLs) participants have varied success cognitively integrating what the IS signer means.

Comparing Measures of IS Comprehension to NSL Comprehension

It was expected that participants would comprehend a NSL presentation better than one in IS, and this is shown from the retell task of videos D and D′. Within two other measures of IS comprehension, scores for IS versus NSL stimulus videos D/D′ and E/E′ are extractable, hence some additional results contribute to the comparison. Differences in comprehensibility ratings of the IS texts A–E and the NSL texts (D′ and E′) align with actual performance measures on the retell task and on the content questions. These are discussed briefly next.

Subjective Comprehensibility Ratings of IS Versus NSL Texts

The first measure of comprehension in this study indicated, not surprisingly, that lectures shown in participants' local NSL were judged

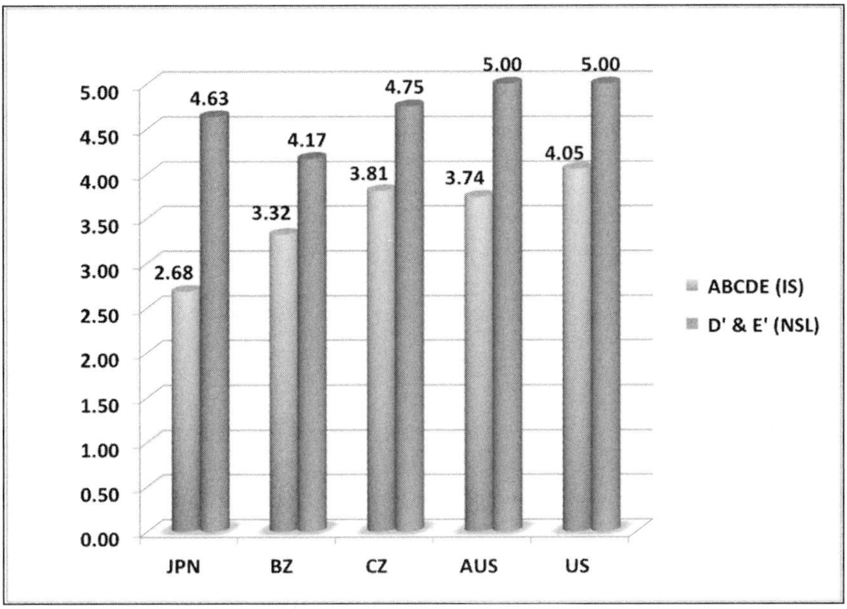

FIGURE 63. *Average comprehension ratings for all IS and NSL texts.*

more comprehensible than IS lectures to a highly significant degree ($p \leq .01$).

The translated NSL versions of IS presentation D′ (JFD Collaborations) and E′ (Boy Scouts) were rated as the most understandable by all participants, more so than the expository IS presentation videos A through E and specifically more so than the IS videos D and E (Figure 63).

Although the results depicted above show differences, for some cohorts these differences are larger than for others. The largest difference is seen from ratings by the Japanese participants, who judged the IS texts on average almost half as understandable as texts in their NSL. The smallest difference is observed in the ratings by the Brazilian participants, who rated the IS texts an average of 3.32 and the NSL version an average of 4.17. There were a small number of participants in each cohort (6–8) and ratings by one or two outliers may have impacted the average. Most participants in all cohort groups generally rated the NSL video version between 4 and 5. One of the Brazilian participants rated understanding of the translated video D′ (JFD Collaborations) with a much lower score of 3, which impacted the overall average of the cohort. Findings indicate consistently that

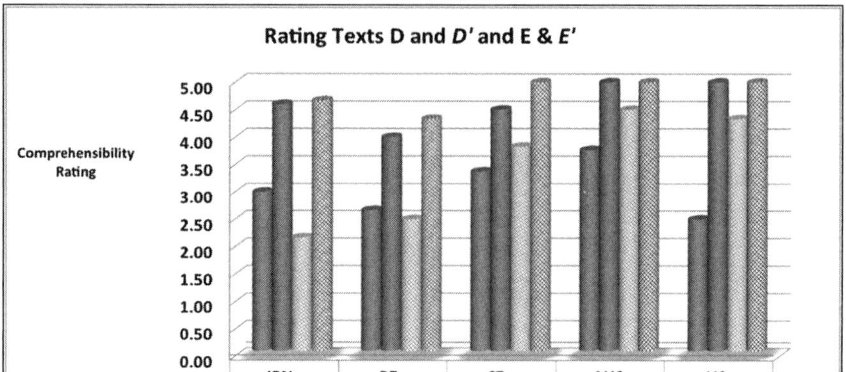

	JPN	BZ	CZ	AUS	US
D	3.00	2.67	3.38	3.77	2.50
D'	4.60	4.00	4.50	5.00	5.00
E	2.17	2.50	3.83	4.50	4.33
E'	4.67	4.33	5.00	5.00	5.00

FIGURE 64. *Average ratings of IS texts D and E and NSL texts D′ and E′ across cohort groups.*

presentations in one's NSL are perceived as more understandable than those viewed in IS.

The above comparison includes all of the IS videos and their ratings with the two translated NSL video ratings. By looking at only ratings for IS videos D and E and comparing them with ratings of NSL videos D′ and E′ across cohort groups, some additional findings are noted. Figure 64 indicates that Japanese participants judged the IS presentation by the JSL native signer (video D) as not as understandable as the actual JSL version; however, they experienced video D to be more understandable than IS video E. This rating is higher than the Brazilian and U.S. participants and close to the average rating given by the Czech Republic cohort. The Australians rated video E (Boy Scouts) as nearly as understandable as the NSL version, which may be due to the signer in video E—an Irish SL native presenting in IS. Both Irish SL and Auslan are variants of the same language, BSL.

This is contrasted with the ratings by three of the four other country cohorts' ratings for both video pairs. The Czech Republic, Australian, and U.S. participants all rated video E as more understandable than video D. The Brazilian cohort rated them almost the same, much less understandable than the versions in their NSL.

Comparing Scores for IS and NSL Detailed Content Questions

Performances on content questions were reported above. Performance on questions about these videos D/D′ and E/E′—different versions of the same content—showed evidence of much less equivalence for audience members who attend IS presentations than their counterparts who see the same content in their known SL.

Significant differences were reported about the comprehension of global information (78%), main points (57%), and details (46%) in IS presentations. Also, this stark difference is shown in comprehension of main points and details from the IS videos, D and E, as opposed to that of the local sign language versions, videos D′ and E′. Table 40 shows these comparative results. Additionally, there was no significant difference in comprehension of global discourse between the two groups (IS and NSL lectures). The fact that differences are shown in main points and details further verifies findings about the quality and level of information that IS audience members glean. By juxtaposing the comprehension differences between the two experimental treatment groups on detailed questions, one sees that some groups understand two or three times less discourse information from IS than from their NSL—much of what appears to be main points and details.

Summary of IS and NSL Comparative Comprehension

From the measures and results reported, it is evident that there are unsurprising substantial differences between comprehension of expository IS lectures and those in a observer's NSL. Not only were IS presentations rated less understandable by participants than NSL presentations, but performance measures on a retell task show an average 24% loss of content from IS lectures than by NSL lectures. In addition, the informational content that appears to not be fully understood by varied IS audience members are discourse details and main points.

Characteristics of Participants Who Comprehend IS Presentations

There is an abundance of quantitative data resulting from these comprehension measures, as reported above. From these data, it is evident that participant understanding of IS presentations is influenced by more than their country and SL origins, and there are some trends that align with earlier findings in the Rosenstock study. Several characteristics are noted by looking at the demographics of participants who were more successful at comprehending IS presentations, as well as analyzing the demographics of participants who demonstrated the least comprehension.

For this study, a benchmark of effective comprehension was posed at 75% or better. There were six participants who met or surpassed this point of reference on the two main measures of comprehension—the lexical identifications task and content question interview. The top third (n = 10) performed with a combined score of 75% or higher on the two measures. Several of them also scored comparatively higher than others on recognition of fingerspelled terms and numbers, and rated IS stimulus videos relatively high compared to the grand mean. Comparing these "comprehenders" with the lowest scoring third (n = 10) indicates sociolinguistic factors for comprehending expository IS.

The next three tables provide summary information about both groups of participants. These are the top 10 who were able to understand IS lectures relatively successfully and the lowest-scoring 10 participants for whom IS is not a contact language of universal access (Table 41). The remaining middle third (n = 12) of participants scored variably around the average scores. None of them demonstrated effective comprehension on the combined comprehension score, although they had mixed success with lexical identifications and questions.

The differences between the two groups' scores for each measurement in Table 41 are statistically significant ($p < .05$). First, I will discuss characteristics of participants who demonstrated successful comprehension of IS lectures (Table 42). One notices several similarities among the top-scoring participants. All but one have some degree of bilingual knowledge

TABLE 41. *Average Percentage Scores for the Top Third and Bottom Third of All Test Participants*

	Lexical IDs	Finger-spelling	Avg Numbers	Content Qs	Combined Score LexlDs+Qs	Mean IS Ratings[B]
Highest Scoring 10	92	60	68	75	84	4.2
Lowest Scoring 10	57	31	29	47	52	3

[B] ratings based on scale of 1 to 5, not percentage score.

TABLE 42. *Sociolinguistic Characteristics of Participants Who Comprehend IS*

First SL	Deaf Parent(s)	Education	Age 1st learned SL	School Info	Use of IS	Travel Experience (# countries)	ASL Knowledge	English Knowledge	# of SLs Known
AUSLAN	Y	G	0	M	SOMETIMES	36	some	L2	3
CZSL	N	G	3	D	OFTEN	17	zero	L2	1
CZSL	Y	G	0	B	REGULAR	15	some	L2	2
ASL	N	G	2	D	SOMETIMES	1	native	L2	1
ASL	Y	F	0	M	RARE	2	native	L2	1
ASL	Mixed	F	0	B	RARE	1	native	L2	1
CZSL	N	E	4.5	D	WEEKLY	8	some	zero	3
ASL	Y	G	0	D	RARE	6	native	L2	5
CZSL	Y	G	0	B	OFTEN	12	zero	L2	1
AUSLAN	N	G	4	B	OFTEN	2	very little	L2	3

Note. Education codes: E = high school diploma; F = some university; G = >15 years/graduated.
School codes: M = mainstreamed; D = sign in and outside classroom; B = sign only outside classroom.

of English, although there is a mix of monolingual NSL users among some with knowledge of other SLs. Nine out of 10 have a university diploma, and 6 out of 10 were raised by at least one deaf parent. Most of them report using IS (self-reported) at least six or many more times per year (or month), and most have extensive travel experience where they have met and interacted with other deaf people. Four of these top third IS performing participants are native ASL users, while most of the others report second-language knowledge of ASL. In terms of primary and secondary education, there are no real trends. Some participants attended schools for the deaf where they used SL in the classroom and/or outside of the classroom with peers. Two attended mainstream educational programs rather than residential schools for the deaf.

Although most of the study participants experienced a large reduction in comprehension of main points and details from IS discourses, the top scoring six (out of the 10 listed in Table 42) gleaned more main points and details than other participants did. The top six performing participant scores on global (87%), main point (83%), and detailed information (68%) fell much closer to one another. Although these six participants were successful at gleaning information from expository IS, as with all other cohort group members main point and detailed information understood from IS videos D and E (72%) was much lower than from their NSL videos D′ and E′ (95%). This group of six were uniquely in a position to gain information from IS compared to the rest of the participants in the study.

Comparing the above demographics with the sociolinguistic characteristics of the lower third of participants (Table 43), one notices that many of the participants performing in the lower third report less knowledge of both English and ASL. Another major difference is seen in that the amount of travel experience and reported use of IS are less frequent. In terms of education, all in this lower third are high school graduates, half of whom have attended some tertiary education but have not yet completed a university diploma. Most of these participants learned their NSL at a young age, although on average it was slightly later than the top third performing cohort. Most of these participants attended schools for the deaf where they used their NSL in class and/or outside class with peers.

Analysis of Variables

Participants were grouped by demographic information, according to scores on measured aspects of comprehension. A series of analyses were made

TABLE 43. *Sociolinguistic Characteristics of Participants Who Did Not Comprehend IS*

First SL	Deaf Parent(s)	Education	Age 1st learned SL	School Info	Use of IS	Travel Experience (# countries)	ASL Knowledge	English Knowledge	# of SLs Known
AUSLAN	Y	E	0	B	SOMETIMES	0	zero	L2	1
LIBRAS	N	F	3	B	RARE	0	zero	zero	1
JSL	N	E	20	B	ZERO	1	very little	some	2
JSL	N	E	2	D	ZERO	0	some	very little	2
LIBRAS	N	F	4	B	RARE	0	zero	zero	1
JSL	N	E	14	D	ZERO	2	some	very little	3
ASL	Mixed	F	2	B	SOMETIMES	2	native	L2	1
AUSLAN	N	E	3	M	ZERO	9	very little	L2	4
LIBRAS	N	F	2	B	RARE	0	some	zero	2
LIBRAS	N	F	1.5	B	SOMETIMES	0	zero	zero	1

Note. Education codes: E = high school diploma; F = some university; G = >15 years/graduated. *School codes*: M = mainstreamed; D = sign in and outside classroom; B = sign only outside classroom.

for several independent and dependent factors. Results indicate sociolinguistic patterns that correlate with improved IS comprehension and are discussed in this section.

The following comprehension measures were of interest: participants' subjective comprehension ratings of IS videos, their lexical identification scores, IS content question scores, and propositional retell scores. These were the established measurements of how well a person understands IS expository text. Certain variables were expected to correlate with higher scores. Results of a series of Pearson *r* correlation tests are shown in Table 44. Across the comprehension measurements the analysis indicates that understanding common lexical signs in IS does relate strongly with better performance on answering content questions and a retelling task. The grand mean of subjective ratings of comprehension was also correlated positively with the grand mean of participants' performances on

TABLE 44. *Correlation Results Between Performance Measures*

Independent variables Performance scores	Dependent variables (Significance at $p \leq .05$)	Correlation (R)
Lexical IDs score	Content questions	$R = .6999$; $p = .000001$[a]
Lexical IDs score (on Video D)	Retell task	$R = .6544$; $p = .0059$[a]
Combined score (Video D Lexical IDs + content questions)	Retell task	$R = .6144$; $p = .0113$[a]
Subjective IS comprehension ratings	Content questions	$R = .7441$; $p = .00001$[a]
Subjective IS comprehension ratings	Retell task	$R = .6999$; $p = .000001$[a]
Subjective comprehension for each video (A–E)	Content questions for each video	A: $R = .259$; $p = .145$ B1: $R = .086$; $p = .632$ B2: $R = .624$; $p = .000$[a] C: $R = .615$; $p = .000$[a] D: $R = .571$; $p = .021$[a] E: $R = .600$; $p = .014$[a] D′: $R = .351$; $p = .200$ E′: $R = .587$; $p = .017$[a]

[a]Positively correlated; significant at the .05 level.

content questions. For the Video D retell task, this was also the case—participants rated their understanding of Video D, which correlated with their actual performance on the retell task. Upon closer analysis, however, participants' rating of understanding did not always correlate with their performance on questions (for videos A, B1, D′).

The amount of sign types, as well as the amount of signs from different origins, was also analyzed against participants' ratings of their understanding of each test video and actual performances on content questions. Main effects were investigated, and results from these analyses showed no significant correlation between linguistic variables of videos and participants' ratings of their understanding of each video; however, there were some correlations between linguistic variables (videos that contained more or less gesture, constructed action, English mouthing, and varied sign origins) and participants' performance on questions. A summary table of correlation and regression findings is shown in Table 45.

TABLE 45. *Summary of Main Effects of Linguistic Factors for IS Comprehension*

Analysis Content question score vs.:	Source	Df	F-value	P-value	Comment
Amount of gesture (Hi, Med, Low)	Factor Error	2 77	10.67	0.00[a]	More gesture → improved score
Amount of CA enactment (Hi, Med, Low)	Factor Error	1 95	0.57	0.45	No relationship
English mouthing (Hi, Low) Ling (Eng, NonEng) SocioLing	Regression Factor Ling FactorSocLing Error	2 1 1 105	4.53 0.43 8.95	0.13 0.52 0.003[a]	More mouthing + English L2 → improved score
Sign Origins ASL Auslan[b] WFD *Gestuno*[b]	Regression VideoSignOrigin SignerL1 Error	7 3 4 53	3.27 2.16 4.33	0.006[a] 0.103 0.004[a]	Sign Origins → Improved score only for ASL L1

[a]The mean differences are significant at the 95% confidence level.

[b]ASL native users performed significantly *lower* on videos with more Auslan and more *Gestuno* signs.

Participants in general performed significantly higher on questions from videos that contained more gesture signs (videos B1 and B2) than those with a moderate amount or much less gesture (A, C, D, and E). However, the topic of video B (both presenters) was previously noted to be very familiar to many deaf people; therefore, it is not known whether the increased amount of gesture alone, or the familiarity of the topic (or both) influenced the higher scores on content questions. Videos with more or less CA enactment did not have a significant relationship to participant comprehension scores—subjective rating or content questions.

Other linguistic variables, such as English mouthings and sign origins, were correlated with higher scores on content questions only for participants who know English as an L2 (for English mouthings) or who are native ASL users. There was no significant difference in content question performances on videos with more or less Auslan, WFD, or *Gestuno* signs for most groups. The exception, however, is that the ASL natives performed significantly lower on videos with more Auslan and more *Gestuno* signs. It is apparent (and not surprising) that the prevalence of English and ASL in international communications benefits understanding of IS for those who know these two languages.

Table 46 reports on several sociolinguistic characteristics and the relationship of these to IS comprehension measures. All results are main effects. Travel experience is a factor in the performance of comprehension tests, lexical IDs, and content question scores. There is no significant difference between comprehension of IS for participants who have some travel experiences (one or two countries) and those with a large amount of travel experience (more than two countries). However, any amount of travel (two or more countries) positively correlates with comprehension when compared to no travel experience, with extensive travel being significant (p = 0.002 and 0.042, respectively, for lexical ID score and content question performance). Participants who are native SL users (with at least one deaf parent or who began learning SL before the age of 3 years) performed significantly better on the combined comprehension score. These 17 participants also met at least one other of the significant factors noted in this variable analysis. Education is one of the other factors for better IS comprehension. Having at least 2 or 4 years of college or university was related to better performance on the measures in this study.

There are also significant comprehension performance differences noted between participants with no use of IS and those who use it at all (regular or rarely). The amount of use of IS is not significantly related to

TABLE 46. *Main Effects of Sociolinguistic Variables and Comprehension Scores*

Sociolinguistic variables Regression analyses	Response	Df	*F*-Value	*P*-Value	Comment
Travel experience (zero, some, extensive)	Lexical ID Score	29	5.96	0.003[a]	Travel experience → Comprehension especially extensive travel
	Content Q score	29	5.46	0.004[a]	
	Combined score	28	8.06	0.001[a]	
Knowledge of ASL (native, some, zero)	Lexical ID Score	29	7.24	0.003[a]	ASL L1 only; some ASL does not predict comprehension
	Content Q score	29	3.77	0.035	
	Combined score	29	6.70	0.004[a]	
Knowledge of English (L2, some, zero)	Lexical ID Score	29	5.61	0.009[a]	English L2 only for Lexical ID score
	Content Q score	29	1.01	0.378	
	Combined score	29	3.46	0.045[a]	
Experience with use of IS (zero, sometimes, often, weekly)	Lexical ID Score	26	2.56	0.052[B]	[B] Zero and often significant
	Content Q score	26	2.10	0.098	
	Combined score	26	2.81	0.037[a]	
Education level (HS, 2-year degree, 4-year degree)	Lexical ID Score	29	3.96	0.030[a]	University degree significant
	Content Q score	29	4.48	0.020[a]	
	Combined score	29	5.17	0.012[a]	
Native SL user/ Deaf parent(s)	Lexical ID Score	30	8.56	0.007[a]	
	Content Q score	30	8.73	0.006[a]	
	Combined score	30	10.68	0.003[a]	

[a] The results are significant at 95% confidence level.

comprehension scores between participants who report using IS regularly, rarely, or weekly/monthly. This means that using IS even rarely is correlated with improved comprehension.

Qualitative Data: Depiction Segments

Meaning construction in SLs includes composite elements that are linguistic and nonlinguistic. Gesture-like enactment that occurs with established, fully lexical signs and partly specified depicting signs are symbolic units created by sign language users, and they are also observed in the mixed contact system of expository IS. Depicting types are signs that contribute to the lexicons of NSLs, and they also appear quite frequently, comprising 10.2% of all sign types in the IS data. Depicting signs are productive in expository IS to convey information about the size and shape of referents and how they move. They also can convey abstract ideas, metaphorically constructing real space blends, as seen in the NSL examples from chapter 3 and the IS examples from the lexical analysis. This next section reports on participants' understanding of several depicting sign segments shown to them from the context of an IS video they had just observed and about which they had answered questions.

Participants were asked to elaborate on the meaning of several short, depicting sequences in IS presentations. These segments are illustrative examples of the kinds of composite constructions employed in expository IS lectures to convey concepts. Defined and described in chapter 3, depiction in SL is a more complex construction that is made up of linguistic and gestural elements (Liddell, 2003; Schembri, 2001). Depicting signs can do either of two things: depict action of a referent and/or depict spatial relationships of referents, both of which involve exploiting visual imagery elements in signed discourse (Dudis, 2011). It is suggested that creative and flexible depicting signs assist audience comprehension of complex relations and abstract ideas. As a result, they "maximize iconic representations without the audience knowing a common vocabulary or a standard lexicon" (Rosenstock, 2004, p. 146).

In total, 20 depicting segments were shown during the comprehension testing. A selection of nine are reported on due to the potentially large scope of analysis of 20 DS segments. These nine depicting segments are noted in Table 47.

Depicting Sign Comprehension

Each selected segment used in this part of the comprehension assessment constitutes a rich, meaningful combination of depicting signs, borrowed and/or conventional lexical signs, space blends, and iconic gestural elements that construct meaning. Participants were shown a few short depicting utterances, which capture points made in the video lecture they watched. A semistructured interview approach is taken by asking the participant questions such as, "What did s/he mean when s/he signed that?" and "What do you think that means?" When participants offer limited, general responses like, "Things are increasing," subsequent follow-up

TABLE 47. *Selected Depicting Segments in Comprehension Test*

Clip ID	Meaning (free translation in context)
DSA2	"A small amount" of information (known about deaf health accessibility, little research)
DSA4	We need to create a clearinghouse for best practices in Deaf Health Care and disseminate this information to global communities.
DSB4	We lobby the government for Deaf people to gain equal (to hearing people's) access to effective education.
DSB5	Collaborations from Deaf associations in other countries contribute to the local (English-speaking African countries) knowledge and improvements.
DSC2	Improvements in Deaf education, SL recognition, and Deaf rights are thwarted by external ignorant social-political influences.
DSC4	(There is no need to) Be defeated and downtrodden, asking for handouts.
DSD2	Over time we have worked and continue to push for the establishment of driving license rights, improved human rights for deaf people, interpreter education, and creating more deaf organizations.
DSD4	Training programs support the development of deaf leaders, who return to their (Asian) communities and influence improvements in Deaf quality of life.
DSE2	Deaf Scout troops evolved out of an original mixed hearing/ deaf troop.

questions are asked, such as, "What sort of things are increasing, from what you understood of that part of the lecture?"

Of keen interest to the question of IS comprehension is the way depicting signs operate across language boundaries. The topic was elaborated on in Chapter 3, where depicting signs feature as one of the meaning-prompting elements in SLs and participate in real space blends (Liddell, 2003). In Chapter 3, the interaction between iconicity and metaphor and Taub's analogue building (AB) framework was introduced (Taub, 2001). Real space blending (Liddell, 2003) and the AB model provide a framework for the analysis of participants' understanding of short, depicting constructions that convey meaning in IS discourse.

Context and Comprehension of Depicting Signs in IS

In the first depiction, labeled DSA2 a single size and shape specifying (SASS) depiction sign was shown from video A. The form is observed

FIGURE 65. *Depicting sign DSA2:* DSS(GCFlat): SMALL-AMOUNT *(Free translation: "A limited amount of information is known about deaf health care access [in the context of research evidence available].").*

in ASL and Auslan and is quite conventionally used to indicate a small amount of an abstract entity. The depicting sign is a single movement, presenting the handshape GCFlat (pictured in Figure 65).

The IS presenter in the video clip uses the depicting sign (size and shape specifier) to mean an insufficient amount or small amount of knowledge or information about health care and accessibility for deaf people worldwide. The context of this utterance is a research initiative on which he and a colleague have been working. The depicting sign appears four times in the video clip shown to all participants, where the signer is giving a summary introduction before his colleague is due to come forth and provide more information about their research work together. Participants view only this 6-minute introduction and summary, not the second presenter. The sign is used 14 times in the IS lexical frequency dataset, and quantifies intangible things such as information and signing skill, as well as amount or size of physical entities such as students, distance, and money.

While this depicting sign may be recognized as a conventional way to describe the relatively small size and shape (and volume) of some object in a variety of SLs, it is nonetheless a partially specified depicting sign, which appears in this utterance to be quantifying the amount of information known about deaf people's accessibility to health care. It fits the category of a partially lexical sign given its gradient meaning potential (Liddell, 2003) and gestural character, since its meaning is dependent on the context in which it is uttered. For example, it could also be used to describe liquid in a bottle, or the length of a piece of licorice candy.

After being shown the depicting sign, participants were asked about what the signer meant by this utterance. Most participants from all test sites were able to identify it as describing a small amount of something in a literal sense, replying, "a little or small amount," with no trends indicating that a person's native SL or country of origin impacted understanding of the depiction. There was, however, overall mixed understanding of the referent and whether it was a small amount of physical objects or abstract ideas. Participants were able to expand on what the signer was referring to in the metaphoric sense ABSTRACT-IDEAS-ARE-PHYSICAL-OBJECTS-TO-BE-MANIPULATED-IN-SPACE, indicating in most cases an understanding that this was not a small amount of tangible objects, but of abstract things. Only two participants (one from Australia and one from Brazil) believed the sign referred to tangible things only but did not indicate what tangible thing the speaker was referencing.

A participant from the United States believed it referred to a small amount of time (response was "almost" or "soon"), and a Brazilian replied it meant some tangible thing that is short in size. For the most part, the general semantic sense of this depiction was understood, as the form is iconic and also a widely recognized emblematic gesture to people who do not know a SL. Nonetheless, all participants saw the form four times in the IS presentation text just minutes before, and only nine of them articulated the exact reference: "a limited amount or small amount of information or knowledge." For those who understood key topic signs, HEALTH and RESEARCH indicated quite precisely that the small information was regarding accessible health care for deaf people. Three participants stated that they did not understand what kind of information was "limited" or "small," except for one who thought it referred to a small amount of information about sign language.

These responses suggest that depicting signs, which are composed of specific yet also nonspecific (gestural) parts, aid comprehension of IS, but only if the context is known. Context plays an influential part in how well depicting signs are understood in expository IS. Contextual information is created by the presentation topic, as well as specific lexical signs used throughout the discourse.

Lexical Signs and Depicting Signs Cooperating in IS Comprehension

The next depicting sign cluster is also from video A, where the presenter describes a need to gather information about best practices in deaf health care access, such as a clearinghouse, and disseminate it or make

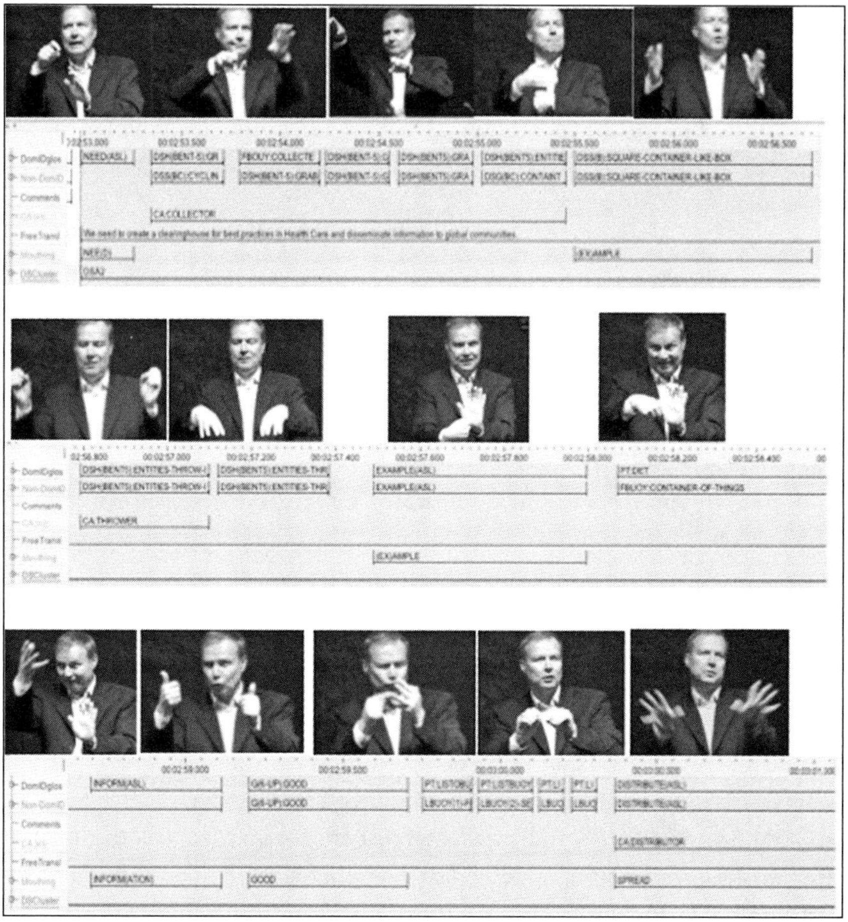

FIGURE 66. *Depiction Segment DSA4 (Free translation: "We need to create a clearinghouse for best practices [in deaf health care] and disseminate this information to global [deaf] communities.").*

it available to deaf people in countries around the world. This construction is shown below and the researcher will elaborate on its elements and participants' understanding from the discourse context.

The segment "DSA4" (Figure 66) incorporates many different types of signs in a composite utterance. These are lexical signs NEED, EXAMPLE, INFORM, DISTRIBUTE, a gesture-like emblem GOOD (thumbs up), constructed action, a list buoy that serves as a token and is pointed to, as well as depicting signs and metaphoric blends (see link to the clip DSA4). List buoys involve holding up fingers and pointing to them in order to list out referents in the discourse. The IS signer in this clip indicates LIST-BUOY: FIRST-THROUGH FOURTH, to point to representative aspects of best practices in deaf health care and accessibility. These aspects are not specified in the utterance, but earlier in the discourse varied elements of accessible health care are noted. The participants' prior knowledge about the domain of health-care access would prompt possible referents, such as adapted health information, provision of interpreting services, and so on.

With two examples of constructed action, the signer uses facial expression and body movements along with enacting gesture signs to "collect" and also "throw into the box" several pieces of information. The box is a metaphorical container for the information about best practices in health care for deaf people. He also employs a depicting sign, a DSS (size and shape specifier) depicting the metaphoric box, which co-constructs the enacted handling behavior THROW-IN-BOX.

Three signs that are conventional in ASL and borrowed into IS appear in this clip. Two of them, INFORM and DISTRIBUTE, use the metaphor ABSTRACT-IDEAS-ARE-PHYSICAL-OBJECTS simultaneously with the CONDUIT-METAPHOR to convey meaning. The individual fingers splayed by the 5 handshape  iconically map plural OBJECTS, which are pieces of information in the iconic blend. This example was given in Chapter 3 with the ASL sign DISTRIBUTE (Figure 15 on p. 77). The head is the starting location of the ASL sign INFORM, compounding the meaning with yet another metaphor, THE-MIND-IS-A-CONTAINER.

DISTRIBUTE also resembles the Auslan sign SPILL, which starts with two closed-fist "S" handshapes. In only one phonological modification of initial starting handshape (two-handed FLAT-O handshape), both conventional signs (ASL and Auslan versions) spread the fingers outward in the second part of sign. Movement of the open hand from the head outward in the sign INFORM and from the signing space outward in the sign DISTRIBUTE maps the conduit and direction.

Applying the framework of Taub's double mapping analogue model, the signs INFORM and DISTRIBUTE can be described as both iconic and metaphoric in their mapping. In both signs, the fingers iconically map individual pieces of information and as an entity, the multiple fingers represent multiple thoughts or ideas (depending on the sign INFORM or DISTRIBUTE). The second, metaphoric, level of mapping occurs with the location where the fingers of the hand are first held. The starting signing space is at the front of the head, which in many cultures represents a container of thoughts and ideas. These thoughts can thus be shared with others. The individual fingers are iconic tokens for representative thoughts; when released outward away from the signer, they are then given to others who receive the information.

In the second sign, the depicting 5 hands  start lower in the signing space, where one can possess something (literally in the physical sense and abstractly). Then, the metaphor that operates in this sign, ABSTRACT-IDEAS-ARE-PHYSICAL-OBJECTS, allows the information that has been collected to move and "spread outward" as if literally targeting them toward varied locations. Those locations are varied countries, which is indicated in the larger discourse context, particularly with the IS fully lexical sign WORLD(GEST).

Several real space and metaphoric blends, therefore, operate simultaneously and/or sequentially through these depicting signs in clip DSA4 to build up the idea that information needs to be collected and placed in a metaphorical box from which pieces of data can be shared with others elsewhere. Metaphors such as SHAPES-ARE-CONTAINERS, THE-CONDUIT-METAPHOR and ABSTRACT-IDEAS-ARE-PHYSICAL-OBJECTS are conceptual devices used to convey meaning in this sequence. UP-IS-GOOD, another common metaphor, is present in this segment through a cross-cultural gestural emblem and the Auslan lexical sign GOOD "thumbs up." Whether participants viewing this segment understood the remaining conventional ASL signs NEED and EXAMPLE is difficult to discern, and they are not among the high-frequency lexical signs shown as part of the lexical identification task. The sign form ID glossed as EXAMPLE is polysemous in ASL and also can mean "show." The composite utterance indicates that good quality examples of access in health care comprise the information (i.e., from research) that can be collected and disseminated to Deaf associations and communities in varied countries.

Participants' responses indicate that several concepts within these metaphoric domains were understood by this depicting sequence, but not all nuances of the message were grasped. Most people did recognize that the physical box being depicted was actually a metaphoric "box" for the collection of something (e.g., information), as opposed to a real physical box. Participants did not always explicitly state the type of information gathered. When asked once again, those who understood key topic signs in the full text—BODY and ANALYZE—replied that it was deaf health-care information and research data to this effect. When the signs NEED and EXAMPLE were fully understood (two native ASL users and one Australian participant), the detail about the type of information (best practices) was understood. Two participants (one Czech and one Japanese) believed there was a meeting or gathering where people were collecting data together. This implies that they both did not understand the container metaphor.

Responses include "research or data being gathered" from "different places in the world" and "a meeting or central location" where "reports are sent out or given" to "different countries." This activity was reportedly happening (present tense) rather than it *needs* to happen. Responses were ambiguous as to time frame. Different responses indicated mixed understanding about whether this activity had happened, was needed, will be happening, or was perhaps currently happening. Recall that the presentation discourse is describing the lack of research on deaf health, and the signer's colleague would next present results from a research survey that was completed by the two of them. From this, he indicates the need for additional information about best practices. There was some confusion about whether this utterance was referring to the previous survey, the results of which would be disseminated. Comprehension of utterance tense was not part of the testing design, so further evidence about tense comprehension in IS would be needed to show whether this is a pattern for IS presentation observers.

In the lexical identifications from this IS text, almost one third of the participants (two from Japan, one from Australia, one from the United States, five from Brazil, and four from the Czech Republic) did not successfully identify both or one of the signs BODY [HEALTH] and/or ANALYZE [RESEARCH]. These same participants' responses to the depicting sequence indicated that they understood the broad meaning, "things or information being collected and disseminated"; however, without knowing the specified lexical signs, they did not demonstrate understanding about the details. Some replies indicated a misunderstanding about where the research best practice information was being disseminated. Some believed it was for the government or to universities, rather than to national Deaf associations. Discourse comprehension was vague with mixed understanding about the type of information collected and that it was best practice examples.

A second example comes from video D, which is a presentation by a JSL native signer about collaboration and training programs that develop leadership skills in deaf youth. The video clip is labeled DSD4 (not pictured here; see DVD media file). Earlier in the text, the presenter discussed youth leadership training as crucial to the continued development of deaf rights and he asserts that there is a need for more leaders to positively impact improvements in the Asia-Pacific region. He uses the depicting signs to indicate "a raising up of something" or an "expansion in the number of some entity," but if participants misunderstood the sign LEADER[LEADER], or the sign YOUTH [YOUNG PERSON], their responses remained vaguely global with "goals are being accomplished." One participant in the Japanese cohort did not understand the discourse mental space builder reference earlier in the text when the topic shifted from a brief recognition and gratitude for the support after the 2011 earthquake in Japan to the main presentation topic. The main presentation topic was the collaborative work of the JFD for human rights issues and improved accessibility to education and interpreters, among other aims. It was evident that the shift in the discourse was not realized, because that particular participant replied, "Well, seeing progress in the reconstruction? I do not know."

Both of the examples in this section illustrate that recognizing the fully lexical signs and other discourse cohesion prompts specific semantic references implied by depicting sign meanings. As a symbolic whole, a balanced combination of telling and showing provides a more complete meaning representation for the observer, and thus increases comprehension of the discourse utterance.

Metaphor and Iconicity in Comprehension of Depicting Signs in IS

A depicting sign cluster from video B is shown in Figure 67. The presenter is discussing the challenges of not having sufficient funding for accessible, effective education for deaf people in her home country of Togo, Africa. She gives many examples such as the lack of knowledge about appropriate, SL-based education, lack of education by qualified teachers who are fluent in the local sign language and spoken language, as well as mixed disability classrooms where deaf people are often overlooked. She points to other issues about access to higher education and

FIGURE 67. *Depicting sign cluster DSB4 (Free translation: "We lobby the government and advocate Deaf people's equal access to effective education.").*

lack of interpreting services. In the stimulus utterance, the signer begins with an ASL sign HIT modified with repetition, which is also iconic, as it depicts a fist striking at the nondominant hand index finger. This sign is also depicting due to the iconic representation of the individual finger-as-person (or entity), which is being subjected to the impact of a striking fist; however, it is a conventional sign in ASL and is used to mean not only to physically hit someone or something, but also to exert a force upon something. Specific to the context of politics, it refers to lobbying government legislators. This sign is borrowed from ASL and has metaphoric meaning in the IS contact situation from the metaphor POLITICAL-IDEAS-ARE-PHYSICAL-FORCES.

The IS user employs a depicting sign at the end of the sequence where her left hand holds a grounded space with a BC handshape as a benchmark of comparison. The depiction is annotated as DSG(BC):HIGH-LEVEL-BENCHMARK and then the dominant right hand raises upward—annotated as DSM(BC):RAISE-UP-TO-EQUAL-POINT—to meet at the same level as the left hand depiction. This final position looks similar to the lexical sign EQUAL in ASL, and that lexical sign is subsequently made at the end of the utterance.

The depiction is iconic to some extent and is also metaphoric in two ways. The sequence creates a general depiction of some action taken by applying force toward some purpose, specified by the ASL sign HIT, the IS sign GOVERNMENT, and the correcting of a disparity of something that is not fully specified. The actors and patients of this action are less clear, but the context and the information that come in the lecture give the depicting sequence its more specified meaning. Participants' understanding of the segment and its specified meaning from the context is of interest in the assessment.

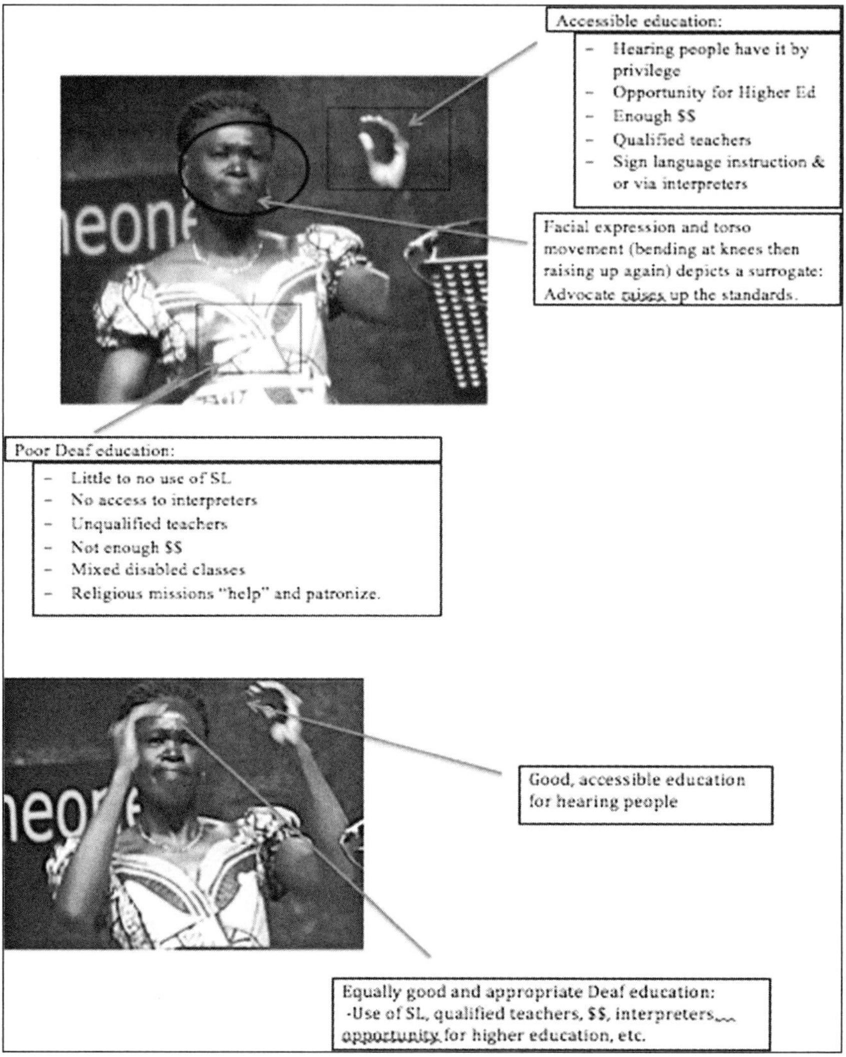

FIGURE 68. *Depicted meaning of* "ADVOCATE FOR EQUAL ACCESS TO EDUCATION."

Meaning is created in the blended space established by the depicting sign DSM(BC):RAISE-UP-TO-EQUAL-POINT. Elements represented by the blend are shown in Figure 68. The depicted spaces are blends that map all of the elements of (on the one hand) "poor, inaccessible Deaf education" and (on the other) "accessible, good quality education." The metaphor of UP-IS-GOOD is operating here, where the higher situated hand instantiates a blended space denoting accessible, good-quality education. This is a depicted characterization of the desired state of education. The two different blended spaces where the left hand and the right hand are articulated indicate metaphorically that LOCATIONS-ARE-STATES-OF-COMPARISON. A combination of lexical signs and depiction and a pointing sign create meaning for the audience and refer back to all of the elements in the domains of inaccessible or comparatively good quality education, given in the larger discourse. Participants are asked to respond to the questions, "What does she mean by that?" and "Equal or better in what way?" with some elaboration and reference to these elements, to show that they fully understand the segment, the depicting sign, and its specific reference given the context of the video B.

Responses to this depicting segment DSB4 show resoundingly that a majority of participants understood the presenter's main point in this utterance. In particular, the concept of "pressuring the government for more equality" (Australian participant) and "lobbying the government for equal educational access for deaf people to that of hearing people" (Czech Republic participant) were clearly articulated by half of the participants, all from varied country cohorts. Several others understood the need to create "equal access," but did not specify educational access. Many of these participants noted the presenter's main point of achieving equality between deaf and hearing citizens, and for some this meant for human rights equality. Only three participants could not fully specify the meaning in the depicting segment. They stated generally that in the presenter's home country "they continue to argue with the government to grow and achieve their aims," "lobbying for better human rights," and that there are "many challenges they have been dealing with." With the exception of these three participants, the other 29 were able to articulate several of the elements in the domains depicted in each of the two comparison spaces, such as lack of access to interpreters, limited funding juxtaposed with an optimal situation with SL instruction or interpreters in class, qualified teachers, and sufficient funding.

The topic of deaf education is a highly familiar one for all deaf people, as mentioned earlier in the comprehension ratings results. The lexical sign STUDY(AUS) featured prominently in this video segment and in the lexical identification task, most participants (87%) successfully understood this sign. In addition to knowing the context and conventional lexical signs, iconicity and real space blends aid the audience in understanding depicting signs in this utterance.

Another interesting construction with a depicting sign comes from video C. The IS presenter incorporates multiple, rich space blends that

FIGURE 69. *Depicting sign cluster DSC2 (Free translation: "Improvements in education, sign language recognition, and Deaf rights are thwarted by external ignorant socio-political influences.").*

are highly metaphoric on several levels, and incorporates iconic elements. Pictured in Figure 69, the signer presents abstract concepts about the struggles and progress deaf people continually experience, in the aim to have SLs recognized, respected, and, in this context, integrated into appropriate and accessible education. The articulation of the upheld hands conveys the image of "signing," resembling the forms in many SLs for sign language, and also is a metaphor for achieving improvements in Deaf education. The signer simultaneously enacts the effort of manipulating in an upward direction SL-based education. Nonmanual markers on the face and his torso movements begin the constructed action, and the first depicting sign employs the 5 handshape  to iconically map and represent multiple SLS (not just one SL or one group of people) in all countries on the individual fingers. The next depicting sign conveys the idea of something being mowed over, or cut off. Again, the 5 handshape depicts (and iconically maps) multiple entities approaching sideways at the nondominant hand. The nondominant hand is a fragment buoy that grounds and depicts the concept from the previous sign, "SLS RAISING-UP." The dominant downward-oriented, 5 handshape repeatedly (three times) cuts across the grounded sign. This conveys the idea that socio-political forces from outside of deaf communities negatively impact the goals and aims toward SL recognition, respect, and inclusion in Deaf education programs.

Participants understood the general message of this complex construction; for some, the metaphoric blend it incorporates was realized. Almost all participants understood the meaning conveyed that "something is improving" or "there is momentum toward something positive." Many people recognized the reference to improvements for deaf people and in particular sign language, and the negative effect of interference or oppression by "others," responding to questions about its meaning with, "It is related to deaf people's progress, improvements, and the use of sign language."

At the same time, varying responses show a mixed understanding of what is being cut off, interfered with, or oppressed. In the presentation discourse, the signer specifically references Deaf education and a respect of SLs; however, some participants were less able to make a full transfer of the metaphoric and blended domains and meaning from the depiction, and their responses indicated a very generalized (albeit globally correct) understanding of the segment. One participant from Australia replied that he was unsure of the referent, but thought that "some people have something and others are taking over or interrupting and getting in the way." Two participants mention the idea of "war," and a negative effect of gunfire or war. One U.S. participant noted that impediments to deaf people's progress come from external force, and it could be government cuts, war, or famine. Another participant from Australia recognized that the first depiction resembled the Auslan sign meaning FIRE and immediately discerned that it could not mean FIRE in that context. A Japanese participant replied with a slightly altered imagery of "fire" by stating, "A fire burning and we have to fight and do our best to overcome the fire in oneself." In fact, four out of the six Australian participants were slightly confounded by this depiction, only understanding basic reference to something being negatively affected. An example response was, "Things are going well, and then it goes wrong. And then something gets taken over or denied. I am not sure of what, specifically." This suggests that a partly specified depicting sign may be motivated iconically but the blended elements are susceptible to being missed or miscued.

Depiction, Tokens, and Pointing Signs

Depicting signs in the next segment interact in the IS discourse alongside pointing signs, specifically those directing focus to a list buoy

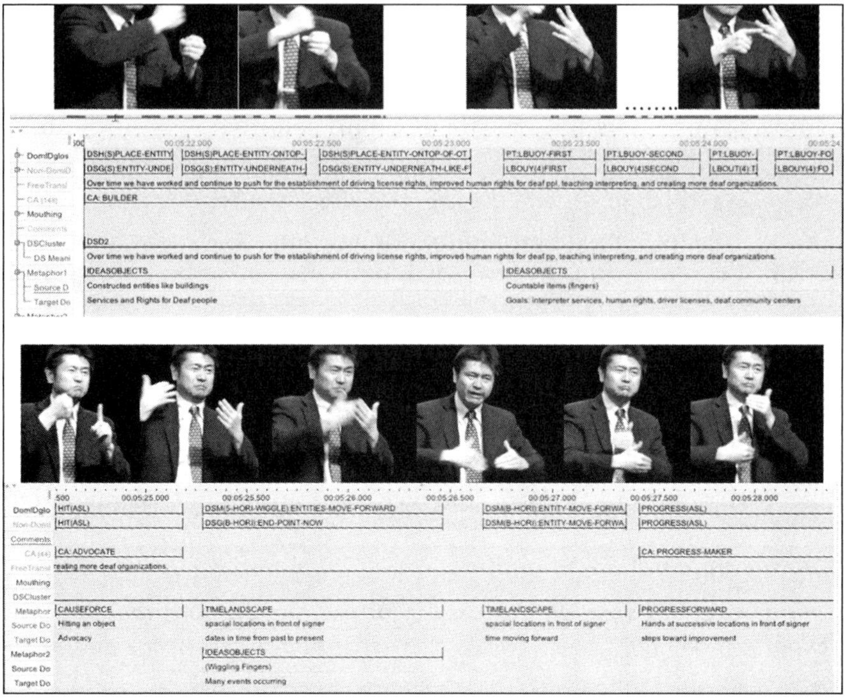

FIGURE 70. *Depicting sign segment DSD2 (Translation: "Over time we have worked for and continue to push for the establishment of interpreter education, driving license rights, improved rights for deaf people, and creating more deaf organizations.")*

(Figure 70). The IS presenter refers back to several aims of the JFD that he introduced a bit earlier in the presentation. Discussed in the results of the retell task, a list buoy (4) is held up in the nondominant hand, and the signer points to each buoy (finger) to tokenize the four aims he previously mentioned. These are (1) driving licenses for deaf people, (2) improved human rights legislation, (3) interpreter training programs, and (4) more organizations by and/or for deaf people. The first depicting sign is a handling depicting sign and co-occurs with nonmanual features that enact (constructed action) the physical setting up of several items. The dominant hand forms the DSH(S) handling depicting handshape, and places it on a DSG(S) "ground" depicting handshape, ENTITY-UNDER-OTHER-LIKE-FOUNDATION. This depiction establishes the figure-ground relationship in the depiction, and then the list buoy elaborates on what is being "built." Following this list buoy, another depicting sign shows the time frame from the past until present, with wiggling fingers from past space to current space to denote these four aims as the entities (wiggling fingers) occurring over time. Then another subsequent depicting sign—a movement depicting sign—conveys the continuity of the work and forward-moving time frame, pushing ahead, and metaphorically "stepping" along a path to the future.

Almost all participants were able to fully realize that the list buoy (4) referred to the goals of the JFD that were mentioned just prior in the discourse. One person was not sure what the referent was (the list buoy and its four token referents may not have been realized earlier in the text), and gleaned the idea that the presenter and his colleagues had success with something. Although several of the participants did not understand or recall all the specific details of the four given goals earlier in the text, most participants were able to grasp the general concept of the organization's aims. For those who did understand the four referred-to goals (tokens), it was not always easy to remember each of them all from seeing this depicting segment again. Working memory or short-term memory impeded recalling this level of detail; however, the utterance was understood by most participants to mean that these four aims of the JFD had been occurring over some unspecified time, and the work was still ongoing.

What is evident in this example is that a depicting sign that establishes a timeline through use of signing space (back to front, or left to right) was a robust and well-understood concept for a variety of participants in this study. TIME-IS-A-LANDSCAPE-WE-MOVE-THROUGH has been shown to be a common metaphor in signed and spoken languages (Lakoff & Johnson, 1980; Taub, 2001; Wilcox, 2000). The depicting signs, however, still required other specific lexical and/or contextual information for the depiction to be fully understood. It is also shown that the pointing signs (PT:LISTBUOY: FIRST-THROUGH-FOURTH) work in combination to give specified meaning to the three depicting signs in the segment. The depiction provides some aspect of the organization of details in the discourse; however, without knowing more detailed information, the depictions might be only vaguely understood, as is seen in several other examples reported in these depicting segment results.

A second depicting sign segment seen in video B (part B2) employs several lexical signs, points, and indicates referents by articulating fully lexical signs in different locations in the signing space (e.g., ASSOCIATION). This depiction segment was first introduced in Chapter 4 as an example of a depicting signs that collaborate with pointing signs and is

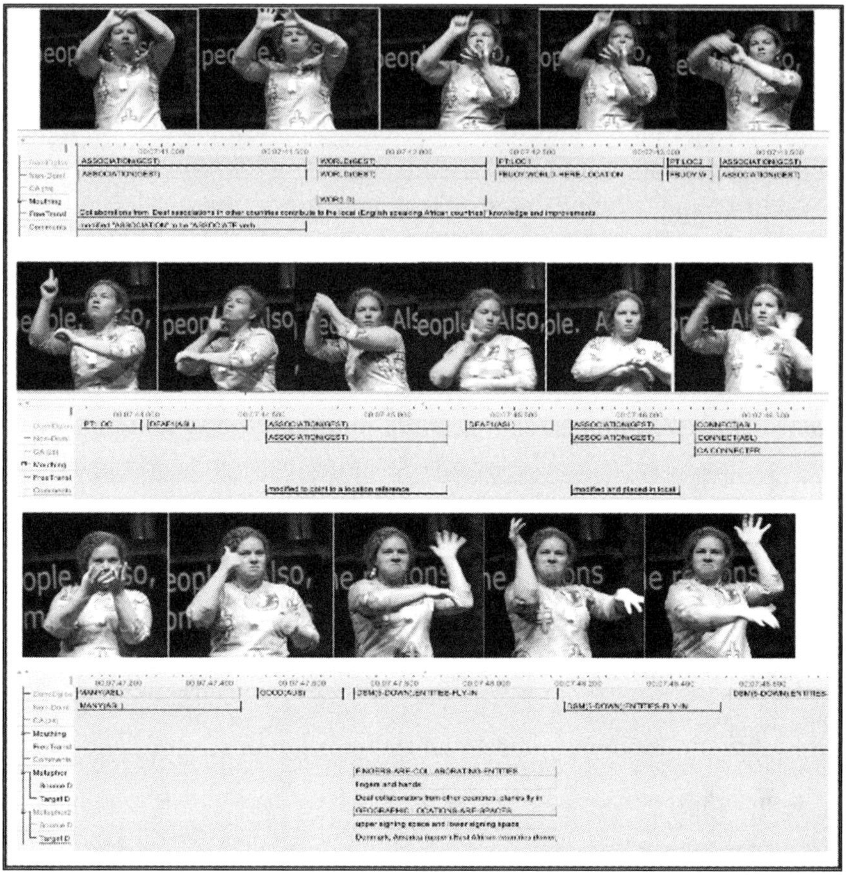

FIGURE 71. *Depicting sign cluster DSB5 (Free translation: Collaborations from Deaf associations in other countries contribute to the local [English-speaking African countries'] knowledge and improvements.).*

again shown in Figure 71. The depicting sign at the end of the complex construction is a blend that shows foreign collaborators flying in to the country (Ghana). The signer's use of referential token space establishes two comparative entities, foreign deaf associations and the local, Ghana deaf association.

The depicting sign aids in building up the discourse to convey one of the main points of this lecture (asked in the content questions section). The signer elaborates on the fact that some French-speaking African countries, like Togo, are not as advanced in their human rights, education, and civic services for deaf people as English-speaking African countries, like

Ghana, are. A main contributing reason comes from Ghana's successful collaboration with and assistance from foreign aid from American and European deaf associations. A majority of participants understood the general reference to relationships with other deaf associations, and some responses specified that there were active collaborations with foreign associations. The depicting sign aided comprehension of the utterance in this depicting segment, and this worked in conjunction with points and tokens in the utterance.

When comparing participants' responses to the content question answered by this video segment, many (24) answered correctly that some communities in Africa were doing better as a result of foreign aid and collaboration. Eight participants did not give the correct answer (varied cohort groups), and these same participants realized from the depicting sign segment that the "relationship" or "collaboration" is a good thing, but they did not realize the connection between this relationship and improved outcomes for Deaf education in those locations. The pointing signs that establish token spaces, and the subsequent fully lexical sign ASSOCIATION, prompt meaning about connections between foreign deaf associations and the local (Ghana) association. All of these symbolic elements in the utterance aid in the comprehension of the depicting sign, and of the main point for many participants.

In the presentation, the signer specifies country names by fingerspelling and also by using the conventional signs FRENCH(ASL), ENGLISH(ASL), and COUNTRY(WFD). Many participants did not catch this information and were unable to correctly answer the main point question, "What are the presenters comparing?" Depicting signs, therefore, can aid to some extent in constructing discourse referents, but the conveyed information tends to be more global and less detailed. A combination of knowledge of these fully lexical signs, and background knowledge about Africa's English-speaking and French-speaking countries aided only one participant in fully understanding this depicting segment, as well as the related content questions from the comprehension test.

Depiction and Gesture, and Constructed Action

Findings from the lexical frequency analysis of the full IS lecture dataset showed that gestural elements and, in particular, constructed action features predominantly in expository IS discourse (572 periods of CA in the full dataset). In the composite utterance shown in

FIGURE 72. *Depicting sign cluster DSC4 (Translation: "[There is no need for us to accept] being defeated and downtrodden, asking for handouts.").*

Figure 72, the presenter employs two depicting signs. In the first, a figure-ground depiction DSM(2-BENT):PERSON-BUCKLE-AT-KNEES in the dominant hand depicts a standing person as defeated and goes on to enact, through constructed action, the gesture of removing one's hand and holding it out like a beggar. In the repeating movement of this constructed action, he indicates the temporal notion of begging as a continual process. His meaning in this segment is aimed at inspiring the audience that deaf people should have a sense of pride and that asking for handouts (literally and figuratively) is not something to be accepted.

Several participants had a difficult time understanding this enactment, not knowing how it was integrated into the presentation, which was a segment in his candidacy speech. The presentation was globally aimed at inspiring the audience and of course convincing them to cast their vote for him. The enactment was understood by all of the U.S. participants as imitating begging. In the United States, holding out a hat is culturally understood as asking for handouts; however, this may look different in other countries, such as by holding out an upturned hand. In addition, the handling depicting sign of holding onto the edge or brim of a cap skews meaning for several of the participants. The depiction (and simultaneous enactment) is annotated on three tiers as follows:

DomIDGloss : DSH(BABYO):REMOVE-HAT-AND-HOLD-OUT-BEGGING
Non-DomIDGloss: DSG(BC-UP):HOLD-HAND-OUT-BEGGING
CA: BEGGAR

In Auslan, this depiction resembles the sign for SHOTGUN. Interestingly, the enactment was misunderstood as "shooting a gun" by seven participants: one Australian, two Czech Republic participants, two Japanese, and two Brazilians. Some replies were, "I am not sure, it looks like dependency and something to do with war," "the shooting of people," "something to do with war…being attacked," and "something to do with shooting; it looked like hats and shooting people. It doesn't make sense!? How does it fit with voting, talking about fires, and shooting people?!" One participant's response indicated that in general, the behavior of gesturing is recognizable yet he states, "I understand the gesturing but I don't know how to explain it…he is holding something, like he's cleaning?" Finally, the depicting signs and enactment prompted one Czech participant to admit, "I do not know what this means. Maybe he refers to feeling mentally or emotionally tired?"

Nonetheless, half of the participants were able to understand the presenter's intended meaning, responding with answers such as, "Deaf people are persecuted, and let down, with no other opportunity other than to beg for handouts (individually) and funding (collectively). This is not fair, we should not be left to feel demoralized" and quite succinctly, "Oppression sucks, it is demoralizing and depressing." These were all participants from the United States, and two or three from each other cohort group.

What these mixed replies show is that using depicting signs with some integration of constructed action adds descriptive information where there may not be sufficient linguistic resources, but it is not always as effective for audience members as intended. Gestural enacting behavior in constructed action is influenced by culture and entrenched NSL sign meanings.

Context and Background Knowledge Informs Depiction in IS Comprehension

In the next clip (Figure 73), the signer employs a token blend through the use of a depicting sign, DSM(BC-DOWN): DEAF-GROUP-MEMBERS-SPLIT-OFF. In addition, conceptual metaphors such as STATES-ARE-LOCATIONS and the CONDUIT METAPHOR interact in the depiction. The two locations establish the mixed deaf and hearing member troop initially. Then, once the new group is established (moving the depicting handshape part of the sign into another location in the signing space), the presenter points to the depicting sign, which has become the blended entity of an all-deaf member troop. The final depicting sign shows the group as a contained group (two BENT5-handshapes ), which then moves gesturally and visibly expanding: DSS(BC):SIZE-OF-GROUP-INCREASES.

Similar to the previous example above, this depicting sign segment is aligned with one of the content questions, "How did the first all-deaf Boy Scout troop start?" When shown this depicting segment, all of the participants, except for two Japanese cohort members who viewed this IS video E, expanded correctly on the depicting sign and its blended elements.

Two of the three Japanese participants who viewed this video in IS did not fully realize the rich meanings that the signer aimed to convey with this utterance. It was not clear to them what exactly was expanding, although the gestural component of the form was understood "something is growing larger." One of the participants who did not fully

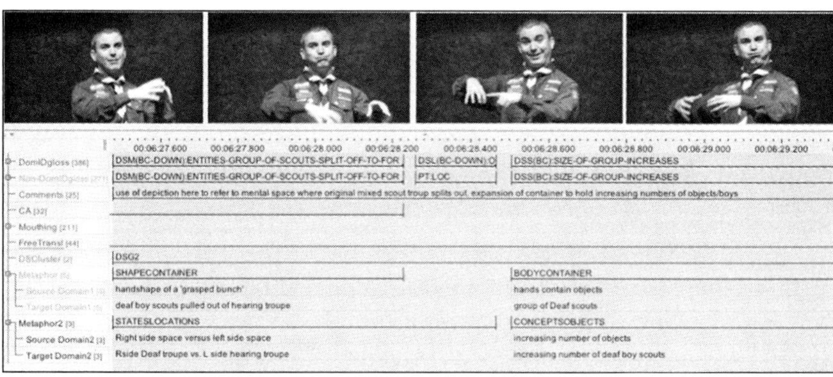

FIGURE 73. *Depicting sign cluster DSE2 (Free translation: "The first Deaf Scout troops evolved out of an originally mixed hearing/deaf troop.").*

understand the utterance guessed the signer was talking about a balloon. The other miscued, responding that the sequence resembled the JSL sign for "hot pot," and he was unsure what the depicting sequence meant. Otherwise, almost all participants (whether they viewed either the IS video E or the NSL video E′) were able to correctly understand the basic meaning in the utterance that something was expanding as shown by the final depiction sign.

It is also notable that one of the Japanese participants, who either misunderstood or did not glean full meaning from the utterance, admitted she had not seen a Boy Scout in uniform in a long time and did not have a frame of reference. Therefore, she had minimal experience to inform background knowledge about the organization. She viewed the JSL version and when shown the original IS signer in this segment, she commented that it seemed what the signer was talking about did not match up with what she thought Boy Scouts did in her minimal experience.

This example provides additional support for what is evident from all of the depicting segment comprehension clips discussed thus far. Depicting signs in IS can aid comprehension of more general discourse organization, but they work in context and coordination with other symbolic material in IS discourse utterances.

Summary of IS Comprehension

In this chapter, several measurements were made to determine comprehension of IS expository discourses. The findings show wide variability in each measurement across individual and group results. It is evident that several sociolinguistic characteristics correlate with successful comprehension of expository IS lectures. Audience observers who successfully understand expository IS presentations are those who have travel experience with exposure to other deaf SL users, a postsecondary education, native knowledge of ASL, knowledge of English, and at least some experience with IS. Knowledge of established (fully) lexical signs in IS improves an observer's ability to glean more discourse content. The majority of diverse SL users in this study understand IS at 56% average, primarily receive information at a global, general discourse level, and misperceive or attempt to guess details and some main points with their own ideas, experience, or imagination.

Chapter 6

Implications and Conclusions

The research presented here sought to determine whether, and to what extent, expository IS created by deaf presenters is understandable to a variety of different sign language (SL) users. It uncovered additional factors previously observed in the literature that correlate with successful and less successful understanding of IS conference presentations. Existing research lacks empirical description about factors for effective comprehension of this SL contact variety, despite a regular reliance on expository IS for communication access at international conferences. This study also makes a quantified description of authentic International Sign (IS) lexicon data, reporting sign types and their distribution in 13 diverse signers' presentation discourses. In particular, it provides the first empirical attempt at measuring comprehension of IS lexicon. It also is the first study to quantitatively and qualitatively compare comprehension of IS to native signed language (NSL) discourse content.

Several research questions were posed at the start of this project. In this chapter I frame the discussion and implications of findings, and formulate conclusions by explicitly addressing each of the stated research questions in turn.

COMPREHENSION OF EXPOSITORY IS

One of the main questions of the research was as follows: "To what extent is expository international contact signing (IS) comprehensible, and for whom?" I have found here that comprehension of expository IS appears to be influenced by *more than* just audience members' NSL origin, a finding in Rosenstock (2004). Those who know the lexifier signed languages in IS, know and lip-read English, have travel experience, have higher education, and have experience using IS performed better across all comprehension measures, although successful comprehension is not always guaranteed. Western SL users demonstrate better understanding of expository IS lectures by deaf presenters than non-Western SL using participants. Further, when comparing the reduced information gleaned from IS versus NSL source texts, the gap between IS and NSL content comprehension is present, although smaller for a majority of Western SL users (but not all).

Forty-five conventionally established, high-frequency, lexical signs were understood with 73.8% accuracy on average, and content questions about information in IS presentations were understood 61.5% on average. After including scores for numerical identifications and fingerspelled terms, four quantitative measurements of comprehension resulted in a mean score of 56% across five different country cohort deaf participants. The current study uses a larger and more robust dataset than the Rosenstock study (2004), but it complements her findings. Rosenstock found that interpreted IS was better understood than direct IS, and the findings from this current work show that IS created by deaf presenters and IS created by interpreters both are understood by a diverse SL-using audience at similar percentages—56% and 54%, respectively.

Global Comprehension Is More Effective Than Main Points and Details

Responses by diverse participants indicate a trend toward better understanding of global discourse pragmatic and goal information (78%), with decreasing ability to determine IS presentation main points (57%) and details (46%).

A common sentiment by several participants was captured by the comment, "I understood at first, but as it went along I did not really follow {the text}." The limitations become evident when comparing IS video observers, who understood 43% of main points and detailed text questions, to NSL video observers, who understood 73% of main points and detailed questions. This 30% gap, taken in consideration with performances on the retell task, indicates a considerable discrepancy in quality of conveyed information from IS compared to one's NSL.

In a study of SL lecture comprehension, global understanding was shown to be a strength for deaf participants, whereas hearing participants performed better on explicit, implicit, and open-ended questions (Rodriguez Ortiz, 2007). Deaf participants also invented more information than hearing counterparts. Rodriguez Ortiz used lectures that were translated into Spanish Sign Language (LSE) and not direct NSL lectures.

Deaf audience members may show great resourcefulness in "filling in the gaps" to comprehend, and the implications are that this resourcefulness may or may not skew the reliability of the information conveyed by anything other than direct NSL communication.

The amount of IS presentation information integrated sufficiently to be immediately retold in fact was quite low—given the average 53% of idea units across participants. One might argue that the low performance scores on IS discourse recall by deaf participants are not purely from poor integration of IS discourse, but from constraints of working memory. Working memory capacity impacts cognitive tasks such as comprehension (Baddeley, 1986), and deaf signers of Auslan (native and non-native) were shown to perform significantly lower than interpreters on working memory tasks (Wang & Napier, 2013). This is because interpreters have much more practice at using working memory due to their professional training. If working memory had any influence on the retell task for Study Two participants, scores for the retelling from those on NSL would also show deficits, but they did not. The average scores across all participants who retold from the NSL version of the lecture was 78%, a 25% difference.

Despite any potential test fatigue and short-term memory constraints, the difference in performance of retell groups (25%) and the 30% gap shown between global and detailed discourse comprehension is significant. Results indicate that the gap in information quality is a loss of main points and details. Reduced understanding of discourse information and quality of the information was evident across all participants, and some groups showed larger differences between the gap (IS versus NSL retell).

Sociolinguistic Factors for Successful IS Comprehension

A small number of participants *do* gain information from expository IS. Only six out of the 32 comprehension test participants performed at a level established as successful, effective understanding of IS expository presentations. The remaining 26 performed around the grand means, with the lowest 20% (seven participants) averaging 39% on the four quantitative measures. Scoring 75% or better on both the lexical identifications and the content questions, the top six participants' ability to access IS information reveals several shared sociolinguistic factors. Characteristics of participants that are strongly related to improved comprehension of IS are those with 2 or 4 years of university education, knowledge of ASL plus bilingual knowledge of English, and/or knowledge of a second sign language (e.g., British Sign Language [BSL], Auslan, or American Sign Language [ASL] for non-ASL natives). Also, another factor is travel experience to other countries where one has interacted with other deaf people. The six top-scoring participants also report they use IS between one or two times per year and one or more times per month. One successful "comprehender" did not know ASL but reported regular (one to five times per month) use of IS and travel experience to more than 15 countries. Although understanding is more successful and relatively effective for the top scorers, it was noted that the quality of information gleaned from IS was still compromised (by a 23% gap), with 72% of main points and details understood rather than 95% from discourses in their NSLs.

An Illusion of Comprehension

As Marschark et al. (2004) note, a disturbing finding in SL lecture comprehension testing is that deaf students have little way of knowing how much of a presentation (interpreted) they missed, given higher predicted comprehension performance than what is actually measured. In terms of direct IS presentations and the NSL version (interpreted), there is mixed correlation between how well participants rate their understanding and their actual performance on content questions. For example, many participants rated the presentation in video B2 as quite understandable; however, scores on content questions averaged lower than would be expected. This also was true for Japanese participants, who rated their understanding of video D (the Japanese presenter) higher compared to others, but their understanding of content questions about it was low. These lower scores were influenced by the large number of main point and detailed questions asked for that video. High subjective comprehension ratings on this video by this cohort may also have been a result of identifying with the IS signer who was a member of the Japanese Deaf community.

Statistical analysis of different variables indicates that generally, participants who highly rated their understanding of a lecture did perform better on content questions about those IS videos and on the video D retell task. But, comprehension scores of 56% (combined score) and 53% (retell task) were lower than perceived comprehension (subjective ratings) of 70% average. IS audiences therefore may not be able to accurately predict their own understanding of IS presentations. Findings are significant here because when some attendees watch an IS lecture they may *think* they are comprehending more than they actually are, because understanding global information and some (but not all) main points may create the illusion of comprehension.

What Is Acceptable for Comprehension of IS Lectures?

It is shown that 100% comprehension does not occur for deaf attendees of interpreted and direct SL lectures (Marschark et al., 2005; Napier & Barker, 2004; Rodriguez Ortiz, 2007). Signed language comprehension (of *interpreted* lectures) often ranges between 50% and 90% (Marschark et al., 2004; Napier & Barker, 2004; Rodriguez Ortiz & Mora Roche, 2008). A study by Rodriguez Ortiz and Mora Roche (2008) established 68% to be an acceptable performance for comprehension of a Spanish SL interpreted lecture.

Global comprehension of expository IS (78%) aligns with what is reported in SL comprehension studies—between 62% and 80%, depending on question format (Rodriguez Ortiz, 2007). Deaf people extract less information from NSL lectures than their hearing peers do, and this current IS study demonstrates even less extracted information from IS lectures than from NSL (although no comparison is made to any hearing group performance here). With average comprehension of direct IS lecture and interpreted IS (Rosenstock, 2004) ranging 54% to 56%, the question lingers about expectations and an acceptable comprehension level.

Because most IS information conveyed is global, rather than detailed, IS can be effective for providing general information, and in certain contexts this may be acceptable. Given the right sociolinguistic profile of users (such as the six "comprehenders" in this study), IS can be an effective auxiliary contact system, which apparently applies to current usage settings in the European Union of the Deaf (EUD), and World Federation of the Deaf (WFD), and to some extent, World Association of Sign Language Interpreters (WASLI). Nonetheless, all participants should be made fully aware that they may not be accessing the full story. The experience of IS comprehension, with its limits, may only be of value if the information missed is not important to the audience and if audiences are aware of this and accept the limitations.

Distribution of Linguistic and Nonlinguistic Elements in IS and Effect on Comprehension

The results reported in Chapter 5 answer the second major research question: "What is the distribution of linguistic elements in the IS lexicon and does this affect comprehension?" (and related subquestions). A quantitative lexical analysis of the distribution of different sign types and tokens in the IS dataset permitted a comparison to similar studies of Auslan, BSL, and other NSLs, and thus enabled an investigation of the sign types and meaning-making to IS comprehension.

Deaf people presenting with expository IS use both linguistic and gestural elements similar to those described in NSLs; however, the sign types are distributed differently than what is reported in NSLs. Although the methodology and theoretical assumptions in this study differ somewhat from prior IS studies, the presence of fully lexical signs, depicting signs, and gestures revealed from this dataset parallels, what has been observed in interpreted IS (McKee & Napier, 2002; Rosenstock, 2004) and in IS contact between deaf people (Allsop et al., 1995; Woll, 1990, 1995). Intuitions about increased gesture and depiction, and a lesser amount of established lexical signs in IS, were in fact demonstrated. A smaller percentage of fully lexical signs (63%) in comparison to similar genre NSL discourses (mean = 73%) shows that there are on average 10% less established, fully lexical signs in expository IS than in NSLs. Depicting signs in IS presentation discourses are more than double (10.2%) compared to similar genre NSL studies (1.6% to 4.2%). Gestural signs comprise 9% of sign types in expository IS, and the large number of constructed action periods—one in every 12 signs—provides additional gestural features IS discourse. Compared to NSL lectures and other more formal types, IS shows more gestural (non-linguistic) material, in some cases twice as much gesture. These findings support prior claims and anecdotal intuitions that IS has an impoverished lexicon (Allsop et al., 1995) and appears to be a type of "language of gestures" (British Deaf Association [BDA], 1975).

The reduced lexical density in IS target interpretations reported by McKee and Napier (2002) create constraints for interpreters attempting to make meaning in interpreted IS lecture. Their study was based on a comparison of signs to spoken words (from the source English texts), rather than a quantified analysis of sign types. As a result, a direct comparison is not possible here. The quantitative data reported by Woll (1990), however, allow cautious comparison from this current study's findings and sign types in the IS data she collected at an international workshop of deaf researchers. The coding of types is different and the genre is a hybrid lecture/discussion format, but the description of her three sign type categories provides insight into where there might be consistent findings. In the Woll study, the reported distribution of "normal" (BSL) signs averaged 74%. The "altered mime" signs averaged 7%, and the "international/invented" signs averaged 18% (1990, p. 5). In this current study, the finding of 63% fully lexical signs and 9% nonlexical gesture signs appears similar to the distribution of "normal" BSL signs and "altered mime" signs in Woll's data. There is not enough detail about the "international/invented" signs to know whether these are depicting or pointing types, or enacted segments; however, the author reports that many signs were similar to "new sign creations" that are seen in many SLs. It is possible that many of the invented/international forms could be characterized as depicting signs. Nonetheless, it appears that the distribution of conventional lexical (fully lexical) forms, gestural types, and other productively constructed (and potentially partly gestural) forms supports intuitions about semiotic material in IS.

IS Signs Sourced from a NSL and Effect on Comprehension

Results regarding fully lexical signs in this study are consistent with the way lexifier languages contribute a large percentage of lexical material in a contact mix (Winford, 2003). A majority of spoken contact pidgins[1] are based in the lexical material of a source language (the lexifier language), with the contact pidgin seeming to be a rough attempt at learning the lexifier language as a second language. However, for many trade pidgins in history, "creators of the pidgin were not [aiming to] learn the other group's language, but to forge some limited practical means of communication. Once it was established, this compromise system, and not the lexifier language, became the **target of learning** for later arrivals on the scene" (Winford, 2003, p. 279; bold emphasis mine). Although IS is a contact variety that may be a target of learning in itself rather than an attempt to learn one of the lexifier languages, this study

1. The term *pidgin* is derived from the English word *business* (Winford, 2003, p. 268), which is a reflection of the trade context normally associated with pidgins.

reveals that citation signs in ASL and Auslan, occur in IS regularly: 58% and 20.8%, respectively.

Recall that a small number of the forms annotated with the origins (ASL) or (AUS) could have been tagged as one or the other, because some belonged to both SLs according to corpus information about these languages. As was explained in the methodology to the current study, the default categorization was ASL; therefore, the high representation of lexical signs in IS described as ASL may not *only* be attributable to ASL. It is likely that some percentage of these signs is also shared by other European SLs (e.g., LSF) and would therefore be recognizable to users of other NSLs; nonetheless, it is evident that ASL is one of the major contributors of superstrate lexical material in expository IS. ASL and BSL are typically noted as first and/or second sign languages of my Study One and Study Two participants (presenters and comprehension test alike), as well as are reportedly known by the majority IS interpreters (de Wit, 2016).[2] ASL's genetic relationship to the historically influential European SL, LSF, may also contribute to the strong correlation that Western SLs have with improved IS comprehension. Until loan forms in IS are cross-linguistically analyzed against other SL corpora, and further historical linguistic studies are undertaken, it will be difficult to determine all of the SLs that contribute to expository IS lectures in the dataset.

The limited studies thus far on IS show that Western SLs predominantly contribute to IS, and it is not known if any of the more established conventional forms include signs that are also shared by Asian, Middle Eastern, or African countries' SLs, or are even unique to them. Though, as reported, publications on IS do exist in which significant numbers of ASL signs appear (e.g., the Korean publication *International Signs*); therefore, signs that might be common to both ASL and other Asian SLs may be represented in Asia-Pacific regional forms of IS contact.

Although NSL forms are observed in direct lecture IS, practitioners who use IS propose that using forms from one's NSL should be avoided, and that aiming for gestural constructions that are iconic will be more

2. In an initial April 2011 scoping study of IS interpreters for this research, it was noted that a majority of the respondents' first language is either ASL or BSL or Auslan, with spoken language fluency mainly in English, or French, German, Spanish, and Dutch, among others. The majority reported knowing either ASL or BSL (BANZSL) or both.

effective.[3] Reliance on iconicity, however, was shown to sometimes create misunderstanding, such as the regularized IS form "PROJECT" (Figure 34 on p. 131) and the use of depicting signs and CA to show begging, elaborated from Figure 72 on p. 264.

In the Study Two findings, it was noted that native users of ASL and BANZSL groups are among the most successful participants in comprehending expository IS lectures, yet it is only one characteristic of the small number of participants for whom IS is effective. Improved performance was only significant for participants whose first language is ASL. This is perhaps owing to the high percentage of recognizable ASL forms in expository IS previously noted. In fact, one U.S. participant stated after viewing the first IS video, "That's ASL!" The presenter in that particular video (A) incorporates 56% ASL forms in his fully lexical signs, which is slightly lower than the average 58% in the IS source dataset. No other participant from other country cohorts made such an observation (about the IS stimulus being ASL or their own NSL); however, it would be interesting to test future participants' impressions about the "language" they think they are seeing, without divulging the fact that the stimulus text is IS.

Results from the lexical identification task demonstrated improved understanding of lexical signs in IS when the form-meaning pair was identical or similar on most parameters to the same lexical sign in participants' NSL (refer to Table 36 on p. 214). Sign forms may be shared between two related SLs, and unrelated SLs can exhibit a similarly articulated sign for the same concept, likely due to shared symbolism and iconicity. However, a language's established lexicon marks one distinction between SLs, exemplified by the ASL-AUSLAN examples in Figure 9 on p. 63 and by findings in cross-linguistic lexical studies (Al-Fityani & Padden, 2008; Guerra Currie, Meier, & Walters, 2002; Johnston, 2003a; McKee & Kennedy, 2000; Woll, 1984; Woodward, 1991). Depending on the coding method and the types of signs (whether one includes number signs), estimates of sign similarities between SLs range from 23% to 40% to as high as 80% for SLs that are known to be genetically related. Established, conventional lexicon provides substantive and semantic specificity of symbolic forms (signs) for people who use the language.

3. In April 2011, my survey of 45 IS interpreters resulted in a large percentage of responses that indicate this belief, that more effective IS is richer in gesture and classifier (depicting) verbs.

There were times, however, that an IS sign matching the same in one's NSL sign was not recognized. The foreign context of the sign created confusion or tentative recognition. It is possible that an unconventional co-location of a NSL sign with a depicting sign or gesture may have provided ambiguity and impeded its recognition. Potentially confounding factors for understanding a contact SL system like IS may arise from what is shown in judgments about sign segmentation. When shown unfamiliar phonemic inventories and combinations, signers use the rules of their own sign language to make sign segmentation decisions (Brentari & Wilbur, 2006). A comparative analysis of word segmentation judgments between users of ASL, Croatian SL (HZJ), or Austrian SL (ÖGS) indicated differences in what may be considered lexical "word" units. Deciphering an IS message may lead to potentially incorrect understanding or miscuing of a minimal symbolic unit. A targeted investigation of sign co-location on IS utterance recognition or comprehension might verify if this is the case.

Furthermore, IS signs that appear similar to, but have different coordinated meaning in one's NSL may cause misunderstanding (e.g., NOW[ASL] meaning SCHOOL in JSL), and potentially impact understanding of the utterance in which the sign appeared. The analysis indicated that improved score on lexical identifications was related to improved understanding of content questions; therefore, the relationship between lexical forms recognized from a participant's NSL positively impacted IS comprehension, particularly for those who recognized the ASL and Auslan lexifier sources in IS presentations. Presence of recognizable lexical signs from one's NSL or shared cognates appears to aid comprehension to some degree, but other factors also contribute to this success. In particular, semantic "verification" seems to come from supplemental spoken language mouth patterns visible to audience members and some gestural enactments as well.

Studies in interlanguage identify strategies that learners of a second language apply as they attempt to understand the L2 (Sasaki, 1991; Tarone, 1980). It is known from studies on L2 acquisition that when people attempt to understand a second language, they bring their L1-based processing strategies for comprehending (Sasaki, 1991). Sasaki's work showed that L2 learners transfer an interpretation strategy from their L1 based on lexical semantics rather than syntax or grammar.

In SLs, different language-specific articulation of phonemes, such as handshape or orientation, may create potential for interference. Signers in contact may realize a sign with an "accent," given an altered articulation of a handshape, and may not integrate the phoneme correctly, mistaking it for a different sign.

In a study of heterogeneous, RSL L1, deaf Russian immigrants to Israel, Yoel (2007) demonstrates that unintentional code-switching and temporary replacement of L1 lexical signs or phrases with L2 forms occurs as an interim solution when the L1 form is temporarily inaccessible, as well as more permanent replacement over time (p. 171). What these studies imply for SLs in contact, is that a signer's L1 lexicon will interfere with comprehension of another language system. Findings in Study Two indicate this fact given the examples of misunderstood signs described from IS "WANT" and JSL "UNDERSTAND" (Figure 54 on p. 217) and several other instances where participants misunderstood signs in IS to be a sign in their NSL having a completely different meaning.

In an expository IS contact system, a majority of signs are borrowed from NSLs, many of which are recognizable citation forms in ASL and Auslan. Because there are a large number of IS forms that are the same in ASL and Auslan, participants from these sign language origins easily identified them; however, there were times that these were doubtfully realized. As participants knew they were watching presentations in IS, they were aware of the "foreign" nature of the signing system. Participants observing IS presentations seem to integrate the forms differently from how they process discourse in their NSL, mainly from the contextual knowledge that they are attending to a mixed language system. Additional research on processing differences between NSL reception and IS or other contact language reception is needed to verify this intuition.

Last, English mouthings and fingerspelled words and acronyms are also borrowed into expository IS, which were clearly shown to be of some benefit for those who know English. Indeed, several participants admitted being aided by English mouthings to improve their comprehension. It is well known that signers articulate mouthed words of the surrounding spoken language of the signing community simultaneously with signs (Quinto-Pozos, 2008, among others). At times mouthings disambiguate concepts (Lucas & Valli, 1992) such as signing HOUSE (plural) while mouthing "village." Mouthings also help construct complex utterances such as signing the word for [BREAD] while mouthing the spoken word [TO EAT] (Crasborn et al., 2008). Mouthings of spoken language words with signs show increasingly in younger generations of deaf people in African countries who have more opportunities for upward mobility and contact (Lule & Wallin, 2010). The long oralist history influencing deaf education influences an effect on deaf peoples' use of speech reading in their SL communication. Spoken language mouth patterns are likely to confound the semiotic stream for IS audience members who do not recognize foreign spoken language lip patterns. It is unknown, however, what impact lip-reading had on the success of participants' scores on lexical identifications. A lexical recognition study that isolates the mouthing component from the lexical sign in IS might provide definitive answers.

Fingerspelling

The comprehension of fingerspelling and number signs was both particularly problematic and was poorly recognized (43% and 49.6%, respectively) by most study participants. This finding is quite different from Rosenstock (2004), which reported mean comprehension scores of 73% and 54%, respectively.

Fingerspelled borrowings typically follow Western letters and English words or acronyms, and three- or four-letter short words or acronyms that are articulated slowly proved more easily understood than longer words. When specific text information comes from fingerspelled borrowings and they are not recognized, the detailed information is often lost to the audience. For example, in video B, the first presenter (B1) fingerspells S-E-C-O-N-D-A-R-Y, when expanding on the lack of higher education available for deaf students in her country. The content questions sought detailed examples of problems that the presenter identified. Although issues in inaccessible deaf education were stated, only two participants actually mentioned the lack of access to higher education. The fingerspelled word was not integrated directly or with contextual support. The form is meant to prompt detailed semantic information and most people did not realize it, thus the point was not given as one possible answer in the content questions. Moreover, participants did not understand the fingerspelled word when it was shown again as a lexical identification. Country cohorts who use a nearly identical one-handed fingerspelling system understood the example given above (S-E-C-O-N-D-A-R-Y); these were all but one U.S. participant, three of the six in Brazil, one from the Czech Republic, one from Australia, and none from Japan.

Numbers represented by holding up fingers on one hand (in a counting manner) are iconic forms understood some of the time. Numbers 1 through 5 are better understood than higher numbers, such as when two-handed numbers are articulated (e.g., TEN-SEVEN). Yet different SL meanings for the same handshape form (Figure 58) are examples of how simple, iconically motivated numbers might not be as iconically representative as expected in an IS contact setting. Misunderstandings about numbers occurred for participants because of this type of confusion (e.g., three and eight in ASL and BSL, and nine and eight in JSL and BSL).

Depiction and Gesture in IS and the Effect on Comprehension

Depicting Signs

A second question relating to the impact of sign types on comprehension was "Do depiction and gesture influence intelligibility of expository IS?" Given that expository IS employs an average of 10% fewer established signs compared to similar genre NSL texts, other semiotic material must be exploited to convey meaning. Depicting signs and gestures comprise 10.2% and 9% of the remaining sign types in IS, with pointing signs also figuring prominently. Since points were not a targeted part of the comprehension testing, I will not include them in this analysis, except to note similarities in the amount of pointing signs in NSLs and in IS.

Depicting signs are one type of symbolic unit in NSLs (and in IS) that instruct the perceiver to construe a representation of a thing, or a process, or both (Wilcox, 2004a). (See Chapter 3.) The productive sublexical forms available in signed languages that are often similar can map imagistic reference to objects, and they are a source of potentially meaningful symbols in IS contact. Users of unrelated SLs and in some cases, nonsigning gesturers employ similar systematic handshapes and movement constructions to refer to objects and motion events (Schembri, 2001); however, nonsigners in Rosenstock's study only understood 25% of depicting sign-centered test questions.

The fact that SL users gain more than nonsigners from depicting type signs (Schembri, 2001) and that those with conventional knowledge (of a sign language) recognize the continuum of handshapes in the linguistic system, shows a linguistic effect in signed language users' interpretation of handshape (classifiers) that differs from the way they are interpreted by hearing, nonsigners (Emmorey & Herzig, 2003 for ASL). The use of depicting sign structures has potential for some universal ways of meaning-making for signers across different signed languages.

This current research showed that depicting signs did contribute to understanding of composite meaning from IS utterances. Shared visual-gestural mechanisms in the form of depicting sign types and a small number of basic handshapes provide what could be thought of as effective contact material for conveying relationships between referents in IS discourse. Depicting signs offer predominantly schematic symbols rather than fully substantive ones, so they are less effective at profiling specific referents unambiguously. However, they appear to help in organizing discourse relationships with some limitations.

Participants' responses to several depicting sign segments provided evidence that depicting signs have the potential to convey some aspects of utterance meaning in expository IS; however, depicting signs co-construct meaningful utterances in IS and appear to provide only partial information. Participants' responses to short depicting sign segments in this study indicated mixed success. The prior research (Rosenstock, 2004) indicated depicting verbs were understood better than other sign types. In the author's discussion, it appeared that most participants understood depicting signs at 70% to 72% success rate and the ASL signers understood close to 100% of depicting sign-centered questions. Successful understanding of depicting sign-related questions comes from more than the depicting sign itself. The author reports the use of a lexical sign BOOK just before the targeted depicting verb that informs the design of the lines of bilingual text (2004, pp. 235–236). As was observed in this current study, the lexical signs in the utterance might have provided a conventional, symbolic unit that contributed to successful realization of depicting sign meaning.

It should be noted that while all SLs use space to organize referents, frame of reference and perspective-taking from observer or from a bird's-eye diagrammatic view is shown to be different from one SL to another (Arik, 2008; Emmorey, 2002). Not all SLs use spatial references the same. For instance, Kata Kolok (a village SL used in northern Bali) employs spatial reference that is absolute, rather than arbitrary (Marsaja, 2008, in Zeshan, 2008). Referents established in absolute space are placed in relation to their real-world location, not token assignments. Hence, the information encoded in a spatial reference is highly contextual, and interlocutors must be aware of exact locations in relation to themselves of what is being discussed (Zeshan, 2008). Some problems with understanding more detailed relationships in IS texts in this study (and also shown in Rosenstock's 2004 study) may be due to constraints posed by specific sign language space and depicting conventions, as was seen in some participants' attempts to understand depicting sign sections in IS.

From the results in this study, a depicting sign in IS may not profile something clearly to an observer, and other times it does successfully prompt the intended semantic profile. This may be from integration with other semantically specific signs, or from a specific contextual use of the depicting sign.

At one point in video A the presenter signs, DSS(BC):SQUARE-ENTITY-PARAGRAPH-ON-PAGE to refer to a particular section (#25) in the human rights document (the CRPD) pertaining to health care. The number following this depiction is TWO-FIVE. Some participants understood and were able to recall the number, yet some did not. Recognition of the depicting sign beforehand was problematic, as one participant indicated she did not understand what DSS(BC):SQUARE-ENTITY-PARAGRAPH-ON-PAGE meant; therefore, she did not integrate the contextual clue and the number, 25. Other participants successfully recognized the iconic TWO-FIVE but many did not know what the number quantified in the utterance. The depicting sign in the utterance would need to be realized as telling and showing the CRPD's [SECTION] or [ARTICLE NUMBER]. Here is where prior knowledge and contextual clues also might have influenced recognition of meaning. Participants may not have experience with the use of the DSS(BC) sign to indicate written documents and legal statutes, nor familiarity with the IS lexicalized sign CRPD. This form is seen regularly on the WFD website, and is a topic of international discussion; however, it was also not recognized by the above-noted participant, and the sign CRPD was one of the less understood signs in the lexical identifications. The profiled semantic structure that normally comes from fully lexical material, as well as the context, the topic, and prior knowledge about the topic, help prompt meaning from the depicting sign by itself. Furthermore, the depicting sign might resemble a fully lexical sign in an audience member's NSL and potentially skew the intended meaning by the IS presenter (e.g., FIRE in Auslan and a depicting sign participant miscue from video C).

Gestures

In terms of gesture and impact on IS comprehension, there were not enough direct ways of assessing comprehension of gesture in this study to make definitive claims. Gestures were not isolated and tested independently from depicting segments. However, some meanings from the gestural aspects of depicting sign segments were understood, such as the movement and spatial displacement parameters in depicting signs that constructed metaphoric blends (UP-IS-GOOD, etc.).

Some trends were noted from participants' judgments about IS presentations and from the short depicting sign utterances where participants were asked to elaborate on meaning. Results of subjective comprehension ratings suggest that diverse audiences believe IS lectures exhibiting increased amounts of gestural signs and enactment are more understandable than those with less; although, in the analysis these were not statistically significant differences. On average, videos with increased gesture were correlated with better actual performance on content questions. A direct relationship between the two was difficult to discern with any statistical significance, but it appears that deaf participants appreciate the use of gestures, whether or not they definitely contribute to improved comprehension or not.

In SL, gesture (nonlinguistic) and linguistic components interact in complex ways, and the lexical analysis of IS indicates presence of a few kinds of gestural material. Gesture-type signs, gestures that contribute to discourse cohesion, gestures and nonmanual signals that create constructed action enactments, and gestural components of depicting and pointing signs are varied ways that gesture appears in expository IS contact signing. Periods of CA were more prevalent in some videos; and accompanied many lexical signs in the IS dataset; however, there was no measured correlation between higher incidence of CA and increased ratings of understanding or improved score on content questions.

In Schembri's (2001) argument that depicting signs are both linguistic and gestural (which is one of the assumptions behind the lexical categories applied in this study), he proposes that some handshapes of depicting signs are used more generally to encode meaning and less systematic or idiosyncratic of a language-specified pattern of use. As evidence, Schembri presents similar sign forms constructed by nonsigners and TSL, Auslan, and ASL signers. Given a hypothetical linguistic—gestural continuum—certain handshapes incorporated into an IS depicting sign may prompt general semantic sense (as in the BC handshape in Figure 74 on p. 284, from IS video E). The same form used in an NSL may point to a more specific meaning, given its pattern of use or conventionality. Without knowing (or understanding) the referent established (and pointed at) in the utterance, or without knowing the conventional patterns of the handshape used, an observer will glean only a general, almost gestural understanding of the form in Figure 74 as "a cluster of entities." The entities fully understood might be a pile of wood, the location of a dome-shaped tent, or a gathering of young scouts. Meaning, of course, will come from the utterance context and other established symbolic units in the utterance.

FIGURE 74. *Depicting Sign DSL(Bent5-DOWN):OTHER-GROUP.*

The gestural, analogue aspect of depicting signs in an unconventional contact system makes them open to being *in*completely semantically specified and therefore not always effective in communicating detailed discourse information. Their gradient semantic nature means that forms are easily applicable to numerous potential referents, such as "large pile of entities" or "individual entities move across to another location." This ambiguity requires the IS observer to rely on prior experience and background domains of knowledge, contextual clues such as written English on an overhead slide, and understanding of specified lexical sign meanings to fully comprehend IS discourse utterances. Often, these more specific details come from individual personal experiences or cultural, local frames of reference. Other times, as one participant reports, "Sometimes I can follow the English lip patterns to know what the signer means" or "I'm not sure the audience would be able to understand her; people may have been watching (as I noticed) the captioning behind the speaker."

Lack of Conventional Forms

Conventionality of form-meaning symbolic units is one of the key features in language use and understanding. Okrent (2002) suggests that conventionality may reside in the form, or it may reside in the patterns of the form's usage, such as the gradient way depicting signs are used to represent a size, shape, location, or movement of an object. The distribution of, and the limited collection of basic handshapes recruited in depicting sign subtypes in IS (shown in Tables 17 and 18 on pp. 129 and 141, respectively, in Chapter 4) suggests that IS signers make assumptions about the way certain sublexical forms might stand for referent objects and actions in IS, perhaps exploiting what they believe are shared basic forms in many SLs. Iconicity and metaphor motivates these forms and their recruitment for meaning construction may be one strategy for creating conventional form-meaning symbols in IS.

The site of conventionalization (Okrent, 2002, p. 190) in a language sets up constraints or restrictions for the way a form-meaning unit (morpheme, single sign, collocations, or string of signs) is used (and understood) in a language. Comprehension test participants exhibited confusion about the meaning of some IS lexical signs, especially when sublexical components of the sign or the whole sign itself were a form with regular, conventional meaning in their own NSL. As fully lexical signs are borrowed into the IS mixture by a presenter, the intention may be to fill the need for conventional, established signs, yet ambiguity can result and skew one's interpretation of the meaning. Perceivers of IS messages may be aided by other material such as visual aids (PowerPoint slide images and English words, as well as English captioning) to fill in gaps in their understanding.

Fully lexical signs in IS are described in this study as the most frequent IS signs in the dataset, yet they are not *exactly* fully lexical signs like those seen in established NSLs. Fully lexical signs in a given language are substantive, symbolic word-level units that have been established through multigenerational use of the language to refer to and profile specific objects, states, and events. Where IS fully lexicalized signs are shared cognates by many audience members, these signs will truly function in the discourse as fully lexical conventional symbols, yet results of lexical comprehension indicate gaps in participants' understanding of forms that are operating as fully lexical. Discussed above, a person's L1 interferes with processing a second language (and in this case a contact language). Similarly, the component parts of a sign in a SL can individually contribute meaning (and they are robustly recruited as evidenced by the high percentage of depicting signs in IS), one or more of these components may prompt a familiar or a different conventional semantic sense to the observer of an IS lexical form. The movement parameter may offer conventional patterns that many signed languages employ construct symbols, but other sublexical components may resemble ideas constrained by one's NSL in the viewer's mind. Potential nuances of understanding may run along a larger scope of options to the observer and thus not be interpreted by the viewer as it was intended by the presenter. The sign form may not be recognized as a fully lexical, form-meaning symbolic unit to all observers, although it is used this way in expository IS. Because findings here showed that IS signers also include additional gestural information (CA enactment) to supplement fully lexical signs (that usually tell without needing to demonstrate meaning), this suggests a lesser degree of conventionality even with what may be perceived as more established signs in IS.

At a schematic level, the IS signer incorporates space blends to show grammatical relationships. Coordinated, two-handed depictions conventionally establish the nondominant hand as background, in figure-ground relationships. Movement and location components are often recruited as conventionally understood gestural material to provide general, schematic meaning. It was reported that some of the elements in blends in depicting sign clusters are understood by participants, but lack of specificity poses a challenge in naming details beyond the force and path information being conveyed. Perceivers of unidirectional IS messages therefore rely on their own background knowledge to interpret the meaning intended, and this may or may not align with the intended meaning of the presenter. The overall gist of the message may be understood, at a general level, but points and details often will be filled in by the audience, which may be conveyed or distorted by one's expansive or perhaps limited knowledge of the speaker's topic.

I have shown how expository IS—as a contact sign variety with a history of usage in specific contexts—frequently draws on gesture and depiction (and borrowed fully lexical signs). I have presented several patterns regarding fully lexical forms and the distribution of depicting signs, points, and gestures. These forms, especially depicting constructions, consistently appear in expository IS and become familiar and somewhat established, if not conventionalized to regular users who use the contact system. Sign forms in the collected source dataset were considered in terms of their degree of potential conventionality within this community of users; yet "community of users" is somewhat problematic in IS, because a majority of users are in contact in an ad hoc manner, rather than in daily routine.

Established forms in a language or contact system provide symbolic units with specified form tied to specified meaning. Given that IS is a system that shows much less fully lexical material, successful comprehension pivots on composite meaning from a variety of forms, contextual clues, and schematic constructions, which may or may not prompt *all* of the meaning intended. Other semiotic clues arise from mouthings, and nonce agreed-upon conventional forms in the usage setting, were also shown to be important. The role of "grammar" in IS as alluded to by Woll (1995): "The grammar has to carry some of the load which would be carried by a larger lexicon in a longer-established language" (p. 2). Perhaps it is not the grammar per se, but the basic building blocks shared by many signed languages that allow for a rudimentary sketch of intended meanings. Using basic, unrefined tools to construct an elaborate concept requires a leap of imagination to a viewer. It also requires the viewer to bring varied experiences with different sorts of concepts, and the ability to recognize and integrate the semantic stretch that the basic tools are referencing.

Fully established NSLs have developed agreed-upon tools to be able to convey the rich description of an elaborate idea, yet IS lacks conventionality of forms and usage patterns to convey the same rich concept. It appears that more than just the grammar takes on what is lacking from conventional patterning, whether linguistic or gestural. Other semiotic clues arise from context, mouthings, audience knowledge and experience, and nonce agreed-upon conventional forms in the usage setting. Expository IS cannot be easily characterized as a universally accessible system at this point in time, given what is lacking in conventionality of form-meaning symbols.

INTERNATIONAL SIGN: IS IT?

The final question posed at the start of this study—"How effective is IS for universal access to lectures?"—is answered to some extent by these research findings. This study of IS comprehension shows that even given a somewhat consistent usage setting, expository IS conference presentations are not well understood by diverse sign language users.

It is generally realized that expository IS is not an equivalent medium for communicating information compared to a person's native SL (NSL). This study showed that gap to be on average 30%. The past several decades, however, have seen the consistent provision of IS interpretation at international conferences and the increasing expectation that deaf presenters will do so using expository IS.[4] In practice, this acknowledges

4. In the months toward the end of this research project, I was asked by a friend who is a (Deaf) leader in my home state in the United States to direct him to resources in IS. I have been asked by at least one other deaf academic to advise on the expected use of IS for academic discourse and dissemination of research. In both cases, they were required to submit a presentation abstract in IS, rather than their NSL to discuss postgraduate or doctoral research work.

expository IS contact to be an acceptable second-best option, given the prohibitive costs of interpreting services for a large number of SLs. Findings in this study respond to the lack of empirical clarity around exactly how much difference there is between IS and NSL communication and indicate that IS is not actually "international."

A large number of participants in this study expressed their opinions throughout their comprehension test experience. One participant noted, "I had to work hard to understand the IS signer; I didn't feel relaxed. I feel like I'm a hearing person trying to understand a signing person!" This sentiment, I believe, sums up the challenges that audience members experience when attempting to understand an expository IS lecture, especially for those who do not fit the sociolinguistic description of the top six performing "comprehenders" in this study.

The IS contact variety in this study exhibits some conventional and recurring form-meaning pairs. IS is not a fully conventional language, and this study shows that limited linguistic conventions make expository IS ineffective as a universal system of access for all audiences. As a contact system, it offers evidence of being effective for only a few, and practical application (for in-depth information exchange) for diverse deaf audiences is not effective.

The contact system allows some *global-level* discourse information to be understood by many types of audience members, which perhaps contributes to its popular appeal. The system, however, is much less effective than a participant's NSL, particularly if main points and details are important to presenters and audience members. IS is only effective in conveying main points and details for relatively few audience members. It was demonstrated from a variety of measures and analyses that a majority of deaf people who might attend an IS presentation would not understand expository IS content, especially if details are important to material shared in a presentation. This poses a conflict with the current rationale for its expanded use in international settings such as academic or scientific conferences, particularly for those attendees who do not fit the sociolinguistic profile of those who do better with IS and where their NSLs are not one of the official conference languages and are not provided via interpreting services.

Following Flay et al. (2005), *effectiveness* needs to consider real-world conditions and some criteria around efficacy. Expository IS is meant to be efficacious for making lecture content accessible to varied SL users, as an auxiliary language. To use an efficacy statement, I can claim from this research that expository IS lecture is efficacious for conveying limited, general, global-level information for many perceivers, but is more efficacious for conveying information effectively only for bilingual and multilingual audiences with experience using IS, knowledge of ASL and English, have a university education, and have traveled amid other Deaf communities. Monolingual signers therefore risk missing large amounts of information in IS. Expository IS will not likely be effective or create language access for monolingual audience members.

INTERNATIONAL SIGN AS A SYMBOL OF DEAF COLLECTIVE IDENTITY

The continued use of expository IS for presentations despite uncertainty around its effectiveness for linguistic access points to the unique sociological and political status that IS seems to hold in international discourse among deaf people. The idea of IS may be more of a symbol that encapsulates a sense of universal Deaf identity and of inclusiveness, rather than a consistently viable contact language that stands up to linguistic scrutiny, as is given in this study. Historical social forces that impede deaf people's access to their own naturally occurring visual languages establishes a sociopolitical environment that begs for a crucible—a symbol that emerges from suppression and hardship, an idea that recognizes the unique visual nature of signed languages. IS as a symbol therefore has its place in international deaf discourse, despite the fact that potentially universal features of signed languages are not fully uncovered.

Given a short history of linguistic study of signed languages, and the fact that many deaf people do not have basic human rights of access to the naturally occurring signed language of their community, it remains to be seen whether promotion of IS—and for what purposes—will benefit deaf communities. If deaf attendees of international events do not expect to effectively understand information in IS, but want to enjoy an illusion of understanding and inclusiveness (even if it means only understanding 54% to 56% or less), this may be the limits of IS. I suggest that appropriate use of IS contact for linguistic access deserves further evaluation and propose that those of us who use IS and interpret with IS continue to question and dialogue about its application in conference interpreting, especially if attendees risk missing important cross-cultural exchange of information.

Interpreters and deaf presenters alike are tasked to make conference material accessible by expository IS. Mediating messages using a system with a smaller established lexicon is challenging for interpreters, which is shown for those working into IS (McKee & Napier, 2002) and from IS (de Wit, 2010). Best, Napier, Carmichael, and Pouliot (2016) suggest that the compact bundles of simultaneous information in IS (what I refer to as composite utterances) are more complex for interpreters to decipher than those in familiar NSLs, which increases cognitive processing load. However, knowing more than one signed language (Moody, 2002), knowing the context and having direct experience with the topic and lexicon of the presentation, as well as and having contributed to a set of agreed, established lexicon (cf. Best et al., 2016), may create improved conditions for more effective IS interpreting. Moreover, interpreters often have time to prepare with an IS presenter and can bring their vast range of experience and multilingual skill to decipher an IS message and render an interpretation into English (or other fully conventional language). It should be noted that audience members watching an IS lecture may or may not have these luxuries. The complex task of "interpreting" a presenter's meaning also falls on the IS audience, and those who fit a highly specific sociolinguistic profile (shown by the six "comprehenders" in my study) may be the only ones equipped with sufficient experience with different conventional systems (multilingual skill) to decipher richer IS messages.

Very little is known about whether audiences understand interpreted IS better than deaf presenters' IS. Additional direct comparison will come in a future study. Results from the Rosenstock study indicate that both types have their limitations, and by her measure, interpreted IS were slightly better understood than a deaf presenter's IS. Lack of conventionality of forms in deaf presenters' IS also appears to impact the amount of information understood by audience members from different SL origins. Lack of established, conventional form-meaning pairs means that discourse information cannot easily transfer equivalent information and meet diverse audience linguistic needs—even with much effort on the part of the interpreter.

It was noted earlier that spoken language conference interpreters and translators are not typically tasked with creating contact language target messages for audiences. A related task in the signed language field, however, comes to mind. English-to-SL *transliterating* is a practice that for several years was credentialed by the Registry of Interpreters for the Deaf (RID) in the United States. Until recently, interpreters were granted national certification in interpreting (CI or certificate of interpretation) and/or in transliterating between English and an English-influenced form of sign language that is often referred to as Signed English (CT, or certificate of transliteration) (RID website).[5] The latter is the only other phenomenon that might be somewhat comparable to creating IS target messages, because transliteration involves working between English and encoded English words in the visual mode—a form of contact signing or mixing (Davis, 1999) that is used by English and ASL bilinguals. Comprehension of transliteration into an English-based signing system was studied and compared to interpreted ASL (Marschark et al., 2004). Marschark compared deaf students' comprehension of transliterated lecture and an interpreted lecture, and found that there was no significant difference in comprehension of one over the other. He also found that sociodemographic and communication preferences do not influence signed (interpreted/transliterated) comprehension; however, in these situations where contact language is used, students in the United States are familiar with both of the languages in the contact mix. I have shown already that this is not the case for all attendees in an IS presentation audience who hope to rely on a contact SL system for communication access. Further, there is much more heterogeneity in an international audience of deaf people than in a group of students in an American classroom or lecture hall.

IS as a contact language poses added complicating factors for interpreting. Multiple languages (not just two known entities) are in the mix, and some audience members are not familiar with the lexifier languages and/or signs that become fully lexical in the system. Even though they may have some understanding of the ways that many SLs exploit space and sublexical components of signs, audience members still need semantically specific signs in IS (as they do in NSLs) to grasp equivalent detail, nuance of meaning, and range of ideas.

The professional duty to render information that is faithful to the source message and intent (at all levels of discourse) and that is most readily accessible to an audience is unavoidably challenged with a contact signed language. A lack of equivalent, conventionalized, and semantically

5. RID URL: https://www.rid.org

specific forms in IS for conveying the rich source message may very well make message faithfulness impossible, except for, as shown in this study, on a global discourse level.

RECOMMENDATIONS FOR IS USAGE AND CONFERENCE LANGUAGE POLICIES

Given the limitations in expository IS effectiveness, and characteristics of the limited number of deaf people who can truly benefit from expository IS, recommendations for IS usage settings is warranted. IS contact phenomenon arises from deaf people who have international contact experiences, and is therefore created by them. The social aspect and benefits of connecting with other deaf people will continue and increase, as long as deaf people and interpreters are engaged across country borders. Varied settings where IS-type contact takes place, such as in international sporting events and (to some extent) in international politics among deaf leaders who know the IS system, seem to be where expository IS offers a reasonable medium for cultural exchange. Over time and in continued usage settings where deaf people interact, expository IS may develop into a more established auxiliary "language." The number of users and their demographic profiles will influence agreed and lexicalized forms in future contact settings.

There is enthusiasm in making contact with users of other SLs, and this research highlights the importance for an open dialogue about the most appropriate use of an IS contact variety on a policy level. This study showed that fully conventional, natively occurring SLs, and their rich, linguistic capabilities communicate more discourse information than a second-best, auxiliary sign language contact system. Although this is expected, it is important to remember that for people who do not know the contact "language," the loss of information is significant. This has implications particularly when vital information impacting Deaf people's quality of life and advancement needs to be communicated. Deaf people are often the last to learn important information, and the reality of imperfect L1 learning experienced by more than 90% of deaf people means that most do not have the luxury of *one* full language, let alone two or more. A contact system appears inadequate for in-depth, scientific, or academic exchange of ideas and in other high-stakes arenas where deaf audiences require complete, fully detailed information. Deaf peoples' human right to their natively occurring community SL is outlined in the UN Convention on the Rights of Persons with Disabilities (UNCRPD). Information about the UNCRPD on the WFD website states:

> *Any forcible purification or unification of sign languages, conducted by governments, professionals working with Deaf people, and organizations for or of the Deaf, is a violation of the UN and UNESCO treaties, declarations, and other policies, including the UN Convention on the Rights of Persons with Disabilities. Deaf people in every country have the sole right to make changes, if necessary, in their own local, provincial, and national sign languages in response to cultural changes.* (WFD website)

Broadening acceptance of a limited contact system at conferences for "universal access" in lieu of fully established NSLs seems a compromise that may set a costly precedent that could impact deaf people's right to their own NSLs in other arenas.

At the recent (2016) Theoretical Issues in Sign Language Research (TISLR12) in Melbourne, Australia, I served the local organizing committee as Interpreter Coordinator and in this role considered the use of IS as a conference lingua franca. One recommendation I can make from the experience and from my detailed research on this topic is that conference registrants should be given the chance to register their first language and second language preferences, before interpreting language provision is decided. Official conference languages should employ the local signed and spoken language of the host country/region (and increasingly English as a pivotal language of academia and interpreting) and take into account the linguistic needs of large blocks of attendees.

For TISLR12, we provided interpreting services between English and the local signed language (Auslan) and ASL (as the predominantly requested and noted first or second language of delegates), with the intention of providing IS if people could not access the conference languages. As it turned out, providing the full program in IS as well as the two official conventional signed languages would not have been financially possible, or would have raised the registration fees to rates that would turn potential attendees away. In the end, by asking registrants to designate their L1 and L2 preferences, we ended up making a successfully accessible conference with less than five attendees who could not access the conference languages. A few delegates brought their own SL interpreters, but other thoughts came to mind about using remote video technology to bring in other SL interpreting, or require presenters not able to present in a conference language to prepare a translation into one of the conference languages for the interpreting team, and still be able to present in their language of choice.

Undoubtedly, each conference will be different in terms of attendees; therefore, it is important to consider the linguistic needs of the audience so that as many attendees can understand full information, as best as is feasible, and through a variety of technology and interpreting solutions that uphold language diversity in our Deaf communities. At TISLR12, IS of course was still a lingua franca outside of the academic program, which continues to serve well to connect Deaf people across language and national borders.

RECOMMENDATIONS FOR IS TRAINING AND ASSESSMENT

There may be benefits to teaching interpreters and other interested users of IS contact strategies about varied semiotic resources used by deaf presenters and observed in this study of expository IS. This research uncovered several factors that contribute to more or less effective IS contact for lecture or expository purposes, as well as provides authentic examples of high-frequency IS lexicon and depicting signs observed in IS lecture. It offers empirical documentation of IS forms that may be more or less effective for some audiences. Knowing at least the agreed-upon lexicon (which comes from regular use) may assist in improved understanding. Although it may show some evidence of increasing conventionalization, the IS expository contact system is in a state of ongoing change. Additional observation and documentation is needed of the forms that are created and implemented by regular IS users. The nature of contact language, however, appears to constrain the widespread use of expository IS for mixed audiences of different SLs. Not just anyone can access the system universally; contact language will be accessible to those who know the system, contribute to it, and use it regularly.

Teaching interpreters and other users an established curriculum is probably quite problematic until IS lecture forms become more stable. In the meantime, this study offers a small collection of what appear to be conventional lexical signs, commonly recruited handshapes and depicting signs, and examples of forms for telling and showing meaning in IS. This and other empirical investigations might offer preliminary curriculum content. One ought to be cautious about teaching a set list of lexical signs, and remain open to a changing group of conventionalizing IS form-meaning symbols. Additional research into shared symbolic forms across SLs may offer additional insights into potential content for IS training efforts. Study of IS conventional lexical signs, contact phenomena and accommodation between SL users, and strategies for maximizing depicting signs and pointing signs used in IS to indicate referents and relationships can inform future curriculum for IS training.

IS will likely continue to be the lingua franca in certain deaf leadership circles, such as at the EUD or in WFD boards and regional secretariats, which is where it originates and perpetuates. IS will likely continue to be recognized and expected in formal contexts such as the European Commission and European Union (EU) parliament meetings, World Federation of the Deaf (WFD) official meetings and congresses, and other international gatherings, particularly given the WFD's recent joint accreditation of IS interpreters with the World Association of Sign Language Interpreters (WASLI).

In an international setting, interpreters and Deaf leaders are in a privileged position to use multilingual resources, contribute to IS forms, and impact deaf persons' access to vital information. These are the people who may benefit most from an IS contact system. Rathmann and Mathur (2000) initially raised concerns about international linguistic access in *The Amsterdam Manifesto*. This study has provided evidence to suggest expository IS is a limited system not as effective as hoped for conveying complex, detailed ideas meant to be shared for academic, scientific, and, perhaps to some extent, economic and political advancement. It is hoped that the results of this study will educate others about IS and prompt additional research on IS contact to inform training and awareness. More information is certainly needed to understand IS and other forms of SLs in contact. Meanwhile, an expectation that deaf people and interpreters could somehow meet competency standards in expository IS when there is not enough information about a "normative," and universally effective form of IS seems premature. While multilingual competency is a reasonable starting point for recognizing the work of those of us who provide interpreting from and into IS, it is my belief that we also need to be cautious with how we claim that contact language interpreting can be "accredited." In light of the endangered status of many deaf communities' NSLs, the lack of accreditation in many countries for interpreters who work with full community signed languages, the active promotion of IS contact in some contexts seems incompatible with channeled efforts toward sign language recognition and language rights for all deaf people.

LIMITATIONS OF THE RESEARCH

With every research project, there are limitations that must be acknowledged. First, assessing comprehension of a contact language is a daunting task with very little methodological precedence. Creative, multiple measurements of IS comprehension were attempted with content analysis and rubrics, despite the fact that there are no "normative" IS texts on which to base an assessment tool. One must begin somewhere, to expand the understanding of IS contact phenomena beyond intuitions of users. There has been and continues to be a need to document and describe SLs using representative samples from authentic and varied usage settings and with corpus-based methods (Johnston, 2010). If conventional, natively occurring SLs are still new to corpus description and documentation (Johnston, 2012), then contact phenomena between SLs are even more elusive and difficult to capture. The collection of live, conference-setting IS data in this study provides authenticity to the source data; the analysis of IS lexicon methods is rigorous and informative. The testing data are experimental, and findings are based on a relatively small sampling of expository IS from quite diverse signers and from one international conference. Assessing comprehension from other international events and capturing and analyzing other samples of expository IS—such as online information and different conference venues—can offer additional insights into IS comprehension.

In addition, deaf communities are characterized as high-context culture types (Hall, 1989), exhibiting interdependent relationships, and intimate, implicit, high-context communications. It has been observed that deaf people in a lecture audience often engage in interactive discussion with their neighbor at times when they seek clarification about the lecture. Deaf people have been acting as "interpreters" or clarifiers, assisting fellow deaf people for many years in education and other such settings (Adam, Stone, Collins, & Metzger, 2011). There was no way to replicate this aspect of being an audience participant in the original lecture; therefore, the comprehension assessment was situated in an experimental setting. Future research might look at whether and what kinds of gaps in understanding might be filled by a neighbor when groups of deaf people attend IS presentations. In fact, I suggest this may offer possible models for summary-type, or escort-style IS interpreting at conferences using experienced Deaf Interpreters and Deaf-hearing interpreter teams.

RECOMMENDATIONS FOR FUTURE RESEARCH

Research findings often uncover more questions. Future investigations might further analyze several phenomena observed in this research such as what, if any, *optimal* constructions are effective for prompting meaning in the minds of audience members from varied and distinctly different SL origins.

Because the main focus of this study was on IS comprehension, much of the collected IS presentation source data are yet to be studied. Basic annotation levels were completed on the dataset for the purpose of lexical description for testing. Further analysis is needed into the way different types of signs (e.g., pointing, depicting and lexical signs) function in complex multisign symbolic units (i.e., grammatical constructions) to create meaning, and whether these constructions adhere to patterns in NSL grammatical constructions. A follow-up study might analyze multisign constructions to explore constituents in terms of grammatical function and role.

A fuller analysis of the variation of lexical forms observed in the IS dataset is also needed. Many types of modifications of forms were observed, and investigation might indicate how and why they are modified (e.g., by reduplication for aspect or manner) and if these modifications pattern like they do in other SLs and if they function similarly.

The lexical study in the first part of the research offers a start to documenting sign forms that show some degree of conventionality in this particular genre of IS. Rosenstock's comparison across five language families for cognates of the most common 162 signs in her data could be compared to the high-frequency signs in Study One of this research, to see if there are noticeable differences in signs employed more than 12 years ago. A comparison of forms in earlier similar settings and future ones would show changes across time, or evidence increasing conventionalization of certain sign forms in IS contact.

It is important to consider establishing glossing conventions and consistent methods for annotating and documenting sign forms that appear repeatedly in IS lectures or presentations at conferences, as well as for those appearing in the increasing number of online examples of expository IS. Any future comparison between research on IS lexicon requires consistent video documentation of forms using rigorous methods and available digital mechanisms currently available for corpus-linguistic analysis of SLs.

Additional study, particularly collaborative research between linguists and signers from non-Western SL with Western SL signers and researchers, would supplement lexical analysis of IS thus far. A comparative study across several NSL and IS using lexicostatistical methods could offer further, more internationally balanced insights about the relationship between sign form-meaning pairs in IS and NSLs. Findings from varied genres of situated IS could enlighten those of us who are interpreters and researchers interested in sign language contact phenomena about recruited semiotic material, and whether recurring forms are becoming more established or shifting.

Finally, further study on IS and other types of SL contact must clearly delineate and define the parameters around the setting, participants, and formality of the contact situation before making any measured conclusions. It also is important to resist the urge to generalize to all SL contact phenomena from even one study's findings.

CONCLUDING REMARKS

I recognize that SL contact phenomena such as the genre investigated in this study come from deaf people, particularly leaders who are in positions to influence other Deaf communities that are severely underrepresented in local, national, and international politics and economies. It is evident that contact effects from spoken languages are also influential in SLs, carrying semiotic and symbolic material from a variety of cultural frames. Interpreters, myself included, who work in these contact settings are tasked with collaborating with Deaf leaders to be mindful of ethnocentric linguistic and cultural influences that may unintentionally marginalize or leave behind other linguistic and culturally distinct deaf communities.

The unique structural similarities that seem to be shared in several studied SLs come from the visual spatial modality. It is this visual spatial modality that deaf people take great pride in, particularly given the long-standing oppression and misunderstanding of SLs. At the same time, empirical research on varied SLs will continue to shed more light on elements that make SLs a special type, similar in some ways, yet also different from one another as well.

This project shows that expository IS discourse is quite variable in terms of its lexicon, and it is understood with even more variation. Expository IS is clearly a moving target, and it is subject to ongoing contact influences. The research reported in this volume provides additional information about some of the limits of expository IS, with implications for potentially appropriate and inappropriate usage settings. It also sheds light on strengths and weaknesses inherent in cross-linguistic signed contact. It is my hope that it informs and also prompts additional, much needed inquiry.

If IS is destined to evolve into a reliable auxiliary tool in international SL communications, additional research is needed to learn about IS constructions that communicate effectively and for what purposes. An ongoing dialogue is also needed about policies for the use of IS. In the meantime, contact between SLs will continue to influence the evolution of SLs. For this reason, there must be more rigorous research on these phenomena in order to understand and describe unique features of existing and evolving SLs within the context of human language.

Appendix A: High Frequency Signs in Expository IS

Rank	ID gloss	Total	Frequency in Full dataset (N=4383)	% Cumul	Rank	ID gloss	Total	Frequency in Full dataset (N=4383)	% Cumul
1	DEAFH(AUS)	139	3.2%	2.9%	28	EXPLAIN(WFD)	31	0.7%	37.0%
2	WHAT(ASL)	99	2.3%	5.2%	29	GROUP-TOGETHER(ASL)	30	0.7%	37.7%
3	DEAF1(ASL)	98	2.2%	7.4%	30	PROGRESS(ASL)	30	0.7%	38.4%
4	SAME(AUS)	96	2.2%	9.6%	31	YEAR(ASL)	29	0.7%	39.1%
5	HAVE(AUS)	94	2.1%	11.7%	32	DISABLED(WFD)	28	0.6%	39.7%
6	SIGN(AUS)	87	2.0%	13.7%	33	NINE(WFD)	27	0.6%	40.3%
7	PERSON(AUS)	85	1.9%	15.7%	34	TWO(ASL)	27	0.6%	40.9%
8	GOOD(AUS)	62	1.4%	17.1%	35	WRITE(ASL)	27	0.6%	41.5%
9	DIFFERENT(ASL)	61	1.4%	18.5%	36	GIVE1(ASL)	26	0.6%	42.1%
10	TEACH(ASL)	61	1.4%	19.9%	37	HOW1(ASL)	26	0.6%	42.7%
11	WORK(GEST)	59	1.3%	21.2%	38	WANT(AUS)	26	0.6%	43.3%
12	ONE(ASL)	56	1.3%	22.5%	39	WOMANB(WFD)	26	0.6%	43.9%
13	IMPORTANT(ASL)	55	1.3%	23.7%	40	HEARING(WFD)	25	0.6%	44.5%
14	ASSOCIATION(GEST)	54	1.2%	25.0%	41	NS:ASIAPACIFIC	25	0.6%	45.1%
15	INTERPRETER(WFD)	50	1.1%	26.1%	42	ZERO(ASL)	25	0.6%	45.6%
16	HELP(ASL)	49	1.1%	27.2%	43	BUT(AUS)	24	0.5%	46.2%
17	WORLD(GEST)	47	1.1%	28.3%	44	EXAMPLE(ASL)	24	0.5%	46.7%
18	CONNECT(ASL)	42	1.0%	29.3%	45	INTERNATIONAL(WFD)	24	0.5%	47.3%
19	CAN(ASL)	41	0.9%	30.2%	46	RESPONSIBLE(ASL)	24	0.5%	47.8%
20	NOW(GEST)	38	0.9%	31.1%	47	BRING(ASL)	23	0.5%	48.3%
21	KNOW(ASL)	37	0.8%	31.9%	48	NEED(ASL)	23	0.5%	48.9%
22	GOVERNMENT(GEST)	35	0.8%	32.7%	49	NONE(ASL)	23	0.5%	49.4%
23	ANALYZE(ASL)	32	0.7%	33.4%	50	CRPD(WFD)	22	0.5%	49.9%
24	FINISH(ASL)	32	0.7%	34.2%	51	PROBLEM(ASL)	22	0.5%	50.4%
25	NS:JAPAN	32	0.7%	34.9%	52	CHILDREN(ASL)	21	0.5%	50.9%
26	THINK(ASL)	32	0.7%	35.6%	53	FIRST2(AUS)	21	0.5%	51.4%
27	COUNTRY(WFD)	31	0.7%	36.3%	54	HAVE2(ASL)	21	0.5%	51.8%

(*Continued*)

Rank	ID gloss	Total	Frequency in Full dataset (N=4383)	% Cumul	Rank	ID gloss	Total	Frequency in Full dataset (N=4383)	% Cumul
55	LANGUAGE3(WFD)	21	0.5%	52.3%	83	LEAD(ASL)	13	0.3%	62.8%
56	LOOK-2H(ASL)	21	0.5%	52.8%	84	RELATE(ASL)	13	0.3%	63.1%
57	SEE-2H(ASL)	21	0.5%	53.3%	85	ACCEPT(ASL)	12	0.3%	63.4%
58	STUDY(AUS)	21	0.5%	53.8%	86	DEAFH.EAR(GEST)	12	0.3%	63.7%
59	LECTURE(ASL)	20	0.5%	54.2%	87	HOW2(WFD)	12	0.3%	63.9%
60	MANY(ASL)	20	0.5%	54.7%	88	MONEY1(ASL)	12	0.3%	64.2%
61	RIGHTS(ASL)	20	0.5%	55.1%	89	OFFER(ASL)	12	0.3%	64.5%
62	COUNTRY2(ASL)	19	0.4%	55.6%	90	OTHER(ASL)	12	0.3%	64.8%
63	IN(ASL)	19	0.4%	56.0%	91	REGIONAL(ASL)	12	0.3%	65.0%
64	SEE(ASL)	18	0.4%	56.4%	92	SCHOOL2(AUS)	12	0.3%	65.3%
65	BODY(AUS)	17	0.4%	56.8%	93	COME(ASL)	11	0.3%	65.6%
66	AGO(ASL)	16	0.4%	57.2%	94	FOR(ASL)	11	0.3%	65.8%
67	EQUAL(ASL)	16	0.4%	57.5%	95	HIT(ASL)	11	0.3%	66.1%
68	LEARN(ASL)	16	0.4%	57.9%	96	IMPOSSIBLE(GEST)	11	0.3%	66.3%
69	SCOUT(ASL)	16	0.4%	58.3%	97	MEET(ASL)	11	0.3%	66.6%
70	THANK(ASL)	16	0.4%	58.6%	98	NEW(ASL)	11	0.3%	66.8%
71	ALL(AUS)	15	0.3%	59.0%	99	SEE1(AUS)	11	0.3%	67.1%
72	COMMUNICATE(ASL)	15	0.3%	59.3%	100	STRONG(ASL)	11	0.3%	67.3%
73	MEAN(ASL)	15	0.3%	59.6%	101	SUPPORT(ASL)	11	0.3%	67.6%
74	NS:DUSKIN	15	0.3%	60.0%	102	TELL(ASL)	11	0.3%	67.8%
75	BOY(ASL)	14	0.3%	60.3%	103	TIME(ASL)	11	0.3%	68.1%
76	FS:WFD	14	0.3%	60.6%	104	WHAT2(AUS)	11	0.3%	68.3%
77	MUST1(GEST)	14	0.3%	60.9%	105	WITH(ASL)	11	0.3%	68.6%
78	NAME(GEST)	14	0.3%	61.3%	106	DEMOTE(AUS)	10	0.2%	68.8%
79	NEXT1(ASL)	14	0.3%	61.6%	107	LOOK(ASL)	10	0.2%	69.0%
80	PEOPLE(ASL)	14	0.3%	61.9%	108	NEXT(AUS)	10	0.2%	69.2%
81	TITLE(ASL)	14	0.3%	62.2%	109	TRAINING(ASL)	10	0.2%	69.5%
82	DEVELOP(ASL)	13	0.3%	62.5%	110	WORD(AUS)	10	0.2%	69.7%

111	BLIND1(ASL)	9	0.2%	69.9%	141	FS:CRPD	7	0.2%	75.6%
112	CONDENSE(ASL)	9	0.2%	70.1%	142	FS:UN	7	0.2%	75.7%
113	CONTACT(ASL)	9	0.2%	70.3%	143	INFORM(ASL)	7	0.2%	75.9%
114	FEEL(ASL)	9	0.2%	70.5%	144	INFORM2(AUS)	7	0.2%	76.0%
115	FIND(ASL)	9	0.2%	70.7%	145	SEVEN(WFD)	7	0.2%	76.2%
116	FIVE(ASL)	9	0.2%	70.9%	146	START(ASL)	7	0.2%	76.4%
117	FLY(AUS)	9	0.2%	71.1%	147	CONGRESS(GEST)	6	0.1%	76.5%
118	LAW(ASL)	9	0.2%	71.3%	148	PRESIDENT(GEST)	6	0.1%	76.6%
119	LEARN-2H(AUS)	9	0.2%	71.6%	149	ENGLISH(OTHER)	6	0.1%	76.8%
120	MORE(ASL)	9	0.2%	71.8%	150	APPROVE(WFD)	5	0.1%	76.9%
121	NOTHING-2H(AUS)	9	0.2%	72.0%	151	DEMOTE(AUS)	6	0.09%	77.0%
122	PROJECT(WFD)	9	0.2%	72.2%	152	ENCOURAGE(ASL)	6	0.09%	77.1%
123	SAME2(ASL)	9	0.2%	72.4%	153	FAR(ASL)	6	0.09%	77.1%
124	SERVICE(ASL)	9	0.2%	72.6%	154	FAST(OTHER)	6	0.09%	77.2%
125	TYPE(ASL)	9	0.2%	72.8%	155	FIRST1(AUS)	6	0.09%	77.3%
126	WHY(ASL)	9	0.2%	73.0%	156	FOUR(ASL)	6	0.09%	77.4%
127	BUDGET1(WFD)	8	0.2%	73.2%	157	FS:JFD	6	0.09%	77.5%
128	ENGLISH(ASL)	8	0.2%	73.4%	158	FS:JICA	6	0.09%	77.6%
129	GIVE(AUS)	8	0.2%	73.5%	159	G:PLUS-SIGN	6	0.09%	77.7%
130	LANGUAGE2(ASL)	8	0.2%	73.7%	160	GO(ASL)	6	0.09%	77.7%
131	MONEY(GEST)	8	0.2%	73.9%	161	INTERPRETER(ASL)	6	0.09%	77.8%
132	START(WFD)	8	0.2%	74.1%	162	OR(WFD)	6	0.09%	77.9%
133	TEN(WFD)	8	0.2%	74.3%	163	PERSON-PL(GEST)	6	0.09%	78.0%
134	YOUNG(ASL)	8	0.2%	74.4%	164	SECOND(ASL)	6	0.09%	78.1%
135	AIM(AUS)	7	0.2%	74.6%	165	THIRD(ASL)	6	0.09%	78.2%
136	CHANGE(ASL)	7	0.2%	74.8%	166	TWO-OF-US(ASL)	6	0.09%	78.3%
137	COMMUNITY(ASL)	7	0.2%	74.9%	167	WAY(ASL)	6	0.09%	78.3%
138	EIGHT(WFD)	7	0.2%	75.1%	168	WIN(ASL)	6	0.09%	78.4%
139	FAMILY(ASL)	7	0.2%	75.2%	169	WOMAN.EAR(GEST)	6	0.09%	78.5%
140	FIRST(ASL)	7	0.2%	75.4%	170	BEFORE(ASL)	5	0.07%	78.6%

(Continued)

Rank	ID gloss	Total	Frequency in Full dataset (N=4383)	% Cumul
171	BUT(ASL)	5	0.07%	78.7%
172	BUY(ASL)	5	0.07%	78.7%
173	CONTROL(ASL)	5	0.07%	78.8%
174	DECIDE(ASL)	5	0.07%	78.9%
175	DIFFERENT-1H(ASL)	5	0.07%	78.9%
176	DISSEMINATE(ASL)	5	0.07%	79.0%
177	FALSE START	5	0.07%	79.1%
178	FINGERSPELLING(ASL)	5	0.07%	79.2%
179	HAPPEN(AUS)	5	0.07%	79.2%
180	HOSPITAL(ASL)	5	0.07%	79.3%
181	HOUSE(ASL)	5	0.07%	79.4%
182	IDEA(ASL)	5	0.07%	79.4%
183	INSTINCT(ASL)	5	0.07%	79.5%
184	KNOW-ZERO(ASL)	5	0.07%	79.6%
185	MIX(ASL)	5	0.07%	79.7%
186	MUST(GEST)	5	0.07%	79.7%
187	NS:AMERICA	5	0.07%	79.8%
188	PT:LBUOY-FOURTH	5	0.07%	79.9%
189	READ(ASL)	5	0.07%	79.9%
190	SEARCH(ASL)	5	0.07%	80.0%
191	SPECIAL(ASL)	5	0.07%	80.1%
192	VISION(WFD)	5	0.07%	80.1%
193	WHEELCHAIR(ASL)	5	0.07%	80.2%
194	WHO(ASL)	5	0.07%	80.3%
195	WORD(ASL)	5	0.07%	80.4%
196	ASSEMBLY(WFD)	4	0.06%	80.4%
197	COLLEGE(GEST)	4	0.06%	80.5%
198	NS:ASIA	4	0.06%	80.5%
199	FOCUS(ASL)	4	0.06%	80.6%
200	GO-POINT(AUS)	4	0.06%	80.6%

Rank	**DEPICTING SIGNS** (n=664)	Total
1	DSS(BENTB):ENTITIES-IN-A- LINE-LISTED-ON-PAGE	17
2	DSS(GC):SMALL-AMOUNT	14
3	DSM(1):ENTITY-GOES-FAR-IN-DEEP	11
4	DSM(5):ENTITIES-GATHER-TOGETHER	8
5	DSL(B-HORI):ENTITY-LOCATED-AT	6
	total	**56**

Rank	**Most frequent GESTURES** (n=632)	Total
1	G(5-UP):WELL	110
2	G(5-UP):HUH	56
3	G(5-UP):SO	51
4	G(5-SHAKE):WOW	24
5	G(1-SHAKE):NO-NO	20
6	G(5-WAVE):NO-NO	10
7	G(F):ALL-OK	9
	total	**279**

Appendix B: Lexical Identification Scoring Sheet

Sign #	IDGloss	Meaning(s)	"1" if correct; "0" if incorrect
1	BODY(AUS)	health (care, physical care)	
2	ANALYZE(ASL)	research, analysis	
3	BOY(ASL)	male person -man or boy	
4	FINISH(ASL)	finish, completed	
5	PROJECT (WFD)	project, initiative	
6	DISABLED(WFD)	person with disabilities, disability	
7	STUDY(AUS)	education, school, study	
8	APPROVE(WFD)	approve, ratify, legalize	
9	GOVERNMENT(GEST)	government	
10	CONNECT(ASL)	connection, relate, connect	
11	CHILDREN(ASL)	children, kids, young people	
12	SAME(AUS)	also, same as	
13	LANGUAGE3(WFD)	grammar or text information	
14	CRPD(WFD)	Legal document giving rights to ppl with Disabilities and Deaf persons	
15	HAVE(AUS)	have, possess, own	
16	DIFFERENT(ASL)	different, varied	
17	HELP(ASL)	help, assistance	
18	ASSOCIATION(GEST)	Deaf associations	
19	WORLD(GEST)	world, global, international	
20	CONGRESS(GEST)	congress, converence	
21	WHAT(ASL)	what	
22	YEAR(ASL)	year	
23	COUNTRY(WFD)	country, region	
24	WANT(AUS)	want	
25	WORK(GEST)	work	
26	PROBLEM(ASL)	problem	
27	PROGRESS(ASL)	progress, move forward/on, advance	

(*Continued*)

Appendix B: (*Continued*)

Sign #	IDGloss	Meaning(s)	"1" if correct; "0" if incorrect
28	KNOW (ASL)	know, aware, knowledge	
29	PERSON(GEST)	person(s)	
30	CAN(ASL)	able, can	
31	ACCEPT(ASL)	accept	
32	NS:ASIAPACIFIC	Asia- Pacific (region)	
33	SEE-2H(ASL)	see, look, view	
34	BRING(ASL)	bring, carry, deliver	
35	INTERPRETER(WFD)	interpreter, translator	
36	SIGN(GEST)	sign language	
37	IMPORTANT(ASL)	important	
38	INTERNATIONAL(WFD)	international (adjective)	
39	NOW(ASL)	now, today, immediate time	
40	SCOUT(ASL)	boy scouts, scouting organization	
41	THINK(ASL)	think, realize, idea	
42	HEARING(WFD)	able to hear, not deaf	
43	DEAF1(ASL)	Deaf	
44	G(6-UP):GOOD	good	
45	DSS(GC):SMALL-AMOUNT	a small amount, little, not enough	

Appendix C: Content Questions Rubric

Questions		Q Types: P= Pragmatic/Discourse G= Goal D=Detail MP= Main Point(s)			
Q #	TYPE	Questions: Clip A	Points	Answers	Participant Score
1	P	What kind of presentation is this?	1	Introduction of a speaker at a large international, formal conference	
2	G	Why is he giving it?	2	Give background and introduce colleague/ co-researcher (Dr. Fellinger)	
3	P	Who is he talking to? (audience)	2	WFD audience- General assembly, mixed signers, Deaf and hearing.	
4	D	Who is the person to his left side?	2	Dr. Fellinger, colleague, a doctor	
5	MP	What did he and that person do together?	2	Created a Deaf Health Initiative, did a survey	
6	MP	Is he talking about research in his home community or elsewhere?	1	globally	
	Total A		10		
		Questions: Clip B			
7	P	What kind of presentation is this? To whom?	3	CONFERENCE, FORMAL PRESENTATION, TO DEAF LEADERS	
8	G	What is she talking about?	2	DEAF EDUCATION IN DEVELOPING COUNTRIES (i.e. TOGO, WEST AFRICA).	
9	MP	In her country, what is happening in Deaf education?	3	LACK of Funding, NO SECONDARY (HIGH) SCHOOL, no opportunity for educational advancement, SCHOOLS GETTING WORSE/ DECLINING, MIXED DISABLED CLASSES/ mainstreaming, prevalence of oralism.	
10	D	Why don't Deaf people in her country understand correspondence/letters?	2	Literacy problems; letters written in English, not in French/native written language	
11	MP	What are the two presenters comparing?	1	Resources in English speaking African countries vs.French speaking ones	

(Continued)

Questions		Q Types: P= Pragmatic/Discourse G= Goal	D=Detail	MP= Main Point(s)
12	MP	What did she say is a big problem with Deaf education in some African countries?	5	NOT ENOUGH FUNDING FOR EDUCATION, ORALISM, TEACHERS WHO ARE NOT TRAINED /DON'T KNOW SIGN LANGUAGE, Not enough interpreters, RELIGIOUS MISSIONS THAT DON'T KNOW HOW TO WORK WITH DEAF PEOPLE. NO SECONDARY (HIGH) SCHOOL, SCHOOLS GETTING WORSE/ DECLINING, MIXED DISABLED CLASSES/mainstreaming.
13	MP	What does the white woman say is the reason some Deaf communities are doing better?	1	collaboration with Deaf associations and outside entities from other countries.
	Total B		17	
		Questions: Clip C		
14	P	What kind of presentation is this?	1	Formal conference
15	G	Why is he giving it?	2	TO INSPIRE THE AUDIENCE, TO GET ELECTED, ENCOURAGE COLLABORATION
16	P	Who is he talking to? (audience)	2	DEAF AUDIENCE of WFD delegates, international Deaf.
17	D	How many Associations make up the WFD?	1	132
18	MP	What does he say Deaf people have that is powerful?	2	THE CRPD AND A COMMON VISION
19	MP	How does he say Deaf people improve their communities?	3	WORKING TOGETHER, GIVING UP TIME TO SERVE COMMUNITY, THE CRPD, CAPACITY BUILDING, DEAF ASSOCIATION WORKING WITH WFD
20	MP	Why does he say Deaf people are unique/special?	1	SIGN LANGUAGE/VISUAL PEOPLE (Deaf pride)
	Total C		12	

		Questions: Clip D		
21	D	How many Deaf people in Japan (JFD?)	1	22,000
22	D	How many people attended?	1	7,000
23	D	What did he say happens every year with the help of WFD?	2	Asia Pacific/regional conferences
	Total D		4	
24	D	What year were the Boy Scouts established?	1	1907
25	D	As of 2011 how many scouts worldwide?	1	41 million
26	MP	What are the goals/mission of the Boy Scouts?	3	develop young people physically, emotionally, spiritually
27	D	Name four activities that Boy Scouts learn about.	4	law, ethics/ confidentiality, health, camping, making campfires, survival, woodworking, crafts, first aid compass navigation (orienteering), hiking,
28	D	What are the 5 age groups in the Boy Scouts?	5	6-8; 8-11; 11-15; 16-18; 18+
29	D	What are the 5 group names?	5	bears (or beavers), cubs, scouts, venturers, rovers
30	MP	How did the first Deaf only Boy Scout troop start?	2	A father of a Deaf boy in his local troop, brought in a Deaf leader, then more Deaf boys got involved, the group split out and formed a Deaf -only group. This expanded Deaf scouting.
	Total E		21	
	Grand TTL		**65**	

Appendix D: Main Idea Unit Scoring Sheet for Video D/D'

Video segment	Idea Units Circle: IS or NSL version Participant #	1 point each	Comments
1a	Before we start, want to share something	1	
1b	There was an earthquake in Japan	1	
1c	It happened March 2011	1	
1d	It caused a large tsunami	1	
1e	The damage was terrible	1	
1f	A nuclear accident and power outage occurred	1	
2a	The world Deaf communities (you) sent messages	1	
2b	Asked if we were ok	1	
2c	Money and donations were sent	1	
2d	We want to thank you for your generosity	1	
2e	This supports the work of the JFD	1	
3a	The JFD is working hard to help Deaf people affected	1	
3b	We are making repairs	1	
3c	Please continue to send donations	1	
4a	The JFD started in 1947	1	
4b	Since then we work towards 4 aims	1	
5a	One is interpreter training	1	
5b	The second is obtaining legal/human rights for deaf people	1	
5c	Thirdly attainment of drivers licenses for Deaf persons	1	
5d	Fourth, establishing more deaf (community service) organizations	1	
6a	Soon Japanese government will pass a law recognizing JSL as a language	1	
6b	We are both very excited about this	1	
7a	The JFD works to assist Deaf people in Japan	1	
7b	There are 22,000 members/Deaf in Japan	1	
8a	We hosted the 1991 World Federation of the Deaf congress.	1	
8b	This happened in Tokyo	1	
8c	7000 people attended	1	
8d	We (Japan/ Asia) were inspired by the world influence	1	
9a	We witnessed a sad situation across Asia	1	

9b	Deaf education is not good	1
9c	Access to interpreters is not good	1
9d	Japan is open to the world to advocate for Deaf people in other (Asian?) communities	1
10a	There is one example of success - Fiji	1
10b	Two Deaf people came from Fiji	1
10c	They came to learn from us (Japan/ JFD)	1
10d	One returned to Fiji	1
10e	He became the president of the Fiji Deaf association	1
10f	He is no longer president	1
10g	But he works as an advocate for better quality of life for Deaf people there	1
10h	He teaches Deaf people in Fiji	1
11a	The second Fiji person studied in Japan	1
11b	He returned to Fiji to teach SL	1
11c	He teaches interpreting	1
11d	There has been much positive development in Fiji	1
11e	We are very happy about this good collaborative work	1
12a	The WFD has an Asia Pacific Regional Secretariat (group)	1
12b	JFD/AP region WFD Sponsors an annual conference	1
12c	The conference is held in different (Asian) countries	1
12d	Delegates gather in that one country	1
13a	Support is given to the hosting country to make improvements for Deaf people	1
13b	The conference improves the AP region	1
14a	Deaf association in the AP region are getting stronger	1
14b	Leadership is important for growth	1
14c	But there are not enough Deaf leaders. We need to develop more.	1
15a	Two organizations provide this training	1
15b	The names of those organizations are JICA (Japan International Cooperative Agency) and Duskin (a business)	1
15c	More leaders are trained and they go back to work in their home communities	1
15d	We are happy to see these improvements	1
	Total # Idea Units - Possible Score	**58**

Appendix E: ELAN Search Documentation

Search: Total numer of signs

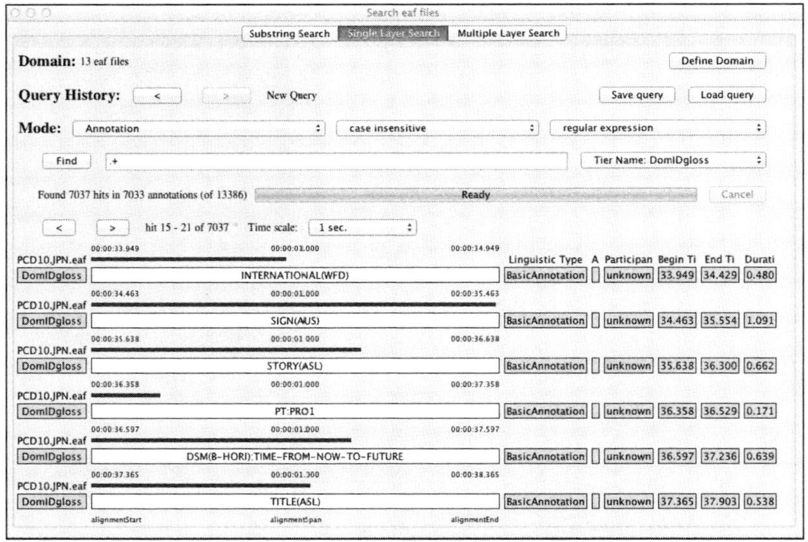

Function	Identifies total signs of the type "DS" in the dataset
Domain	All 13 signers in the IS dataset (or 6 in the comprehension video sub set)
Mode	Annotation, case insensitive, regular expression
Tier Name	Dominant hand ID gloss tier
Search regular expression	.+ (any character one or more times)
Notes	This search finds all dominant hand ID-gloss annotations. At times one-handed signs are made on the non-dominant hand, however de Beuzeville, et al. (2009) show that missing these examples does not have a significant effect on the approximate number of signs in the search.

Search: Frequency of signs by type

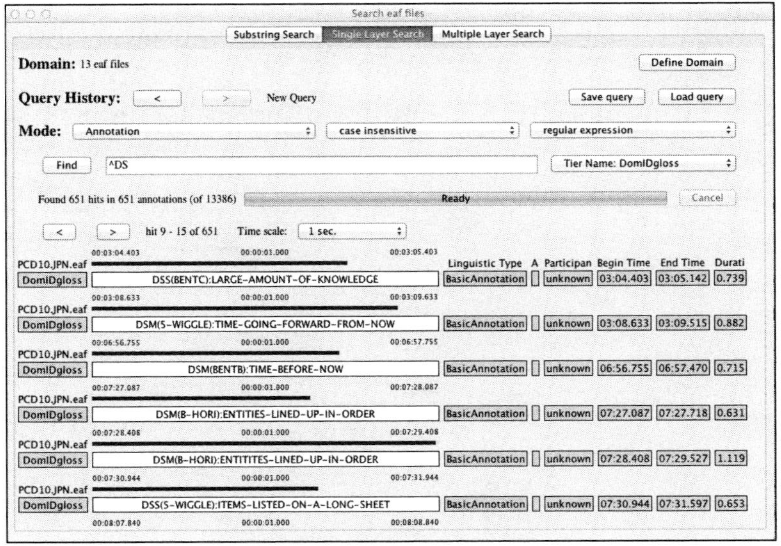

Function	Identifies total signs of the type "DS" in the dataset
Domain	All 13 signers in the IS dataset (or 6 in the comprehension video subset)
Mode	Annotation, case insensitive, regular expression
Tier Name	Dominant hand ID gloss tier
Search regular expression	^DS (an annotation that begins with the letters DS)
Variations on this search	^DSS (signs that depict size and shape); ^DSM (signs that depict the movement of entities); ^DSH (handling depicting signs); ^DSL (signs that depict location); ^DSG(signs that depict ground, usually in relation to other hand in a depicting sequence) ^PT (pointing sign annotations), ^FS (fingerspelling annotations); ^G\: (gesture, an annotation that starts with a G then a colon; ^G\ (non-manual gesture or constructed action, an annotation that begins with the letter G followed by a parenthesis)
Notes	This search finds dominant hand ID-gloss annotations. At times one-handed signs are made on the non-dominant hand, however de Beuzeville, et al. (2009) show that missing these examples does not have a significant effect on the approximate number of signs in the search.

(*Continued*)

APPENDIX E: (*Continued*)

Search: Frequency and distribution of signs by origin

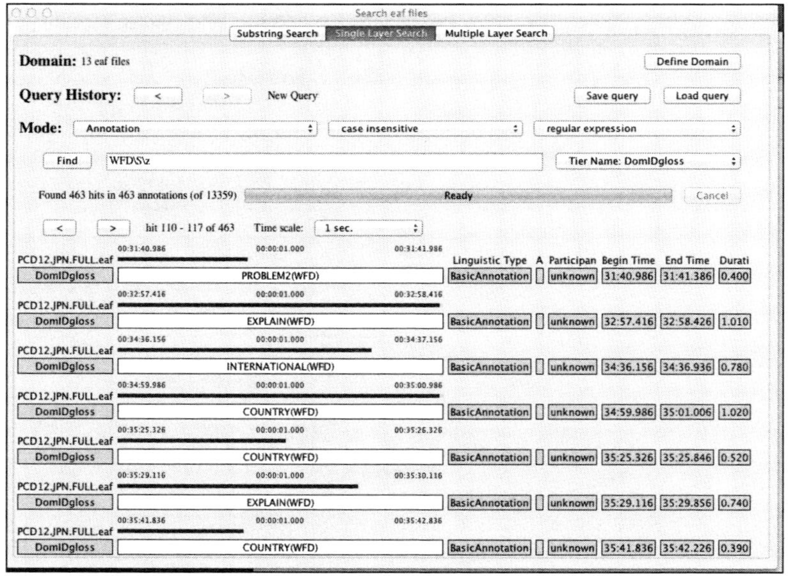

Function	Identifies total signs of the type X(WFD)
Domain	All 13 signers in the IS dataset (or 6 in the comprehension subset)
Mode	Annotation, case insensitive, regular expression
Tier Name	Dominant hand ID gloss tier
Search Regular Expression	WFD\S\z (an annotation that contains the sequence WFD and is followed by one non-white space that ends the annotation)
Variations on this Search	ASL\S\z (an annotation that contains and ends with the sequence ASL; all signs of the type X(ASL); AUS\S\z (an annotation that contains and ends with the sequence AUS; all signs of the type X(AUS); GEST\S\z (an annotation that contains and ends with the sequence GEST; all signs of the type X(GEST); UNKNOWN\S\z (an annotation that contains and ends with the sequence X(UNKNOWN).

References

Adam, R. (2012). Language contact and borrowing. In R. Pfau, M. Steinbach, & B. Woll (Eds.), *Sign language: An international handbook* (pp. 841–861). Berlin, Germany: De Gruyter Mouton.

Adam, R., Stone, C., Collins, S., & Metzger, M. (Eds.). (2014). *Deaf interpreters at work*. Washington, DC: Gallaudet University Press.

Alreck, P. L., & Settle, R. B. (1995). *The survey research handbook* (2nd ed.). Chicago, IL: Irwin.

Al-Fityani, K., & Padden, C. (2008). A lexical comparison of sign languages in the Arab world. In R. M. de Quadros (Ed.), *Sign languages: Spinning and unraveling the past, present and future. TISLR9, forty-five papers and three posters from the Ninth Theoretical Issues in Sign Language Research Conference*, Florianopolis, Brazil, December 2006 (pp. 2–14). Petrópolis, RJ, Brazil: Editora Arara Azul.

Allsop, L., Woll, B., & Brauti, J. M. (1995). International Sign: The creation of an international deaf community and sign language. In H. Bos & G. Schermer (Eds.), *Sign language research 1994: Proceedings of the Fourth European Congress on Sign language research* (pp. 171–188). Hamburg, Germany: Signum Press.

Arik, E. (2008). Locative constructions in Turkish Sign Language (TID). In R. M. de Quadros (Ed.), *Sign languages: Spinning and unraveling the past, present and future. TISLR9, forty-five papers and three posters from the Ninth Theoretical Issues in Sign Language Research Conference*, Florianopolis, Brazil, December 2006 (pp. 15–31). Petrópolis, RJ, Brazil: Editora Arara Azul.

Armstrong, D. F., Stokoe, W. C., & Wilcox, S. (1995). *Gesture and the nature of language*. Cambridge, UK: Cambridge University Press.

Aronoff, M., Meir, I., & Sandler, W. (2005). The paradox of sign language morphology, *Language*, *81*(2), 301–344. doi:10.1353/lan.2005.0043

Auslan Signbank (2014). Retrieved from http://ww.auslan.org.au

Baddeley, A. D. (1986). *Working memory*. Oxford, UK: Oxford University Press.

Bartlomiejczyk, M. (2006). Strategies of simultaneous interpreting and directionality. *Interpreting*, *8*(2), 149–174.

Battison, R. (1978). *Lexical borrowing in American Sign Language*. Silver Spring, MD: Linstok Press.

Battison, R. (2000). American Sign Language Linguistics 1970–1980: Memoir of a Renaissance. In K. L. Emmorey & H. Lane (Eds.), *The signs of language revisited: An anthology to honor Ursula Bellugi and Edward Klima*. Mahwah, NJ: Lawrence Erlbaum.

Battison, R., & Jordan, I. K. (1976, Spring). Cross cultural communication with foreign signers: Fact and fancy. *Sign Language Studies, 10*, 52–68.

Bavelier, D., Newport, E. L., & Supalla, T. (2003). Children need natural languages, signed or spoken. *Cerebrum, 5*, 19–32.

Bergmann, A. (1990). Extra rational responses: International Sign—Language? *SignPost*, *4*(3), 2–3.

Berry, J. W. (2004). Fundamental psychological processes in intercultural relations. In D. Landis, J. M. Bennett, & M. J. Bennett (Eds.), *Handbook of intercultural training* (3rd ed., pp. 166–184). Thousand Oaks, CA: Sage.

Best, B., Napier, J., Carmichael, A., & Pouliot, O. (2016). From a Koine to Gestalt: Critical points and interpreter strategies in interpretation from International Sign into spoken English. In J. Napier & R. Rosenstock (Eds.), *International sign: Linguistic, usage, and status issues* (pp. 136–166). Washington, DC: Gallaudet University Press.

Biber, D., Johansson, S., Leech, G., Conrad, S., & Finegan, E. (1999). *Longman grammar of spoken and written English*. Essex, UK: Pearson Education.

Boutla, M., Supalla, T., Newport, E. L., & Bavelier, D. (2004). Short-term memory span: insights from sign language. *Natural Neuroscience*, *7*(9), 997–1002.

Boyes Braem, P. (2003–2005). Linguistic descriptions of DSGS, as printable texts in four CD-ROMS. Zurich, Switzerland: Schweizerischer Gehorlosenbund-DS.

Bradford, A., Sagara, K., & Zeshan, U. (2013). *Multilingual and multimodal aspects of "cross-signing"—A study of emerging communication in the domain of numerals*. Paper presented at the 11th Theoretical Issues in Sign Language Research conference (TISLR11), University College London, July 13–15.

Brennan, M. (1990). Productive morphology in British Sign Language: Focus on the role of metaphors. In S. Prillwitz & T. Vollhaber (Eds.), *Current trends in European Sign Language research: Proceedings of the Third European Congress on Sign Language Research Hamburg, July 26–29, 1989* (pp. 205–228). Hamburg, Germany: Signum Verlag.

Brennan, M. (1992). The visual world of BSL: An introduction. In D. Brien (Ed.), *Dictionary of British Sign Language/English* (pp. 1–133). London and Boston: Faber and Faber.

Brentari, D. (Ed.). (2001). *Foreign vocabulary in sign languages: A cross-linguistic investigation of word formation*. Mahwah, NJ: Lawrence Erlbaum.

Brentari, D. (2010). *Sign languages*. New York, NY: Cambridge University Press.

Brentari, D., & Padden, C. A. (2001). Native and foreign vocabulary in American Sign Language: A lexicon with multiple origins. In D. Brentari (Ed.), *Foreign vocabulary in sign languages: A cross-linguistic investigation of word formation*. Mahwah, NJ: Lawrence Erlbaum.

Brentari, D., & Wilbur, R. (2006). A cross-linguistic study of word segmentation in three sign languages. In R. M. de Quadros (Ed.), *Sign languages: Spinning and unraveling the past, present and future. TISLR9, forty-five papers and three posters from the Ninth Theoretical Issues in Sign Language Research Conference,* Florianopolis, Brazil, December 2006 (2008).

Brislin, R. W. (1970). Back-translation for cross-cultural research. *Journal of Cross-Cultural Psychology, 1*, 185–216.

Brislin, R. W. (1980). Translation and content analysis of oral and written materials. In H. C. Triandis & J. W. Berry (Eds.), *Handbook of cross-cultural psychology: Methodology* (pp. 389–444). Boston, MA: Allyn and Bacon.

British Deaf Association (BDA). (1975). *Gestuno: International Sign Language of the Deaf: A revised and enlarged book of signs agreed and adopted by the Unification of Signs Commission for the World Federation of the Deaf.* Carlisle, England: BDA.

Cheng, L., & Gao, L. (2002). Passage dependence in standardized reading comprehension: Exploring the College English Test. *Asian Journal of English Language Teaching, 12*, 161–178.

Chomsky, N. (1965). *Aspects of the theory of syntax*. Cambridge, MA: MIT Press.

Clark, H. H., & Gerrig, R. J. (1990). Quotations as demonstrations. *Language, 66*(4), 764–805.

Cokely, D. (1992a). The effects of lag time on interpreter errors. In D. Cokely (Ed.), *Sign language interpreters and interpreting* (pp. 39–70). Burtonsville, MD: Linstok Press.

Cokely, D. (1992b). *Towards a sociolinguistic model of the interpretation process*. Washington, DC: Linstok Press.

Corazza, S. (1993). The history of sign language in the Italian education of the Deaf. In R. Fischer & H. Lane (Eds.), *Looking back: A reader on the history of Deaf communities and their sign languages* (pp. 219–229). Hamburg, Germany: Signum.

Cormier, K., Fenlon, J., Rentelis, R., & Schembri, A. (2011). Lexical frequency in British Sign Language conversation: A corpus-based approach. In P. K. Austin, O. Bond, L. Marten, & D. Nathan (Eds.), *Proceedings of the Conference on Language Documentation and Linguistic Theory 3*, London, UK: School of Oriental and African Studies.

Cormier, K., Schembri, A., & Woll, B. (2013). Diversity across sign languages and spoken languages: Implications for language universals. *Lingua 120* (2010), 2664–2667.

Council of Europe. (2011). *Common European Framework of Reference for Learning, Teaching, Assessment.* Council of Europe. Retrieved from http://www.coe.int/t/dg4/linguistic/Cadre1_en.asp

Crasborn, O., & Sloetjes, H. (2008). Enhanced ELAN functionality for sign language corpora. In: *Proceedings of LREC 2008, Sixth International Conference on Language Resources and Evaluation.*

Crasborn, O., van der Kooij, E., Waters, D., Woll, B., & Mesch, J. (2008). Frequency distribution and spreading of different types of mouth actions in three sign languages. *Sign Language and Linguistics*, *11*, 45–67.

Croker, R. A. (2009). An introduction to qualitative research. In J. Heigham & R. A. Croker (Eds.), *Qualitative research in applied linguistics: A practical introduction* (pp. 135–164). New York, NY: Palgrave Macmillan.

Crystal, D. (2003). *English as a global language* (2nd ed., first ed., 1997). Cambridge, UK: Cambridge University Press.

Davis, K. A. (1995). Qualitative theory and methods in applied linguistics research. *Tesol Quarterly*, *29*(3), 427–453.

Davis, J. (1989). Distinguishing language contact phenomena in ASL interpretation. In C. Lucas (Ed.), *The sociolinguistics of the Deaf community* (pp. 85–102). San Diego, CA: Academic Press.

Davis, J. (2005). Evidence of a historical signed lingua franca among North American Indians. *Deaf Worlds, 21*(3), 47–72.

Davis, J. (2007). North American Indian Signed Language Varieties: A comparative historical linguistic assessment. In D. Quinto-Pozos (Ed.), *Sign languages in contact* (pp. 85–122). Washington, DC: Gallaudet University Press.

DeafPlus. (2012). *International Sign*. Korea: Signbooks.

de Beuzeville, L., Johnston, T., & Schembri, A. (2009). The use of space with indicating verbs in Auslan. *Sign Language and Linguistics, 12*(1), 53–82.

Deuchar, M. (1984). *British sign language*. London: Routledge.

de Wit, M. (2010, December). EUMASLI Module 3.1—*Linguistic coping strategies from International Sign to English*, European Master in Sign Language Interpreting (Research Report) (pp. 1–23).

de Wit, M. (2016). International Sign: An exploration into interpreter preparation. In R. Rosenstock & J. Napier (Eds.), *International sign: Linguistic, usage, and status issues* (pp. 105–135). Washington, DC: Gallaudet University Press.

Dudis, P. (2004). Body partitioning and real-space blends. *Cognitive Linguistics, 15*(2), 223–238.

Dudis, P. (2011). The body in scene depictions. In C. Roy (Ed.), *Discourse in signed languages* (pp. 3–45). Washington, DC: Gallaudet University Press.

Emmorey, K. (1999). Do signers gesture? In L. S. Messing & R. Campbell (Eds.), *Gesture, speech and sign* (pp. 133–160). Oxford, UK: Oxford University Press.

Emmorey, K. (2002). *Language, cognition, and the brain: Insights from sign language research*. Mahwah, NJ: Lawrence Erlbaum.

Emmorey, K., & Corina, D. (1990). Lexical recognition in sign language: Effects of phonetic structure and morphology. *Perceptual and Motor Skills*, 71, 1227–1252.

Emmorey, K., & Herzig, M. (2003). Categorical versus gradient properties of classifier constructions in ASL. In K. Emmorey (Ed.), *Perspectives on classifier constructions in sign languages* (pp. 221–224). Mahwah, NJ: Lawrence Erlbaum.

Enfield, N. J. (2009). *The anatomy of meaning: Speech, gesture and composite utterances*. Cambridge, UK: Cambridge University Press.

Engberg-Pedersen, E. (1993). *Space in Danish Sign Language: The semantics and morphosyntax of the use of space in a visual language*. Hamburg, Germany: Signum Press.

Engberg-Pedersen, E. (2003). From pointing to reference and predication: Pointing signs, eyegaze, and head and body orientation in Danish Sign Language. In S. Kita (Ed.), *Pointing: Where language, culture, and cognition meet* (pp. 269–292). Mahwah, NJ: Lawrence Erlbaum.

Ethnologue. (2012). *Languages of the world: Deaf sign language* (16th ed.). Retrieved from http://www.ethnologue.com/subgroups/deaf-sign-language

EUDICO Linguistic Annotator (ELAN) (Version 4.7.2). Nijmegen, Netherlands: Max Planck Institute for Psycholinguistics, The Language Archive. Retrieved from http://tla.mpi.nl/tools/tla-tools/elan/

European Union of the Deaf (EUD). (n.d.). *International Sign position paper*. Retrieved July 18, 2016 from http://www.eud.eu/about-us/eud-position-paper/international-sign-guidelines/

Evans, V., & Green, M. (2006). *Cognitive linguistics: An introduction*. Edinburgh, Scotland: Edinburgh University Press.

Fauconnier, G. (1985). *Mental spaces: Aspects of meaning construction in natural language*. Cambridge, UK: Cambridge University Press. Reprinted 1994, Cambridge, MA: MIT Press.

Fauconnier, G. (1997). *Mappings in thought and language*. Cambridge, UK: Cambridge University Press.

Fauconnier, G., & Turner, M. (1996). Blending as a central process of grammar. In A. Goldberg (Ed.), *Conceptual structure, discourse, and language* (pp. 113–130). Stanford, CA: CSLI Publications.

Fenlon, J., Denmark, T., Campbell, R., & Woll, B. (2007). Seeing sentence boundaries. *Sign Language and Linguistics, 10*(2), 177–200.

Fenlon, J., Schembri, A., Rentelis, R., Vinson, D., & Cormier, K. (2014). Using conversational data to determine lexical frequency in British Sign Language: The influence of text type. *Lingua, 143*(May), 187–202.

Ferguson, C., & DeBose, C. (1977). Simplified registers, broken language and pidginization. In A. Valdman (Ed.), *Pidgin and creole linguistics* (pp. 99–125). Bloomington, IN: Indiana University Press.

Ferrara, L. (2012). *The grammar of depiction: Exploring gesture and language in Australian Sign Language (Auslan)*. Doctoral dissertation, Macquarie University, Sydney, Australia.

Ferrara, L., & Johnston, T. (2014). Elaborating who's what: A study of constructed action and clause structure in Auslan (Australian Sign Language). *Australian Journal of Linguistics, 34*(2), 193–215. doi:10.1080/07268602.2014.887405

Fillmore, C. J. (1982). Frame semantics. In The Linguistic Society of Korea (Eds.), *Linguistics in the morning calm* (pp. 111–137). Seoul, Korea: Hanshin Publishing.

Fischer, R. (2002). The study of natural sign language in eighteenth-century France. *Sign Language Studies, 2*(4), 391–406.

Fischer, S. (1978). Sign language and creoles. In P. Siple (Ed.), *Understanding sign language through sign language research* (pp. 309–331). New York, NY: Academic Press.

Fischer, S. (1998). Critical periods for language acquisition: Consequences for deaf education. In A. Weisel (Ed.), *Issues unresolved: New perspectives on language and deaf education* (pp. 9–26). Washington, DC: Gallaudet University Press.

Flay, B. R., Biglan, A., Boruch, R., Gonzalez Castro, F., Gottfredson, D., Kellam, S., . . . Ji, P. (2005). Standards of evidence: Criteria for efficacy, effectiveness and dissemination. *Prevention Science*, *6*(3), 151–175.

Fleischer, L. R. (1975). *Language interpretation under four interpreting conditions*. Unpublished doctoral dissertation, Brigham Young University, Provo, UT.

FoxTree, E. (2009). Meemul Tziij: An indigenous sign language complex of Mesoamerica. *Sign Language Studies, 9*(3), 324–366.

Friedman, L. A. (1975). Space, time, and person reference in American Sign Language. In W. Bright (Ed.), *Language: Journal of the Linguistic Society of America* (Vol. 5, pp. 940–961). Baltimore, MD: Waverly Press.

Fu, Y., & Mei, C. (1986). *Longren Shouyu Gailun* [Sign Language of the Deaf]. Shanghai, China: Xuelin.

Geertz, C. (1973). *The interpretation of cultures*. New York, NY: Basic Books.

Geertzen, J. (2012). Inter-rater agreement with multiple raters and variables. Retrieved from https://nlp-ml.io/jg/software/ira/

Gile, D. (2009). *Basic concepts and models for interpreter and translator training*. Amsterdam/Philadelphia: John Benjamins.

Giles, H. (1973). Accent mobility: A model and some data. *Anthropological Linguistics, 15*, 87–105.

Gish, S. (1987). "I understood all the words, but I missed the point": A goal to detail/detail to goal strategy for text analysis. In M. McIntyre (Ed.), *Proceedings from the Sixth National Convention of Interpreter Trainers.*

New Dimensions in Interpreter education: Curriculum and Instruction (pp. 125–137). Chevy Chase, MD: RID Publications.
Goldin-Meadow, S. (2003). *Hearing gesture: How our hands help us think.* Cambridge, MA: Harvard University Press.
Golos, D. (2010). Literacy behaviors of deaf preschoolers during video viewing. *Sign Language Studies, 11*(1), 76–99. doi:10.1353/sls.2010.0001
Grady, J. (1997). *Foundations of meaning: Primary metaphors and primary scenes.* Unpublished doctoral dissertation, University of California, Berkeley.
Graesser, A. C., Ozuru, Y., & Sullins, J. (2010). What is a good question? In M. McKeown & L. Kucan (Eds.), *Bringing reading research to life* (pp. 112–141). New York, NY: Guilford Press.
Granger, S. (2002). A bird's eye view of learner corpus research. In S. Granger, J. Hung, & S. Petch-Tyson (Eds.), *Computer learner corpora, second language acquisition, and foreign language* (pp. 3–36). Philadelphia, PA: John Benjamins.
Green, E. M. (2014). Building the tower of Babel: International Sign, linguistic commensuration, and moral orientation. *Language in Society, 43*(4), 445–465.
Gries, S. Th. (2009). What is corpus linguistics? *Language and Linguistics Compass, 3*(5), 1225–1241.
Grosjean, F. (1989). Neurolinguists, beware! The bilingual is not two monolinguals in one person. *Brain and Language, 36,* 3–15.
Guerra Currie, A. P., Meier, R. P., & Walters, K. (2002). A crosslinguistic examination of the lexicons of four signed languages. In R. P. Meier, K. Cormier, & D. Quinto-Pozos (Eds.), *Modality and structure in signed and spoken languages* (pp. 224–236). Cambridge, UK: Cambridge University Press.
Haiman, J. (1983). Iconic and economic motivation. *Language, 59*(4), 781–819.
Hall, E. T. (1989). Deaf culture, tacit culture and ethnic relations. *Sign Language Studies, 65,* 291–304.
Hallgren, K. A. (2012). Computing inter-rater reliability for observational data: An overview and tutorial. *Tutorials in Quantitative Methods for Psychology, 8*(1), 23–34.
Halliday, M. A. K. (1975). *Learning how to mean: Explorations in the development of language.* London: Edward Arnold.
Harkness, J. A., Pennell, B-E., & Schoua-Glusberg, A. (2004). *Methods for translating survey questionnaires.* Paper presented to American Association for Public Opinion Research, Montreal, Canada, May 2006.
Haug, T. (2005). Review of sign language assessment instruments. *Sign Language and Linguistics, 8*(1–2), 59–96.
Haug, T. (2011). Approaching sign language test construction: Adaptation of the German Sign Language receptive skills test. *Journal of Deaf Studies and Deaf Education, 16*(3), 343–361.

Heine, B., & Kuteva, T. (2005). *Language contact and grammatical change.* New York, NY: Cambridge University Press.

Hiddinga, A., & Crasborn, O. (2011). Sign languages and globalization. *Language in Society*, *40(*4), 483–505.

Hodge, G. (2013). *Patterns from a signed language corpus: Clause-like units in Auslan (Australian sign language)*. Unpublished dissertation, Macquarie University, Sydney, Australia.

Hodge, G., & Johnston, T. (2014). Points, depictions, gestures and enactment: Partly lexical and non-lexical signs as core elements of single clause-like units in Auslan (Australian sign language). *Australian Journal of Linguistics*, *34*(2), 262–291.

Hohenberger, A. (2007). The possible range of variation between sign languages: Universal grammar, modality, and typological aspects. In P. M. Perniss, R. Pfau, & M. Steinbach (Eds.), *Visible variation: Comparative studies on sign language structure* (pp. 341–383). Berlin, Germany: Mouton de Gruyter.

Hoyer, K. (2007). Albanian Sign Language: Language contact, international sign, and gesture. In D. Quinto-Pozos (Ed.), *Sign languages in contact* (pp. 195–234). Washington, DC: Gallaudet University Press.

Hoza, J. (2011). The discourse and politeness functions of HEY and WELL in American Sign Language. In C. B. Roy (ed.), *Discourse in sign languages* (pp. 69–95). Washington, DC: Gallaudet University Press.

Hu, G. (2009). *Cognitive mechanisms underlying second language listening comprehension*. Dissertation. Atlanta, GA: Georgia State University.

Hymes, D. (1974). *Foundations in sociolinguistics: An ethnographic approach.* Philadelphia, PA: University of Pennsylvania Press.

Ivankova, N. V., & Creswell, J. W. (2009). Mixed methods. In J. Heigham & R. A. Croker (Eds.), *Qualitative research in applied linguistics: A practical introduction* (pp. 135–164). New York, NY: Palgrave Macmillan.

Jacobs, L. R. (1977). The efficiency of interpreting input for processing lecture information by deaf college students. *Journal of Rehabilitation of the Deaf, 11*, 10–14.

Jakobson, R. (1964). Efforts towards a means-ends model of language in interwar continental linguistics. In J. Vachek (Ed.), *A Prague school reader in linguistics*. Bloomington, IN: Indiana University Press.

Jansma, S., Knoors, H., & Baker, A. E. (1997). Sign language assessment: A Dutch project. Deafness and education. *Journal of the British Association of the Teachers of the Deaf, 21*(3), 39–46.

Janzen, T. (2004). Space rotation, perspective shift, and verb morphology in ASL. *Cognitive Linguistics, 15*(2), 271–306.

Janzen, T. (2014). *From pragmatics through intersubjectivity: Do interpreters need a theory of language?* Keynote presentation, Gallaudet University Research Symposium, March, Washington, DC.

Janzen, T., & Shaffer, B. (2002), Gesture as the substrate in the process of ASL grammaticization. In R. Meier, K. Cormier, & D. Quinto-Pozos (Eds.), *Modality and structure in signed and spoken languages* (pp. 199–223). Cambridge, UK: Cambridge University Press.

Johnson, R., & Liddell, S. K. (1986). ASL compound formation processes, lexicalization, and phonological remnants. *Natural Language and Linguistic Theory, 4*, 445–513.

Johnson-Laird, P. N. (1981). Comprehension as the construction of mental models. *Philosophical Transactions of the Royal Society of London. Series B, Biological Sciences, 295*, 353–374.

Johnston, T. (1989). *Auslan: The sign language of the Australian deaf community.* Unpublished doctoral dissertation, University of Sydney, Australia.

Johnston, T. (1991). Spatial syntax and spatial semantics in the inflection of signs for the marking of person and location in Auslan. *International Journal of Sign Linguistics, 2*(1), 29–62.

Johnston, T. (2003a). BSL, Auslan and NZSL: Three signed languages or one? In A. Baker, B. van den Bogaerde, & O. Crasborn (Eds.), *Cross linguistic perspectives in sign language research, selected papers from TISLR 2000* (pp. 47–69). Hamburg, Germany: Signum Verlag.

Johnston, T. (2003b). Language standardization and signed language dictionaries. *Sign Language Studies, 3*(4), 431–468.

Johnston, T. (2004). The assessment and achievement of proficiency in a native sign language within a sign bilingual program: The pilot Auslan receptive skills test. *Deafness and Education International, 6*, 57–81.

Johnston, T. (2008). The Auslan archive and corpus. In D. Nathan (Ed.), *The endangered languages archive.* London: Hans Rausing Endangered Languages Documentation Project School of Oriental and African Studies University of London. Available at: http://elar.soas.ac.uk/languages

Johnston, T. (2010). From archive to corpus: Transcription and annotation in the creation of signed language corpora. *International Journal of Corpus Linguistics, 15*(1), 104–129. doi:110.1075/ijcl.1015.1071.1005joh

Johnston, T. (2012). Lexical frequency in sign languages. *Journal of Deaf Studies and Deaf Education, 17*(2), 163–193. doi:10.1093/deafed/enr036

Johnston, T. (2013a). Towards a comparative semiotics of pointing actions in signed and spoken languages. *Gesture, 13*(2), 109–142.

Johnston, T. (2013b). Formational and functional characteristics of pointing signs in a corpus of Auslan (Australian sign language): Are the data sufficient to posit a grammatical class of "pronouns" in Auslan? *Corpus Linguistics and Linguistic Theory, 9*(1), 109–159.

Johnston, T. (2014, June 10). *Auslan Corpus annotation guidelines.* Retrieved from http://media.auslan.org.au/attachments/Johnston_AuslanCorpusAnnotationGuidelines_14June2014.pdf

Johnston, T., & Ferrara, L. (2012). Lexicalization in signed languages: When is an idiom not an idiom? *Proceedings of the Third UK Cognitive Linguistics Conference, University of Hertfordshire, July 6–8, 2010* (Vol. 1, pp. 229–248). Retrieved from http://www.uk-cla.org.uk/proceedings

Johnston, T., & Schembri, A. (1999). On defining lexeme in a sign language. *Sign Language and Linguistics*, *2*(2), 115–185.

Johnston, T., & Schembri, A. (2007). *Australian Sign Language (Auslan): An introduction to sign language linguistics*. Cambridge, UK: Cambridge University Press.

Johnston, T., & Schembri, A. (2010). Variation, lexicalization and grammaticalization in signed languages. *Langage et societé, 131*(March), 19–35.

Jordan, I. K., & Battison, R. (1976). A referential communication experiment with foreign signers. *Sign Language Studies, 10*, 69–81.

Kellett Bidoli, C. J., & Ochse, E. (2008). *English in international Deaf communication*. Bern, Switzerland: Peter Lang.

Kendon, A. (1980). A description of a deaf-mute sign language from the Enga Province of Papua New Guinea with some comparative discussion—Part I: The formational properties of Enga signs. *Semiotica, 31*(1–2), 1–34.

Kendon, A. (2004). *Gesture: Visible action as utterance*. Cambridge, UK: Cambridge University Press.

Kintsch, W., & Keenan, J. (1973). Reading rate and retention as a function of the number of propositions in the base structure of sentences. *Cognitive Psychology, 5*, 257–274.

Kintsch, W., & van Dijk, T. A. (1978). Toward a model of text comprehension and production. *Psychological Review, 85*, 363–394.

Klima, E. S., & Bellugi, U. (1979). *The signs of language*. Cambridge, MA: Harvard University Press.

Kraska-Miller, M. (2014). *Nonparametric statistics for social and behavioral sciences*. Boca Raton, FL: CRC Press, Taylor and Francis Group.

Krippendorff, K. (2004). *Content analysis: An introduction to its methodology* (2nd ed.). Thousand Oaks, CA: Sage.

Kyle, J. G., & Woll, B. (1988). *Sign language: The study of Deaf people and their language*. Cambridge, UK: Cambridge University Press.

Ladd, P. (2003). *Understanding Deaf culture: In search of Deafhood*. Clevedon, UK: Multilingual Matters.

Lakoff, G. (1987). *Women, fire, and dangerous things: What categories reveal about the mind*. Chicago, IL: University of Chicago Press.

Lakoff, G., & Johnson, M. (1980). *Metaphors we live by*. Chicago, IL: University of Chicago Press.

Lakoff, G., & Johnson, M. (1999). *Philosophy of the flesh: The embodied mind and its challenge to Western thought*. New York, NY: Basic Books.

Landis, J. R., & Koch, G. G. (1977). The measurement of observer agreement for categorical data. *Biometrics, 33*, 159–174.

Lane, H. (1985). *When the mind hears: A history of the Deaf*. New York, NY: Random House.

Lang, C. (2012). *Phonological variation in International Sign*. Unpublished paper, Gallaudet University, Washington, DC.

Langacker, R. W. (1987). *Foundations of cognitive grammar. Volume 1: Theoretical prerequisites*. Stanford, CA: Stanford University Press.

Langacker, R. W. (1990). Subjectification. *Cognitive Linguistics, 1*(1), 5–38.

Langacker, R. W. (1991). *Foundations of cognitive grammar. Volume 2: Descriptive application*. Stanford, CA: Stanford University Press.

Langacker, R. W. (2001). Discourse in cognitive grammar. *Cognitive Linguistics, 12*(2), 143–188.

Langacker, R. W. (2005). Construction grammars: Cognitive, radical, and less so. In F. J. R. d. M. Ibanez & M. S. P. Cervel (Eds.), *Cognitive linguistics: Internal dynamics and interdisciplinary interaction* (pp. 101–158). Berlin, Germany: Mouton de Gruyter.

Lawrence, S. (1994). Interpreter discourse: English to ASL expansion. In E. A. Winston (Ed.), *Mapping our course: A collaborative venture. Proceedings of the Tenth National Convention of the Conference of Interpreter Trainers* (pp. 205–216). Washington, DC: Conference of Interpreter Trainers (CIT).

Liddell, S. K. (1995). Real, surrogate, and token space: Grammatical consequences in ASL. In K. Emmorey & J. Reilly (Eds.), *Language, gesture, and space* (pp. 19–41). Hillsdale, NJ: Lawrence Erlbaum.

Liddell, S. K. (2000). Indicating verbs and pronouns: Pointing away from agreement. In K. Emmorey & H. Lane (Eds.), *The signs of language revisited: An anthology to honor Ursula Bellugi and Edward Klima* (pp. 303–320). Mahwah, NJ: Lawrence Erlbaum.

Liddell, S. K. (2003). *Grammar, gesture, and meaning in American Sign Language*. Cambridge, UK: Cambridge University Press.

Liddell, S. K., & Metzger, M. (1998). Gesture in sign language discourse. *Journal of Pragmatics, 30*, 657–697.

Livingston, S., Singer, B., & Abramson, T. (1994). A study to determine the effectiveness of two different kinds of interpreting. In *Proceedings of the Tenth National Convention of the Conference of Interpreter Trainers—Mapping our course: A collaborative venture* (pp. 175–197). Sacramento, CA: Conference of Interpreter Trainers (CIT).

Long, D. R. (1990). What you don't know can't help you: An exploratory study of background knowledge and second language listening comprehension. *Studies in Second Language Acquisition, 12*(1), 65–80.

Lucas, C. (1994). Language contact phenomena in Deaf communities. In I. Ahlgren, M. Bergman, & M. Brennan (Eds.), *Perspectives on sign language structure* (pp. 261–268). Durham, UK: ISLA.

Lucas, C., & Valli, C. (1989). Language contact in the American deaf community. In C. Lucas (Ed.), *The sociolinguistics of the Deaf community* (pp. 11–40). San Diego, CA: Academic Press.

Lucas, C., & Valli, C. (1990). ASL, English and contact signing. In C. Lucas (Ed.), *Sign language research theoretical issues* (pp. 288–307). Washington, DC: Gallaudet University Press.

Lucas, C., & Valli, C. (1992). *Language contact in the American Deaf community.* San Diego, CA: Academic Press.

Lule, D., & Wallin, L. (2010). Transmission of sign languages in Africa. In D. Brentari (Ed.), *Sign languages* (pp. 113–130). New York, NY: Cambridge University Press.

Magliano, J. P., Millis, K., Ozuru, Y., & McNamara, D. S. (2007). A multidimensional framework to evaluate reading assessment tools. In D. McNamara (Ed.), *Reading comprehension strategies: Theories, interventions, and technologies* (pp. 107–136). Mahwah, NJ: Lawrence Erlbaum.

Maller, S. J., Singleton, J. L., Supalla, S. J., & Wix, T. (1999). The development and psychometric properties of the American Sign Language Proficiency Assessment (ASL-PA). *Journal of Deaf Studies and Deaf Education, 4*, 249–269.

Marsaja, I. G. (2008). *Desa Kolok—A deaf village and its sign language in Bali, Indonesia.* Nijmegen, the Netherlands: Ishara Press.

Marschark, M., Pelz, J. B., Convertino, C., Sapere, P., Arndt, M. E., & Seewagen, R. (2005). Classroom interpreting and visual information processing in mainstream education for deaf students: Live or Memorex©? *American Educational Research Journal, 42*, 727–761.

Marschark, M., Sapere, P., Convertino, C., & Seewagen, R. (2005a). Access to postsecondary education through sign language interpreting. *Journal of Deaf Studies and Deaf Education, 10*(1), 38–50.

Marschark, M., Sapere, P., Convertino, C., & Seewagen, R. (2005b). Educational interpreting: Access and outcomes. In M. Marschark, R. Peterson, & E. Winston (Eds.), *Sign language interpreting and interpreter education* (pp. 57–83). New York, NY: Oxford University Press.

Marschark, M., Sapere, P., Convertino, C., Seewagen, R., & Maltzen, H. (2004). Comprehension of sign language interpreting: Deciphering a complex task situation. *Sign Language Studies, 4*(4), 345–368.

Mayberry, R. I. (1993). First language acquisition after childhood differs from second language acquisition: The case of American Sign Language. *Journal of Speech and Hearing Research, 36*, 1258–1270.

Mayer, M. (1969). *Frog, where are you?* New York: Dial Press.

McBurney, S. L. (2002). Pronominal reference in signed and spoken language: Are grammatical categories modality-dependent? In R. Meier, K. Cormier, & D. Quinto-Pozos (Eds.), *Modality and structure in signed and spoken languages* (pp. 329–369). Cambridge, UK: Cambridge University Press.

McKee, D., & Kennedy, G. (2000). Lexical comparison of signs from American, Australian, British and New Zealand sign languages. In K. Emmorey & H. Lane (Eds.), *The signs of language revisited: An anthology to honor Ursula Bellugi and Edward Klima* (pp. 49–76). Mahwah, NJ: Lawrence Erlbaum.

McKee, R., & Napier, J. (2002). Interpreting into International Sign pidgin: An analysis. *Sign Language and Linguistics, 5*(1), 27–54.

McNeill, D. (1992). *Hand and mind: What gestures reveal about thought.* Chicago, IL: University of Chicago Press.

McNeill, D. (2005). *Gesture and thought.* Chicago, IL: University of Chicago Press.

Mehrpour, S., & Rahimi, M. (2010). The impact of general and specific vocabulary knowledge on reading and listening comprehension: A case of Iranian EFL learners. *System, 38*(2), 292–300.

Meier, R. (1990). Person deixis in American Sign Language. In S. D. Fischer & P. Siple (Eds.), *Theoretical issues in sign language research. Vol. 1: Linguistics* (pp. 175–190). Chicago, IL: University of Chicago.

Meier, R. (2002). Why different, why the same? Explaining effects and non-effects of modality upon linguistic structure in sign and speech. In R. P. Meier, K. Cormier, & D. Quinto-Pozos (Eds.), *Modality and structure in signed and spoken languages* (pp. 1–26). Cambridge, UK: Cambridge University Press.

Mesch, J. (2010). *Perspectives on the concept and definition of international sign.* Retrieved from http://wfdeaf.org

Metzger, M. (1995). Constructed dialogue and constructed action in American Sign Language. In C. Lucas (Ed.), *Sociolinguistics in Deaf communities* (pp. 255–271). Washington, DC: Gallaudet University Press.

Metzger, M. (2005). Interpreted discourse: Learning and recognizing what interpreters do in interaction. In C. Roy (Ed.), *Advances in teaching sign language interpreters* (pp. 100–122). Washington, DC: Gallaudet University Press.

Metzger, M., & Bahan, B. (2001). Discourse analysis. In C. Lucas (Ed.), *The sociolinguistics of sign languages* (pp. 112–144). Cambridge, UK: Cambridge University Press.

Moody, B. (1979). La communication international chez les sourds. *Rééducation orthophonique, 17*(107), 213–224.

Moody, B. (1987). Sign language: International gestures. In J. V. van Cleve (Ed.), *Gallaudet encyclopedia on deaf people and deafness* (Vol. 3, pp. 81–82). New York, NY: McGraw-Hill.

Moody, B. (1994). *International Sign: Language, pidgin or charades?* Paper presented at the "Issues in Interpreting 2" conference, April, University of Durham, Durham, UK.

Moody, B. (2002). International Sign: A practitioner's perspective. In D. Watson (Ed.), *Journal of interpretation* (pp. 1–47). Alexandria, VA: Registry of Interpreters for the Deaf.

Moody, B. (2007). *The role of international sign interpreting in today's world.* Paper presented at the World Association of Sign Language Interpreters (WASLI) conference, July. Segovia, Spain.

Morford, J. P., & MacFarlane, J. (2003). Frequency characteristics of American Sign Language. *Sign Language Studies, 3*(2), 213–223.

Morford, J. P., & Mayberry, R. I. (2000). The "early" of early exposure: Timing and language acquisition. In C. Chamberlain, J. P. Morford, & R. I. Mayberry (Eds.), *Language acquisition by eye* (pp. 112–127). Mahwah, NJ: Lawrence Erlbaum.

Mori, S. (2011). *IS Interpreter in Asia and Pacific region: From experience as IS Interpreter for JICA-JFD Deaf leadership training programme.* Paper presented at the World Association of Sign Language Interpreters (WASLI) Conference, Durban, South Africa. Retrieved from http://efsli.blogspot.de/2011/07/is-interpreter-in-asia-and-pacific.html

Mufwene, S. (2007). What do Creoles and Pidgins tell us about the evolution of language? In B. Kaks, S. Cleuziou, J. Demoule, & P. Encrevé (Eds.), *The origin and evolution of languages: Approaches, models, paradigms* (pp. 272–297). London, UK: Equinox.

Mufwene, S. (2008). *Language evolution: Contact, competition and change.* London, UK: Continuum International.

Murphy, H. J., & Fleischer, L. R. (1977). The effects of Ameslan versus Siglish upon test scores. *Journal of Rehabilitation of the Deaf, 11*, 15–18.

Napier, J. (2002). *Sign language interpreting: Linguistic coping strategies.* Coleford, UK: Douglas McLean.

Napier, J., & Barker, R. (2004). Sign language interpreting: The relationship between metalinguistic awareness and the production of interpreting omissions. *Sign Language Studies, 4*(4), 369–399.

Napier, J., McKee, R., & Goswell, D. (2006). *Sign language interpreting: Theory and practice in Australia and New Zealand.* Sydney, Australia: Federation Press.

Nardi, M. (2008). To boldly go . . . Abroad? In C. J. Kellett Bidoli & E. Ochse (Eds.), *English in international Deaf communication,* Linguistic Insights (Vol. 72, pp. 279–303). Bern, Switzerland: Peter Lang Verlagsgruppe.

Neidle, C., & Vogler, C. (2012). A new web interface to facilitate access to corpora: Development of the ASLLRP data access interface, *Proceedings of the Fifth Workshop on the Representation and Processing of Sign Languages: Interactions between Corpus and Lexicon, LREC 2012,* Istanbul, Turkey.

Newport, E. (1999). Reduced input in the acquisition of signed languages: Contributions to the study of creolization. In M. DeGraff (Ed.), *Language creation and language change: Creolization, diacrony, and development* (pp. 161–178). Cambridge, MA: MIT Press.

Newport, E. L., & Supalla, T. (2000). Sign language research at the millennium. In K. Emmorey & H. Lane (Eds.), *The signs of language revisited: An anthology to honor Ursula Bellugi and Edward Klima* (pp. 103–114). Mahwah, NJ: Lawrence Erlbaum.

Nonaka, A., Mesch, K., & Sagara, K. (2015). Signed names in Japanese Sign Language: Linguistic and cultural analyses. *Sign Language Studies. 16*(1), 57–85.

Okrent, A. (2002). A modality-free notion of gesture and how it can help us with the morpheme vs. gesture questions in sign language linguistics (or at least give us some criteria to work with). In R. Meier, K. Cormier, & D. Quinto-Pozos (Eds.), *Modality and structure in signed and spoken languages* (pp. 175–198). New York, NY: Cambridge University Press.

Orfanidou, E., Adam, R., Morgan, G., & McQueen, J. M. (2010). Segmentation in signed and spoken language: Different modality, same segmentation procedure. *Journal of Memory and Language, 62*, 272–283. doi:10.1016/j.jml.2009.12.001

Oyserman, J. (2016). Complexity of International Sign for inexperienced interpreters: Insights from a Deaf IS instructor. In R. Rosenstock & J. Napier (Eds.), *International sign: Linguistic, usage, and status issues.* Washington, DC: Gallaudet University Press.

Ozuru, Y., Briner, S., Kurby, C. A., & McNamara, D. S. (2013). Comparing comprehension measured by multiple-choice and open-ended questions. *Canadian Journal of Experimental Psychology, 67*(3), 215–227.

Padden, C. (1986). Verbs and role-shifting in American Sign Language. In C. Padden (Ed.), *Proceedings of the Fourth National Symposium on Sign Language Research and Teaching*, Las Vegas, Nevada (pp. 44–57). Silver Spring, MD: National Association of the Deaf.

Peirce, C. S. (1955). *Philosophical writings of Peirce.* Justus Buchler (Ed.), [1940] Routledge and Kegan Paul. Reprinted 2001. New York: Dover.

Pizzuto, E., Boyes-Braem, P., & Volterra, V. (1996). Seeing through signs' iconicity: A crosslinguistic-crosscultural study of Signers and Speakers. Paper presented to *The Fifth International Conference on Theoretical Issues in Sign Language Research*, September 19–22, Montreal, Quebec, Canada.

Pollard, R. Q. (2002). Ethical conduct in research involving deaf people. In V. A. Gutman (Ed.), *Ethics in mental health and deafness* (pp. 162–178). Washington, DC: Gallaudet University Press.

Pollard, R. Q., DeMatteo, A., Lentz, E., & Rediess, S. (2007). A prose recall test using stories in American Sign Language. *Rehabilitation Psychology, 52*(1), 11–24.

Pollard, R. Q., Rediess, S., & DeMatteo, A. (2005). Development and validation of the Signed Paired Associates Test. *Rehabilitation Psychology, 50*, 258–265.

Prillwitz, S., & Zienert, H. (1990). Hamburg Notation System for sign language: Development of a sign writing with computer application. In S. Prillwitz & T. Vollhaber (Eds.), *Current Trends in European Sign Language Research: Proceedings of the Third European Congress on Sign Language Research Hamburg July 26–29, 1989* (pp. 355–379). Hamburg, Germany: Signum Verlag.

Quer, J., Mazzoni, L., & Sapountzaki, G. (2010). Transmission of sign languages in Mediterranean Europe. In D. Brentari (Ed.), *Sign languages* (pp. 113–130). New York, NY: Cambridge University Press.

Quinto-Pozos, D. (2002). *Contact between Mexican Sign Language and American Sign Language in two Texas border areas*. Dissertation, University of Texas at Austin.

Quinto-Pozos, D. (Ed.). (2007). *Sign languages in contact*. Washington, DC: Gallaudet University Press.

Quinto-Pozos, D. (2008). Sign language contact and interference: ASL and LSM. *Language in Society, 37*, 161–189. doi:10.10170S0047404508080251

Ramsay, C. M., & Sperling, R. A. (2010). Designating reader perspective to increase comprehension and interest. *Contemporary Educational Psychology, 35*, 215–227.

Rathmann, C., & Mathur, G. (2000). *The Amsterdam Manifesto* (retrieved directly from the authors). Document also available at http://www.deafacademics.org /conferences/amsterdam_manifesto.pdf

Rickheit, G., Schnotz, W. L., & Strohner, H. (1985). The concept of inference in discourse comprehension. In G. W. Rickheit & H. Strohner (Eds.), *Inferences in text processing* (pp. 3–49). Amsterdam, the Netherlands: Elsevier.

Rodriguez Ortiz, I. R. (2007). Sign language comprehension: The case of Spanish Sign Language. *Journal of Deaf Studies and Deaf Education, 13*(3), 378–390.

Rodriguez Ortiz, I. R., & Mora Roche, J. (2008). The efficiency of information transmission for sign and spoken language. *American Annals of the Deaf, 152*(5), 480–494.

Rosenstock, R. (2004). *An investigation of International Sign: Analyzing structure and comprehension*. Doctoral dissertation, Gallaudet University, Washington, DC.

Rosenstock, R. (2008). International sign: Surprising sources of the lexicon. In R. M. de Quadros (Ed.), *Spinning and unraveling the past, present and future, TISLR 9, forty-five papers and three posters from the Ninth Theoretical Issues in Sign Language Research Conference Sign Languages,* Florianopolis, Brazil, December 2006, Arara Azul, Petropolis/RJ, Brazil.

Rosenstock, R. (2016). Comprehension of expository international sign. In R. Rosenstock & J. Napier (Eds.), *International sign: Linguistic, usage, and status issues*. Washington, DC: Gallaudet University Press.

Rosenstock, R., & Napier, J. (2016). *International sign: Linguistic, usage, and status issues*. Washington, DC: Gallaudet University Press.

Rost, M. (1994). On-line summaries as representations of lecture understanding. In J. Flowerdew (Ed.), *Academic listening: Research perspectives* (pp. 92–128). Cambridge, UK: Cambridge University Press.

Roy, C. (1989). Features of discourse in an American Sign Language lecture. In C. Lucas (Ed.), *The sociolinguistics of the Deaf community* (pp. 231–251). San Diego, CA: Academic Press.

Roy, C. (2000). *Interpreting as a discourse process*. New York, NY: Oxford University Press.

Roy, C. (Ed.). (2011). *Discourse in signed languages*. Washington, DC: Gallaudet University Press.

Saldanha, G., & O'Brien, S. (2013). *Research methodologies in translation studies*. Manchester, UK: St. Jerome Publishing.

Sandler, W., & Lillo-Martin, D. (2006). *Sign language and linguistic universals*. Cambridge, UK: Cambridge University Press.

Sasaki, D. (2007). The lexicons of Japanese Sign Language and Taiwan Sign Language: A preliminary comparative study of handshape differences. In D. Quinto-Pozos (Ed.), *Sign languages in contact* (pp. 123–150). Washington, DC: Gallaudet University Press.

Sasaki, Y. (1991). English and Japanese interlanguage comprehension strategies: An analysis based on the competition model. *Applied Psycholinguistics, 12*, 47–73.

Schembri, A. (2001). *Issues in the analysis of polycomponential verbs in Australian Sign Language (Auslan)*. Unpublished doctoral dissertation, University of Sydney, Australia.

Schembri, A. (2003). Rethinking "classifiers" in signed languages. In K. Emmorey (Ed.), *Perspectives on classifier constructions in signed languages* (pp. 3–34). Mahwah, NJ: Erlbaum.

Schembri, A., Cormier, K., Fenlon, J., & Johnston, T. A. (2013, June). *Sign languages and sociolinguistic typology*. Paper presented at ICLaVE, Trondheim, Norway.

Schembri, A., Fenlon, J., Rentelis, R., & Cormier, K. (2011). *British Sign Language Corpus Project: A corpus of digital video data of British Sign Language 2008–2011* (First Edition). London: University College London. URL: http:www.bslcorpusproject.org

Schembri, A., Jones, C., & Burnham, D. (2005). Comparing action gestures and classifier verbs of motion: Evidence from Australian Sign Language, Taiwan Sign Language, and nonsigners' gestures without speech. *Journal of Deaf Studies and Deaf Education, 10*(3), 272–290.

Schembri, A., Wigglesworth, G., Johnston, T., Leigh, G., Adam, R., & Baker, R. (2002). Issues in development of the test battery for Australian Sign Language morphology and syntax. *Journal of Deaf Studies and Deaf Education, 7*, 18–40.

Schick, B. S. (1990). Classifier predicates in American Sign Language. *International Journal of Sign Linguistics, 1*(1), 15–40.

Schiefele, U. (1996). Topic interest, text representation, and quality of experience. *Contemporary Educational Psychology, 21*, 3–18.

Schiffrin, D. (1994). *Approaches to discourse.* Cambridge, MA: Blackwell.

Scott-Gibson, L., & Ojala, R. (1994). *International sign interpreting.* Paper presented to the Fourth East and South African Sign Language Seminar, Uganda, Africa.

Seleskovich, D. (1978). *Interpreting for international conferences.* Washington, DC: Pen and Booth.

Slobin, D. (2005). Issues of linguistic typology in the study of sign language development of Deaf children. In B. Schick, M. Marschark, & P. E. Spencer (Eds.), *Advances in the sign language development of deaf children* (pp. 20–45). Oxford, UK: Oxford University Press.

Smith, W. H., & Tang, L. (1979). *Shou neng sheng chyau* [Your hands can become a bridge]. Taipei, Taiwan: Deaf Sign Language Research Association of the Republic of China.

Smith, W. (1987). Taiwan Sign Language. In J. V. Van Cleve (Ed.), *Gallaudet encyclopedia of deafness and deaf people* (Vol. 3, pp. 113–116). New York, NY: McGraw-Hill.

Stamp, R., Schembri, A., Fenlon, J., Rentelis, R., Woll, B., & Cormier, K. (2014). Lexical variation and change in British Sign Language. *PLoS ONE*, *9*(4), e94053. doi:10.1371/journal.pone.0094053

State of Victoria Electoral Commission (Producer). (2012). *Auslan guide to voting in Victorian elections* [Video]. Retrieved from http://www.vec.vic.gov.au/Voting/AssistanceForVoters.html

Stokoe, W. C. (1960). Sign language structure: An outline of the visual communication systems of the American Deaf. *Studies in linguistics: Occasional papers 8*. Buffalo, NY: University of Buffalo. Reprinted in (2005) *Journal of Deaf Studies and Deaf Education 10*(1), 3–37.

Stone, C. (2011). Register, discourse, and genre in British Sign Language (BSL). In C. B. Roy (Ed.), *Discourse in signed languages* (pp. 121–154). Washington, DC: Gallaudet University Press.

Supalla, T. (1978). Morphology of verbs of motion and location in American Sign Language. In F. Caccamise & D. Hicks (Eds.), *American Sign Language in a bilingual, bicultural context: Proceedings of the Second National Symposium on Sign Language Research and Teaching* (pp. 27–46). Coronado, CA: National Association of the Deaf.

Supalla, T. (1982). *Structure and acquisition of verbs of motion and location in SL*. Unpublished doctoral dissertation, University of California, San Diego.

Supalla, T. (1986). The classifier system in American Sign Language. In C. Craig (Ed.), *Noun classification and categorization* (pp. 181–214). Philadelphia, PA: Benjamins.

Supalla, T. (1990). Serial verbs of motion in ASL. In S. Fischer & P. Siple (Eds.), *Theoretical issues in sign language research* (pp. 127–152). Chicago, IL: University of Chicago.

Supalla, T. (2008a). Prologue. In *A handbook on international sign*. Spanish National Association of the Deaf (CNSE) and FAXPG.

Supalla, T. (2008b). Sign language archeology: Integrating historical linguistics with fieldwork on young sign languages. In R. M. de Quadros (Ed.), *Sign languages: Spinning and unraveling the past, present and future. TISLR9, forty-five papers and three posters from the Ninth Theoretical Issues in Sign Language Research Conference*, Florianopolis, Brazil, December 2006 (pp. 575–583). Petrópolis, RJ, Brazil: Editora Arara Azul.

Supalla, T., & Webb, R. (1995). The grammar of international sign: A new look at pidgin languages. In K. Emmorey & J. S. Reilly (Eds.), *Language, gesture, and space* (pp. 333–352). Hillsdale, NJ: Lawrence Erlbaum.

Sutton-Spence, R., & Woll, B. (1999). *The linguistics of British Sign Language: An introduction*. New York, NY: Cambridge University Press.

Talmy, L. (2000). *Toward a cognitive semantics* (Vol. 1). Cambridge, MA: MIT Press.

Tannen, D. (1986). *That's not what I meant! How conversational style makes or breaks your relations with others*. London, UK: J. M. Dent & Sons.

Tarone, E. (1980). Communication strategies, foreigner talk, and repair in interlanguage. *Language Learning, 30*(2), 417–431.

Taub, S. F. (2001). *Language from the body: Iconicity and metaphor in American Sign Language*. Cambridge, UK: Cambridge University Press.

Thomason, S. G. (2001). *Language contact*. Washington, DC: Georgetown University Press.

Thomason, S. G., & Kaufman, T. (1988). *Language contact, creolization, and genetic linguistics*. Berkeley, CA: University of California Press.

UEA-Universala Esperanto Asocio (Universal Esperanto Association). *An update on Esperanto*. transl. by D. Ryan. Retrieved from http://uea.org/info/angle/an_ghisdatigo.html

UNESCO: *Culture*. (2003, April). A message from the World Esperanto Association. Retrieved from http://portal.unesco.org/culture/en/ev.php-URL_ID=8523&URL_DO=DO_PRINTPAGE&URL_SECTION=201.html

van den Broek, P., & Kremer, K. (2000). The mind in action: What it means to comprehend during reading. In B. Taylor, M. Graves, & P. van den Broek (Eds.), *Reading for meaning: Fostering comprehension in the middle grades* (pp. 1–31). New York, NY: Teachers College, Columbia University.

van Dijk, T. A. (1985). Semantic discourse analysis. In T. A. van Dijk (Ed.), *Handbook of discourse analysis* (Vol. 2, pp. 103–136). London, UK: Academic Press.

van Dijk, T. A. (2008). *Discourse and context: A sociocognitive approach.* Cambridge, UK: Cambridge University Press.

van Dijk, T. A. (2011). Discourse studies and hermeneutics. *Discourse Studies, 13*(5), 609–621.

van Dijk, T. A., & Kintsch, W. (1983). *Strategies of discourse comprehension.* New York, NY: Academic Press.

Waas, M. (1996). *Language attrition down under: German speakers in Australia.* New York, NY: Lang.

Wang, J., & Napier, J. (2013). Signed language working memory capacity of signed language interpreters and deaf signers. *Journal of Deaf Studies and Deaf Education, 18*(2), 271–286. doi: 10.1093/deafed/ens068

Webb, R., & Supalla, T. (1994). Negation in international sign. In I. Ahlgren, B. Bergmann, & M. Brennan (Eds.), *Perspectives on sign language structure: Papers from the Fifth International Symposium on Sign Language Research, Vol. 1*, Salamanca, Spain, May 25–30, 1992 (pp. 173–186). Durham, UK: ISLA.

Whynot, L. (2013). *Assessing communicative effectiveness and the conventions of international sign.* Gallaudet Department of Interpretation Colloquium Series. September 24. Paper presentation, Gallaudet University Department of Interpretation, Gallaudet University Regional Interpreter Education Center, and the Interpretation and Translation Research Center, Washington, DC.

Whynot, L. A. (2015). *Assessing comprehension of international sign lectures: Linguistic and sociolinguistic factors.* Unpublished doctoral dissertation, Macquarie University, Sydney, Australia.

Wilbur, R. (1994). Eyeblinks and ASL phrase structure. *Sign Language Linguistics*, 84, 221–240.

Wilcox, P. (2000). *Metaphor in American Sign Language.* Washington, DC: Gallaudet University Press.

Wilcox, S. (2004a). Cognitive iconicity: Conceptual spaces, meaning, and gesture in signed languages. *Cognitive Linguistics, 15*(2), 119–147.

Wilcox, S. (2004b). Gesture and language: Cross-linguistic and historical data from signed languages. *Gesture, 4*(1), 43–73.

Willgerodt, M. A., Kataoka-Yahiro, M., Kim, E., & Ceria, C. (2005). Issues of instrument translation in research on Asian immigrant populations. *Journal of Professional Nursing, 21*(4, July–August), 231–239.

Winford, D. (2003). *An introduction to contact linguistics.* Malden, Oxford, UK: Blackwell Publishing.

Winston, E. (1991). Spatial referencing and cohesion in an American Sign Language text. *Sign Language Studies, 73*(Winter), 397–409.

Winston, E., & Monikowski, C. (2003). Marking topic boundaries in signed interpretation and transliteration. In M. Metzger, S. Collins, V. Dively, & R. Shaw (Eds.), *From topic boundaries to omission: New research on interpretation* (pp. 187–227). Washington, DC: Gallaudet University Press.

Wolf, M. B. W. (2005). Memory for narrative and expository text: Independent influences of semantic associations and text organization. *Journal of Experimental Psychology: Learning, Memory, and Cognition, 31*(2), 359–364.

Woll, B. (1984). Comparing sign languages. In F. Loncke, P. Boyes-Braem, & Y. Lebrun (Eds.), *Recent research on European sign languages* (pp. 79–92). Lisse, the Netherlands: Swets and Zeitlinger.

Woll, B. (1990). International perspectives on sign language communication. *International Journal of Sign Linguistics, 1*(2), 1–14.

Woll, B. (1995). *International sign: A sign language interlanguage.* Unpublished paper, City University, London, UK.

Woll, B., Sutton-Spence, R., & Elton, F. (2001). Multilingualism: The global approach to sign languages. In C. Lucas (Ed.), *Sociolinguistics of sign languages* (pp. 8–32). New York, NY: Cambridge University Press.

Woodward, J. (1973). Some characteristics of Pidgin Sign English. *Sign Language Studies, 3*, 39–46.

Woodward, J. (1978). Historical bases of American Sign Languages. In P. Siple (Ed.), *Understanding language through sign language research* (pp. 333–348). New York, NY: Academic Press.

Woodward, J. (1991). Sign language varieties in Costa Rica. *Sign Language Studies, 73*, 329–346.

World Federation of the Deaf (WFD). (2008). *Suggested international signs for use at the World Federation of the Deaf (WFD) general assembly.* A 25-minute digital media production by the World Federation of the Deaf, Norwegian Association of the Deaf, and Ål Experiential College and Conference Center for Deaf People, and Døves Media.

Yoel, J. (2007). Evidence for first-language attrition of Russian Sign Language among immigrants to Israel. In D. Quinto-Pozos (Ed.), *Sign languages in contact* (pp. 153–191). Washington, DC: Gallaudet University Press.

Young, R. (1993). Functional constraints on variation in interlanguage morphology. *Applied Linguistics, 14*(1), 76–97.

Zeshan, U. (2000). *Sign language in Indo-Pakistan: A description of a signed language.* Philadelphia, PA: Benjamins.

Zeshan, U. (2004). Interrogative constructions in signed languages: Cross-linguistic perspectives. *Language, 80*(1), 7–39.

Zeshan, U. (2008). Roots, leaves, branches—The typology of sign languages. In R. M. de Quadros (Ed.), *Sign languages: Spinning and unraveling the past, present and future. TISLR9, forty-five papers and three posters from the Ninth Theoretical Issues in Sign Language Research Conference, Florianopolis, Brazil, December 2006* (pp. 671–695). Petrópolis, RJ, Brazil: Editora Arara Azul.

Zeshan, U. (2015). "Making meaning": Communication between sign language users without a shared language. *Cognitive Linguistics, 26*(2), 211–260.

Zheng, Y., Cheng, L., & Klinger, D. A. (2007). Do test formats in reading comprehension affect second-language students' test performance differently? *TESL Canada Journal, 25*(1), 65–80.

Zimmer, J. (1989). Toward a description of register variation in American Sign Language. In C. Lucas (Ed.), *The sociolinguistics of the Deaf community* (pp. 253–272). San Diego, CA: Academic Press.

Index

Figures and tables are indicated by f and t respectively.